American Popular Music

Blues

American Popular Music

Blues
Classical
Country
Folk
Jazz
Rhythm and Blues, Rap, and Hip-Hop
Rock and Roll

General Editor: Richard Carlin

Editorial Board:

Barbara Ching, Ph.D., University of Memphis

Ronald D. Cohen, Ph.D., Indiana University-Northwest

William Duckworth, Bucknell University

Kevin J. Holm-Hudson, Ph.D., University of Kentucky

Nadine Hubbs, Ph.D., University of Michigan

Craig Morrison, Ph.D., Concordia University and McGill University

Albin J. Zak III, Ph.D., University at Albany (SUNY)

American Popular Music

Blues

Dick Weissman

Foreword by Craig Morrison, Ph.D.
Concordia University and McGill University

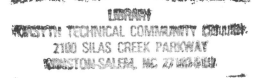

Facts On File
An imprint of Infobase Publishing

American Popular Music: Blues

Copyright © 2006 by Dick Weissman

Facts On File, Inc.
An imprint of Infobase Publishing
132 West 31st Street
New York NY 10001

Library of Congress Cataloging-in-Publication Data

Weissman, Dick.
    American popular music : blues / Richard Weissman ; foreword by Craig Morrison.
        p. cm.
    Includes bibliographical references (p.) and index.
    ISBN 0-8160-5310-3 (hc : alk. paper)
    1. Blues (Music)—Encyclopedias. 2. Blues Musicians—Biography—Dictionaries. I. Title.
    ML102.B6W45 2006
    781.643'0973'03—dc22   2004027586

Facts On File books are available at special discounts when purchased in bulk quantities for businesses, associations, institutions, or sales promotions. Please call our Special Sales Department in New York at (212) 967-8800 or (800) 322-8755.

You can find Facts On File on the World Wide Web at http://www.factsonfile.com

Text design by James Scotto-Lavino
Cover design by Nora Wertz

Printed in the United States of America

VB FOF 10 9 8 7 6 5 4 3 2 1

This book is printed on acid-free paper.

Contents

Foreword

The blues as a genre of music is now more than 100 years old. In that time it has gone from a music localized in the American South and made by and for blacks to a music that is known internationally and cherished by people of diverse racial and cultural backgrounds. The people who created and developed the blues, at least the ones who managed to get recorded, have been acknowledged in numerous ways. Though only some of them lived to see it, their lives have been researched, their music has been made available in various formats, and their place in history is now assured. Among music fans, the most famous artists are household names, including BESSIE SMITH, ROBERT JOHNSON, MUDDY WATERS, B. B. KING, and JOHN LEE HOOKER. From postage stamps to music festivals to historical plaques marking significant locations, the blues heroes have been honored. They now stand alongside the greats in any other field, musical or otherwise.

The blues has triumphed by its indomitable human spirit over the oppressive forces that gave it birth. Because that spirit comes through, on records and CDs, and in performances, the blues continues to inspire and uplift those who can hear its messages. Into it generations of men and women—whether entertaining an audience, trying to get a hit record, or giving themselves solace when alone—have poured their frustrations, joys, hopes, and observations about the business of living life. The lyrics of the blues can be remarkably direct, beautifully poetic, or both at the same time. Its musical form is deceptively simple: The basics can be learned by fledgling musicians in a matter of minutes. However, the blues takes years to master, because the notes and chords are only the outline; the rest must be filled in by experience. Because of its apparent simplicity, it is easy to grasp on an intuitive level. Even listeners who do not understand English are capable of feeling it, for its emotions are expressed not just in lyrics but are conveyed in the singing and in the musical mood.

The journey of the blues is as fascinating as the lives of its performers. It appears to have crystallized at the end of the 1800s, decades after slavery was officially abolished (but while the oppression of blacks was as bad, if not worse, than ever). Its roots are deep in the cultural intermingling that took place when the slaves brought from Africa to the United States encountered the music of their overseers whose background was European. On European instruments and ones adapted from Africa, the slaves and their descendants blended these traditions, along with traces of others, into something unique. Indications point to MISSISSIPPI as the place where the blues began, and musicians from that state have had an inordinate influence on the music's history.

From its rural origins, the blues was taken into cities, adopted by professional bandleaders like W. C. HANDY who composed sophisticated variations, and played by jazz musicians. It was recorded by a music industry that finally realized, in the 1920s, that it existed and that there was a market for it. As we can hear in the records made from then until now, the blues blossomed into a variety of styles.

Each is a product of its time and the creativity of a series of individuals. Blues influenced and was influenced by other genres, particularly jazz, country, gospel, and, since the 1950s, rock and roll.

Fanatical interest by British musicians was the catalyst for an international awareness of the blues. The object of their affection, in the 1950s, was folk blues; their response to it led to skiffle, a style that the Beatles played in the earliest part of their career. In the 1960s, the electric blues coming out of the cities, especially CHICAGO, was highly appealing; the British response created blues rock. The ROLLING STONES, the Who, the ANIMALS, the YARDBIRDS, JOHN MAYALL, ERIC CLAPTON, LED ZEPPELIN, and FLEETWOOD MAC, while forging ahead with their own music, all helped to direct their audiences to the blues. A related development occurred in America, first with the folk revivalists, some of whom rediscovered veteran blues musicians and brought them to festival stages and back into recordings studios, and then the blues rockers, such as the PAUL BUTTERFIELD Blues Band, CANNED HEAT, and JIMI HENDRIX (an American who first came to prominence in England).

While the musicians were in the spotlight, behind the scenes were record collectors, some of whom would go "junking" by calling from door to door in black neighborhoods with a car parked nearby or even just a wheelbarrow to carry whatever records they were able to purchase. Because of their efforts, a lot of music that would have been lost was recovered. There were writers, many of them dedicated amateurs, who transcribed lyrics, created discographies, interviewed blues players, published magazines and books, and wrote liner notes for the multitude of reissued records. An industry sprang up around the teaching of the blues. It included private lessons, workshops, summer camps, instructional videos, and books of transcribed songs showing the guitar and piano techniques used on recordings.

In learning about the blues and its history, we gain a sense of the broader context of historical events and conditions. Among them are migrations, racial issues, wars, advances in technology, and factors of economics and geography. In hearing the music and the lyrics, modern listeners can have insight into facets and values of the culture in which the blues is situated. A study of the music of notable artists can provide a glimpse into their personalities. We begin to see how each involves himself creatively and subjectively in his music.

There is a world of sound in the blues. The singer's voice, grainy or smooth, shouting or crooning, and with inflections that can betray a regional upbringing, is the focal point for most presentations. Also up front usually is the GUITAR, an instrument capable of a seemingly endless array of colors. One single player with an ACOUSTIC GUITAR can make a room full of people dance, draw a crowd to a sidewalk performance, or make a recording so full of subtleties that generations of later musicians devote themselves to making the same sounds. The steady drone of a guitarist's thumb bouncing between two low strings can give a foundation for plucking fingers that pick out a lively tune on the higher ones. A chugging beat generated by strumming two low strings together (with some minimal finger movement on the higher of the strings) can make for an infectious sound that can drive a band or a dance floor. Notes can be made to whine by sliding up and down the strings with a tube of glass, metal, or bone placed over one of the fingers. Anguish can be conveyed by the fretting hand bending and releasing the strings. On electric guitar the expressive possibilities are further increased with more sustain, tonal variations, and greater volume and presence.

Pianists can make thundering, hypnotic train rhythms with the left hand or shimmering, cascading phrases with the right. The HARMONICA, so rustic sounding when played acoustically, transforms into something entirely different when played into a microphone plugged into a distorting amplifier. A single sax can ignite an auditorium with a honking solo that sounds at times like screaming. A horn section fills out a band with harmonious punctuations and featured spots for each of the instruments to display its own characteristic tones. If there is a rhythm section, the bass and drums work together, locking into a groove that unifies the band and connects with the listeners on a visceral level. Whether playing straight, even subdivisions of the pulse, the more jazzy shuffle rhythm, or borrowing Latin dance patterns like the rumba beat, a good rhythm section can make the standard blues chord progression seem to be something so fresh and natural that its inevitability is forgotten with the very vitality of the rhythm that propels it.

In the lyrics sung by blues artists, "the blues" is presented as something real, a presence, almost like a person, to be talked to and spoken about. The blues is personal. It is about day-to-day life, the tribulations, the wondering and hoping, the scheming and dreaming. There is a lot of direct talk, a lot of "you" and "me." You're a no-good woman, you're a cheating man, why don't you write me? are you ever coming back? before you accuse me take a look at yourself, I've got rambling on my mind, I'm going back down South, I'm being mistreated, I can't hold out. As LITTLE WALTER declared, it's a "Mean Old World." Because the blues acknowledges that in a way that is real and still finds something to celebrate, it will continue to speak, with endless and subtle variations, across generations, races, and cultures.

Craig Morrison
Concordia University and McGill University

Preface

American popular music reflects the rich cultural diversity of the American people. From classical to folk to jazz, America has contributed a rich legacy of musical styles to the world over its two-plus centuries of existence. The rich cross-fertilization of cultures—African-American, Hispanic, Asian, and European—has resulted in one of the unique musical mixtures in the world.

American Popular Music celebrates this great diversity by presenting to the student, researcher, and individual enthusiast a wealth of information on each musical style in an easily accessible format. The subjects covered are:

Blues
Classical music
Country
Folk music
Jazz
Rock and Roll
Rhythm and Blues, Rap, and Hip-Hop

Each volume presents key information on performers, musical genres, famous compositions, musical instruments, media, and centers of musical activity. The volumes conclude with a chronology, recommended listening, and a complete bibliography or list of sources for further study.

How do we define *popular music*? Literally, any music that attracts a reasonably large audience is "popular" (as opposed to "unpopular"). Over the past few decades, however, as the study of popular music has grown, the term has come to have specific meanings. While some might exclude certain genres covered in this series—American classical music leaps to mind—we felt that it was important to represent the range of musical styles that have been popular in the United States over its entire history. New scholarship has brought to light the interplay among genres that previously were felt to be unrelated—such as the influence of folk forms on classical music, opera's influence on jazz, or the blues' influence on country—so that to truly understand each musical style, it is important to be conversant with at least some aspects of all.

These volumes are intended to be introductory, not comprehensive. Any "A to Z" work is by its very nature selective; it's impossible to include *every* figure, *every* song, or *every* key event. For most users, we hope the selections made here will be more than adequate, giving information on the key composers and performers who shaped each style, while also introducing some lesser-known figures who are worthy of study. The Editorial Board and other outside advisers played a key role in reviewing the entry lists for completeness.

All encyclopedia authors also face the rather daunting task of separating fact from fiction when writing short biographies of performers and composers. Even birth and death dates can be "up for grabs," as artists have been known to subtract years from their lives in their official biographies. "Official" records are often unavailable, particularly for earlier artists who may have been born at home, or for those whose family histories themselves are shrouded in mystery. We have attempted to draw on the latest research and most reliable sources whenever possible, and have also pointed out when key facts are in dispute. And, for many popular performers, the myth can be as important as the reality when it comes to their lives, so we have tried to honor both in writing about their achievements.

Popular music reflects the concerns of the artists who create it and their audience. Each era of our country's history has spawned a variety of popular music styles, and these styles in turn have grown over the decades as new performers and new times have arisen. These volumes try to place the music into its context, acknowledging that the way music is performed and its effect on the greater society is as important as the music itself. We've also tried to highlight the many interchanges between styles and performers, because one of the unique—and important—aspects of American cultural life is the way that various people have come together to create a new culture out of the interplay of their original practices and beliefs.

Race, class, culture, and sex have played roles in the development of American popular music. Regrettably, the playing field has not always been level for performers from different backgrounds, particularly when it comes to the business aspects of the industry: paying royalties, honoring copyrights, and the general treatment of artists. Some figures have been forgotten or ignored who deserved greater attention; the marketplace can be ruthless, and its agents—music publishers, record producers, concert promoters—have and undoubtedly will continue to take advantage of the musicians trying to bring their unique voices to market. These volumes attempt to address many of these issues as they have affected the development of individual musicians' careers as well as from the larger perspective of the growth of popular music. The reader is encouraged to delve further into these topics by referring to the bibliographies in each volume.

Popular music can be a slave itself to crass commercialism, as well as a bevy of hangers-on, fellow travelers, and others who seek only to make a quick buck by following easy-to-identify trends. While we bemoan the lack of new visionary artists today like Bessie Smith, Miles Davis, Pauline Oliveros, or Bob Dylan, it's important to remember that when they first came on the scene the vast majority of popular performers were journeymen musicians at best. Popular music will always include many second-, third-, and fourth-tier performers; some will offer one or two recordings or performances that will have a lasting impact, while many will be celebrated during their 15 minutes of fame, but most will be forgotten. In separating the wheat from the chaff, it is understandably easier for our writers working on earlier styles where the passing of time has helped sort out the important from the just popular. However, all the contributors have tried to supply some distance, giving greatest weight to the true artists, while acknowledging that popular figures who are less talented can nonetheless have a great impact on the genre during their performing career—no matter how brief it might be.

All in all, the range, depth, and quality of popular musical styles that have developed in the United States over its lifetime is truly amazing. These styles could not have arisen anywhere else, but are the unique products of the mixing of cultures, geography, technology, and sheer luck that helped disseminate each style. Who could have forecast the music of Bill Monroe before he assembled his first great bluegrass band? Or predicted the melding of gospel, rhythm and blues, and popular music achieved by Aretha Franklin during her reign as "Queen of Soul"? The tinkering of classical composer John Cage—who admitted to having no talent for creating melodies—was a truly American response to new technologies, a new environment, and a new role for music in our lives. And Patti Smith's particular take on poetry, the punk-rock movement, and the difficulties faced by a woman who leads a rock band make her music particularly compelling and original—and unpredictable to those who dismissed the original rock records as mere "teenage fluff."

We hope that the volumes in this series will open your eyes, minds, and, most important, your ears to a world of musical styles. Some may be familiar, others more obscure, but all are worthy. With today's proliferation of sound on the Web, finding even the most obscure recording is becoming increasingly simple. We urge you to read deeply but also to put these books down to listen. Come to your own conclusions. American popular music is a rich world, one open to many different interpretations. We hope these volumes serve as your windows to these many compelling worlds.

Richard Carlin,
General Editor

Introduction

The first enslaved Africans landed in the English colonies of North America in 1619. From the earliest days of these dreadful oceangoing voyages, there were reports of slaves singing laments on the ships that brought them from Africa. Prior to their emancipation in 1863, slaves were reported to be excellent fiddlers and banjoists (the banjo being an instrument of African origin), often playing for the entertainment of their masters. Music was also a vehicle for expressing their hopes, dreams, and frustrations. In the period following the Civil War, the newly-freed slaves began to apply their skills in a remarkable variety of styles and genres. MIGRATION from the southern states to the north and west spread these styles throughout the United States. Some African-American musicians joined or formed minstrel companies, refining and expanding this musical mix by adding syncopated cakewalks and dances and song. It also influenced the composition and performance styles of American popular music. Civil War soldiers abandoned brass instruments all over the South, and former slaves learned to play these instruments, forming brass ensembles and, later, jazz bands. On the vocal front, groups such as the Fisk University Jubilee Singers brought spirituals to white audiences in the United States and in Europe starting in the 1870s. Soloists such as black operatic artist M. Sissieretta Jones sang operatic arias on tour. Black theater began to flourish in New York City, with music composed and performed by black musicians. For years the Ziegfeld Follies featured singer-comedian Bert Williams, one of the biggest stars of vaudeville. New

black evangelical churches incorporated music into their services. RAGTIME piano later grew out of earlier versions of this music played on the banjo, and it became one of the main ingredients of the early 20th-century music called jazz.

But another, less-documented musical development was taking place away from the urban areas. Rural blacks became interested in the instruments played by their equally poor white counterparts, especially the guitar. Creative musicians took instruments already in use, such as the banjo and the violin, and developed hybrid techniques incorporating elements of both white and black instrumental techniques. Borrowing and building on the Anglo-American folk music of the 19th century and incorporating elements of the old slave songs, rural African-American musicians at the turn of the 20th century gradually developed a new and highly personal music: the blues.

Although a few early white artists recorded music based on the blues, the first major recorded blues artists were closer to the vaudeville and popular music traditions than to the more rural forms of the blues. MA RAINEY and BESSIE SMITH were the most important singers in this style, known as the classic blues. W. C. HANDY, CLARENCE WILLIAMS, and T. A. DORSEY (later a gospel composer) were among the most important composers of early blues. The rougher, more rural blues style appeared on records in the mid-1920s and was popular through the 1930s, when the Great Depression all but eliminated the sale of these "race records" to the blues audience. During the late 1930s to the mid-1940s, southern blues musicians began using guitars with pickups plugged into amplifiers, and instruments and singers were utilizing microphones in performances. They had previously been available only in recording studios. The combination of these elements, along with the addition of drums and bass, led to blues combos, and then to the genre called rhythm and blues, or R&B. This was one of the primary sources of rock and roll. With the addition of amplified HARMONICA and SAXOPHONE and/or trumpet, the blues became more organized in terms of both rhythm and harmonic structure.

While the blues "went underground" in the 1950s, largely replaced by the newer rhythm and blues combo styles, the newly awakened interest in roots music by white musicians during the late 1950s and 1960s led to the rediscovery of rural blues performers who had not played publicly, or even recorded for two decades or more. The general interest in American roots music that emerged during the 1960s led to the reissue of many blues recordings on long-playing records, notably the recordings of Bessie Smith and ROBERT JOHNSON. Rock musicians (especially in the United Kingdom) became enamored of blues music, both honoring its stars and re-creating it in a rock music style. The interest in rural and urban blues continued to wax and wane in succeeding decades. Although few young African-American performers appeared in this early blues revival, by the 1990s a number of such musicians emerged on records and in performance.

By this time the blues had become established as a specific musical genre in the world of American popular music. Blues festivals were presented in all regions of the United States, drawing thousand of blues fans and creating more future fans. There were local blues singers recording and performing in every major city of the United States, and the House of Blues nightclubs had opened a number of blues venues where performers sang and played the blues, and everything from T-shirts to vintage guitars were on sale. B. B. KING went from playing to an older black audience to becoming an internationally-known artist with his own nightclubs in several cities. The U.S. Congress declared 2003 to be the year of the blues, and a series of radio and TV programs brought relatively obscure aspects of the blues to the attention of millions of Americans. The television series called *The Legacy of the Blues* consisted of seven two-hour television programs. The executive producer of the series was the famous film director Martin Scorsese. He directed one of the films and commissioned a number of other directors, including Clint Eastwood, to do the other six programs. The videos were also available for purchase, and Scorsese was also the impetus for a book about the blues, as well as a series of CD reissues of artists whose work was included in the soundtracks of the various programs.

This volume of the *Encyclopedia of American Popular Music* provides a comprehensive overview of the blues, focusing on its origins, and history during the course of more than 100 years, culminating in its revival in the mid-20th century, and looking at its present and future. It then discusses blues trends and styles, important composers and performers, the cultural and commercial impact of the music, and essential recordings. The book also highlights the ways that American blues has influenced and been influenced by other musical styles. It also includes discussions of the social issues crucial to the evolution of rural and urban blues. The accomplishments of women in the blues field is documented, and key figures in the transmission of the music are discussed. In addition to composers, musicians, and performers, both folklorists and commercial record producers are covered, and their importance in the evolution of the music is evaluated. There are alphabetical listings for these people, and a series of articles is included that is intended to highlight the history, structure, and evolution of the blues.

Origin and History of the Blues

It is generally believed that the blues began sometime around the 1890s or at the turn of the 20th century. The first written references that we have to anyone actually hearing the blues are W. C. Handy's and Ma Rainey's reports that they first heard something resembling the blues in 1903. Howard Odum was the first folklorist who collected blues songs, and his work began in 1908. We know that before the blues began there were other genres of African-American music found in the southern United States. These musical styles included the following:

◆ FIELD HOLLERS were unaccompanied songs sung while the singer was actually doing farm work. The musical form of field hollers was very free, because there were no instruments or voices accompanying the singer.

◆ *Street cries* were sung in the cities by vendors selling or delivering food or merchandise.

◆ *Spirituals* were the traditional religious music of African Americans. Spirituals often used a call-and-response pattern with the leader singing a verse, and the other singers answering with short refrains, or repeated phrases, such as "Oh my Lord." Many of the spirituals repeated a line two or three times, with a final line as a sort of answer or commentary to the first line of the song.

◆ *Work songs*, sung by groups of people at work, often used a call-and-response pattern in the same style that spirituals did. Work songs tended to be sung either on plantations or on prison gangs, where large groups of people were working.

◆ RAGTIME was a complex instrumental style that developed out of the dances and banjo playing in the minstrel era. Ragtime centered on the piano, although accomplished banjoists and guitarists played rags on their instruments, and they were also played by bands. Ragtime tunes had as many as four parts and often used key changes in the different sections. The first published ragtime pieces appeared in 1892, which was at the very beginning of or just prior to the birth of the blues.

W. C. Handy was an African-American composer and bandleader. Out of his experiences listening to itinerant rural guitar players he wrote a number of famous blues, including the "Memphis Blues" and the "St. Louis Blues." "Memphis Blues" was the third blues published in sheet music form, and the only one of the three (all of which appeared in 1912) that is still well known today.

A number of white vaudeville performers such as Morton Harvey, Marian Harris, Norah Beyes, and Marie Cahill sang and recorded blues before 1920. Many of these performances were closer to ragtime and vaudeville styles than to the blues, although ELIJAH WALD, in his book *Escaping the Delta,* quotes W. C. Handy as saying that Harris's performances were sufficiently convincing that many listeners thought she was black.

The Classic Blues

The second recorded performance of blues by a black singer was Mamie Smith's recording of "Crazy Blues" in 1920. The first was her earlier record, "That Thing Called Love," backed with "You Can't Keep a Good Man Down." That recording did well enough for Okeh Records to ask her to record again. Because "Crazy Blues" had unexpectedly high sales of 75,000 copies in the first month of its release, all the record companies became extremely interested in blues, at least the sort of vaudeville blues that Smith was singing. The classic blues songs tended to be pop-oriented, and the singers came out of tent shows and early vaudeville performances. Among these early blues recordings were performances by IDA COX, VICTORIA SPIVEY, Clara Smith, Lucille Hegamin, Edith Wilson, Rosa Henderson, SIPPIE WALLACE, and ALBERTA HUNTER. Virtually all blues music critics and fans consider Ma Rainey and Bessie Smith to have been the most significant of the classic blues artists. Rainey had toured widely throughout the South, playing in theaters and for medicine shows during performances where allegedly powerful medicines were sold to the gullible consumer. Smith, a younger singer, seems to have been influenced by Ma Rainey's work. Smith met Rainey in 1912, when Bessie joined the Moses Stokes company. Rainey was a singer with the Stokes Group. Scholars argue about the extent of Rainey's influence on Smith.

Of all the classic blues singers Rainey was the closest to embracing the folk roots of the music, sometimes recording with jug band accompaniment that included a variety of homemade instruments like kazoos, combs, and jugs. Smith preferred to record with jazz musicians, even recording with Louis Armstrong on cornet.

Blues Form and Content

The subject matter of the classic blues, like that of the folk blues, was most often love and romantic difficulties. Most of the songs used repeated lines. A typical verse might have lyrics like the ones below:

It rained today, and I don't know where to go,
Yes, it rained today, and I don't know where to go
Wish I was in California, safe from all this rain and snow.

Notice that the first two lines are identical, except for the word "yes" added to the beginning of the second line. Spoken interjections at the beginning or end of lines were a common feature in the blues. Sometimes lines might be repeated three times, with the fourth line containing the "answer" line. Some blues historians believe that the earliest blues contained one line that was repeated three or four times without the answer line. Although love was the most common subject, classic blues singers also sang about travel and sometimes about hard times or natural disasters, such as floods. We discuss the music of the blues in the next section, and further details about the lyrics of the blues appear in the entry BLUES LYRICS.

Folk Blues

Inevitably the record companies began to realize that besides the urban female singers, most of whom did not play instruments, there were quite a few rural blues singers who accompanied themselves on GUITAR or other instruments. The majority of these artists were men. From a record company standpoint, a solo artist who used no studio musicians was extremely cheap to record.

The first popular folk blues artist was PAPA CHARLIE JACKSON, who accompanied himself on six-string BANJO, an instrument tuned and played like a guitar but that sounds like a banjo. Jackson sang comic songs, vaudeville, and minstrel-sounding material, so he was sort of a human bridge between the pre-blues styles of black music and the blues. Jackson fits into a category called *songster,* an older-generation artist who pursues a variety of styles, including the blues. In addition to his solo recordings, he made records with Ma Rainey and Ida Cox, and even with jazz trumpet man Freddie Keppard. Jackson's recording career started in 1924 and lasted into the 1930s.

The most influential blues man of the 1920s was BLIND LEMON JEFFERSON. Jefferson, originally from Texas, recorded over 80 songs between 1926 and 1929. He wrote mostly blues songs, but he also recorded a few religious songs. Jefferson wrote about whatever was on his mind, hard times, wars, women, animals, and travel, for example. He could come up with original songs, which became very important to record companies and record producers. Record companies needed to establish and feed a market for their products, and obviously they could not keep recording the same songs over and over. The record companies were also eager for artists to come up with new songs, because the record company, or sometimes the record producer, typically owned the publishing rights to the songs. Usually songwriting and publishing rights are split on a 50-50 basis, with the songwriter receiving half the income and the publisher getting the same amount. Record companies often acquired the songwriters' rights as well, by buying them for minimal amounts of money from the artists. Most of the artists were quite happy to sell off the rights, because they had no notion that the songs had any economic value. Some of the artists knew better, but assumed that the record companies would never pay them royalties anyway.

Many of the so-called composed folk blues were actually collections of blues verses that most blues singers had heard in one place or another. Often when a blues singer was singing a song and needed another verse or two, he would reach into his mental song bag and come up with traditional verses to complete the song.

Blues Styles and Other Artists

As the blues developed, there were different regional styles in different parts of the country. Although there was some overlap between the various styles, the early folk styles are usually classified as Piedmont blues, Texas blues, and Delta blues. The Piedmont blues were found in the Carolinas, Georgia, and Florida, and tended to show ragtime and vaudeville influences. Delta blues came from the MISSISSIPPI Delta, and tended to be more intense, often using more heavily textured guitar and vocal styles. Texas blues, often characterized by lighter vocal quality, were harder to pin down, but were neither as intense as the Mississippi styles nor as relaxed and fun-loving as the Piedmont blues tended to be.

The first Delta artist to record was ISHMON BRACEY, who cut his first records in 1927. Other notable Mississippi artists who followed included CHARLEY PATTON, SON HOUSE, ROBERT JOHNSON, and, later, MUDDY WATERS. Piedmont artists included BLIND BOY FULLER, GARY DAVIS, JOSH WHITE, BUDDY MOSS, BROWNIE MCGHEE and SONNY TERRY. Huddie "LEAD BELLY" Ledbetter, TEXAS ALEXANDER, and HENRY "RAGTIME TEXAS" THOMAS were among the early Texas artists.

By the end of the 1920s many bluesmen started to migrate to Memphis or Chicago, and therefore to some extent the styles lost their original differences: for example, ROBERT JOHNSON, who traveled widely, recorded one tune called "They're Red Hot," which sounds much more like a Piedmont blues than his customary Delta blues fare.

MEMPHIS MINNIE (Douglas) was among the few folk blues women artists to achieve popularity. She generally recorded duets where she played lead guitar, and her accompanist was one of her three husbands. When she divorced, she would marry invariably another guitar player. During her career she recorded over 200 sides. Only a handful of other women both sang and played, none as popular as Memphis Minnie.

Chicago and Combo Blues

LEROY CARR grew up in Louisville and Indianapolis. He was a very influential singer and pianist in the late 1920s and early 1930s, writing some blues songs that were later recorded by other artists. Carr sang in a gentler, almost pop music style compared with artists like Blind Lemon Jefferson or any of the Mississippi performers. He teamed up with guitarist FRANCIS "SCRAPPER" BLACKWELL, who developed a melodic accompaniment style that would influence many other musicians. The two of them popularized the piano-guitar duo, and Carr brought a new sophistication to blues, in terms of both his songwriting and his smoother vocal performances.

TAMPA RED and BIG BILL BROONZY were among the blues artists that migrated to CHICAGO. Broonzy moved from ARKANSAS to Chicago in 1920, and TAMPA RED, who had lived in Missouri and Georgia, moved to Chicago in 1925. Both began to experiment with blues combos of various sorts. Broonzy recorded with washboard accompaniment, and later with saxophone and drums. Tampa Red recorded in many different contexts, ranging from "hokum" jug bands to crooned pop songs in a sort of nightclub style. He also recorded a number of humorous duets with pianist T. A. DORSEY, then known as Georgia Tom, who later moved into the gospel music field. Broonzy had a bouncy and rhythmic guitar style, while Tampa played slide guitar, but in a sweet, melodic way, rather than using the slide in an intense and rhythmic way like Delta Players. Both Tampa and Big Bill wrote hundreds of songs and made dozens and dozens of records. Tampa's house in Chicago was a sort of blues central headquarters.

He had a rehearsal studio complete with two pianos and a variety of instruments. When a new singer came to town, he would gravitate to Tampa's house, where he could meet other blues musicians and make contacts that would lead to playing jobs and even recording work.

Rhythm and Blues

The combo style of blues, together with the performances of LOUIS JORDAN and other pop-oriented swing musicians, led to the beginnings of rhythm and blues. The electric guitar was a major player in the development of R&B, and it seemed as though every R&B recording had either a solo by electric guitar or saxophone. Folklorist Alan Lomax used to refer to bluegrass as "folk music with overdrive," and one could say the same thing about the relationship between blues and R&B. *Billboard* magazine, the major music trade paper, changed the name of its black music pop charts from "race records" to "rhythm and blues" by the late 1940s. By 1945 the style had taken hold, and in Chicago it was adopted by a number of artists with deep blues roots, especially Muddy Waters. Muddy was a Delta musician who had been recorded in Mississippi by ALAN LOMAX in 1941, and he moved to Chicago in 1943. He and fellow Delta musician ELMORE JAMES adapted the acoustic Delta blues style to electric guitar, utilizing heavy bass and drums to anchor the rhythm. Instead of using a saxophone, Waters used an amplified harmonica to play lead melody lines. When played by harmonica great LITTLE WALTER, the sound was exciting and ushered in a new era in the blues. Waters was also a major figure because so many excellent musicians, like BUDDY GUY and JUNIOR WELLS, passed through his bands, or at least recorded with him. All these artists were blues men, but their records appeared on the R&B charts.

T-BONE WALKER was another influential electric guitarist. Walker was a Texan who had roots in the blues dating to his childhood when he was a lead boy for Blind Lemon Jefferson, leading him through the Dallas streets and holding his tin collection cup. Walker used the ELECTRIC GUITAR to play melody lines. Little Walter pursued a similar path on the harmonica. Walker also recorded with INSTRUMENTAL COMBOS that included horns. He was a major influence on B. B. KING, who straddled the line between R&B and blues. King refined Walker's technique of using his left hand to bend notes, and to achieve a vibrato sound that he made by rocking back and forth with a left-hand finger on a single string. B. B. in turn was an important influence on such other artists as ALBERT KING, FREDDIE KING, and JOHNNY COPELAND.

Rhythm and blues was succeeded by soul music in the early 1960s. Soul was a sort of fusion of black gospel music and blues, with a touch of country influence as well. It featured artists like Otis Redding and Aretha Franklin. Meanwhile America was experiencing a folk music revival, and many of the folk enthusiasts crossed over into blues music. A series of rediscoveries of old blues men produced a new, white audience for such blues singers as SKIP JAMES, SON HOUSE, BUKKA WHITE, and MISSISSIPPI JOHN HURT. This in turn stimulated a whole generation of young white blues singers, including JOHN HAMMOND, DAVE VAN RONK, KOERNER RAY and GLOVER, MIKE BLOOMFIELD, and PAUL BUTTERFIELD, to begin their own blues careers. On the other side of the Atlantic a number of young English artists, including, Steve Winwood, ERIC CLAPTON, Mick Jagger, and Mick Fleetwood, bought records by American blues singers and began to pursue what would become major careers as rock stars. Many of the recordings by British artists sold millions of copies, and the ROLLING STONES requested American blues men like HOWLIN' WOLF, Sonny Boy Williamson, and Buddy Guy not only as their opening acts but on American television. Other British rock stars toured with American blues artists in Europe, and played on their records as well. This brought the blues to the attention of many rock fans who had never experienced the music before. The British acts also often mentioned artists like B. B. King, who were relatively unknown to white audiences in the United States.

The Blues Today

By the 1980s there were blues festivals, an increasing number of blues record labels, and many reissue albums available on CD. BONNIE RAITT, originally billed as a white blues artist, achieved great success recording both blues and pop songs, and playing slide guitar. ROBERT JOHNSON was an obscure Delta bluesman who had been forgotten all through the 1940s and 1950s. He achieved some notoriety through LP reissues of his work, beginning in 1961, but he became a world-famous figure when his complete works appeared in a double CD set in 1990. It has sold almost two million copies to date. There are dozens of books, and thousands of blues CDs available. Documentary videos cover the lives of various blues figures, and the Martin Scorsese specials brought the works of many relatively obscure bluesmen to network television. Some young white performers, like JONNY LANG and KENNY WAYNE SHEPHERD, have brought their versions of the electric blues to another set of fans. Although there were only a few young black blues artists performing during the 1960s, the mid-1990s saw the emergence of a half dozen prominent black performers, returning the music to its original identity as an African-American art form.

Behind the Scenes

Behind the scenes of blues recording were record company personnel, folklorists, and songwriters. Mamie Smith's recording happened because a black songwriter and businessman named Perry Bradford pestered the people at Okeh Records until they finally agreed to allow her to record. Alan Lomax, as already mentioned, was inadvertently responsible for Muddy Waters's recording career, when he recorded him in Mississippi. Supposedly when Muddy heard his voice played back on Lomax's recorder, he realized he was ready to give up his life in Mississippi and to become a professional musician.

Many of the record companies had people that worked for them on a formal or informal basis,

seeking to find new blues singers. RALPH PEER, FRANK WALKER, ART SATHERLY, and Don Law were among the companies' record producers, and H. C. SPEIR in Jackson, Mississippi, and J. B. LONG in Kingsport, Tennessee, acted as talent scouts, seeking out potential recording artists and bringing them to record companies.

Starting in the 1960s a young generation of white blues scholars and enthusiasts, especially Stefan Grossman, transcribed dozens of blues songs and guitar solos, and edited them into blues instruction books. Jerry Silverman published one of the first blues songbooks, and as the blues became more popular, some of the music publishers, particularly ARC Music in Chicago, printed anthologies of blues sheet music. Another group of white blues fans were responsible for the rediscovery of elderly bluesmen. Acting as detectives, they used old song lyrics, personal contacts made through lengthy trips to the South, and hunches to locate many of the older bluesmen. A generation of blues scholars began to emerge at the same time, and their work also helped to spread information about the blues. SAMUEL CHARTERS and Paul Oliver were the first generation of these blues specialists; they were followed by BRUCE BASTIN, JEFF TODD TITON, DAVID EVANS, and others. They wrote books about the blues, and Titon published a collection of blues lyrics. Other blues researchers and enthusiasts, such as Francis Davis, Peter Guralnick, Steven Colt, Paul Garan, and Gayle Dean Wardlow, researched and wrote about many aspects of the blues. ELIJAH WALD is among the most recent of these scholars, with books about JOSH WHITE and a searching study of the legend of Robert Johnson to his credit.

More than ever before information on the blues is available in every conceivable form—on CD and DVD, in textbooks and songbooks, and on the Internet.

How to Listen to the Blues

Although the blues is often discussed as though it is a single unified musical style, a variety of musical styles are found in blues music. The classic blues was a musical marriage between blues vocals and jazz-flavored accompaniments, often including such instruments as trumpets, trombones, and clarinets. Many of the folk blues recorded in the 1920s, such as the recordings of Blind Lemon Jefferson, feature a vocal with the singer accompanying himself on guitar. The guitar keeps the rhythm of the song and also often comments on the lyrics in the spaces at the end of each line, or between the verses.

The blues appeal to the emotions and also make listeners want to dance or move their body in time to the music. The music usually has an underlying feeling of sadness, yet it can be a positive, happy experience as well. In Mississippi blues guitar players often use a knife held in the left hand or bottleneck worn on a left-hand finger. As the player slides up and down the strings, he simulates the sound of a human voice crying. In Piedmont blues the guitar is intended to highlight the party and dance feeling of the song. In other instances the guitar is played in a style called fingerpicking, where the guitarist keeps the rhythm and plays the melody at the same time. The first time that a listener hears this style of playing, it sounds as though two guitars are playing at the same time. Most of the early folk blues artists accompanied themselves by playing finger-style guitar. Later many of the musicians started to wear fingerpicks, which are worn over the fingernails of the right hand. Fingerpicks allow a musician to play louder and faster, but they usually produce very little variation in sound. Playing with the right-hand fingers enables the player to play with more variations in tone, but the volume is softer. As the electric guitar developed, many musicians started to use a flat pick held in the right hand between the thumb and the index finger. Using the flat pick enables the player to play rapid single-note passages, or to play rhythm without much effort. The disadvantage of a flat pick is that guitarists can play only one note at a time. It is possible to use the flat pick together with the right-hand fingers, but this is a difficult technique.

The guitar is usually tuned E A D G B E, from the lowest (sixth) string to the highest (first) string. One of the musical characteristics of blues is that dominant 7th quality chords are interchangeable with major chords, so that in the key of C, the typical (I, IV, and V chords) C F G7 progression can be modified, so that the C and F chords can become C7 and F7, and the G7 can become a G chord.

One may notice that when musicians play SLIDE GUITAR they often use other TUNINGS, especially the G tuning, D G D G B D, or the D tuning, DF#DF#AD. In the G tuning strumming across the open strings gives the player a G chord, or in the D tuning a D chord. To play the IV and V chords in G tuning (the C and D chords), the player has only to use the slide or a finger straight across to cover all the strings on the fifth fret and then the seventh fret. The same holds true in the D tuning, where the chords are D, G, and A. The G chord is on the fifth fret and A is at the seventh fret.

The piano can be used as a solo instrument, but when piano and guitar play together, either one may be the lead instrument, with the other instrument either playing the rhythm or offering melodic comments. An accompanying banjo follows the same general patterns that a guitar would use. Occasionally blues records are made with guitar and MANDOLIN, with the mandolin usually playing lead parts, while the guitar keeps the rhythm going. The instrumentation in jug band combos often included a banjo, FIDDLE, or mandolin, a washboard, a washtub bass, and a jug or kazoo. Usually one of the instruments would play the lead, and the other ones would keep the rhythm going.

Blues are usually sung by a single vocalist, although in a number of instances there are two voices. When two voices perform a song, usually they do not sing in harmony, but one voice answers the other, or offers spoken comments to the first verse.

When rhythm and blues began, the instrumentation changed. The harmonica and guitar were amplified, and bass and drums were added. As R&B, developed, the acoustic bass was often replaced by an electric bass, and piano became more common. The piano mostly played rhythm parts, with the occasional solo. Saxophone solos were also featured on many R&B records. In soul records the GUITAR often became reduced to a rhythmic role, although sometimes, as in the records of such artists as James Brown, the rhythm guitar was prominent.

The blues arose about 15 or 20 years or so after the end of slavery. Almost all blues have a feeling of sadness or loss in their lyrics, the performances, or the music itself. The early blues artists usually sang about the various aspects of their lives—love, lost love, loneliness, self-pity, traveling, places they had been or wanted to go to, tragedies such as floods or tornadoes, and commentaries on the social world that the blues was born into. These commentaries involved such subjects as jail, hard times, poverty, and even racial prejudice. Many blues also included humorous aspects of life, such as exposing a hypocritical preacher or making fun of a town.

Early blues lyrics often do not tell a single story but are almost like a tour through the mind of the singer. The first verse might be about a train, the second about a woman or man, and the third might be an explanation of why the singer is feeling sad. Later on blues songs became more like pop songs with a beginning, a middle, an ending, and a coherent story line. For those who have not listened to folk blues before, it takes time to get used to the idea that the song is not attempting to tell a single story.

Those who are interested in learning how to play the blues will find many useful books to help master blues styles on the piano, guitar, harmonica, or other instruments. Many of these books come with CDs or videos. A detailed listing of these resources appears in the back of this book.

A-to-Z Entries

acoustic guitar

The guitar has six strings, tuned E A D G B E in normal tuning. The guitar is the single most popular instrument identified with the blues, and there is a rich history of players over the last 80 years or so. The first mention of the blues guitar in print is W. C. HANDY's report of seeing a MISSISSIPPI guitarist playing guitar with a knife outside a railroad station in 1903. The first recorded blues guitarist was SYLVESTER WEAVER, who accompanied SARA MARTIN in 1923 on an Okeh recording, and apparently sufficiently impressed the producer that he recorded to guitar instrumentals at the end of Martin's recording session. One selection was the bottleneck instrumental "Guitar Blues," and the other was called "Guitar Rag."

The floodgates for blues guitar popularity were opened by BLIND LEMON JEFFERSON's 1926 recordings. During the next five years there was a rapid succession of popular blues guitarists, playing a variety of styles. Piedmont guitarist BLIND BLAKE recorded as a solo artist playing his ragtime-flavored instrumentals and songs, and as an accompanist. LONNIE JOHNSON moved over from the fiddle to the guitar, and other guitarists of that period included MISSISSIPPI JOHN HURT, FURRY LEWIS, TOMMY JOHNSON, ISHMON BRACEY, and CHARLEY PATTON.

There were fairly radical differences between the Piedmont and Delta guitar styles. The Piedmont artists were fingerpickers; this means that their right-hand techniques alternated the use of the right thumb and index finger. This technique also became important in white country music, ultimately developed to a complex style utilized by such guitarists as Merle Travis, Chet Atkins, and

Gibson Blues King acoustic guitar (Gibson Guitars)

1

Jerry Reed. Piedmont songs also tended to use more chords than the Delta songs did. They used a harmonic structure that was indebted to ragtime and vaudeville tunes, and some of the performers, like Furry Lewis and John Hurt, performed folk ballads as well as blues.

Delta guitar technique often made use of a slide, sometimes in the form of a knife, sometimes a piece of a bottle. Delta blues focused more on the rhythm and melody than on chords as such. Often the guitar simply doubled the melody and didn't play full chords. Delta blues had a heavy, almost oppressive musical texture, while the Piedmont blues were more gentle and used a lighter rhythmic texture. When Piedmont musicians like TAMPA RED played with a slide, it was to achieve a sweet, almost Hawaiian kind of guitar sound.

Certain techniques are common to virtually all blues guitarists. "Hammering on" is a left-hand technique where the player picks a note with the right hand, then plays another note on the same string at a higher fret with the left hand by pressing down, or "hammering on" with a finger of the left hand while the first note is still resonating. When a player masters this technique, it also becomes possible to play the note with a finger of the left hand alone, although it requires more pressure from the finger to get a good sound.

"Pulling off" occurs when the guitarist plucks the string with the fretting hand. Pulling off and hammering on are often combined in the same song, or even the same musical phrase.

"Slides" (with the finger, not with a device held or worn on the left hand) involve moving from one fret to another on the same string with the left hand. The player picks the note, then the left hand slides up to another note on the same string. Part of the appeal of slides is that the listener hears the notes between the notes that begin and end the slide.

There is a difference between the sound of open (not fingered with the left hand) and stopped (a string finger with the left hand) strings. Open strings tend to ring, and the length of the ring cannot really be controlled specifically. If the left hand is finger-

Gibson J-185 12-string guitar (Gibson Guitars)

ing a note, when the left hand moves off that note the sound stops. Open strings are useful if the sound the musician wants is a sort of clangy, slightly out-of-control tone, as in the playing of Charley Patton or SON HOUSE. Jazz players dislike the sound of open strings, and they look for chord formations that never include them. The sound is much more clipped and controlled, which works particularly well with swing guitar, where the guitar chugs along playing a chord on every beat of the song.

Some guitarists did not fit conveniently in either Delta or Piedmont style. Lonnie Johnson often played individual notes, in the same way that a horn might do. He was probably the first blues guitarist equally comfortable playing jazz, playing with Louis Armstrong's Hot Seven group, and later even playing with jazz composer-bandleader Duke Ellington.

During the 1930s other musicians became influential in the development of blues guitar. Although ROBERT JOHNSON is a tremendously influential and popular blues guitarist today, some 70 years after his death, during his lifetime his importance lay mostly in his contact with a handful of blues guitarists like ELMORE JAMES, and through several of his songs, like "Dust My Broom" and "Sweet Home Chicago," which became staples in the blues repertoire.

Because so many of the early blues guitarists played alone, their music was free and somewhat spontaneous. Without a bass player or a drummer, guitarists could add or subtract a beat or a whole bar of music, and slow down or speed up the tempo without worrying that other musicians might have had trouble following him. If only two people were playing together, like Son House and WILLIE BROWN did, for example, such changes in the music were still possible, provided the two musicians were accustomed to each other's styles. When bass players and drummers became an important part of the scene, as later happened in CHICAGO, it became more difficult to create this level of empathy between the various musicians in a band. In the louder venues, like the Chicago blues clubs, it also was more difficult for musicians to hear one another over the din of the crowd.

Another influential guitarist of the late 1920s was FRANCIS "SCRAPPER" BLACKWELL, who played guitar with pianist-songwriter LEROY CARR. Blackwell's single note lines paralleled what Lonnie Johnson was doing. In Blackwell's case he probably developed this style partly to stay out of the way of the piano.

The mid-1930s saw the development of the combo blues sound, with artists like BIG BILL BROONZY forming ensembles of four or five musicians, featuring bass and drum players, and even saxophone. This sort of music led to the development of rhythm and blues, a musical style that wasn't comfortable with the acoustic guitar, because it lacked the power to compete with the heavy R&B rhythm sections.

MEMPHIS MINNIE stood out during the 1930s as the only well-known and popular female guitarist, usually playing lead guitar in her guitar duets with KANSAS JOE MCCOY and Ernest "Little Son Joe" Lawlar. Other good women guitarists recorded, like Mattie Delaney and Geechie Wiley, but they never achieved great popularity, and they did not record on a regular basis.

Several other important guitarists were comfortable moving between blues and jazz styles. White studio guitarist Eddie Lang made a remarkable series of blues guitar duet recordings with Lonnie Johnson. Teddy Bunn was a New York guitarist who played in all sorts of musical contexts, from blues to jazz. He recorded under his own name, and with such other musicians as trumpet player Tommy Ladnier. During the 1930s Bunn had a group called The Spirits of Rhythm, a good-time trio that included two other musicians on a small 10-string guitar-like instrument called the tiple.

Some of the blues guitarists began to use a flat pick instead of playing guitar with their right-hand fingers. Eddie Lang was one of them, playing either single-note passages or heavily chorded sequences with a pick. Teddy Bunn sometimes played with a pick and sometimes with his thumb and index finger. One of the few country folk players who used a flat pick was the fairly obscure Louie Lasky, whose flatpicking technique is an odd fusion of white country picking and blues.

During the 1930s the electric guitar was introduced and became popular. The acoustic guitar was temporarily eclipsed, only to return during the folk and blues revival of the late 1950s and early 1960s. During this revival some of the blues musicians who had been playing electric guitar, like Big Bill Broonzy, MUDDY WATERS, and LIGHTNIN' HOPKINS, reinvented themselves as folk blues artists, in accord with the demands of their new white audience.

The young white revivalists like DAVE VAN RONK and JOHN HAMMOND were fascinated by acoustic blues guitar techniques, and together with the rediscovered Mississippi John Hurt, Son House, and SKIP JAMES, among others, acoustic blues guitar styles were once again in fashion. BROWNIE MCGHEE played finger style but used a thumb pick and two finger picks, instead of playing with his bare fingers. Fingerpicks enabled a player to achieve more volume and speed, although they tended to produce a uniform tone with fewer musical dynamics than were available to a finger-style player.

Today there is less formal opposition between acoustic and electric guitarists. A number of musicians move comfortably from one style to another, depending on the demands of the particular music they are playing. Other musicians, like RY COODER and KELLY JO PHELPS, integrate acoustic blues styles into other styles of music, in a way that none of the original blues guitarists tried to do.

Gibson Southern Jumbo acoustic guitar (Gibson Guitars)

Alexander, Texas (Alger Alexander)
(1900–1954) *singer*

Texas Alexander was an influential singer who recorded 66 sides (the equivalent of 33 records). Alexander was unusual for a folk blues artist because he did not play any musical instruments and had to rely on accompanists. His accompanists varied from the brilliant guitar work of LONNIE JOHNSON, to jazz musicians and the MISSISSIPPI SHEIKS string band. Over the years Alexander toured with a number of famous blues musicians, including BLIND LEMON JEFFERSON, LOWELL FULSON, HOWLIN' WOLF, and LIGHTNIN' HOPKINS. He had a hard life, working in cotton fields and on railroad gangs, and serving two jail terms. Most of his recordings were made during the period 1927–30, and many of his songs reflected his work experiences or the time he spent in jail.

aliases

Many blues artists have recorded under a variety of names. Some aliases were meant to highlight geographic affiliation, such as TAMPA RED. Sometimes the recording company made the decision to use more than one name for an artist for a specific reason. For example, Delta blues artist CHARLEY PATTON recorded some religious music under the alias Elder J. J. Hadley. Paramount Records felt that Patton's audience would not care for religious music, and that the audience for religious music would not consider a blues artist an appropriate person to record spiritual music. JOSH WHITE began to record when he was only 16 years old. White's mother was very religious, and he did not want her to know that he was recording blues. At the same time he made some religious records under the name Joshua White, The Singing Christian.

Most blues pseudonyms were created for contractual reasons. When artists record for a record label, they generally demand the exclusive rights to the use of their name during the duration of a contract. They are allowed to record for other labels only if their record company gives permission. This is why references appear on some albums to the effect that a particular artist appears courtesy of a certain record company.

Most blues artists recorded for flat fees and received no ROYALTIES. As a result of this practice, many of the blues artists recorded for as many companies as they could, using assumed names. Possibly the artist who used the most aliases was JOHN LEE HOOKER, who recorded for a variety of labels under the names Texas Slim, Delta John, Birmingham Sam, Little Pork Chops, Johnny Williams, John Lee Booker, Johnny Lee, and the Boogie Man. Technically most of these recordings were made illegally, but many of the companies undoubtedly were aware that Hooker was doing this, because he had an unusual and very identifiable sound.

Another unusual use of aliases related to the popularity of recently deceased blues artists. When LEROY CARR died, Bill Gaither recorded under the name Leroy's Buddy. Similarly, when BLIND BOY FULLER died, BROWNIE MCGHEE recorded as Blind Boy Fuller #2. Both of the deceased artists were extremely popular, and this was clearly an attempt by record companies to cash in on that popularity. McGhee recorded under a number of different names, including Tennessee Gabriel, Spider Sam, Big Tom Collins, Henry Johnson, and Blind Boy Williams. All these recordings were made for different record labels, and according to blues historian Paul Oliver, McGhee used these aliases so that the public would not tire of him. The idea was that the consumer would actually believe that all these artists were different people.

Alligator Records

Bruce Iglauer was a shipping clerk for Delmark Records. He wanted the label to record HOUND DOG TAYLOR, but when he asked owner BOB KOESTER to record Taylor, Koester refused. Iglauer took $2,500 of his own money and recorded Taylor. This was the start of Alligator Records, which is now the single largest blues record company.

Among Alligator's artists are LUTHER ALLISON, LONNIE BROOKS, The Kinsey Report, Son Seals, KOKO TAYLOR, and Katie Webster.

Allison, Luther (1939–1997) *singer and guitarist*

As a child Luther Allison had a gospel music background. He grew up in ARKANSAS but moved to CHICAGO, where he attended high school. He formed a band with his brother and later played many local clubs. He recorded for a variety of record labels, and was one of the few blues artists ever to record for soul label Motown Records. Allison lived in France from 1980 until 1994. That year, toward the end of his life, Allison returned to the United States and signed with ALLIGATOR RECORDS, and his career picked up steam. Although Allison was a renowned blues player, he also integrated aspects of other pop styles into his performances, sometimes recording with horns. His life was cut short by lung cancer.

Luther Allison (Bruce Polonsky Photography)

Allison, Mose (b. 1927) *songwriter, singer, and pianist*

Mose Allison is a unique figure in the blues. A white MISSISSIPPI native, he earned his original musical reputation as a jazz pianist and composer. His first recordings were made for Prestige Records in 1956 in NEW YORK, and soon he began to feature his vocals. Although Allison has retained his abilities as a jazz pianist, most of his success has come through his witty and catchy songs, which reflect his Mississippi upbringing and rhythm and blues influences. His songs have been recorded by BONNIE RAITT, the Who, Leon Russell, and Van Morrison; in addition to recording his own songs Allison has cut songs by WILLIE DIXON, MUDDY WATERS, and SONNY BOY WILLIAMSON II. Allison has recorded many CDs, quite a few of them on the ATLANTIC label. With one foot firmly in the jazz world and the other deep in the blues, he is a difficult artist to categorize.

Allman Brothers and Duane Allman

Duane Allman and his brother Gregg had a brief and unsuccessful career as Liberty Records recording artists in California. They returned to Florida, where they established the Allman Brothers Band. Gregg was the lead singer and organ player, and Duane played lead guitar. They added Dickie Betts as a second guitarist, and Berry Oakley on bass and two drummers—Johanny Johanson (Jaimoe) and Butch Trucks. The band made several extremely successful recordings on Capricorn Records, featuring original songs and also some blues, notably BLIND WILLIE MCTELL's "Statesboro Blues." Never a pure blues band, the group moved further and further in a pop music direction, especially after Duane's death in 1971, followed soon thereafter by the death of bassist Berry Oakley. The group has reformed with various personnel changes, and continues to perform.

Duane had a separate career as a studio musician, playing on recordings by Aretha Franklin, King Curtis, and Wilson Pickett in Muscle Shoals, ALABAMA. Possibly his most famous recording is his guitar duet with ERIC CLAPTON on Clapton's song "Layla." Duane was particularly renowned for his explosive slide guitar work.

Anderson, Pink (1900–1974) *singer and guitarist*

An exponent of the Piedmont blues style, Pink Anderson also performed a variety of folk tunes, pop tunes, and songs from the minstrel era. Like many Carolina guitarists, he used a finger-picking style. He recorded with his playing partner Simmie Dooley for Columbia Records in 1928, and they played in various medicine shows. After the duo broke up, Anderson continued on his own. In the early 1960s he recorded an album for Prestige-Bluesville, and he gained many white fans for his music. Among them was British rocker Syd Barrett, who referred to Anderson when naming his band Pink Floyd. Anderson's music is good-time party music, with an emphasis on humor and a real zest for life. Folk revivalists continue to perform his song "Traveling Man."

Animals, The

The Animals were a British rock group that featured vocalist Eric Burdon (b. 1941) and pianist Alan Price (b. 1942). They were big blues and R&B fans, and recorded tunes by JOHN LEE HOOKER and Sam Cooke. Their major hit was the American folk song "The House of the Rising Sun," which they performed in an arrangement inspired by one created by NEW YORK bluesman DAVE VAN RONK. They learned Van Ronk's version from a record by his friend BOB DYLAN. The Animals' version was a number-one pop record in 1964 in both Great Britain and the United States. Later the band moved in a more pop direction, and Burdon left in 1968 to form his funk band War.

Arhoolie Records

Arhoolie started in 1960 when a young Austrian immigrant named CHRIS STRACHWITZ was introduced to songster blues artist MANCE LIPSCOMB by blues scholar Mack McCormick. Strachwitz was teaching high school in Los Gatos, CALIFORNIA, at the time, but by 1962 he had quit teaching and moved to Berkeley.

The label's initial big success story was that Strachwitz had recorded the first Country Joe and the Fish record, and he owned the music publishing rights to the song, "I-Feel-Like-I'm-Fixin'-To-Die-Rag." That song made a considerable amount of money, because it was on the soundtrack recording of the Woodstock Festival, and also was in the film itself. The saga has continued, because Chris owns half of the music publishing rights for the song "Mercury Blues," by K. C. Douglas. That song was a major hit for country artist Alan Jackson, and was then turned into a long-running commercial, with the Mercury changed into a Ford truck.

Strachwitz also owns a large record store, Down Home Music, in El Cerrito, California, and there is an associated mail-order service, Roots & Rhythm, which he eventually sold off to former employee Frank Scott.

Among the blues artists that Arhoolie has recorded are Fred McDowell, zydeco master CLIFTON CHENIER, and BIG JOE WILLIAMS; the label has also been a pioneer in compiling albums of Tejano music, the music of the Texas-Mexico border.

Arkansas

Helena, Arkansas, near the Mississippi River, was the home of SONNY BOY WILLIAMSON II (RICE MILLER), who initiated the famous King Biscuit Radio Show there, along with ROBERT LOCKWOOD, JR., ROBERT JOHNSON's stepson. The show was broadcast live from 1941 to 1969, and resumed as a taped show in 1986. It is now broadcast from the Delta Cultural Center, a museum on the life of the Delta that includes some blues exhibits.

Frank Frost, who was featured in the blues movie *Crossroads*, also lived in Helena and often performed there, where there is now a street named after him.

Armstrong, Howard (1909–2003) *fiddler, guitarist, and mandolinist*

Tennessee-born Howard Armstrong had a lengthy and colorful music career, embracing many musical genres. He played blues, ragtime, pop music, and jazz standards on the fiddle, mandolin, and guitar.

He also taught himself to speak Polish, Italian, and German, and he delighted in playing songs in these languages for appropriate audiences, who were generally amazed that a black musician was familiar with their language and musical traditions. Armstrong performed in a trio with Ted Bogan and Carl Martin, touring Appalachia and settling in CHICAGO. Martin died in 1978, and a 1985 film *Louie Bluie* shows Armstrong and Bogan rehearsing. Armstrong is portrayed as a fascinating and multifaceted musician, who also had talent as a painter.

Armstrong, Louis (1901–1971) *bandleader and trumpet player*

Louis Armstrong, also known as Satchmo, was a major jazz talent; in fact, he is generally acknowledged as jazz's first superstar. His career crossed over into the blues in his role as a cornet accompanist for MA RAINEY, BESSIE SMITH, and other blues artists. Although Armstrong is best known as a brilliant trumpet soloist with a very advanced rhythmic sense, he was also a bandleader. He displayed considerable artistry in his thoughtful accompaniments for blues singers. Armstrong was also renowned as a singer, and his scat singing, using nonsense syllables, used more of a jazz style than anything else. Armstrong recorded a large number of records as a bandleader, toured internationally, and through his many memorable performances and recordings became a beloved icon all around the world.

Arnold, Kokomo (James Arnold) (1902–1968) *guitarist and singer*

Georgia-born, Kokomo Arnold began his music career in the early 1920s in Buffalo, NEW YORK. During Prohibition, Arnold's main job was trading in illegal liquor as a bootlegger, and he played music on the side. The end of Prohibition found Arnold in CHICAGO, where he recorded 88 sides for Decca, beginning in 1934. Arnold was a spectacular slide guitarist who could play long melodic passages at very rapid tempos. ROBERT JOHNSON recorded two of Kokomo's songs. One, "Milk Cow Blues," was recorded 20 years later by Elvis Presley, and another, "Original Kokomo Blues," was changed into "Sweet Home Chicago." It is played by dozens of blues artists today, in and out of Chicago. In 1938 Arnold left the music business and his rediscovery in 1962 resulted only in a performance at the Gate of Horn nightclub in Chicago. Arnold had little interest in performing, and none in recording again.

Asch, Moses (Moe) (1905–1986) *founder of Asch and Folkways Records*

The son of famed novelist Sholem Asch, Moe Asch was a major figure in the folk music and blues revival. Asch entered the record business with his own company, Asch Records, was briefly a partner in Asch-Stinson Records, and later founded Folkways Records. Asch's goal was to record material that was of little or no interest to commercial record companies. He recorded folksinger Woody Guthrie, blues and folksinger Huddie "LEAD BELLY" Ledbetter, and many other artists. Folkways made many recordings of music from exotic places, usually recorded by folklorists and ethnomusicologists, and most of the recordings came with extensive album notes that described the music in detail. Among the blues singers that Asch recorded were BROWNIE MCGHEE and SONNY TERRY (separately and together), LONNIE JOHNSON, DAVE VAN RONK, LEAD BELLY, and numerous little-known folk artists who were recorded on field trips. Asch also reissued many old blues, country, and folk records from the 1920s and 1930s without the permission of the companies that owned the records. Asch felt that these companies would never issue these valuable historical items, so he felt justified in bending the legal rules.

Folkways was one of the first companies to issue boxed sets of recordings with extensive documentation, and later to do multiple CDs devoted to a specific project. Among these sets were "Lead Belly's Last Sessions" and a series devoted to field recordings of Alabama music. Both of these albums were produced by jazz historian and scholar Fredrick Ramsey Jr.

When Asch donated the company to the Smithsonian Institution in 1986, the terms provided that all the recordings would always be available to the public. The records are copied upon customer demand, according to what a customer wishes to order.

Atlanta

Decatur Street in Atlanta, Georgia, was the center of the Georgia blues scene. Atlanta was particularly noted as being home to a group of 12-string guitarists. The 12-STRING GUITAR was a relatively unusual instrument in the blues, but BLIND WILLIE McTELL and brothers CHARLIE and ROBERT HICKS (BARBECUE BOB) all were finger-picking 12-string players. McTell and PEG LEG HOWELL were both noted as songsters, with a broad repertoire of songs that dated back to the minstrel era. "GEORGIA TOM" DORSEY, blues composer, MA RAINEY's bandleader and later the father of gospel music songwriting, was originally from Atlanta.

Today Atlanta is widely known as an important city for rap and soul music artists and record producers.

Ninety miles from Atlanta is Columbus, Georgia, where Ma Rainey lived after her retirement. Her home has been restored and is listed on the National Register of Historic Places.

Atlantic Records

In 1949 Nesuhi and Ahmet Ertegun, two fanatic jazz fans who were the sons of the Turkish ambassador to the United States, borrowed money from their dentist and, together with NEW YORK record entrepreneur Herb Abramson, founded Atlantic Records. The label's first releases were commercially unsuccessful jazz recordings, but the label found its bearings in recording R&B records for white audiences.

Although Atlantic had its own recording studio, unlike the major labels, it recorded in cities all over the country when necessary or appropriate. In fact, when Jerry Wexler joined the company in 1953, he recorded Atlantic's artists in places like Muscle Shoals, ALABAMA, and MEMPHIS. He could employ tighter budgets in these places, because the musicians were happy to be paid union scale and did not demand the overtime payments that were part of the highly unionized scene in New York City. Atlantic also distributed the Stax Records releases in the 1960s, which included such artists as Otis Redding and Sam & Dave.

Atlantic experienced tremendous success, first with Ruth Brown, with R&B groups, then crossed over into pop, like The Drifters and The Coasters, then later with RAY CHARLES and Aretha Franklin. Periodically the label recorded blues artists like Blind Willie McTell in Atlanta, Professor Longhair in New Orleans and blues pianist Jimmy Yancey in CHICAGO.

Atlantic was sold to Warner Brothers–Seven Arts in 1967 and began to move heavily into the rock and roll business, experiencing tremendous financial success with the British band LED ZEPPELIN. Ahmet, though well along in years, is still the chief operating officer of the company.

Austin, Lovie (Cora Calhoun) (1887–1972)
arranger and instrumentalist

Lovie Austin was one of the few women instrumentalists active in blues and Chicago jazz. She led her own band, the Blues Serenaders, and accompanied a number of the classic blues singers, including MA RAINEY, IDA COX, ALBERTA HUNTER, and ETHEL WATERS. She coauthored "Downhearted Blues," BESSIE SMITH's biggest hit, with ALBERTA HUNTER, and was also a skilled arranger, writing musical parts for various instruments.

Austin also performed with a number of important jazz musicians, such as clarinet kings Johnny Dodds and Jimmie Noone, and trumpet player Tommy Ladnier. Austin lived in Chicago, but she led bands in theaters on the Theater Owners Booking Association (TOBA) circuit in various cities. After World War II, Austin ended her public musical career, playing instead for a dance school, and occasionally recording.

"Baby, Please Don't Go" (1935) *blues song written by Big Joe Williams*

Big Joe Williams is a bit of a forgotten figure in the blues. An inveterate traveler, Williams played his nine-string guitar all over the country. Among many others, Bob Dylan and Michael Bloomfield encountered Williams and were influenced by him. Although Williams is not particularly known as a songwriter, this song, recorded in 1935, was his big hit. Cover versions have been recorded by MOSE ALLISON, PINK ANDERSON, BIG BILL BROONZY, JOHN LEE HOOKER, LIGHTNIN' HOPKINS, and MUDDY WATERS. It has also been a favorite of rock bands, with recordings by AC-DC, Aerosmith, Curved Air, and Them. The direct lyric is simply a plea to the singer's woman not to leave.

"Backwater Blues" (1927) *blues song composed by Bessie Smith*

Many blues songs refer to natural disasters, and this one, composed by BESSIE SMITH, is one of the most moving of them all. Written in 1927, it tells the story of a woman who loses her home and explains that "there's thousands of people ain't got no place to go." The inspiration for the song came from a flood that Smith witnessed while on tour. At the time the record was released, 600,000 people, half of them black, lost their homes when the Mississippi River flooded its banks.

Baker, Etta (b. 1913) *guitarist*

Etta Baker was a Piedmont guitarist born in North Carolina. She learned how to play guitar from her father, and she also sings and plays FIDDLE, BANJO, and PIANO. Her playing was limited to family functions until she appeared on a 1956 field recording titled *Instrumental Music of the Southern Appalachians*. This album became a staple of the folk revival, and after Baker's children grew up she pursued music as a profession, recording an album in 1991 at the age of 78, and another one eight years later at the age of 86.

Baker is an excellent finger-picking guitarist, and her music highlights the connections between white and black musical styles, including folk ballads and country songs, as well as blues and ragtime tunes.

Baldry, Long John (b. 1941) *singer*

Long John Baldry was one of the first British artists to sing the blues. He sang in Alexis Korner's blues band, Blues Incorporated, which included future ROLLING STONES Mick Jagger and Charlie Watts, then toured with Cyril Davies's R&B band. Baldry later formed three bands of his own; among the members of these bands were singers Rod Stewart and Elton John. Later Baldry drifted into pop music, then returned to blues.

Ball, Marcia (b. 1949) *pianist and singer*

Pianist and singer Marcia Ball was one of the mainstays of the blues scene in Austin, TEXAS, during the

1960s and 1970s. She was often identified with fellow blues women Lou Ann Barton and ANGELA STREHLI, and made one recording with them. Ball was the only one of the three who also was an instrumentalist. In the Clint Eastwood piano video produced by Martin Scorsese as part of his *Legacy of the Blues* series, Ball talks about being influenced by New Orleans piano players PROFESSOR LONGHAIR and Allan Toussaint.

All three women often appeared at Antone's, a blues club in Austin, and the album they recorded together appeared on the club's own record label.

banjo

There are quite a few kinds of banjos that have different numbers of strings or use different tunings. There are two four-string banjos, the tenor banjo, and the plectrum banjo. The five-string banjo is used in bluegrass and old-time country bands. The six-string banjo, or banjo-guitar, is essentially a guitar with a banjo skin. Finally, the banjo-mandolin is a mandolin that has a banjo head.

The tenor banjo has four strings and is tuned C G D A. The tenor banjo has a relatively short scale and a "chunky" sound. It is generally played with a pick, in one of two styles. It can be used to play chords, which is often the case in Dixieland bands, or it can play single-string melodies. Some folk players like Blind Jimmy Strothers, who was recorded by the Lomaxes, fingerpick the instrument.

The plectrum banjo also has four strings, but it has a longer scale, with a longer neck than the tenor banjo. The plectrum banjo is usually tuned C G B D, although it can also be tuned D G B D. These are the same tunings commonly used on the five-string banjo. Like the tenor banjo, the plectrum is usually played with a pick, and it is used in the same way that a tenor banjo is played.

Four-string banjos were quite common in jug bands, sometimes played alongside another banjo, either a five- or six-string instrument. There were a number of four-string banjo virtuosos in the United States during the 1920s and 1930s, notably Perry

Bechtel, Harry Reser, and Eddie Peabody. None of these musicians, all of whom were white, were blues players. Many of the jazz guitarists of the 1940s, like Barry Galbraith and Bucky Pizzarelli, started their musical careers playing the tenor banjo.

The five-string banjo is tuned G D G B D, although a number of other tunings are often used by folk and country players. The five-string banjo is

Standard style tenor plectrum banjo (OME Banjos)

oddly constructed, with a fifth string that does not run all the way up the neck. In addition the fifth string is the *highest* note in pitch, which means that the highest and lowest notes of the instrument are immediately adjacent to each other. This unique musical arrangement differs from the way string instruments are generally constructed. The cello, mandolin, violin, guitar, and viola, for example, all have the notes lowest in pitch closest to the player's left thumb, and each string is higher than the last one. A West African instrument called the *halam* also has a short high string. Most slaves in the United States were originally from West Africa.

Because of the odd way that the five-string banjo is constructed, the right-hand techniques used to play it are quite different from the way all other banjos are played. The right thumb generally plays the fifth string, and the index and/or middle finger of the right hand plays the other strings. Probably the first technique used to play the instrument had the thumb playing the fifth string, while the first finger picked up, or toward, the player's body. Called two-finger picking, this was probably the way that older black players played the instrument.

Another odd aspect of the five-string banjo is that it was used by both black musicians and the white players in the southern Appalachian mountains to play square dance tunes and to accompany songs. For many years it was thought that black musicians simply abandoned the banjo as a reaction to the racist stereotypes of the minstrel era, but the research of various music scholars has proven otherwise. Musicians and scholars such as Stuart Jamieson, Cecilia Conway, and Kip Lornell turned up quite a few black musicians like Odell Thompson and Dink Roberts who played square dance tunes and old songs from the minstrel era. Some of these musicians played a fretless banjo. Frets, the metal bars that run down the length of the instrument, tell the musician where to place left-hand fingers. The mandolin and guitar, for example, have frets. The violin, viola, cello, and string bass do not use frets. The lack of frets requires the musician to have a superior ear to play the notes in tune.

GUS CANNON, who had a band called Cannon's Jug Stompers, played the five-string banjo. Cannon is most famous for his role in writing the song "Walk Right In," which became a major pop hit during the folk music revival, as performed by the Rooftop Singers. Their recording did not use banjo, although Erik Darling, the leader of the group, was an excellent banjo player.

Several white musicians, notably Dock Boggs and Doc Walsh, were five-string banjo players who became enamored of the blues. Walsh even recorded playing the banjo with a knife, while Boggs wrote a number of songs, like the "Country Blues," that combined the vocal sound of mountain music with his blues-inflected banjo techniques.

Three basic right-hand styles of playing the instrument developed before 1940. We have already mentioned the thumb and index finger approach. Another technique, variously called "frailing," "down picking," or "clawhammer" style involved using the index and middle finger to pick down on the strings using the fingernails of these fingers. This unusual technique had little in common with other instrumental styles, although some slide guitarists, like Son House, played the guitar in this way. The third technique was called up-picking, where the index finger picked up on the strings instead of down. This technique is easier to use than down-picking, and was later popularized by folksinger Pete Seeger. A more contemporary style called bluegrass was synthesized by Earl Scruggs around 1940. It involves playing complicated right-hand patterns with two fingers and the thumb of the right hand. Metal fingerpicks are worn on the fingers, and a plastic thumb pick is used on the thumb. Except for the more recent "newgrass" banjo players, most of the bluegrass players did not specialize in blues playing.

A number of blues musicians, including GARY DAVIS, and songsters JOHN JACKSON and ELIZABETH COTTON played banjo as well as guitar, their primary instrument. A number of white folksingers, like Pete Seeger and Billy Faier, played blues on the banjo, but neither played a large number of blues tunes. Some of the new generation of black blues revivalists, like KEB MO', and GUY DAVIS play the banjo. TAJ MAHAL has played banjo throughout his long career, and Otis Taylor plays electric and acoustic banjo as well as guitar.

Six-string banjo-guitar (OME Banjos)

The six-string banjo is played and tuned like the guitar, but it has a skin head, usually a rather large one. Because the instrument is set up like a guitar, it can be played either with the right-hand fingers or with a flat pick. The early jazz banjoists like Johnny St. Cyr, who played with Louis Armstrong's Hot Five, and Bud Scott, who played with Jelly Roll Morton, used the six-string instrument. Banjo players probably preferred it to the other banjos because the six-string instrument enabled them to play more complicated chords than the other banjos permitted. In terms of the blues, the banjo-guitar can be found in a number of jug bands, but it was most prominent in the work of Papa Charlie Jackson, who was the first country blues artist to make records, starting his career in 1925. Jackson's repertoire was a mixture of blues, ragtime, and vaudeville songs, and the instrument seemed well suited to his old-fashioned songs. On today's music scene the six-string banjo is mostly a novelty instrument used by guitar players to get a slightly different sound without having to master a different tuning.

The banjo-mandolin is a small-bodied banjo with four double strings. It is tuned exactly like a mandolin, GG DD AA EE. The paired strings are tuned exactly the same. Because the paired strings are so close together, the banjo-mandolin is almost invariably played with a flat pick. It is mostly found on jug band records and early vaudeville-ragtimey recordings of such acts as Ciro's Club Coon Orchestra or The Versatile Four. These were West Indian bands that recorded in England from 1917 to 1919. Of all the banjos, the banjo-mandolin is probably the least suited for solo work.

Bankston, Dick (1899–?) *violinist and guitarist*
Dick Bankston, who played violin and guitar, was a contemporary of Charley Patton, Tommy Johnson, and Willie Brown. Not much is known about him, but in addition to playing blues he played in a string band with his brother.

Barbecue Bob (Robert Hicks) (1902–1931)
guitarist
Barbecue Bob was one of a group of guitarists sometimes referred to as songsters, because in addition to playing blues he played minstrel songs, hymns, and folk songs. Hicks, who settled around Atlanta, played both six- and 12-STRING GUITAR, but usually he recorded playing the 12-string. He also played SLIDE GUITAR. There were a number of Atlanta 12-string artists, including BLIND WILLIE MCTELL and SYLVESTER WEAVER. Bob learned to play guitar from his brother Charley, who was also a recording artist. Bob's career was cut short by pneumonia, but he still managed to record 62 sides.

Barker, Danny (1909–1994) *singer and musician*
Danny Barker was a New Orleans singer, banjoist, and guitarist who toured with pianist Little Brother Montgomery. He moved to New York in 1930, appearing in a Broadway show with burlesque actress Mae West, then played with many famous jazz musicians and bands. He also played in a duo with his wife, singer Blue Lu Barker. During the 1960s Barker moved back to New Orleans, wrote his autobiography, and recorded a solo album.

bass and drums
The bass and drums make up the core rhythm section of a band. Their function is to keep the beat going and to make the music danceable. Full-sized stand-up acoustic basses became a feature of the CHICAGO combo scene of the mid-1930s. The bass is plucked either with the right-hand fingers or, when the player wants to sustain notes, with a bow. For blues playing, a bow is generally irrelevant.

Although the acoustic bass has a warm and rich sound, it is huge and clumsy to transport. It also has no frets, which means that guitar players, for example, often have difficulty transferring their skills to the bass. In the 1950s the Fender Company started to manufacture electric basses. Electric basses are much smaller and they usually have frets, so that a guitar player can learn to play electric bass without much difficulty. A few players used fretless electric basses, which enables them to continue to slide between pitches, but still use amplifiers to play at higher levels of volume. Some of the more traditional bass players amplified the full-sized acoustic bass by attaching a pickup to it. This enabled the bass to play louder, but it did not match the sort of volumes that solid-body electric players were achieving. In the days of the jug bands, bass players often used a one-string bass mounted on a washtub. This sound blended well with jugs and kazoos but wasn't suitable for complex guitar playing.

Electric basses can be played either with the right-hand fingers or with a flat pick. Guitarists tended to play with a pick, because the right-hand finger-style bass technique was different from guitar technique.

Two of the acoustic bass players active on the Chicago scene during the 1940s and 1950s were Ransom Knowling and WILLIE DIXON. Knowling played with BIG BILL BROONZY and was part of the "Bluebird beat" sound, while Dixon was a session leader and master songwriter who worked primarily at Chess Records.

As rock blues developed, bass players began to play more and more complex parts. Many of them virtually competed with lead guitars in these bands. In the last ten years bass players accentuated this trend by adding extra strings to the bass. Five-string basses became fairly common, and some electric players even added a sixth string. (Another instrument, a six-string bass tuned like a guitar but an octave lower, was used in the music for some of the James Bond films.)

Drum setups may include two bass drums, several cymbals, and extra tom-toms and other percussion devices. Most of this hardware would be considered superfluous for blues playing, although rock-blues bands might feel otherwise. Jazz drummers sometimes had trouble playing blues, as supposedly Elgin Evans did in the early part of his career with MUDDY WATERS. Jazz drummers like to improvise, most of them enjoy the opportunity to play extended solos, and they make good use of cymbals. Most blues artists want to hear the bass and snare drums forcefully keeping the beat, and they regard cymbals as a distraction that clouds the beat. In the blues the function of a drummer is to keep time, not to play extensive solos. FRED BELOW was a popular Chicago blues drummers. He also played with Waters. When a bass player and drummer play well together, we refer to them as "locking in" or finding a comfortable rhythmic groove.

Drummers seldom become band leaders, especially in the blues. Sammy Lay, whose varied career has included playing in the PAUL BUTTERFIELD Blues Band and also as the backup band for BOB DYLAN's electric debut at the Newport Folk Festival in 1965, playing drums with the JAMES COTTON band, playing on a number of CHESS RECORDS sessions, and working with the Siegel-Schwall Band, is also a band-leader. Unlike most drummers, Lay also sings, and he has made a half dozen albums as a leader. Most drummers do not sing because playing drums requires a good deal of hand and foot coordination. Also the drummer, stuck behind the drum set, cannot wander around the stage the way that guitarists can. The same thing holds true in rock and roll—Don Henley of The Eagles is one of the few drummers who also functioned as a lead singer, although he shared the latter role with Glenn Frey.

Bastin, Bruce (unknown) *blues scholar*
Bruce Bastin is a British blues scholar whose specialty is the Piedmont blues. He has written two books on that field, *Crying for the Carolinas* and *Red River Blues*. He has published numerous magazine articles about Piedmont blues and blues artists, and he runs a British record Company, Flyright, which reissues old blues recordings.

Bell, Carey (b. 1936) *harmonicist*
There is a dynasty of Chicago HARMONICA players, and Carey Bell took lessons from LITTLE WALTER and BIG WALTER HORTON. Bell's recording career began in 1968, and he played with MUDDY WATERS

and WILLIE DIXON. His son Lurie (b. 1958) was taught to play guitar by his father from an early age. He has gone on to make records under his own name and is noted for his explosive guitar style.

Below, Fred (1926–1988) *drummer*
Fred Below was a CHICAGO drummer. Originally a jazz player, Below became comfortable with the blues and became the house drummer for CHESS RECORDS. He played on records by Muddy Waters, CHUCK BERRY, and Bo Diddley, and also played on JIMMY REED's recordings for Vee Jay Records. Many of these recordings became hit songs on the rhythm and blues charts, and even on the pop charts.

Berry, Chuck (b. 1926) *singer, songwriter, and legendary performer*
St. Louis–born Chuck Berry was the first blues-oriented artist who crossed over into major pop music success. His early recordings were on the CHESS label, and his first hit, "Maybelline," was based on the country song "Ida Red." Berry is noted for his songwriting skills, his ability to capture the teenage market, his dynamic guitar playing, and his prancing duck-walk dance, where he hops across the stage like a duck while playing the guitar. Even in his mid-70s Berry was still doing the duck walk. Berry served several jail terms and returned to performing, but he always used pickup bands and did not rehearse with them. He also demands payment before doing his show, or he refuses to go on. Berry wrote an autobiography, and videos are also available about his musical career. Berry is a master of songwriting, and many of his songs, such as "Memphis," "Roll Over Beethoven," and "Johnny B. Goode," are known by virtually every rock and roll musician.

See also CHESS RECORDS and LEONARD CHESS.

Bibb, Eric (b. 1951) *singer and musician*
Eric Bibb is the son of 1960s folksinger Leon Bibb. Born in NEW YORK, he met many blues and folk

performers through his father. He began his career in Europe, and he lives and works in Sweden, performing and teaching. In addition to singing and playing the blues, Bibb has a repertoire on his half-dozen recordings that crosses over into folk, gospel, and soul music.

Big Maceo (Maceo Merriweather)
(1905–1953) *pianist and songwriter*
Maceo Merriweather recorded with guitarist and friend TAMPA RED for Bluebird Records in 1942. He wrote a number of songs and original PIANO pieces, including his most famous song, "Worried Life Blues," and influenced Otis Spann and many other blues pianists. Maceo mastered the art of using both hands independently. His left hand would play bass notes while his right hand played chords or offbeat melodies. Although many piano players do this, Maceo's right hand improvisations were more adventurous than those of most other blues pianists. He was less significant as a singer, varying his style between singing and reciting the lyrics as though they were poems.

Big Maybelle (Mabel Louise Smith)
(1924–1972) *singer*
Big Maybelle was a blues shouter who had a reputation as an R&B singer. Although she never became widely known, she recorded "Whole Lotta Shakin' Goin' On" two years before rockabilly artist Jerry Lee Lewis turned it into a major pop hit.

Bishop, Elvin (b. 1942) *guitarist and vocalist*
Elvin Bishop moved to CHICAGO from his hometown of Tulsa, Oklahoma, to attend the University of Chicago. While in school there, Bishop fell in love with the blues and began to hang out in black South Side clubs with MICHAEL BLOOMFIELD and PAUL BUTTERFIELD. The three of them were among the first important white blues musicians. Elvin also sat in with such blues heavyweights as MUDDY WATERS and BUDDY GUY. He later played in the Paul Butterfield Blues Band, where he and Bloomfield played extensive double-guitar leads and jams. This sort of jam-band music later became popular in San Francisco, especially in the Grateful Dead band, and it continues to be popular today.

Bishop had a brief but successful journey into pop music with his hit song "Fooled Around and Fell in Love," then returned to performing blues. He has lived in the San Francisco Bay area for some years, and he continues to tour and to record.

black-owned record labels
Although there have been many independent record labels, and many of them have specialized in blues and R&B music, it is surprising how few of them have been owned and operated by African Americans. Black Swan was the first to emerge in the 1920s.

Blackwell, Francis "Scrapper" (1903–1962)
guitarist
Scrapper Blackwell is best known for his duets with pianist-songwriter LEROY CARR, who was enormously popular during the late 1920s and early 1930s. Blackwell, a self-taught guitarist, later developed a jazz-oriented PIANO style of playing single notes with both guitar and piano having an important role in his recordings. Blackwell is often mentioned with guitarist LONNIE JOHNSON as being an important influence on moving the blues into more of a jazz vein. In addition to his work with Carr, Blackwell also recorded with T. A. DORSEY and classic blues singer BERTHA "CHIPPIE" HILL. After Leroy Carr's death in 1935, Blackwell left the music business entirely until he was rediscovered in Indianapolis in 1958. He then recorded a solo album for Prestige Records, produced by a young white folk scholar and banjo virtuoso, Art Rosenbaum. Unfortunately, as his career appeared to be reviving, Blackwell was shot to death in 1962.

Blake, Blind (Arthur Phelps) (c. 1890s–1933)
ragtime guitarist

Blake is considered the king of ragtime guitarists. He recorded 80 titles in a period of six years, starting in 1926. Originally from Jacksonville, Florida, Blake, who was blind, is believed to have moved to Georgia before starting his extensive recording career. He was a fingerpicker who mastered the art of syncopation, playing on and off the beat at will. He composed many songs and was a pleasant enough singer, but it was his guitar skills that made him stand out. In addition to his own records, Blake played on records with a variety of artists, including six-string banjoist PAPA CHARLIE JACKSON, classic blues singer MA RAINEY, and jazz clarinet player Johnny Dodds. Some of Blake's recordings were solo guitar pieces, some were songs, and some were spoken-word pieces in which he would play solo guitar while doing a recitation. Blake's work has been reissued, including a five-volume boxed set.

Bland, Bobby "Blue" (b. 1930) *vocalist*

Bobby "Blue" Bland's music varies from almost pop crooning to a more intense gospel sort of vocal delivery. He plays no instruments and has achieved considerable popularity with black audiences, as well as on the R&B record charts. Early in his career Bland was mentored by his bandleader, Joe Scott, a music arranger and trumpet player who led a band that later backed Bland on records and on tour. Bland performed with B. B. KING when both were beginning their careers, and in recent years he has recorded two albums with King. Bland's hits were for the PEACOCK label in Houston, which has long since disappeared. Today he records for MALACO, a Jackson, MISSISSIPPI, label that specializes in R&B-flavored blues for black audiences.

blind musicians and singers

There have been a large number of blind singers and musicians. In David Evans's book, *Big Road Blues,* he maintains that blind musicians virtually dominated the Piedmont blues scene with their virtuoso guitar styles. There were also quite a few blind "guitar evangelists," singers who made a living on the streets singing and playing religious songs, often with blues guitar accompaniments. As a young boy JOSH WHITE acted as a lead boy for a whole string of blind guitarists, including Blind Man Arnold and BLIND JOE TAGGART. Lead boys would guide blind guitarists/musicians through the city streets, and often held the collection cup for the musician.

The more famous blind musicians included Piedmont blues musicians, BLIND BOY FULLER, Willie Walker, BLIND WILLIE MCTELL, and harmonica player SONNY TERRY (Saunders Terrell). BLIND BLAKE was originally from Florida, but he became a superb CHICAGO studio guitarist who recorded both under his own name and accompanying other artists. BLIND LEMON JEFFERSON was one of the most important blues musicians who ever lived; he spent time in both his native Dallas and in Chicago. Snooks Eaglin is a contemporary musician who plays blues, rhythm and blues, and pop music in New Orleans. Holy blues blind performers include the influential GARY DAVIS, originally from South Carolina but transplanted to New York, and Texan BLIND WILLIE JOHNSON.

But these performers were just the tip of the iceberg. Other blind blues guitarists include such relatively obscure figures as Blind Cliff, Blind Teddy Darby, Blind Norris Davis, Blind Arvella Gray, Blind Johnnie, Blind Log, Blind Willie Davis, and Blind Pete. Not as numerous as the guitarists but still on the scene were blind pianists Blind Bobby Bryant, Blind Homer, Blind Joe, Blind Ted, and Blind Ivory Moore. Gospel-blues performers include pianists Arizona Dranes, Blind Mamie Forehand, and Blind Roosevelt Graves, and banjoist Blind Jimmie Strothers. Some of these musicians like Taggart and Dranes made commercial records; some like Jimmie Strothers were recorded for the Library of Congress by JOHN LOMAX; others were obscure figures whose names emerged in interviews with blues artists like pianist LITTLE BROTHER MONTGOMERY. College-trained HENRY BUTLER is a contemporary blind pianist who plays blues, soul music, and jazz, and even includes country elements in his music.

Blind musicians retain a place in today's music, with such artists as Stevie Wonder, gospel performers the Five Blind Boys of Alabama, and their friendly competitors the Blind Boys of Mississippi. On the country side of American music are guitarist and singer Doc Watson, guitarist Riley Puckett, and country-pop artist Ronnie Milsap.

Since blind blues artists could not write and few of them were conversant with braille, it is quite possible that they utilized a system of song structure, traditional verses, and improvisation for remembering songs. Certainly Blind Lemon Jefferson's dozens of recordings marked him as a composer as capable of writing new material as any sighted musician. Because many folk blues contained interchangeable verses, one can imagine the singer putting together a song in his head, and adding one of these traditional verses if nothing new came to mind.

There are some obvious reasons why so many blind black southerners turned to music. It was one way that a blind person could make a living in a culture that offered few options even to sighted African Americans. A number of books mention that passersby or social caseworkers who dealt with some of these blind musicians either were entirely unaware of just how talented they were, or were amazed at their abilities. Blind Willie McTell, for example, was an incredible repository of songs, ranging from slavery day ballads, to vaudeville, to folksongs and blues. Gary Davis and Willie Johnson were both excellent and original guitarists whose styles are still being absorbed by blues musicians and fans. Lemon Jefferson was also a superior guitarist, with a variety of styles at his fingertips, and both Jefferson and Fuller were extremely popular artists.

Another aspect of the work of nonliterate blind musicians is that the most blind artists of the 1920s and 1930s had limited educational opportunities. In a sense their songs and their lives were frozen at the point where they had lost their sight. Many of them became blind in childhood because of accidents or disease.

Another interesting sidelight is that the recorded songs of these blind singers virtually never refer to their lack of sight. The great exception was Gary Davis's "There Was a Time That I Was Blind," which describes his plight in great detail, and another of his songs called "People Who Used to See, Can't See No More." It is difficult to know whether record producers discouraged blues artists from singing such songs because they were not commercial or whether the singers themselves felt these sorts of constraints.

Simon Ottenberg's *Seeing with Music: The Lives of Three Blind African Musicians* is a study of blind singers in Africa. However, Ottenberg maintains that these individuals were quite unusual in their homeland of Sierra Leone, and that there are few blind musicians in the culture.

Blind Pig Records

Blind Pig was originally a blues club founded in Ann Arbor, Michigan, in 1977. The club led to the founding of the label of the same name, which has been in existence for over 25 years. A few of the artists who have recorded on the label are LUTHER ALLISON, CAREY BELL, DEBORAH COLEMAN, JAMES COTTON, BOB MARGOLIN, CHARLIE MUSSELWHITE, PINETOP PERKINS, JIMMY ROGERS, and MUDDY WATERS.

Block, Rory (b. 1949) *blues musician, singer, and songwriter*

Rory Block's father, Allan, played the FIDDLE and held Saturday jam sessions at his sandal shop in NEW YORK's Greenwich Village. From an early age Rory was exposed to a wide selection of folk music styles. With her friend blues scholar and musician Stefan Grossman, Block became deeply involved in the blues. She studied the styles of such blues guitarists as SON HOUSE, MISSISSIPPI JOHN HURT, and GARY DAVIS. Davis had moved from South Carolina to New York, and was blues teacher and role model to many young white musicians. Rory was one of the few white women who performed blues at this time.

Over the years Block has made a number of recordings, as well as instructional tapes, CDs, and videos, teaching various blues guitar styles. She and Stefan Grossman made one of the first instructional recordings on how to play the blues. Besides being an excellent blues musician, Block is also a singer-songwriter, and for some time her albums have alternated between her own songs and those of her original heroes and role models.

Bloomfield, Michael (1944–1981) *guitarist*

Born into a wealthy CHICAGO family, Michael Bloomfield was another young musician like ELVIN BISHOP, hanging out in Chicago's South Side clubs and learning the blues from such masters as MUDDY WATERS and ALBERT KING. Bloomfield also spent time accompanying Delta blues singer BIG JOE WILLIAMS, a creative and somewhat unpredictable musician. He also played alongside Bishop in the PAUL BUTTERFIELD Blues Band, and in 1965 Bloomfield and Butterfield accompanied BOB DYLAN at the Newport Folk Festival, where Dylan unveiled his controversial but eventually very popular electric sound. Bloomfield also played on Dylan's first electric album, *Highway 61 Revisited.*

Bloomfield left the Butterfield band and formed a short-lived but dynamic band called The Electric Flag, one of the first blues-rock bands that featured horns. Bloomfield enlisted his Chicago friends keyboard player Barry Goldberg, singer Nick Gravenites, and black drummer Buddy Miles, and added session bass player Harvey Brooks. The band was based in Mill Valley near San Francisco, and their wide-ranging music included elements of blues, rock, rhythm and blues, and even psychedelic rock.

Bloomfield also played on a best-selling album called *Super-Session,* with Al Kooper and guitarist Stephen Stills. Bloomfield's unsuccessful battle with drug problems put an early end to his life and career.

blues lyrics

Although the blues certainly arose out of difficult circumstances for African Americans in the late 19th and early 20th centuries, all blues are not sad. Jug band tunes and tunes from the Piedmont area in general tend to be more like party dance music than intense and reflective songs.

The most common subject of the blues is relationships between men and women, and this may involve breakups, one partner distrusting another one, or leaving the partner for another. The singer's attitudes vary from self-pity to an assertion that the singer has other partners available. An excellent example of this sort of confidence is BESSIE SMITH's "Young Woman's Blues." The song describes her lover leaving her after saying that he doesn't want to be tied down. Smith responds by singing "I'm a young woman, and I ain't done running around."

Folklorist Harry Oster, writing in his extensive collection of songs *Living Country Blues,* makes a distinction between the lyrics of country and city blues. He describes the earlier rural blues as having a wider range of subjects, a less specific form, and simpler chord structures than are found in the more sophisticated urban blues. He found that city blues also use more predictable music and lyric structures, the subject matter tends to concentrate on love, and the songs are meant for groups of musicians rather than solo performers or duos.

The notion of a less specific form deserves more attention. Some folk blues are simply collections of miscellaneous verses, which may appear to be entirely unrelated to one another. In BLIND LEMON JEFFERSON's song "Wartime Blues," he starts out by asking a woman what she will do when her man goes off to war. She replies that she will "drink muddy water, go sleep in a hollow log." The second verse is an exercise in self-pity, asserting that the women don't care about him, and the "men don't need me here." The song goes on to threaten suicide if he does not find his woman, refers to shining his light on Colorado rain, discusses a train wreck, describes his real woman friend as living in

Memphis, and finally complains that his woman friend is causing him trouble.

A listener who first hears this sort of lyric has the impulse to regard the whole song as nonsense. The best way to interpret this sort of lyric is to see it as an exercise in what psychologists call free association, where one thought suggests another, often unconnected idea. Whether the singer actually has a coherent story in mind is unclear. It is also important to remember the circumstances involved in recording before the introduction of tape recorders in 1945. Songs had to be less than three minutes long, and recording was done "direct to disc." As the singer was recording, the cutting machine was actually making a physical record of the performance, which would later be processed into thousands of copies of that performance. If the singer or any musician made a mistake, the wax master recording was scrapped, and the performance had to start all over again. A red light indicated that recording had started, and 10 or 15 seconds before the three-minute deadline the red light would blink to signal the singer that the performance needed to stop. When the performer was blind, as Jefferson was, someone would physically give a tap on the shoulder to signal that time was running out. Under these circumstances it isn't too surprising that some blues songs may appear to end abruptly.

It is also possible to interpret the lack of a coherent story by making an analogy to Japanese haiku, a form of poetry that presents simple verses as riddles for the reader to figure out. One of the collections of blues lyrics, Eric Sackheim's *The Blues Line*, does exactly that, interpolating Asian and other poetry into blues lyrics and quotes from blues singers in the last part of the book.

In addition to songs with verses that appear to be essentially unrelated to one another, other folk blues may have verses that can be regarded as a story but do not clearly belong together. For example, look at the lyric below:

I'm going to climb that mountain, look out on the sea
I'm going to climb up the mountain, and look out on the sea,
Every time I smiled, she turned her back on me.

Tell me woman, what are you trying to do,
Yeah tell me sister, what are you trying to do,
You know you can't love me, and love my buddy too.
Colorado mountains, are all wrapped in snow,
The Colorado mountains get covered up in snow,
If you leave me now, I don't know where I'll go.

Note that in this lyric the subject is clearly a difficult relationship, where a man distrusts his woman. The description of the snow, and setting the song in Colorado, may appear to be unrelated, but they could be regarded as part of the singer's thought process, as he is trying to resolve his romantic problems. This lyric would represent an intermediate step between the vagueness of Lemon's song, and a song like B. B. KING's big hit, "The Thrill Is Gone," with its specific and definite storyline about a failed relationship. Notice that in the lyric printed above, although the first line is repeated each time, there are small changes made by adding or omitting a word here and there. This is a typical pattern in blues. Some singers used pet phrases like Peetie Wheatstraw's interjection of the phase *"well well"* in many of his songs.

The classic blues singers were a kind of bridge between folk and urban blues. The majority of their songs were about love and romance, but quite a few other subjects were also covered. A number of IDA COX's songs were about death; other songs on this subject include Sara Martin's "Death Sting Me Blues," Bukka White's classic "Fixin' to Die" ("I wouldn't mind dyin', but I can't stand to see me children cry.") Blind Lemon's much-recorded "Six White Horses," also called "See That My Grave Is Kept Clean," and LEAD BELLY's "Death Letter Blues." Other songs, like VICTORIA SPIVEY's "T. B. Blues," MEMPHIS MINNIE's "Memphis Minnie-Jitis Blues," Blind Lemon's "Pneumonia Blues," and JOSH WHITE's "Silicosis Blues," dealt with illness and disease.

Another group of songs dealt with disasters, and blues singers seemed to be particularly fascinated by floods. CHARLEY PATTON contributed "High Water Everywhere"; one of Bessie Smith's best songs, "Backwater Blues," had the sad lyric "my house fell down, and I can't live there no more." Other songs about flooding include SLEEPY JOHN ESTES's "Floating Bridge," KOKOMO ARNOLD's "Wild Water Blues," and Robert Pete Williams's "Mississippi Heavy Water Blues." Another sort of disaster, the sinking of the ship *Titanic,* inspired songs by Henry Brown and Lead Belly. Lead Belly's song about the disaster is particularly interesting, because he attributes the sinking to God's revenge against the ship's racially discriminatory policies.

A number of blues singers referred to some sort of black magic in their songs. Muddy Waters's songs in particular refer to various forms of black magic or superstition. In "Louisiana Blues" he declared that he was "going down in Louisiana, and get him a mojo hand." A mojo hand is a bag of magic charms that can be worn around the neck, which supposedly makes the wearer of the charm successful in romance. Another Muddy Waters recording insists that he's got his "mojo working." In "Gypsy Woman," Muddy relates that his mother went to see the gypsy woman, and she declared that he was going to "make pretty women jump and shout," because he is the "hoochie coochie man." BLIND BOY FULLER referred to his "Mojo Hiding Woman," and both SONNY BOY WILLIAMSON I and Robert Pete Williams sang blues about "hoo doo", or black magic.

Regarding the blues of the 1920s and 1930s, a number of other themes emerge. There are quite a few songs about politics and social conditions. Peetie Wheatstraw's "Working on the Project" was about the federally-sponsored Works Project Administration, which provided work to thousands of people during the Great Depression of the 1930s. Similar songs include Bessie Smith's "Poor Man Blues," Ramblin' Thomas's "No Jobs Blues," and other self-explanatory titles like "Tough Times," "Hard Times Blues," "Starvation Farm Blues," "Stockyard and Blues," "Welfare Store." Racial and social injustice emerge as subjects in songs like LIGHTNIN' HOPKINS's "Tim Moore's Farm," which discusses a (presumably white) farm boss who does not think there will be time to bury the singer's wife. Josh White recorded many songs about racial

injustice and an entire album of chain-gang songs, and Lead Belly and BIG BILL BROONZY, who were popular among radical groups in New York and Chicago, respectively, also wrote songs about social and racial injustice. During the 1960s and 1970s Chicago blues artist J. B. LENOIR recorded a number of songs about racial injustice, the Vietnam War, and various American presidents.

Given the unfortunate fact that for many years African Americans could be thrown in jail at the whim of the local sheriff, police officer, or wealthy farmer, it is not much of a surprise to find a large body of songs that describe going to jail, rough conditions in jail, or mean prison guards. Some blues singers, like BUKKA WHITE, actually spent time in jail, and White described his experiences in "Parchman Farm Blues." Other singers lament that they would not have been sent to jail if not for an unfaithful or mean lover as described in Blind Lemon Jefferson's "Prison Cell Blues," where Lemon complains that he is tired of sitting in his low-down prison cell, where he would not have been sent "had it not been for Nell." Other songs about prisons include Sam Collins's "The Jailhouse Blues," Lightnin' Hopkins's "Grosbeck Blues," and other recorded songs like "The Jailhouse Blues," "Nashville Stonewall Blues," "Death Cell Blues," "Prison Bound," "The Big Rock Jail," "Judge Harsh Blues," "Free Again," "Pardon Denied Again," and "Electric Chair Blues." Folklorist Harry Oster spent a great deal of time recording in the Louisiana prisons, and his song collection includes dozens of songs by various prisoners, especially Robert Pete Williams, in which they discuss jail conditions and such events as trials and pardons.

Violence is another subject that appears in many blues songs. Much of the violence referred to was hypothetical, usually a warning to a mate that there would be grave consequences for misbehavior. Blind Boy Fuller's song "Pistol Slapping Blues" warns that he feels like "snapping some pistol in your face," while the Memphis Jug Band claims that they will "Whip My Woman with A Single Tree." LEROY CARR threatens to chase his woman with his

"Shinin' Pistol," and the same artist's "Suicide Blues" says that he was "tired of living, but wasn't afraid to die." Several other songs use the caliber of a gun as their title, including SKIP JAMES's "22–20 Blues," also recorded by ROBERT JOHNSON, who changed the caliber to .32–20, and Walter Roland's "45 Pistol Blues." No folk blues about lynchings have ever been recorded. Since lynchings generally occurred in situations where African Americans were accused of having sex with white women, or at least propositioning women, possibly this subject was simply too painful and too close to home for blues artists to memorialize it in song. It is also possible that had they done so, the white-owned record companies would have been less than eager to release or promote songs on this highly sensitive subject. BLIND BLAKE recorded a two-part song called "Rope Stretchin' Blues" that places him in jail after he has killed a man. Presumably he is waiting for the hangman.

Another important subject found in the folk blues is travel. The songs point to locations that the singer wants to go to, such as Denver, San Francisco, Louisiana, "sweet home Chicago," Tennessee, Kansas City, MEMPHIS, Kentucky, and New York. It is important to understand this desire to travel among African Americans in terms of the restrictions that they lived under during slavery, when they could go nowhere unless their master chose to take them, and when free blacks traveling were in danger of being arrested as escaped slaves. After the end of slavery African Americans could travel by train, and many of them "hoboed," riding freight trains and not paying railroad fares. In both blues and country music, musicians were fascinated by the sound and speed of railroad trains. They sang songs and created instrumentals imitating the sounds of trains, like black Grand Ole Opry star De Ford Bailey's harmonica tunes "Pan-American Express," "Dixie Flyer Blues;" Bukka White's "The New 'Frisco Train," "Special Stream Line," and "Black Train Blue"; Kokomo Arnold's "Southern Railroad Blues"; the Memphis Jug Band's "K. C. Moan;" and many other songs and instrumental tunes.

After the emergence of the automobile in the early 1900s and the building of highways, musicians had access to buses and cars, or they could hitchhike. Big Bill Broonzy's version of "Key to the Highway," which claimed "I'm gonna leave here runnin' 'cause walkin's most too slow" was a classic highway song, and others included JOE WILLIAMS's "Highway 49 Blues," ROOSEVELT SYKES's "Highway 61 Blues" and Washboard Sam's "Gonna Hit the Highway." SONNY TERRY promised to ride a Greyhound bus "until the tongue touches the ground" in his "Greyhound Bus Blues," and Bill Wilber also sang that he was ready to hit the highway in his "Greyhound Blues."

Any number of songs celebrate drinking, partying, and romantic conquests. Some are simply happy-go-lucky songs that describe drinking as part of partying, like Blind Blake's "Bootleg Rum Dum Blues," or STICKS MCGHEE's much later R&B hit "Drinking Wine Spo-De-O-Dee." Other songs describe alcoholics, like Tommy McLennan's "Whiskey Headed Woman" or Lucille Bogan's "Sloppy Drunk Blues." Other blues simply describe drinking, like MA RAINEY's "Moonshine Blues," or Bessie Smith's "Gin House Blues." The blues were often performed in rough environments, like barrel houses, juke joints, or other rowdy bars, where it was common for people to get drunk and fights to break out because of jealous husbands or wives suspecting their mates of stepping out on them. There were also quite a few songs about gambling, like PEG LEG HOWELL's "Georgia Skin Game," Blind Lemon Jefferson's "Jack of Diamonds" ("Jack of diamonds is a hard card to play"), Clifford Gibson's "Bad Luck Deck," and Blind Blake's "Poker Woman Blues" and his "Playing Policy Blues." Policy was a game that entailed choosing lucky numbers, like the lotteries that most states currently run. It was privately run, and technically illegal, but common in urban ghettoes. In Blake's song he tries various numerical combinations, but keeps losing. Nevertheless he tells us he intends to "keep playing until some good luck comes."

Of course, as in many types of music, love was and remains the primary subject of the blues. Even a rough listing of songs about positive or negative romantic situations would fill a book. To examine songs about love or sexual encounters, one should remember that under slavery no respect was given to black families. To many plantation owners, the only purpose of black families was to breed more slaves. In other words African Americans were regarded as breeders, in the same way that the owner might wish to establish a strong bloodline for his livestock. Families were broken up at the master's will, if he decided to sell off the mother or father to another plantation. Other slave families must have been broken up because one of the parents ran away without the other. It is also important to acknowledge that although sexual contact between male African Americans and white women was strictly forbidden, white masters often sought sexual favors from female slaves, whether or not the female slave was married to another slave. Any male slave that objected to such unions was literally taking his life in his hands. When many of these illicit relationships produced mixed-blood children, those children in turn also contributed to confusion in the structure of African-American families. When mixed-blood children grew up, they were often neither clearly white nor black. Unless their skin color was so light that they could pass as whites, they were compelled to seek blacks as mates. The presence of partially white slaves or ex-slaves created a class system among African Americans, where lighter-skinned blacks had a higher status than pure blacks. Many songs refer to these mixed bloods, sometimes calling them "high yallers," one of the many slang terms for mixed bloods. People who were obviously of mixed blood also reduced the coherence or solidity of the black family unit.

In the folk and classic blues songs, romance is presented with considerable suspicion. Many of the songs are either pitiful, boastful, or both. The blues singer sings of distrust for a romantic partner, then claims nor to really care, because other women are available to him. Self-pity is expressed in complaints of loss of a romantic partner and also in terms of homelessness or poverty. Sometimes the homelessness is expressed as losing a home because the singer's partner has thrown him or her out of the house.

There is also often an element of vengeance and violence in the lyrics. The singer sings that if her man leaves, she may cut him with a razor, or shoot him with a gun. Although there are expressions of romantic love and tenderness, it is much more common to discuss the sexual attributes of one's partner, whether positively or negatively. There are also references to bisexuality, where the singer complains, for example, that she is losing her lover to a "sissy," or homosexual partner. Ma Rainey's recordings of T. A. DORSEY's "Sissy Blues" refers to how she "found her man in a sissy's arms," and in her song "Prove It on Me," Rainey flaunts her own sexuality, asserting that she "don't like no men." Both Rainey and Smith were openly bisexual, although Smith, unlike Rainey, does not seem to have sung about it.

Many of the classic blues singers refer to frequent traveling, an opportunity not open to many black or even white women in the early part of the 20th century. These early blues women were feminist role models, but without the political motivations of the feminist movement that would spring up some 50 years later among white middle-class women. Since there were few white listeners to this music during the 1920s, most of these messages were received only by African-American women. Songs by both male and female performers often utilize double entendres—expressions that can be given a sexual interpretation in addition to their literal meaning. Many songs refer to cars. For example, taking a ride in a car may represent physical lovemaking. Other songs, like T. A. Dorsey's "Terrible Operation Blues," present the doctor as the one to cure the singer's love problems. Sexual metaphors can be found in Blind Boy Fuller's "Custard Pie Blues," or Blind Lemon Jefferson's "Peach Orchard Mama," and dozens of other songs as well.

When rhythm and blues became popular in the mid- to late 1940s, folklorist Oster's breakdown of song subjects becomes even more accurate, although periodically such singers as B. B. King sang about social conditions in the ghetto and in American society in general. This was increasingly true in the 1960s, when soul singer CURTIS MAYFIELD in particular was closely identified with the civil rights movement. Many of Mayfield's songs, like "People Get Ready," used metaphors in the lyric, words that appeared to have a specific meaning but stood for something else. In that particular song Mayfield continually refers to a train going to Jordan, but many of his listeners understood that he was talking about a freedom train where there were no Jim Crow cars. Similarly his calls to "move on up," in his song "Keep on Pushin," referred to race pride in improving one's position. In the same song he talks about a stone in the road that needs to be moved aside. The stone stood for racism and barriers to equality and justice for African Americans.

In addition to the forms mentioned earlier, some blues contain lines or phrases called *refrains*. A refrain is simply a repeated phrase. For example, look at the following lyric:

Goin' to the Rocky Mountains, just as far as I can see,
Everytime I start to smile, you turn your back on me.
Everything I ever had is gone.

Add another verse;

I'm headed to the river, just as far as can swim,
My mama always told me, someday I was bound to win.
Everything I ever had is gone.

The last line, "everything I ever had is gone," is a refrain. A famous example of a refrain is Leroy Carr's song "How Long," which contains the refrain "how long, how long, baby, how long."

When an entire section of a song is repeated, the repeated portion is called a chorus. This is a common occurrence in pop songs but unusual in blues songs, yet not unknown.

Blues Project

The Blues Project was one of the first blues-rock bands. New York guitarist Danny Kalb and drummer Roy Blumenfeld were in it until the end, and along the way guitarist Steve Katz and pianist Al Kooper were members. Katz and Kooper went on to start the hit jazz-rock band Blood, Sweat and Tears. The Blues Project's recordings varied from their own original tunes to covers of songs by blues artists like MUDDY WATERS and WILLIE DIXON and even to folk-pop tunes of the time. Kalb was one of the first folk guitarists to turn to electric blues guitar, and the band was quite popular in New York City.

blues revival

The 1960s brought the folk and folk blues revivals. First there was the rediscovery of such legendary blues artists and songsters as SKIP JAMES, SON HOUSE, MISSISSIPPI JOHN HURT, and BUKKA WHITE. These inspired a whole generation of white blues revivalists like JOHN HAMMOND and DAVE VAN RONK. Another set of white blues revivalists like ELVIN BISHOP, MICHAEL BLOOMFIELD, and PAUL BUTTERFIELD learned their trade by going to the rough South Side CHICAGO clubs and sitting in with the various black blues bands. This set of revivalists were more attuned to the electric guitar and rhythm and blues than to country blues music.

The late 1970s were not kind to blues artists. Chicago blues musicians had trouble finding work, and pop music was dominated by disco and heavy metal music. Some of the Chicago artists gave up on music as a full-time job and limited their performances to weekend gigs.

In the mid-1970s a blues scene developed in Austin, TEXAS, around a nightclub called Antone's. Out of this scene developed a group of musicians who generated long performing careers. Among these white blues artists were Lou Ann Barton, ANGELA STREHLI, MARCIA BALL, JIMMY and STEVIE RAY VAUGHAN, and Kim Wilson. During the 1980s Stevie Ray became something of a rock blues superstar, and his brother Jimmy had great success with his band, the Fabulous Thunderbirds. Black bluesman Robert Cray also tasted success with his smooth vocal stylings and songs that used stylistic devices found in pop songs, like choruses and hooks.

Once the rediscovered country blues artists died or retired from performing, there were comparatively few young black musicians playing the blues. TAJ MAHAL was virtually the only one with national popularity, and his music included musical styles far afield from the blues. A second generation of Chicago bluesmen like Lurie Bell did appear on the scene. These were artists whose fathers or close relatives were themselves active in the blues. Many of these artists were comfortable with R&B and soul music styles, and their music went back and forth between the various styles.

During the mid-1990s a group of mostly younger black blues revivalists began to perform and record. ERIC BIBB, GUY DAVIS, Ben Harper, COREY HARRIS, ALVIN YOUNGBLOOD HART, and KEB MO' all started their careers in the blues at about the same time, although Mo' was a veteran of the Los Angeles soul scene. All these artists featured ACOUSTIC GUITAR, although they all played electric blues as well. They rerecorded many staples of the PIEDMONT and Delta repertoire and also wrote their own material. For the first time in many years, Taj Mahal had company in his lifelong quest to keep the blues alive. Meanwhile younger white blues rock artists like KENNY WAYNE SHEPHERD and JONNY LANG are continuing to bring the rock sensibility to the blues.

In the early years of the 21st century, the blues style included a little bit of everything. The Chicago electric blues have become a tourist attraction, moving beyond the ghetto to the north side of the city. White and black revivalists, some no longer young, still perform the blues of BLIND BLAKE and ROBERT JOHNSON. Rhythm and blues has turned into soul music, but it is still essentially the same idiom—gospel-flavored intense vocals, with strong rhythm sections and horns.

The outlets for the performance of blues have changed over the years. Today there are dozens of blues festivals all over the world, especially in summer. Live performances still occur at everything from small southern juke joints to ghetto bars to tourist attractions like the House of Blues nightclubs. The South has recognized that there is a worldwide interest in the blues. In formerly racist enclaves like Clarksdale, Mississippi, blues museums are devoted to the music, and the state tourist bureau invites visitors to tour the "blues highways." A steady stream of new CDs, CD reissues, and blues videos helps keep the blues alive.

boogie-woogie

Boogie-woogie is essentially a piano style intended for dancing. Some musicians have also written boogie-woogie tunes for other instruments or swing bands. One example is the hit record "Guitar Boogie," written and recorded by Arthur "Guitar Boogie" Smith, who was a country and western instrumentalist who also wrote the tune "Dueling Banjos," used in the movie *Deliverance*.

Classic boogie-woogie performances were invariably piano solos whose playful energy contrasted with the generally more thoughtful style of blues piano. The confusing part of this picture is that many pianists, like JIMMY YANCEY, were excellent players in both styles. A further complication is that occasional boogie-woogie passages also appear in published ragtime pieces, dating back as early as 1909. Some of the more proficient piano players, like LITTLE BROTHER MONTGOMERY and CHARLES "COW COW" DAVENPORT, slid comfortably into all three of these styles of piano playing, sometimes even in a single piece.

Boogie-woogie employs a number of musical devices. There is a heavy left-hand bass part, with the left hand playing more notes than the right hand. In another pattern the left hand plays a repetitious rhythmic figure that moves from one chord to the next in a sort of mirrored style; for example, in the key of C, the left hand might play the rising notes C E G A C A G E on the C chord, and use the same musical distances between the notes while moving to the F chord and playing F A C D F D C A. The right hand then improvises melodic passages that fall in front of or behind the beat.

Starting in the 1850s a large black labor force was employed clearing forests in the southern United States, especially in Alabama, ARKANSAS, Florida, Louisiana, MISSISSIPPI, Oklahoma, and TEXAS. The men worked in rough work camps, and the labor force grew greatly between 1890 and 1910. In his authoritative book *A Left Hand Like God: A History of Boogie-Woogie Piano*, Peter J. Silvester writes that black saw and planing mill employees increased from 17,276 in 1890 to 108,811 in 1910, while significant though less dramatic increases of black lumbermen, raftsmen, and turpentine farmers and laborers took place during the same period. Silvester writes that these logging camps had large bunkhouses that could be converted to railroad boxcars for easy portability. One of the bunkhouses also functioned as a dancehall and gambling parlor, and prostitution was also prevalent in these isolated locations. This recreational bunkhouse became known as a barrelhouse, honky tonk, or juke joint, names that persist to this day in the South.

At these barrelhouses the early styles of boogie-woogie developed, practiced by little-known musicians who hoboed on freight trains to get from one camp to another.

The first recorded tune with the words "boogie-woogie" in the title was "Pinetop's Boogie," recorded by (Clarence) Pinetop Smith in 1928. As the form evolved, such musicians as Albert Ammons and MEADE "LUX" LEWIS developed a more structured approach to the music. This was partly because of the difference between recording music, where people actively listen to what is being played, and playing for an audience, which viewed music primarily as a background for dancing. Another reason for the development of more structured performances was that pianists started to play duets and trios, so that it became necessary for each musician to have some notion of what the other players were doing. Ammons and Lewis were childhood friends and often played piano duets.

The better players developed sophisticated compositions that used the form to imitate natural sounds, notably Lewis's classic "Honky Tonk Train Blues," his signature tune, first recorded in 1927.

Boogie-woogie was a prominent feature of CHICAGO rent parties during the 1930s. Admission was charged to the party, and the musicians were paid to entertain the patrons. During the Great Depression rent parties were quite literally used to raise enough money to pay the rent.

In 1938 JOHN HAMMOND presented his groundbreaking From Spirituals to Swing jazz history concerts at Carnegie Hall in New York City. Hammond included three boogie-woogie pianists Albert Ammons, Meade "Lux" Lewis, and PETE JOHNSON—and some tunes also included blues shouter Joe Turner singing with Johnson. The three pianists played solos, duets, and trios, and they were a sensation. The three went on to perform at a club called Café Society, and did an encore at the 1939 edition of Hammond's Carnegie Hall presentation.

Another aspect of boogie-woogie is that it formed an ingredient of a more complex style called stride piano, practiced by such fluent jazz players as James P. Johnson, Willie "The Lion" Smith, Lucky Roberts, and Fats Waller. Stride utilized a powerful left hand that featured a great deal of motion, often alternating single bass notes and chords. It also used more complex rhythmic and melodic figures than were found in boogie-woogie, and the left hand sometimes played intervals that required a long reach in the left hand, like tenths (for example, a stretch from the C to the E more than an octave above). Fats Waller had such a long reach in his left hand that he could even play the interval of a twelfth, a G an octave and a fifth above the C note. All these piano players were New York–based musicians who played jazz and blues boogie, and sometimes utilized elements of classical music in their compositions.

If the barrelhouse piano of the southern lumber camps was the first phase of boogie, and the development of the idiom by Ammons, Lewis, Johnson, Jimmy Yancey, and others was the second part of boogie history, the third development of the style took place during the 1930s, when it was adapted and orchestrated by white swing bands. Although the original practitioners and inventors of the style were all black, such white bandleaders as Bob Crosby, Tommy Dorsey, Woody Herman, and Benny Goodman used white piano players like Joe Sullivan, Bob Zurke, and Johnny Guarneri, who were fluent in boogie-woogie as well as swing piano technique. Pop vocal groups like the Andrews Sisters added to the boom by singing songs that referred to the style, like "Boogie Woogie Bugle Boy." By 1945 the big bands had greatly declined in popularity, the original boogie pianists had either died or were relegated to musical obscurity, and the fad had ended. Today boogie-woogie survives among well-rounded piano stylists for whom it is one of many piano techniques, and with a few European and American players who have dedicated themselves to preserving an art form barely recognized today in the United States. Many of the original recordings are available on CD reissues.

Blues scholar ELIJAH WALD credits ROBERT JOHNSON as being the guitarist who introduced the use of boogie-woogie bass figures to the guitar.

Book Binder, Roy (b. 1943) *Piedmont vocalist and guitarist*

In the mid-1960s Roy Book Binder devised one of the more interesting ways to learn guitar. He became Reverend Gary Davis's chauffeur, driving him to concerts. In turn Davis taught Book Binder to play his complicated Piedmont style of guitar. Book Binder went on to play with Homesick James, New York guitarist LARRY JOHNSON, and BIG BOY CRUDUP. Starting in 1973 he had a duo with violin player Fats Kaplan. They recorded and toured until 1976, when they broke up. Book Binder then bought a mobile home, and since then he has traveled in the motor home, touring, recording, and incorporating his droll sense of humor into his storytelling shows.

Book Binder's specialty is singing and playing Piedmont music, with a bit of country music thrown in.

Booker, James (1939–1985) *New Orleans pianist*

James Booker was one of the most influential New Orleans piano players, along with PROFESSOR LONGHAIR. He sang, and his music encompassed jazz, gospel, and pop, as well as blues. By the time he was 14 years old he had his own band.

Booker's career was a roller coaster, because of his struggles with drug addiction and a series of mental problems. He was a flamboyant individual known to rent extravagant costumes and a Rolls Royce car for some of his personal appearances. He was a spectacular piano player who could imitate other people's styles, as well as playing his own versions of tunes. Booker even played piano on some Fats Domino records where he basically imitated Fats' own style. In his odd musical approach he might throw in snatches of classical and jazz pieces in the middle of a blues number.

"Bourgeois Blues" (1938) *protest blues recorded by Lead Belly*

This unusual social protest blues tells the story of how LEAD BELLY and his wife, Martha, together with ALAN LOMAX and his wife, and a New York college professor were unable to get served in either white or black restaurants in Washington, D.C. Lead Belly recorded the song in 1938 for the Library of Congress, and it has been reissued as a CD on the ROUNDER RECORDS label. RY COODER, Arlo Guthrie, Pete Seeger, and TAJ MAHAL have all recorded the song.

There are several interesting things about this song. Lead Belly developed a way of creating narratives for many of his songs. Often the narratives were like little theatrical pieces, lasting as long as the songs themselves. In this instance the story is a true one, as described above. Lead Belly was friendly with a number of people involved in left-wing causes, including Lomax. Presumably that is where he picked the word *bourgeois* (middle class and conventional). The song also has a chorus, which it repeats many times.

Boyd, Eddie (1914–1994) *singer, songwriter, and pianist*

A CHICAGO pianist, singer, and songwriter, Eddie Boyd enjoyed his greatest success with his 1952 song "Five Long Years." In 1965 he moved to Helsinki, Finland, and later to Paris, France. Boyd was one of several piano-playing blues singers who did better in Europe than in the United States. Champion Jack Dupree, MEMPHIS SLIM, and Curtis Jones were some of his fellow blues pianists who moved to Europe.

Bracey, Ishmon (1901–1970) *singer*

Ishmon Bracey was an unusual performer whose voice varied from his low register to the soprano vocal range. He often played with another MISSISSIPPI bluesman, Tommy Johnson. As a teenager, like a number of other blues musicians, Bracey acted as a guide and traveling companion to BLIND LEMON JEFFERSON. Bracey recorded for Victor in 1928 and Paramount in 1930. During the 1930s he toured with Tommy Johnson, but when Johnson became an alcoholic, Bracey became an ordained minister and sang gospel hymns for the rest of his life.

Brooks, Lonnie ("Guitar Junior") (b. 1933) *guitarist*

Louisiana-born Lonnie Brooks plays a blend of cajun, country and western, gospel, blues, and rock music. He played with zydeco accordion master CLIFTON CHENIER, and moved to CHICAGO in 1960, playing with Jimmy Reed's band. In the late 1970s Brooks began to establish his solo career through a series of blues recordings on Chicago's ALLIGATOR label.

Broonzy, Big Bill (1893–1958) *composer, bandleader, and guitarist*

Big Bill Broonzy made over 300 recordings of his own songs and was noted as a composer, guitarist, and bandleader. Before he took up the guitar he had a career as a country fiddler.

Broonzy took the MISSISSIPPI blues and put a CHICAGO rhythmic polish on them. In addition to his many solo recordings, he accompanied many other artists. In 1938 JOHN HAMMOND SR. brought Broonzy to NEW YORK's Carnegie Hall to play at the Spirituals to Swing Concert. Originally Hammond was trying to find ROBERT JOHNSON, but when he discovered that Johnson was dead, he brought Broonzy in to sing the blues. Broonzy is credited with writing the blues standard "Key to the Highway," which has been performed and recorded by dozens of other blues musicians. He also wrote socially-conscious songs that openly criticized racial inequality. One was called "When Will I Get to Be Called a Man?" This song is a reference to white southerners calling an adult black man a boy. Another song protesting social conditions that Broonzy wrote was "Black, Brown and White." This song refers to the preference given to lighter-skinned African Americans, and complains about various ways in which African Americans have been restricted from achieving a proper place in America.

In the late 1930s Broonzy recorded with the Chicago Five, a combo that foreshadowed how rhythm and blues music would evolve, featuring bass, drums, and piano. Broonzy toured Europe in 1951 and 1952, presenting himself as much more of an authentic rural product rather than the sophisticated Chicago musician he actually was. He referred to himself as "the last of the blues singers." In 1955 French writer Yannick Bruynoghe wrote an informative biography of Broonzy called *Big Bill Blues*. Broonzy told the author a series of stories about his life and music, which Bruynoghe wrote up in book form. Among the stories is an amusing one about a blues contest with MEMPHIS MINNIE. Minnie won the contest, but Broonzy ran off with the prize, a bottle of liquor.

Brown, Charles (1920–1998) *pianist*

Charles Brown modeled his approach to piano as a member of Johnny Moore's Three Blazers after playing piano in jazz musician Nat King Cole's Trio. Brown pioneered a subdued pop-blues style that became very popular in California. He studied classical piano in his hometown of Galveston, TEXAS, and earned a college degree in chemistry. After graduation he taught school, but feeling he was not being paid properly, he moved to Los Angeles in the mid-1940s, and freelanced as a pianist until he joined the Three Blazers. His major hit song was "Driftin' Blues," recorded in 1945. After leaving Moore's group, Brown continued to tour widely in various clubs.

In an interesting interview in author Alan Governar's book, *Meeting the Blues,* Brown said that he simplified his style on records to make it easily identifiable, but when he appeared in person the band "sounded ten times better than the records." When Brown tried to persuade his record producer Eddie Mesner at Aladdin Records to allow the group to record live, Mesner rejected the idea, not wanting to argue with a successful string of records.

Brown had retired in the early 1980s when blues singer-songwriter BONNIE RAITT recorded several duets with him and brought him on tour. After that, Brown's career was reborn, and he toured and recorded once again.

Clarence "Gatemouth" Brown (Bruce Polonsky Photography)

Brown, Clarence "Gatemouth" (b. 1924) *multi-instrumentalist*

Gatemouth Brown is a multi-instrumentalist, playing blues guitar, country FIDDLE, MANDOLIN, viola, and drums. His father, an engineer on the Southern Pacific Railroad, played music on the weekends, including fiddle, banjo, mandolin, and guitar. This accounts for Gatemouth's own musical versatility. His brother Bobby was a drummer, and James "Widemouth" Brown, another brother, was a blues guitarist and singer.

Brown is convincing as a hoedown fiddler, but, ironically, his versatility has probably led to his being underrated as a blues guitarist. Influenced by pioneering electric blues guitarist T-BONE WALKER, Brown has himself influenced a number of musicians. As a composer, he has recorded prolifically, including one album with country and western guitarist Roy Clark. Brown has toured widely, both stateside and abroad, including an African trip. In addition to his musical accomplishments he was the deputy sheriff of San Juan County, New Mexico, in the 1970s.

Brown, James (b. 1933) *singer and enigmatic performer*

Not really a blues performer, James Brown is known as the Godfather of Soul and the "hardest working man in show business." His shows are dramatic and energetic, and he appears in a black cape, sometimes pretending to be overcome by emotion, only to be revived by a valet. Brown's music is a mixture of gospel-flavored vocals, heavy rhythm and blues drums, female backup singers, horns, and a bluesy guitar. During the 1960s Brown's music became somewhat political, and he began to emphasize black pride ("Say It Loud, I'm Black and I'm Proud"). Brown is a living R&B musical legend.

Brown, Ruth (b. 1928) *vocalist*

Ruth Brown was the first major star on ATLANTIC RECORDS, recording many R&B hits during the 1950s, including "So Long," "Teardrops in My Eyes," and "5-10-15 Hours". Her songs were often ballads, sung with a gospel singer's emotional approach. During the 1970s and 1980s she appeared in several Broadway and touring shows, and also in films. Through a chance meeting with corporate lawyer Howell Begle, Brown won a lengthy legal battle with Atlantic Records as a result of which Atlantic paid her back royalties (she had never previously received any). The same action achieved a similar result for other artists and led to the founding of the Rhythm & Blues Foundation, an organization initially funded by record companies that provides relief and sometimes medical treatment for older artists lacking financial resources. Her life story and the battle with Atlantic is detailed in her autobiography, *Miss Rhythm: The Autobiography of Ruth Brown, Rhythm and Blues Legend* (Da Capo Press, 1999).

Brown, Willie (1900–1952) *singer*

In ROBERT JOHNSON's recording of his famous song "Crossroads Blues," he sings "go tell my friend Willie Brown, I'm standing at the crossroads and I believe I'm sinking down." Willie Brown was generally regarded as one of the finest Delta guitar players. He recorded only a handful of solo records but was an accompanist on some of the recordings of Delta pioneer bluesman CHARLEY PATTON. Other than his brief commercial recording career Brown recorded "Make Me a Pallet on Your Floor" and other songs for folklorist ALAN LOMAX, working for the Library of Congress in 1941. Brown was a close friend of SON HOUSE, even moving briefly to Rochester, New York, to join him, before returning to Mississippi.

Brozman, Bob (b. 1954) *slide guitarist*

Bob Brozman is a SLIDE GUITAR artist who specializes in the blues, but his musical background and abilities include ragtime and early jazz. Like RY COODER,

Bob Brozman (Larry Sandberg)

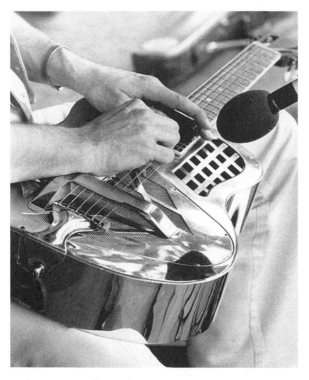

Bob Brozman on lap steel guitar (Larry Sandberg)

Brozman's interests include music from a number of musical cultures from other parts of the world. He has recorded Hawaiian music with Hawaiian musicians, as well as delving into world music through recordings and festival appearances with Okinawa musician Takashi Hirayasi, Djeli Moussa Diawara from Ghana, and musicians from other music cultures. He has also recorded with American guitarist Woody Mann and mandolin virtuoso David Grisman. In addition to his slide guitar talents, Brozman sings and plays ukulele and lap steel guitar.

Buchanan, Roy (1939–1988) *electric guitarist*
Roy Buchanan was a spectacular though relatively little-known electric guitarist, playing in a blues-rock style. He played in the Ronnie Hawkins band in the late 1950s with some of the musicians who later formed The Band, and recorded a number of albums. He never achieved commercial success but was known as a musician whom other musicians enjoyed and appreciated. His song "The Messiah Will Come Again" is one of his best known. Problems with drugs and alcohol put Buchanan in a jail cell, where he committed suicide, never achieving the popularity that many musicians felt he deserved.

Bumble Bee Slim (Amos Easton) (1905–1948)
pianist, guitarist, and recording artist
Bumble Bee Slim had a prolific recording career, cutting 150 songs, 30 in 1935 alone. He was popular in the 1930s, and he recorded with BIG BILL BROONZY and MUDDY WATERS. The peak of his popularity occurred in CHICAGO during the 1930s. Slim played both piano and guitar, and was heavily indebted to the work of LEROY CARR and SCRAPPER BLACKWELL. He moved to Georgia in 1935, and to Los Angeles in 1940, where he continued to record sporadically through the 1950s.

Burnside, R. L. (b. 1926) *guitarist*
R. L. Burnside is a Delta-style guitarist who has made some adventurous recordings. He recorded one album with Jon Spencer's Blues Explosion, a sort of garage rock version of a blues band. Burnside studied with Delta guitarist Fred McDowell and occasionally recorded with acoustic guitar. His specialty is raw down-home blues, with JOHN LEE HOOKER one of the artists who have influenced him. Burnside lived in CHICAGO and MEMPHIS before returning to his native MISSISSIPPI. His son and son-in-law have been members of his band. Burnside has a coterie of worshipful young white fans.

Butler, Henry (b. 1951) *musician*
Henry Butler studied PIANO, SAXOPHONE, trombone, and drums at the Louisiana School for the Blind, then earned two college music degrees in piano and

voice. His music includes a wide variety of stylistic influences, including jazz, soul, blues, Caribbean music, and country.

Butler's albums reflect his broad interests and influences. During the 1980s he lived in Los Angeles and New York, but after a brief stint teaching music at Eastern Illinois University in Charleston, he returned to New Orleans. He has recorded with black blues revivalist COREY HARRIS.

Butterfield, Paul (1941–1987) *harmonicist*

Associated with MIKE BLOOMFIELD and ELVIN BISHOP, Paul Butterfield is a white blues musician who hung out in black clubs on the South Side of CHICAGO. Like Bishop, he was also a University of Chicago student. Butterfield was a dynamic HARMONICA player who studied with blues harmonica masters LITTLE WALTER and JUNIOR WELLS, and like them played amplified harmonica. His band mixed white and black blues musicians. The bass player and drummer, Jerome Arnold and Sam Lay, respectively, were black, and the guitarists, Bishop and Bloomfield, and keyboard player Mark Naftalin were white. This was an unusual group for the time. "East-West," the title cut on their second album, was based on an Indian raga and became popular during the psychedelic rock period of the 1960s. Its long jam session format was taken up by the Grateful Dead and is still popular today. After Bloomfield left the band, Butterfield added a horn section that included a young David Sanborn playing alto, tenor, and soprano saxophone and a new rhythm section. Butterfield later formed another band called Better Days with singer-guitarist GEOFF MULDAUR and Canadian guitarist Amos Garrett. After this group broke up, two commercially unsuccessful albums followed, and Butterfield died of a heart attack stimulated by his drug and alcohol problems.

California

LOS ANGELES

Los Angeles was an important city in the development of rhythm and blues. The style of R&B that developed on the West Coast was a softer and less raucous version than was coming out of New York or New Orleans. Many of the California-based artists, like CHARLES BROWN, were influenced by jazz-pop pianist-crooner Nat King Cole, whose trio records during the 1940s, followed by his later enormously successful career as a pop singer, were widely circulated. Cole's vocal style tended more toward crooning than the blues idiom. Although Cole was not a rhythm and blues singer, he occasionally recorded songs in or close to that style, like his 1943 recording "Straighten Up and Fly Right." Other important R&B and blues artists working out of Los Angeles were early electric guitarist T-BONE WALKER, AMOS MILBURN, and PEE WEE CRAYTON.

After World War II, Los Angeles became a major center for the record industry. Capitol Records was the first major label to headquarter here, but some of the small blues companies like the various labels run by the Bihari Brothers, who recorded many of B. B. KING's early records, had offices in Los Angeles. By the 1970s many of the large companies, like Warner Brothers, were also established there.

During the folk and blues revival of the 1960s, the Ash Grove, a nightclub on Melrose Avenue in Hollywood, was an important outlet for the blues, presenting many of the rediscovered blues singers, as well as the younger white revivalists. One of the B. B. KING

blues clubs is now open in Los Angeles, and McCabe's, an acoustic music store and a concert venue on the weekends, carries on in the tradition of the Ash Grove.

SAN FRANCISCO BAY AREA

The African-American migration to Oakland and San Francisco occurred much later than did the population shift to CHICAGO. World War II produced a large demand for workers in the shipbuilding industry, and this population influx also brought a number of blues artists. They included MISSISSIPPI bluesman K. C. Douglas and blues artists PEE WEE CRAYTON, LOWELL FULSON, and JIMMY McCRACKLIN. Many of these artists had moved from Texas, and record producer–label owner Bob Geddins also moved in, starting his first record company in Oakland in 1945. Geddins remained active for many years, starting various labels and producing records for other companies.

During the 1960s white blues singer Barbara Dane ran a club, Sugar Hill, in San Francisco's North Beach where she and other blues artists performed, among them Jesse Fuller, who had moved to Oakland from Georgia. Fuller even wrote a famous and oft-recorded song, "San Francisco Bay Blues." CHRIS STRACHWITZ founded Arhoolie Records in El Cerrito, California, in 1960. He has recorded LIGHTNING HOPKINS, MANCE LIPSCOMB, and many other blues artists.

Years later, JOHN LEE HOOKER opened his Boom Boom Room, which is still open today. Other venues, like the Great American Music Hall in San Francisco and the Freight & Salvage in Berkeley, sometimes present blues artists. Berkeley-based

Fantasy Records has reissued many blues numbers recorded by Prestige Records during the 1960s, and BLIND PIG RECORDS is also headquartered here. HighTone Records, which at one time recorded influential bluesman ROBERT CRAY and now records important white blues revivalists GEOFF MULDAUR and CHRIS SMITHER, is based in Oakland.

Canned Heat

The peak of Canned Heat's career came in the late '60s, when they achieved success on the pop charts with the blues songs "Goin' Up the Country" and "On the Road Again." The original impetus for the band was the meeting of two fanatical blues fans—Bob "The Bear" Hite (1945–81) and Al "Little Sunflower" Wilson (1943–70). Hite was a serious collector of blues recordings, and Wilson, originally a trombone player, had become fascinated by the blues. He accompanied SON HOUSE while earning a music degree. Hite and Wilson formed a jug band, which later became Canned Heat. After Wilson's premature death, the band continued and exists today, although Hite's own death greatly diminished its popularity. Canned Heat was named after a song by Delta blues artist TOMMY JOHNSON. The band brought down-home country blues to the attention of millions of listeners unfamiliar with the music. The only pop music group that had comparable roots in the blues was the LOVIN' SPOONFUL.

Cannon, Gus (1883–1979) banjo player

Gus Cannon was one of the most important figures in jug band music. He played the five-string banjo, sometimes with a knife, and had a jug strapped around his neck so that he could play both at the same time. Cannon's Jug Stompers were popular around Memphis during the 1930s. Cannon made one album for Folkways Records in 1956, but his place in history was secured when the folk group Rooftop Singers had a number-one pop recording of Cannon's tune "Walk Right In." They copyrighted the song in their own names, but after some

controversy his name was later added to the songwriting credits. The song reappeared in the soundtrack to the movie *Forrest Gump*.

Carr, Leroy (1905–1935) composer and vocalist

During his seven-year recording career, pianist Leroy Carr recorded almost 200 songs. Carr is credited as one of the most important artists who transformed folk blues into a smoother urban style. He was also one of the best composers of blues songs, writing the blues standards "How Long, How Long Blues," "Blues Before Sunrise," and "In the Evening." Teamed with guitarist SCRAPPER BLACKWELL, their relaxed vocal and instrumental style influenced many other musicians and singers. Carr had a persistent problem with alcohol, which led to his premature death. Thousands attended his funeral, and fellow musician Bill Gaither recorded under the name Leroy's Buddy, as a tribute to Carr.

Carter, Bo (1893–1964) singer

Bo Carter was a member of the Chatmon Family, who had an influential string band called the MISSISSIPPI SHEIKS. Bo also recorded over 100 titles as a soloist. His songs tended to be humorous and were usually about romantic situations between men and women. The songs were playful and musically often displayed some of Carter's ragtime roots.

censorship

Censorship is the attempt to suppress speech or ideology. In connection to music in the 21st century, the sort of censorship that immediately comes to mind is the attempt to restrict the radio or television play given to gangsta rap music. However, censorship is a much more complicated process than limiting broadcast time, and there are many other aspects of the issue.

The first sort of censorship is self-censorship. Self-censorship is not necessarily a bad thing. An artist may decide that a song isn't good enough, and therefore change, or even abandon it. Other reasons for self-censorship may be more complex. An artist might want to write a blues song about a controversial issue, such as a white policeman killing a black teenager. The artist may guess that his record company won't like the song. He might base this assumption, correct or otherwise, about the record company or previous experiences with it.

Economic censorship can take place when a manager, record company, or business manager tells an artist that she is better off not releasing a particular record because it won't sell. A record company may believe that it will not get any radio play. A manager might feel that the song hurts an artist's image. Some in the music industry would rather avoid any sort of controversy, so they may be unwilling to release a record because they know it will alienate part of an artist's audience. A record producer may refuse to record an artist's song, or in effect sabotage it by devoting less time to the recording process. This might include such things as not carefully crafting a musical arrangement, devoting fewer hours to putting the song together in the final mix, or telling the artist that an inferior performance is adequate, and later removing that particular song from the songs that will actually appear on an album. Another form of economic censorship takes place in the process of record distribution, where a record company may release a recording but decide to spend little or no money promoting it. It can decide not to send promotional albums to music critics, who will then not review a recording, or the company might send very few copies of an album to radio stations, which hampers airplay and consequently limits sales. Under those circumstances, the only way that an artist can fight back is by widely performing a song; this, of course, assumes that the artist already has an audience.

Moral censorship is another limit to free speech. Moral censorship might involve a particularly outrageous video that shows people partially undressed, or it might involve a record that uses obscenities. Outrageous events shown on television can lead to censorship. For example, because of pop singer Janet Jackson's live performance on television at the 2004 Super Bowl, where her costume seemingly deliberately self-destructed and exposed one of her breasts, at least one performance by a rock star at a sports event was canceled, and probably many more will simply never be considered.

Moral censorship is handled in different ways by different media. In the early 1980s the PMRC-Parent's Music Resource Center called for record companies to place parental advisory stickers on recordings that used "unacceptable" language. Some record companies and artists deliberately created two versions of their music, the "clean" version with obscene words omitted, and another version. The movie industry has developed a different system, creating letter ratings for movies suggesting that parents supervise their children because of violence or sexually explicit scenes in a movie. The lowest R rating restricts the right of children to see a film without the presence of an adult.

Because most of the blues of the 1920s and 1930s were recorded by black artists for black audiences, there was comparatively little censorship of records. But many of the songs recorded and released during those years would be regarded as unacceptable today, when the audience for blues is now interracial and worldwide. This is because the songs used curse words or because the subject matter was sexually explicit. There were even certain artists, like Bo Carter and Lucille Bogan, who specialized in writing and performing such songs.

The last sort of censorship practiced is political censorship, where a record company will not release a recording, or a radio station won't play it because it takes an unpopular or controversial political position. For years no record company was willing to record BIG BILL BROONZY's song "Black, White and Brown Blues" because it referred to the oppression of black people by the white majority.

There is little question that political and moral censorship, sometimes by artists themselves, took place when folklorists did field recordings of blues artists. Folklorist LAWRENCE GELLERT collected many songs about racism when other collectors found few if any songs on that subject. It is not difficult to imagine that a blues artist would be quite suspicious of a white middle-class folklorist or record producer. The artist may well have felt that singing any political songs could be dangerous to the artist long after the folklorist or record producer disappeared. It is also possible that many of the artists felt that the folklorists might be racists themselves and, at the very least, not welcome songs that referred to issues of racial prejudice. Folklorists also censored songs that they regarded as being sexually explicit or "immoral." Newman I. White dealt with this situation by not printing such songs in his book, but by including them in the collection that he donated to the Harvard Library.

More than 30,000 CDs are released every year, and no one could have the time to listen to all of them. Although not strictly speaking censorship, limitation of space in a record store and the inability of artists to obtain distribution of their work limits available music.

Cephas, John (b. 1930) *Piedmont guitarist*
John Cephas is a Piedmont-style guitarist who lives in the Washington, D.C., area. He hooked up with the much younger harmonica player Phil Wiggins (b. 1954) in 1976. Together the two have toured the world and carried on the duo tradition established by BROWNIE MCGHEE and SONNY TERRY some 20 years earlier. Their repertoire is a blend of traditional blues and original songs, and both are excellent instrumentalists and fine singers.

Charles, Ray (1930–2004) *blues legend*
RAY CHARLES had a long and successful music career. As did a number of other musicians, he overcame the handicap of blindness. A trained musician with a music degree, Charles was renowned as a singer, composer, blues PIANIST, and jazz arranger. He spent many years developing his own musical style, which is a unique blend of gospel music and rhythm and blues. He usually used female backup singers, calling

them the Raelettes. Charles experienced great success in the 1950s recording for Atlantic Records. His early Atlantic recordings were a bit controversial, because he sometimes took religious songs and totally changed the lyrics to describe romantic situations. In the early 1960s Charles recorded two commercially successful albums of country and western standards, adding his own soulful vocals. Years later he recorded some country albums in Nashville produced by Billy Sherrill. Among the tunes was "Seven Spanish Angels," a hit country duet with Willie Nelson. Since then his work varied from jazz albums to Pepsi Cola commercials. Ray Charles became an American musical institution, and several books including an autobiography entitled *Brother Ray* and detailed biographies are available for those who want to know more about his life.

Charters, Samuel (b. 1929) *blues scholar*
Samuel Charters was one of the first blues scholars. His influential book, *The Country Blues,* appeared in 1959. He followed the book with an album of songs by some of the artists discussed in the book. Charters has written a half dozen books about the blues, covering such subjects as the relationship between African music and the blues, biographical portraits of various blues artists, books about ROBERT JOHNSON, New Orleans jazz, Swedish folk fiddlers, and poetry. He has also produced several records, including some important recordings by West Indian guitarist Joseph Spence and Country Joe and the Fish.

Charters has a descriptive and clear writing style. Some critics have objected to his work, feeling that it is overly romanticized and not based on serious, detailed research. Nevertheless, he has introduced many readers to the blues with his books and records. Charters lived in Sweden for many years, beginning in 1970.

Chenier, Clifton (1923–1987) *zydeco musician*
If there ever was a king of blues accordion, Clifton Chenier deserves the title. Chenier sang rhythm and

blues songs, often in French. The musical style that he worked in is called zydeco, and the instruments played usually include a metal washboard played with thimbles. It is related to cajun music, but cajun has more of a country feel, with FIDDLE often playing the lead parts. In Chenier's music, the accordion played the leads, in a sort of blues version of the way the accordion is used in the music of southern Texas and northern Mexico. CHRIS STRACHWITZ started an independent record label, ARHOOLIE RECORDS, and recorded a number of albums with Chenier. Toward the end of his life Chenier leaned more toward rhythm and blues music and included electric instruments in his band. His son C. J. continues the tradition, but with more emphasis on rhythm and blues and jazz.

Chess Records and Leonard Chess (1917–1969)

Leonard Chess had a long music business career. He and his younger brother Phil arrived in the United States from Poland in 1928. By 1947 he was running a CHICAGO nightclub. In addition to Chess Records, the company also owned WVON, a black music radio station, and formed Arc Music, an important music publishing company. Chess's partners in Arc were clarinetist Benny Goodman's brothers Gene and Harry.

The Chess Brothers formed their first record company, Aristocrat, in 1947. One of their first artists was Delta bluesman MUDDY WATERS, who had moved to Chicago. By 1952 the brothers had bought out their partner and founded Chess and later Checker Records. Among the artists whom they recorded were LITTLE WALTER, HOWLIN' WOLF, CHUCK BERRY, BO DIDDLEY, and Muddy Waters. Many of these artists' recordings were successful on the R&B charts, and in Berry's case the pop charts as well. The artists and Chess experimented with adding electric guitar, amplified harmonica, and drums to a more traditional blues instrumentation. The company also developed a sort of house rhythm section that played on many recordings. This included drummer FRED BELOW and bass player, songwriter-arranger WILLIE DIXON.

The company achieved enough success that it acquired its own building, which included an office and recording studio. Leonard's son Marshall joined the company and experimented by adding psychedelic guitar and heavy rock beats to recordings of Howlin' Wolf and Muddy Waters. The results were questionable and controversial. The company was sold to GRT Records in 1969, shortly before Leonard's death. It never recaptured its original feel or popularity, but today many of the original recordings are available on CD reissues.

Leonard Chess was an old-school record man, and many controversies developed over his business practices. Many of his artists complained that they did not receive the royalties promised in their contracts. Willie Dixon ending up suing Arc Music, the company's publishing wing, and he received a cash settlement and ownership of his publishing rights. At the same time, ETTA JAMES told author David Ritz that although she received no royalties from Chess, Leonard bought her a house and made sure she kept it even during the years when she was a heroin addict. Chess liked to attend recording sessions, and opinions vary about his role in the process of making music. The most famous musical story about Chess is that he once dismissed a drummer and banged on a bass drum himself to capture the beat that he wanted to capture on the record. Whatever Chess's business practices or musical participation were, most of his artists made their best recordings for Chess, whether or not they got better business deals elsewhere. Interest in the history of Chess Records has led to three books on the subject, including *Machers and Rockers: Chess Records and the Business of Rock & Roll* (Norton) and *Spinning Blues Into Gold: The Chess Brothers and the Legendary Chess Records* (St. Martin's Press).

Chicago

Chicago, Illinois, is one of the most important cities in tracing the development of the blues. The blues in Chicago developed from the migration of African Americans to the city from the South, especially from the MISSISSIPPI Delta. In addition to the migration of blues artists, the presence of record companies and music business entrepreneurs played a significant role in the development of Chicago blues.

BLIND LEMON JEFFERSON was the first major artist to record in Chicago. Jefferson traveled back and forth from his Texas home to Chicago, recording dozens of successful records during the period 1925–29. BLIND BLAKE was another important recording artist who recorded from 1926 to 1932. Blake was a Piedmont artist who had lived in Florida and Georgia before coming to Chicago.

During the 1930s, record producer and entrepreneur LESTER MELROSE recorded many artists of that period, including BIG BILL BROONZY. Aside from TAMPA RED, another artist who lived in Florida and

Arvella Gray (Art Thieme)

Georgia before coming to Chicago, Melrose's artists all came from Mississippi, ARKANSAS, or LOUISIANA. The Delta artists are generally identified with the Chicago blues. MUDDY WATERS and ELMORE JAMES were among the major artists who developed the electric blues. In addition to electric guitar, which James played with a slide, their bands included bass, drums, and piano. As the style evolved and younger musicians like J. B. Hutto and BUDDY GUY came on the scene, electric bass replaced acoustic bass, and the guitarists played more modern, solid-body electric guitars with larger amplifiers, which allowed them to play at higher volume.

The early black migrants to Chicago lived mostly on the South Side of the city, and a number of clubs, such as Theresa's, became major venues for blues artists. In later years the black population also expanded to the West Side of the town, and other clubs opened there.

Until recently the Maxwell Street Market in a racially mixed ghetto on the South Side also played an important role as a performing place for blues artists. On Sundays it was an outdoor marketplace filled with pushcarts and stalls where peddlers sold food, clothing, and appliances. Blues artists played in the market for tips, and it was a rendezvous where new blues artists could come to town and quickly meet some of the established musicians. In more recent years the street has become more of a flea market. The area is now being redeveloped by its landlord, the University of Chicago.

Another important landmark on the South Side was the home of Chess Records, the label that recorded Muddy Waters, LITTLE WALTER, BO DIDDLEY, and most of CHUCK BERRY's hits. The building is located at 2120 S. Michigan Avenue and tours are available. The building now belongs to the Blues Heaven Foundation, Inc., an organization founded by blues songwriter WILLIE DIXON and originally financed by a portion of his songwriting royalties. The building also houses a collection of photographs of blues artists.

Another group of artists came from Texas, notably Texas Alexander, who sang but did not play, and Blind Lemon Jefferson, who dominated folk blues during the late 1920s. The Texas style had a foot in each of the other styles, but Lemon himself was quite eclectic, varying his style from song to song. Some artists, notably LONNIE JOHNSON, cannot be pigeonholed. Growing up in New Orleans, living variously in St. Louis and Chicago, Johnson assimilated many jazz and blues styles, and sometimes his singing approaches pop crooning as much as it does blues.

Chicago was the place where blues combos developed, starting with Tampa Red's and Big Bill Broonzy's work in the period 1935–40. The combos included drums, string bass, and saxophone. When the electric guitar came into use, it was quickly adopted by blues artists as a way of being heard over the rest of the band in loud venues. This combo style, referred to as the "Bluebird Beat" after the record company of that name, led to early rhythm and blues records.

BOOGIE-WOOGIE was another style that largely developed out of Chicago, with piano players Pinetop Smith, Albert Ammons, and MEADE LUX LEWIS all living in the same building, and playing as a trio, in duos, or as soloists. Boogie-woogie was essentially a piano style, but as the fad developed, it was orchestrated and band leaders like Tommy Dorsey had hits with band versions of boogie. By 1950 the fad for boogie-woogie had evaporated.

When electric guitars entered the scene in the late 1930s and early 1940s, the Chicago electric blues bands developed. Muddy Waters, HOWLIN' WOLF, and SONNY BOY WILLIAMSON II (RICE MILLER) were the major figures, and practically every Chicago blues musician of the 1960s and 1970s spent time playing with one or more of them. The harmonica also was amplified, and Waters's bands and many of the other Chicago bands featured such harmonica players as Little Walter, Junior Wells, JAMES COTTON, and BIG WALTER HORTON. Harmonicas played lead parts that paralleled the horn lines found in jazz bands.

Today Chicago continues to house many clubs where the blues are performed on a regular basis, but the clubs are now located all over the city, including the suburbs. ALLIGATOR RECORDS, the largest blues record company, is headquartered here, as is Earwig Records and Delmark. Delmark, the oldest of the group, records both jazz and blues; it also operates the Jazz Record Mart, a well-stocked record store with a large blues stock.

Chicken Shack

One of the first British pop-blues bands, Chicken Shack scored a British top-20 hit with their recording of "I'd Rather Go Blind." Stan Webb was the guitarist and lead singer, until pianist Christine Perfect joined the group in 1967. She stayed in the group until 1969, then married John McVie and became a member of FLEETWOOD MAC. The band showed both R&B and blues influences. It disbanded in 1973 and reappeared during the 1980s.

Clapton, Eric (b. 1945) *guitarist*

Eric Clapton is one of the most influential British blues artists. He started out in an R&B band at the age of 17, became the guitarist in the YARDBIRDS, and left after their big hit "For Your Love" moved the band in more of a pop direction. He then joined JOHN MAYALL's Bluesbeakers, leaving to form his influential trio CREAM, and after that band broke up was briefly in Blind Faith, a short-lived "supergroup," with drummer Ginger Baker, bass player Rick Grech, and vocalist-keyboard player Steve Winwood. Clapton then recorded in a band he called Derek and the Dominos, with slide guitarist Duane Allman. Clapton's early influences were electric guitarists Freddie Albert, B. B. KING, ROBERT JOHNSON, and MUDDY WATERS.

In the early part of his career Clapton was noted for his spectacular electric guitar solos, but in recent years he has played more acoustic guitar, rearranging his hit "Layla" for acoustic guitar. Guitar maker Martin Guitars has marketed a limited-edition guitar that is an Eric Clapton signature model. Clapton wrote some of the album notes for box-set CD reissues of Robert Johnson's recordings. He has recorded an album with B. B. King and recently made an album entirely devoted to the songs of Robert Johnson.

classic blues

The first black blues recordings were the classic blues recordings of the 1920s, with the first one made by MAMIE SMITH. When record companies found that there was a market for the blues, they immediately recorded several dozen classic blues singers, all of whom were women. None played an instrument on her recordings, although SIPPIE WALLACE was capable of doing so. It simply happened that she had a younger brother who was a superb instrumentalist.

The musical style of classic blues was a blend of vaudeville, ragtime, pop music, and blues. All the classic blues artists were experienced performers, and many of them played in theaters. Some also appeared in plays and films. The two most famous artists were Ma Rainey and BESSIE SMITH. Although Smith became famous, "Downhearted Blues," her first record, was the most popular one she ever made. Ma Rainey wrote or coauthored most of her own songs, and a few of the other classic blues artists, like IDA COX, VICTORIA SPIVEY, and Sippie Wallace, were also talented songwriters. Smith did not write as many, but she also recorded more songs than anyone else, and the songs that she did write, like "Backwater Blues," were imaginative and interesting.

Because classic blues singers were not instrumentalists, their recordings featured everything from jug band accompaniments to small or medium-sized jazz bands. A number of the bands consisted of jazz musicians who played on these records because they were a source of income.

Because classic blues singers were all experienced performers, for the most part they enunciated well, and the lyrics of the songs were easy to understand. Heard today on reissue albums, these recordings remain easy to follow. The exception is Ma Rainey, due to a combination of poor recording quality and

a countrified accent. By 1930 the vogue for classic blues singers had died down, and the onset of the Great Depression crippled record sales. Smith died in 1937, and by that time none of the classic blues singers was actively singing the blues.

Just as folk blues artists were rediscovered during the late 1950s and into the 1960s, some of the classic blues singers reemerged and resumed their careers. This group included Ida Cox, ALBERTA HUNTER, BERTHA "CHIPPIE" HILL, Victoria Spivey, and Sippie Wallace. Many other classic blues singers were dead, or their whereabouts were unknown.

Clearwater, Eddy (b. 1935) *guitarist*

MISSISSIPPI-born Eddy Clearwater moved to Chicago in the early 1950s and became one of the leading exponents of the so-called West Side CHICAGO blues guitar styles. Clearwater's music combines elements of blues, gospel, rock and roll, and soul music. He plays the guitar left-handed and often appears in an Indian headdress.

Coleman, Deborah (b. 1956) *electric guitarist*

Deborah Coleman stands out in the blues field because she is a black woman who plays strong electric lead guitar while leading her own band. Coleman, who grew up in a musical family, is a former nurse and electrician. Her father played piano, and two of her brothers and sisters also played guitar or piano. At the age of eight Coleman was inspired to take up the guitar after seeing the Monkees TV show.

Her recordings are a blend of blues and original songs, featuring her powerful Jimi Hendrix–influenced guitar work.

Collins, Albert (1932–1993) *guitarist*

One of the important TEXAS-raised blues guitarists and a cousin of Houston bluesman LIGHTNIN' HOPKINS, Albert Collins was an innovative guitarist who played the guitar in minor tunings and also

Albert Collins (Larry Sandberg)

used a capo high up on the neck of the guitar. (A capo is a mechanical device that enables guitarists to play in difficult keys with simple chords.) A minor tuning tunes all the strings to a minor chord; for example, an E Minor tuning might be E B E G B E. Collins had a reputation as a superb showman whose performances were so explosive that no one wanted to go on stage after he performed.

Connor, Joanna (b. 1962) *slide guitarist, singer, and songwriter*
Joanna Connor developed a reputation as a forceful slide guitarist, singer, and songwriter. She has been a professional musician since the age of 10, growing up in Worcester, Massachusetts. Joanna was seven years old when she saw Bonnie Raitt perform at a coffeehouse. Connor's original instrument was the saxophone. She moved to Chicago in 1984 and played for other singers before starting her own band.

Cooder, Ry (b. 1947) *slide guitarist and composer*
Ry Cooder is an extremely versatile musician, but his roots are definitely in the blues. He grew up in Los Angeles, and as a teenager would periodically take guitar lessons from musicians passing through town. In the early 1960s he formed a blues-rock band with TAJ MAHAL called the Rising Sons. Cooder played on the ROLLING STONES' *Let It Bleed* album, and has recorded numerous solo albums for Warner Brothers. He plays mandolin, banjo, and many styles of guitar but is best known for his dynamic and creative slide guitar playing. On his recordings Cooder is fond of creating original musical stylings by combining instruments that usually would not play together, such as Tex-Mex accordion and slide guitar. In recent years Cooder has concentrated on writing film scores, among them the music for *Paris, Texas; The Long Riders;* and *Crossroads.* He has also become increasingly interested in music from different parts of the world, recording with Cuban, African, and Indian musicians. His Cuban recordings with the band Buena Vista Social Club have been particularly popular and are also documented on film.

Copeland, Johnny (1937–1997) *electric guitarist and vocalist*
Johnny Copeland was a dynamic electric guitarist who experimented by recording with African and jazz musicians. Vocally his singing shows the influence of soul music. He made a successful trio album with Robert Cray and ALBERT COLLINS. His daughter Shemekia (b. 1979) turned professional at the age of 16, toured with her father, partly to help take care of his heart condition, and later won several W. C. HANDY Blues awards.

Shemekia Copeland (Bruce Polonsky Photography)

"Cortelia Clark" (1972) *tribute song written by Mickey Newbury*

Cortelia Clark was one of many blind street singers who could be found all over the southern United States and in many northern cities as well. Many of these musicians had disappeared by the 1950s, but Clark plied his trade on the streets of Nashville into the 1960s. One day Felton Jarvis, a producer for RCA Records whose artists included ELVIS PRESLEY, saw Clark near his company's office and decided to record him. The 1966 album won a Grammy Award, but Clark quickly disappeared into the streets, dying a few years later. Mickey Newbury was one of the most creative and original of the numerous songwriters in Nashville, and

he wrote this song, not a blues, but a ballad that pays tribute to the bluesman, ending by asking God "can you save a street in glory, for Cortelia Clark?"

Newbury recorded the song in 1972, and it subsequently has been recorded by a recent version of the Kingston Trio, and in 2002 by JOSH WHITE Jr. Since White's father led blind singers on the streets of the Carolinas at the age of ten, it seems particularly appropriate that his own son would sing this song.

Cotton, Elizabeth (1895–1987) *songwriter, singer, and guitarist*

Elizabeth Cotton was a songster who performed turn-of-the-century songs and ragtime tunes in the vein of Piedmont guitar styles. She played the guitar left-handed and upside down, so it is impossible for a right-handed guitarist to duplicate her technique. Cotton also played BANJO.

Cotton was working as a maid for ethnomusicologist Charles Seeger and his wife, Ruth Crawford Seeger, when one day their daughter Peggy saw her playing the guitar. As a result, Cotton was invited to become a part of the 1960s folk revival. Cotton also wrote some of her own tunes, and her song "Freight Train" became a hit when performed by British artist Nancy Whiskey. Many other folk revivalists went on to play and record it as well.

Cotton, James (b. 1935) *harmonicist*

One of the masters of blues harmonica, James Cotton actually went to ARKANSAS from his birthplace of Mississippi to seek out SONNY BOY WILLIAMSON I and stayed with him for six years. He played for HOWLIN' WOLF and spent 11 years in MUDDY WATERS's band. He has also often appeared with blues-rock musicians like Johnny Winters, Steve Miller, and ELVIN BISHOP. Cotton is known as an excellent live performer, and he has appeared at a large number of blues festivals and night clubs.

country blues

The country blues style began earlier than the classic blues did, but the songs were not recorded until 1925. Once PAPA CHARLIE JACKSON recorded, the floodgates opened. The early country blues artists usually wrote songs that had no choruses, just verses. The verses were often disconnected; in other words, the song did not tell a single story, in the way that pop songs do. The primary stylistic division in country blues was between the Piedmont style, which was gentle, had a strong ragtime influence, and was sometimes talked as much as sung, and the Delta style, which featured intense and tortured guitar playing and singing.

Piedmont artists of importance included BLIND WILLIE MCTELL, "BARBECUE BOB" HICKS, Buddy Moss, BLIND BOY FULLER, and later BROWNIE MCGHEE and SONNY TERRY. The style dominated

Elizabeth Cotton (Larry Shirkey)

music in the Carolinas and around Atlanta. Delta guitarists included Charley Patton, considered possibly to be the father of the style, SON HOUSE, TOMMY JOHNSON, ISHMON BRACEY, SKIP JAMES and, briefly, ROBERT JOHNSON. Some scholars feel that the musical differences between the styles reflect the living conditions in the two areas. Life was relatively good in the Piedmont region, racism was less flagrant, and there seemed to be more musical contact between the races, to judge from a number of country musicians who claimed that they were influenced by black blues artists early in their careers. A few of the pioneering Delta bluesmen are alive today, like ROBERT LOCKWOOD Jr. and DAVID "HONEYBOY" EDWARDS.

Jug bands have some of the same musical characterics as the Piedmont blues, such as upbeat songs and ragtime chord progressions. Jug bands utilized cheap and homemade instruments, including jugs, kazoos, washboards, combs, harmonicas, and washtub basses, together with stringed instruments like banjos and fiddles. The jug bands were akin to the string bands, black bands that played country music, often for white audiences. The jug bands developed in various places, especially Cincinnati, Ohio, Louisville Kentucky, and MEMPHIS, TENNESSEE, and the string bands could be found around the southern mountains but also in MISSISSIPPI and New Orleans. This is "good time music," the lyrics tend to be humorous, and the emphasis is on partying, rather than on the expression of deep or sorrowful sentiments.

Another group of artists came from TEXAS, notably TEXAS ALEXANDER, who sang but did not play, and BLIND LEMON JEFFERSON, who dominated folk blues during the late 1920s. The Texas style had a foot in each of the other styles, but Lemon himself was quite eclectic, varying his style from song to song. Some artists, notably LONNIE JOHNSON, cannot be pigeonholed. Growing up in New Orleans, living variously in St. Louis and CHICAGO, Johnson assimilated many jazz and blues styles, and sometimes his singing approaches pop crooning as much as it does blues.

Cox, Ida (1896–1947) *singer and songwriter*

One of the classic blues singers of the 1920s, Ida Cox was also known as a songwriter. Many of today's artists have covered her song "Wild Women Don't Have the Blues." Cox was also a capable businesswoman; she owned and managed a touring company and produced stage shows. Her touring group included 16 chorus girls, comics, and backup singers. She appeared at the second JOHN HAMMOND Spirituals to Swing concert in 1939 at Carnegie Hall, subsequently recording with such famous jazz musicians as guitarist Charlie Christian.

Cray, Robert (b. 1953) *songwriter, singer, and guitarist*

In 1986 Robert Cray had a big hit with his song "Strong Persuader." The album of the same name won a Grammy award in 1986. At that time Cray was one of the few younger black blues artists. A songwriter, singer, and guitarist, Cray has concentrated more on the guitar in recent years. He has also used horns on his records, which now are placed more in the soul tradition of Stax Records in Memphis, than in traditional blues. Cray writes or cowrites many of his songs. They all show blues influences, but some are structured more like pop songs.

Crayton, Pee Wee (Connie Curtis) (1914–1985) *electric guitarist*

As a young Texan inspired by the dynamic guitar playing of Charlie Christian, Pee Wee Crayton took up the electric guitar, falling under the spell of pioneering electric bluesman T-BONE WALKER. Crayton moved to Los Angeles in 1935, where he had a lengthy performing and recording career, recording for a half dozen different labels. Though Crayton was an excellent guitarist with a long career, he has not been well represented on CD reissues.

"Crazy Blues" (1920) *breakthrough recording by a black artist*

The significance of "Crazy Blues" is that it was the first successful blues song recorded by a black artist. It was actually MAMIE SMITH's second recording for the Okeh label, but the first one that achieved popularity, supposedly selling some 100,000 copies. Before this no record company imagined that there was such a large audience for black popular music. Perry Bradford, who wrote the song, lobbied numerous record companies about the market for black music before convincing Okeh to take a chance on Smith.

Ironically, "Crazy Blues" was not really a blues, but more of a pop song, despite its title and the recurrence of the word "blues" in the refrain. Other artists who recorded the song include the Alabama Jug Band, Original Dixieland Jazz Band, JIMMY RUSHING, Noble Sissle, and Mary Stafford.

Cream

CREAM was ERIC CLAPTON's most successful band, featuring the lead singing and bass playing of Jack Bruce and the powerful drumming of Ginger Baker. Bruce and Baker brought a jazz influence to the band, combining with Clapton's blues-rock background. The band recorded some blues classics, like ROBERT JOHNSON's "Crossroads" and WILLIE DIXON's "Spoonful." They also wrote their own more rock-oriented songs, of which "Sunshine of Your Love" and "White Room" became major pop hits. In both his solo career and his band performances, Clapton has always paid the royalties due to the original blues composers. Not all his British blues-rock colleagues have followed his lead, some of them claiming that the works are folk songs, while others have tried to obtain a share of the writer's royalties.

crossroads

The crossroads is the mythical place where ROBERT JOHNSON allegedly made his deal with the devil, exchanging his immortal soul for learning how to play the blues better than anyone else. Clarksdale blues fans claim the crossroads to be at the junction of highways 61 and 49 in Mississippi. Other communities have claimed the crossroads as their own.

"Crossroads Blues" (1936) *classic blues by Robert Johnson*

One of ROBERT JOHNSON's most famous songs, "Crossroads Blues" was recorded in 1936. In the song Johnson goes down to the crossroads and prays to the Lord for mercy. He then complains that he cannot get a car to pick him up to get out of there, and that he has no "sweet woman." He then asks the listener to tell his friend WILLIE BROWN, who was SON HOUSE's friend and known as an excellent guitarist, that Johnson is sinking down.

The song has long been identified with the legend that attributes Johnson's guitar skills to his making a deal with the devil at the crossroads. The movie *Crossroads* was also loosely based on this legend. Johnson's self-pitying lyrics and his intense performance also make the song particularly memorable. It was recorded by ELMORE JAMES, ERIC CLAPTON and his band CREAM, the electric blues ALLMAN BROTHERS BAND, and the rock group Lynyrd Skynyrd.

Crudup, Arthur "Big Boy" (1905–1974)
songwriter, composer, and guitarist

Arthur Crudup did not start playing guitar until he was 30 years old. He took up music as a career alternative to farming. Crudup had an unsuccessful career as a recording artist but achieved more success as a composer. After his recording career did not deliver the results Crudup hoped for in Chicago, he returned to Mississippi and became a successful bootlegger.

Crudup never received royalties for his songs on his early recordings. His "That's All Right Mama" became a hit when ELVIS PRESLEY recorded it, and some of his other songs, including "Mean Old Frisco," were covered by other blues and R&B acts, including BOBBY "BLUE" BLAND, BIG MAMA THORNTON and BROWNIE MCGHEE, and SONNY TERRY. Toward the end of his life, Crudup was represented by agent-manager-blues fan Richard Waterman. Waterman got Hill & Range Music, the publishers of Presley's material, to agree to pay Arthur the royalties for Presley's recording. Crudup drove up from Georgia, where he was then living, to the New York publisher's office. A lawyer came out of the office and told Crudup and Waterman that he was going upstairs to get his boss, Julian Aberbach, to sign a considerable check for the monies due Crudup. Fifteen minutes later the lawyer returned, his face turning ashen. Aberbach simply could not bring himself to sign the check. Waterman tells the story that he was extremely embarrassed that Crudup had driven all the way from Georgia for nothing, but Crudup assured him that he realized he had done his best. Crudup then turned around and drove back to Georgia. Waterman continued the battle, and although Crudup died before it was won, his children eventually received their proper legacy in the form of a massive royalty check. These payments continue today.

Unfortunately the denial of royalties for songwriting and recorded performances is a common and consistent pattern in the story of the blues.

Davenport, Charles (Cow Cow) (1894–1955) *pianist*

Charles Davenport was one of the early boogie-woogie and blues pianists, recording his "Cow Cow Blues" in 1928. It was one of the first recorded examples of boogie-woogie and is a standard part of the blues piano repertoire. Alabama-born Davenport got his odd nickname from the cow-catcher mounted to the front of engine cars.

Davenport performed in Birmingham, Atlanta, and New Orleans and toured with singer Dora Carr. He wrote a number of songs but never received any royalties because he sold the rights.

Davies, Debbie (b. 1952) *electric guitarist and singer*

Debbie Davies is one of the blues women who emerged during the 1970s. Born in Los Angeles, she toured with ALBERT COLLINS as an opening act and also played in his band. She is an electric guitarist known for her prowess on the Fender Stratocaster guitar, and she is also a songwriter and singer who has recorded several albums.

Davis, Blind John (1913–1985) *pianist*

John Davis served as a house piano player for Lester Melrose's Bluebird record label in the 1930s and 1940s. He accompanied such well-known blues artists as TAMPA RED, SONNY BOY WILLIAMSON I and BIG BILL BROONZY on records, and went on the first European blues tour in 1952 with Broonzy. Davis could play blues, ragtime, jazz, and boogie-woogie piano. He began playing piano because his father, who owned a bar, promised him a job if he would learn how to play.

Davis, Gary (aka Reverend Gary Davis) (1896–1972) *composer, singer, and guitarist*

Gary Davis was a gospel music composer and singer who accompanied himself by playing blues guitar. His music has accurately been described as "holy blues." Davis spent approximately 45 years in the Carolinas, where he mastered the art of ragtime guitar. He moved from South Carolina to Durham, North Carolina, in the mid-1920s. Durham's active blues scene included local musicians BLIND BOY FULLER and SONNY TERRY. Davis was an important influence on Fuller, who played a simplified version of Davis' style. Davis was a streetsinger who mastered a broad repertoire that included John Philip Sousa marches, blues, rags, and spirituals. In 1937 Davis became an ordained minister, after which he gave up performing blues in public. From time to time he could be coaxed into performing this part of his repertoire at private gatherings.

In the early 1940s Davis moved to New York City, where he sang on the streets, using a tin cup to collect tips—a difficult life. Two Gibson J200 guitars were stolen from him during his streetsinging career. By the 1950s Davis would go down to Manhattan's Lower East Side and play informally every Tuesday night at the home of Tiny Ledbetter, LEAD BELLY's niece, who lived in the same apartment building where Lead Belly had spent the last years of his life. Word spread about Davis's phenomenal guitar abilities, and young white guitarists started to jam with him at Tiny's. Many of them then took guitar lessons from him. Some of his prominent students included Stefan Grossman, who transcribed and later published many of Davis's tunes, and New York studio musician Barry Kornfeld, a young Roy Book Binder, the talking-blues performer RY COODER, David Bromberg, the blues performer, and Jorma Kaukonen, of the rock group Jefferson Airplane. Other folk musicians sometimes found at these jam sessions were Erik Darling, Andy Cohen, and John Gibbon. DAVE VAN RONK, one of the most important white bluesmen in the blues of the 1960s revival, also spent time with Davis. It would be hard to overestimate Gary's influence on all these musicians and the many other players who saw him perform or bought his records. Davis was a stern teacher, and he acknowledged only a rare few, like BLIND BLAKE or WILLIE WALKER, as his equal. For many of his young students, and even for the casual listener, an evening spent with the pianist was a total immersion into unique emotional musical territory.

Early in Davis's career he broke his left wrist, and when it was reset, it was placed at an odd angle. He did not play barre chords (in which the first finger of the left hand covers all six strings); instead, he used his left thumb. This made it difficult to follow him by watching. In addition to six-string guitar, he played five-string BANJO and 12-STRING GUITAR.

Most of Davis's songs had religious themes, often taken from the Bible. He also was fond of inserting spoken sermons into the songs. "The Day When I Went Blind" was a rare autobiographical song about his condition and how difficult it was for him. Peter, Paul & Mary recorded Davis's song "If I Had My Way (Samson and Delilah)," from which he received considerable royalties. The Grateful Dead also recorded it.

Davis appeared at the Newport Folk Festival, and two documentary films were made about him. His recording career began in the 1930s in Durham, when he recorded spirituals and blues for the

Gary Davis (Larry Shirkey)

American Record Company. He did not record again until he moved to New York. He made many commercial recordings during the 1970s and 1980s, and a number of people recorded him in nonstudio live situations as well. Twelve-string guitarist Fred Gerlach also recorded some unissued tapes of Davis preaching at a storefront church in New York's East Bronx. Several Gary Davis songbooks and a tribute CD have been issued, and there is an out-of-print British biography written in 1993 about him entitled *Reverend Gary Davis* by Aaron Stang.

Davis, Guy (b. 1952) *multi-instrumentalist and singer*

Guy Davis is the son of actors Ruby Dee and Ossie Davis, and his career has gone back and forth between acting and music. He recorded a little-known album for FOLKWAYS RECORDS in 1978, then acted in the Broadway play *Mulebone,* and in an Off-Broadway show about the life of Delta blues-man ROBERT JOHNSON. Davis wrote and directed a show called *In Bed with the Blues; The Appearance of Fishy Waters.* He has also written several scores for television shows. He sings and plays six- and 12-string guitars, slide guitar, banjo, mandolin, bass, keyboards, and harmonica. Davis specializes in blues composed before World War II, although he also plays electric guitar. In 1995 Davis began to concentrate on his music, and his recordings began to circulate on a wider basis. Currently he actively tours and records.

Davis, Walter (1912–1964) *pianist, singer, and songwriter*

During the 1930s, St. Louis was home to a group of piano players–singers–songwriters that included Davis, St. Louis Jimmy Oden, and Henry Brown. Davis was born in MISSISSIPPI but moved to St. Louis in 1924. He was the most prolific of the group, recording about 150 songs. His first recording, "M & O Blues," started his career off with a bang. Davis played simple, straightforward piano, often accompanied by local guitarist Henry Townsend. More than most blues artists, Davis wrote many rather romantic songs that celebrated love, like "Please Remember Me," and he had a fondness for writing blues songs in minor keys, a somewhat unusual practice for the blues, especially during that period.

Dawkins, Jimmie (Fast Finger Jimmy Dawkins) (b. 1936) *"West Side sound" guitarist*

A MISSISSIPPI-born artist, Dawkins moved to CHICAGO in 1955. He is one of the most important guitarists involved in the creation of the so-called West Side sound, a more modern version of electric blues, contrasted with the blues from the South Side of Chicago. Dawkins is more experimental than most blues guitarists, employing amplifier feedback and trying to sustain notes longer than they are

usually held. His songs deal with politics as well as the usual love situations found in the blues. Two of his songs that contain social commentary are "Welfare Line" and "Born in Poverty."

DeLay, Paul (b. 1952) *harmonica virtuoso, singer, and songwriter*

In many parts of the country there are musicians who make most of their living playing where they reside. Paul DeLay is a Portland, Oregon, singer, songwriter, and harmonica virtuoso. He plays chromatic harmonica, the more complicated instrument that LITTLE WALTER favored because, unlike the small harmonica most players use, it is easily capable of playing sharps and flats. The smaller instrument requires the player to bend the notes to get these pitches. In recent years DeLay has toured Europe and Canada to go with his performances in the Pacific Northwest. He has recorded about a dozen albums.

Delmark Records

Delmark Records began as a one-man show. The founding father and sparkplug of the operation was Bob Koester, who founded the company in St. Louis in 1953, when he was a college student. Koester moved the company to CHICAGO in 1958, opening a jazz record store, the Jazz Record Mart, which has often had to support the activities of the label.

Over the years Delmark has divided its recording efforts between jazz and blues. The company has issued four SLEEPY JOHN ESTES albums, and it recorded JUNIOR WELLS, BIG JOE WILLIAMS, BUDDY GUY, and MAGIC SAM. Koester has also functioned as a sort of record company guru for a number of his employees, who went on to start their own record companies. Michael Frank started blues label Earwig, Jim O'Neal opened Rooster Blues Records, and BRUCE IGLAUER started ALLIGATOR RECORDS in 1970. Alligator has gone on to become the largest blues record company in existence; curiously, it began with an argument between Koester and

Iglauer. Koester refused to record HOUND DOG TAYLOR, and Iglauer then started his own company.

Koester still operates the record store and the label, and has issued and reissued many albums in his large catalog. The record store also operates a large mail-order blues and jazz business.

Detroit

Detroit, Michigan, is best known in the world of popular music as the home of the Motown sound, the hit-making, R&B-flavored pop music of the 1960s. Before the Motown sound ever existed, the east side of the city had a thriving blues scene centered around Hastings Street. Chicago-based BLIND BLAKE sang that "there must be something about that Hastings Street," and years later JOHN LEE HOOKER asserted that he knew the town better than anyone "because I rambled it through and through." Hooker arrived in the city in 1943 and became its best-known blues artist during his five-year sojourn working in a steel mill during the day and playing music at night and on the weekends. Pianist BIG MACEO also had a regular gig at Brown's Bar on Hastings Street, and Hooker teamed up with guitarist-singer Eddie Kirkland for many of his hit records.

Today Motown is gone, but there is a museum in the building where so many hit records were recorded.

Bo Diddley (Lynn Goldsmith/Corbis)

Diddley, Bo (Ellas McDaniel) (b. 1928)
guitarist

Bo Diddley studied violin as a child and plays guitar and harmonica. He was born in MISSISSIPPI but moved to CHICAGO in 1934. His career paralleled CHUCK BERRY's, and both recorded for CHESS RECORDS. Although Bo Diddley has not had as many hits as Berry turned out, he has had his moments on the pop charts. He dresses outrageously, portraying different characters, as in his gunfighter period, where he dressed like a cowboy. Another part of his show is his box-shaped guitars, which always cause a stir among guitar players in the audience. A number of rock bands have covered his songs, including a lengthy early jam session version of "Who Do You Love?" by the late 1960s psychedelic rock group Quicksilver Messenger Service, and other recordings by the YARDBIRDS, rock and roll legend Buddy Holly, and the New York Dolls. Bo Diddley's original stage show included interplay between Bo and his maracas player, Jerome Green. Bo's trademark rhythmic figure ("shave and a haircut—five cents") is known to every rock and blues player, and was used by Buddy Holly, among many blues and rock artists.

"The Dirty Dozens" (1929) *battle of words*

"The Dirty Dozens" was a game between two black males. Each one would insult the other's family, particularly his opponent's mother. Usually the language used was bawdy and insulting. Eventually one of the players would run out of insults, and the other one became the victor.

The first recording of "The Dirty Dozens" was made in 1929 by piano player RUFUS "SPECKLED RED" PERRYMAN. The recording is in a sort of talking blues format, half spoken and half sung. The language in recorded versions of "The Dirty Dozens" has always been cleaned up. Folklorist Roger Abrahams printed the way the dozens are practiced on the street in his book, *Deep Down in the Jungle*.

Dixon, Willie (1915–1992) *composer, session leader, and arranger*

Willie Dixon probably deserves to be considered the outstanding blues composer of all time. His songs were recorded by such artists as LITTLE WALTER, MUDDY WATERS, HOWLIN' WOLF, and SONNY BOY WILLIAMSON I. British rock groups ROLLING STONES and LED ZEPPELIN also recorded his tunes, selling millions of records in the process. Among his dozens of well-known songs are "My Babe," "Little Red Rooster," "Spoonful," and "Wang Dang Doodle." Dixon abandoned a career as a boxer to become a musician. During the 1960s he was the house bass player for CHESS RECORDS, and he also served as an arranger and music contractor, hiring other musicians to play on the sessions. Many of Dixon's songs were about romantic situations and problems, but he wrote about many other subjects as well.

Dixon was a session leader, bass player, and arranger for LEONARD CHESS's Chess Records. As such he had easy access to many of the Chess artists. He wrote "I Just Want to Make Love to You," "I'm Your Hoochie Coochie Man," and "The Seventh Son" for Muddy Waters. He wrote "Spoonful," "Little Red Rooster," and "Back Door Man" for

Howlin' Wolf. He wrote "Wang Dang Doodle" for KO KO TAYLOR, "You Can't Judge a Book by Looking at the Cover" for BO DIDDLEY, and "My Babe" for Little Walter. He also wrote songs for blues artists Junior Ells, Magic Sam, OTIS RUSH, and Sonny Boy Williamson II (RICE MILLER.)

Dixon achieved his greatest popularity in the many recordings of these same songs by rock blues artists, particularly British bands. American rockers the Doors recorded "Back Door Man"; among the many British recordings were "Spoonful" by CREAM, "I Just Want to Make Love to You," and "Little Red Rooster" by the Rolling Stones; "You Shook Me," "I Can't Quit You Baby," and two other songs that ended in payments to Dixon's publisher by Led Zeppelin; "I'm Your Hoochie Coochie Man" by American expatriate JIMI HENDRIX; and other recordings by Aerosmith, GEORGE THOROGOOD & the Destroyers, and the ALLMAN BROTHERS.

What was so special about Dixon's songs, for one thing, was that although they had the repeated lines often found in blues verses, many of them, like "My Babe" or "I'm Your Hoochie Coochie Man," had the sort of memorable and catchy choruses found in pop and rock songs. Dixon also had a knack for coming up with memorable titles, like "Spoonful" or "Wang Dang Doodle." Sometimes he used material that had been around for years in these titles, or in the case of "My Babe," he borrowed the title of a traditional spiritual called "This Train." Certainly of all the blues composers, to this day Dixon is the one who wrote the most songs for the most artists.

After the decline of Chess Records, Dixon played with pianist Memphis Slim, performing at the Newport Folk Festival and in Europe. He later led a Chicago all-star blues band on a number of European tours. In 1982 he established the Blues Heaven Foundation, funded with his own extensive royalty checks. The purpose of the foundation was to bring blues programs into the schools, provide financial aid for poor older blues musicians, and create scholarships for needy students. His autobiography, *I Am the Blues,* is still in print.

Dr. John (The Night Tripper, Mac Rebbenack, Malcolm John Rebennack Jr.) (b. 1940)
keyboardist and vocalist

Dr. John created an outrageous character for himself, dressing in extravagant Mardi Gras costumes and spraying magic powder on the stage. He also wore long robes and hung necklaces, bones, and crosses around his neck. He named himself after a New Orleans resident named Dr. John who was involved in voodoo. Beyond this stagecraft is a superb piano player. Dr. John has a distinctive growling voice, and in 1973 he recorded his biggest hit, "Right Place, Wrong Time." During the 1980s he did spoken voice parts for radio and television commercials, and wrote his autobiography, *Under a Hoodoo Moon.* Dr. John may be a fabricated stage name, but his keyboard playing is seriously steeped in New Orleans blues piano, especially the work of PROFESSOR LONGHAIR and JAMES BOOKER. He has made an instructional videotape about New Orleans piano styles for Homespun Tapes, and he has demonstrated New Orleans piano styles in the documentary film *Piano Blues,* directed by Clint Eastwood.

Dorsey, T. A. (Georgia Tom) (1899–1993)
pianist and composer

Georgia-born Dorsey arrived in Chicago in 1916. He had two different careers, crossing over from blues into gospel music. As a blues pianist and composer he played with TAMPA RED and was MA RAINEY's bandleader. He wrote over a 100 blues songs and was a studio musician, playing on records by MEMPHIS MINNIE, JIM JACKSON, and many other artists. His song "It's Tight Like That" sold a million copies and popularized "hokum music," good-natured humorous dialogue songs. After his wife died during childbirth, he left the blues to concentrate on writing gospel songs. Two of his songs, "Precious Lord" and "Peace in the Valley," have become gospel standards, recorded by numerous artists. Country and western artist Ernest Tubb made an enormously successful recording of "Peace in the Valley," as did ELVIS PRESLEY. Dorsey was particularly associated with gospel singers Sallie Martin and Mahalia Jackson, both of whom performed his songs.

For years Dorsey was the choral director at Pilgrim Baptist Church in Chicago. A gospel movie that includes considerable material about Dorsey, *Say Amen, Somebody,* appeared before his death, and in 1992 author Michael W. Harris wrote a book about him, *The Music of Thomas A. Dorsey in the Urban Church.*

Because Dorsey was such a towering figure in the world of gospel music, his contributions to the blues have not been recognized as much as they deserve to be.

"Downhearted Blues" (1922) *Bessie Smith's biggest hit*

This song was written in 1922 by classic singer Alberta Hunter and pianist LOVIE AUSTIN. Hunter's recording was considered successful, but she felt that the song could have a renewed life if she could get BESSIE SMITH to record it. Hunter solicited Frank Walker, Bessie's producer, to record the song. A year later she did, and it became Bessie's biggest hit. It sold somewhere between 250,000 and 750,000 copies, depending upon which account is to be believed.

The lyric complains that the singer's man destroyed her life through mistreatment, but it also claims that she will eventually be in control over him. Such ambivalence about a singer's husband, wife, boyfriend, or girlfriend is typical of many blues songs. Many other artists have recorded the song, including white blues-jazz artist Mildred Bailey, jazz entertainer Cab Calloway, jazz and blues artist JIMMY RUSHING, and blues singer Mamie Smith.

Dupree, Champion Jack (1909–1992) *pianist*
Jack Dupree had a long career, going through many different phases. He was an orphan who learned how to play piano in New Orleans bars and barrel-

houses. He was also a professional boxer who fought 107 bouts. Dupree came to New York City in the 1940s and recorded with BROWNIE MCGHEE and SONNY TERRY and rhythm and blues guitarist Mickey Baker. In 1958 Dupree went to England to perform, then he took up residence variously in France, Switzerland, Denmark, and England. Before finally settling in Germany in the mid-1970s, he continued to record and tour in Europe and made a triumphant return to his hometown, playing at the New Orleans Jazz & Heritage festival in 1990.

"Dust My Broom" (aka "I Believe I'll Dust My Broom," "Dust My Blues") (1936) *blues song written by Robert Johnson*

This tune became the theme song of Delta blues artist Elmore James, who was one of the first electric blues players when he moved to Chicago. He had learned it from ROBERT JOHNSON, who had recorded it a few years before electric guitars came on the scene. According to blues scholar Elijah Wald, Johnson's powerful version is the first recorded example of boogie-woogie played on the guitar. He also traces the song back to two other songs by Chicago slide master KOKOMO ARNOLD and the melody to LEROY CARR.

This tune was so successful that James recorded it over and over again, hoping to recapture the magic. Many have recorded the song, especially blues rockers. These artists include HOWLIN' WOLF, CANNED HEAT, Spencer Davis Group, FLEETWOOD MAC, FREDDIE KING, ALBERT KING, and ARTHUR "BIG BOY" CRUDUP. Johnson's recording was made in 1936, and the first of the many James recordings was made in 1951. The lyric of the song describes an unfaithful girlfriend whom the singer can't seem to find.

Dylan, Bob (Robert Zimmerman) (b. 1941) *singer, literary songwriter, and performer*

There are many books available about the life and career of Bob Dylan. Dylan is known as a country-folk-rock songwriter, performer, and recording artist. A number of his songs reveal some of his roots in blues music. Such songs as "Highway 61 Revisited," "Tombstone Blues," "Maggie's Farm," "Blind Willie McTell," and "High Water (written for Charlie Patton)" reveal that Dylan has listened closely to the blues. More than any other artist he was responsible for bringing rock into folk-rock music, when he appeared at the Newport Folk Festival in 1965 with a loud electric band that featured guitarist MICHAEL BLOOMFIELD and PAUL BUTTERFIELD's blues band. Because Dylan's music moves into so many different musical areas, it is impossible to classify him under a single category.

Bob Dylan (Bettmann/Corbis)

Eaglin, Snooks (Fird Eaglin Jr.) (b. 1936)
singer
Snooks Eaglin is a self-taught, blind New Orleans street singer with an extremely varied musical repertoire. His music encompasses jazz, gospel, rhythm and blues, and the blues. As a child he sang in churches, and later he performed in an R&B band called The Flamingoes, with legendary pianist Allen Toussaint. After the band broke up, he sang on the streets of New Orleans and later at the Playboy Club. He was recorded in 1960 by folklorist Harry Oster, and later he recorded for Imperial Records and other labels. He has also recorded with his friend pianist PROFESSOR LONGHAIR.

Eaglin, though a spectacular and versatile guitarist, has never achieved the sort of popularity that his talent merits, possibly because his repertoire is so varied.

Earl, Ronnie (Ronald Horvath) (b. 1953)
Versatile guitarist Ronnie Earl's playing includes elements of jazz, soul, blues, and rock music in his performances. He took up guitar while attending Boston University. Earl changed his name, using the Earl in honor of Chicago blues guitar player Earl Hooker. Earl had enough ability to replace guitarist Duke Robillard in the band Roomful of Blues. He remained in the band from 1979 to 1987, then formed his own band, The Broadcasters.

Earl has made a number of solo albums, some of them instrumental. He has had to overcome prob-

lems with drugs, alcohol, and depression, but he continues to tour and record today.

Edwards, David (Honeyboy) (b. 1915) *Delta blues guitarist*
David Edwards is one of the last of the original Delta blues guitarists. He learned how to play by listening to recordings of local guitarists Tommy McClennan and Robert Petway. He then became a protégé of BIG JOE WILLIAMS, playing jobs with him at the age of 14. He also met harmonica ace BIG WALTER HORTON and mandolinist YANK RACHELL at about this time. Edwards claims to have been with ROBERT JOHNSON when Johnson was poisoned in 1938, and he is one of the few links left to many of the early and important Delta musicians. ALAN LOMAX recorded him for the Library of Congress in 1942. Edwards moved to Chicago in 1950, and during the 1970s and 1980s he toured Europe and Japan. Edward's autobiography *The World Don't Owe Me Nothing,* is in print, and he has recorded as recently as 1999, at the age of 84. Edwards is not a major original stylist but a fine representative of a musical style that can be re-created by younger players, but whose music is best represented by those who lived and worked in the Mississippi Delta.

electric guitar
During the mid-1930s urban blues artists started to perform with groups of other musicians in combos. These groups included saxophone or harmonica,

piano, string bass, and drums. BIG BILL BROONZY, a CHICAGO blues artist, performed with such a five-piece group. In this environment an acoustic guitar tended to get drowned out. Before 1935 guitarists tried to remedy this problem by using either resonator guitars or guitars that have f-holes on either side of the fingerboard instead of a round hole in the body. The resonator guitars had steel bodies and the resonators were metal cones. Even with this help the resonator guitars still drowned out the acoustic guitar.

In 1935 "Floyd's Guitar Blues," the first record using amplification, was recorded. Electromagnetic pickups were attached beneath the steel strings in the body of the guitar. Jazz guitarist Charlie Christian immediately started to play and popularize these primitive electric guitars. Blues artist T-BONE WALKER, who had met Christian, picked up on the idea as well.

Besides allowing the guitar to be played at louder volumes, certain left-hand tricks or effects became easier for the audience to hear. One of these techniques was bending the strings, where the player pushes the string with a left-hand finger, raising its pitch. It was also now possible to sustain the sound of a note for a longer time.

These early electric guitars often sounded distorted, and unpleasant feedback resulted that the player could not control. In 1940 Les Paul designed a solid-body electric guitar. His awkwardly large instrument was called "The Log." Paul mounted the strings and pickups on a solid piece of wood that minimized hum and feedback. He then worked out his design with the Gibson Guitar Company, which manufactured the highly successful Les Paul model guitar. The guitar was introduced in the late 1940s, and it is still one of Gibson's best-selling electric guitars.

Not long after, guitar designer Leo Fender mass-produced his own solid-body guitars. He designed and produced the Telecaster and the Stratocaster, which were equally successful and have had an equally long time in the marketplace.

Many of the blues players, including MUDDY WATERS and T-Bone Walker, chose to play the Fender guitars. These guitars could be turned up to high volumes, and guitarists started to experiment with deliberately distorted sounds, which were now possible to achieve without feedback.

A number of jazz-blues guitarists began to appear on the scene. Players like Eric Gale and Cornell Dupree, "Wild Jimmy" Spruill, Billy

Gibson ES-335 electric guitar (Gibson Guitars)

Butler, and Lawrence Lucie played on dozens of recording sessions for R&B stars like Aretha Franklin. Some of the jazz guitarists, like Kenny Burrell and CHICAGO studio session guitarist Phil Upchurch played on many recordings, and CURTIS MAYFIELD developed a technique of playing catchy guitar figures that enlivened many of the hit records by the Impressions. In Los Angeles players like ROBBEN FORD and Barney Kessel fulfilled similar roles.

Rock-blues bands like the ROLLING STONES and LED ZEPPELIN played in large venues like outdoor stadiums or concert halls that held thousands of people. It was inevitable that they would demand larger and more powerful amplifiers that could be heard clearly anywhere in these venues. Rock-blues guitarist JIMI HENDRIX played guitar at almost deafening volumes, and he would deliberately try for special distorted effects, creating "ghost" notes of almost excruciating feedback. During the 1960s a great deal of "outboard gear" was introduced. This included a number of guitar pedals, such as the wah wah pedal and the volume pedal. The guitarist could then control much of the sound through foot pedals. MIDI (musical instrument digital interface) and other special effects also enlarged the menu of available electric guitar sounds.

Although T-Bone Walker was the acknowledged pioneer of electric blues guitar, B. B. KING is probably the most famous of the many electric blues players. King used the electric guitar in some of the ways described above for bending the notes and extending their length by using extensive left-hand vibrato. Bending guitar strings became much easier because string manufacturers introduced much lighter-gauge strings. It became possible for players like ALBERT KING to bend the notes up a whole tone (two frets or more).

Many of the Chicago West Side guitarists were electric players from the beginning. They utilized the electric guitar not only to play louder but to create all sorts of special effects.

Although some electric guitarists play with their fingers, the style of electric playing usually involves the use of the flat pick. New ways of playing rhythm guitar also evolved, partly due to the rhythm and blues influences on electric guitar. Some of the rhythm styles involve much busier playing, with 16th notes in use instead of eighth notes, and sometimes special sounds; for example, a high-pitched "chick" sound could be obtained by hitting the strings with a pick, and then quickly muffling the sound with the left-hand fingers.

Today many blues artists play electric guitar. One of the most popular is BUDDY GUY, who is capable of playing good down-home acoustic guitar and recently recorded an album of Jimi Hendrix's tunes.

There are far too many white electric players to cover in details. Almost all the British rock bands featured electric guitar, and the Rolling Stones' Keith Richards, Jimmy Page of Led Zeppelin, ERIC CLAPTON of CREAM and other bands, and Jeff Beck were among the most prominent. In America, Billy Gibbons of ZZ TOP is among many rock-blues artists. STEVIE RAY VAUGHAN was an influential blues-rock guitarist of the 1980s, and Johnny Winter has pursued a long and successful career, turning increasingly toward blues in recent years. The much younger generation of white blues-rock guitarists includes JONNY LANG and KENNY WAYNE SHEPHERD.

Guitar technology has moved on too, and it is now possible to buy guitars that have different sets of pickups designed to give a player the ability to get the sounds identified with the Fender Telecaster and the Gibson Les Paul models and dozens of other options.

Estes, Sleepy John (1899–1977) *composer and blues stylist*

An original blues stylist and composer, Sleepy John Estes is hard to place in a specific blues category. He recorded about 50 titles from 1929 to 1941, then disappeared. He was rediscovered by BOB KOESTER in 1961. Koester operated the Chicago blues and jazz label DELMARK, and he produced concerts featuring Estes and recorded him as well. Playing with him, just as they did some 20 years earlier, were harmonica player Hammie Nixon and mandolinist YANK RACHELL. The musical effect is music somewhere between the blues and the stringed band tradition. The black string band tradition, best represented by the MISSISSIPPI SHEIKS, fuses white string band music, the blues, and ragtime. Some of Estes's songs, especially "Drop Down Mama," "Going to Brownsville," and "Diving Duck Blues," are performed by blues revivalists today.

Evans, David (b. 1944?) *blues scholar and ethnomusicologist*

David Evans is an ethnomusicologist and blues scholar who runs the Southern Regional Music program at the University of Memphis. Evans has written several books about the blues, notably *Big Road Blues*. He is also a musician who plays guitar and keyboards and a record producer, and he started a record label at his university to record Memphis roots music. The label is called High Water Records. Evans has also recorded some CDs of his own music.

Fabulous Thunderbirds

The two founding members of the Thunderbirds and primary soloists were guitarist JIMMY VAUGHAN, who is STEVIE RAY VAUGHAN's brother, and harmonica player and vocalist Kim Wilson. Vaughan was in the band from 1974 to 1990, and left to form a duo with his brother, then pursued a solo career. The other members of the band have changed several times over the years and have included the jazz-oriented DUKE ROBILLARD and studio bassist Harvey Brooks. Wilson has stayed with the band except for the period 1993–95, when the band broke up. The band was known as an outstanding Texas blues band and had a hit recording in the 1980s, "Tuff Enuff." The Thunderbirds play a blend of blues, rock and roll, and rhythm and blues. They have recorded for a half dozen labels in their lengthy career.

Fahey, John (1939–2001) *guitarist and ethnomusicologist*

John Fahey's name does not often appear in books about the blues, because John practically invented the art of playing newly-composed finger-style guitar pieces. Fahey was responsible for rediscovering SKIP JAMES and BUKKA WHITE while he was a graduate student in ethnomusicology at UCLA. He also wrote a book about Delta blues artist Charley Patton and, toward the end of his life, compiled a lavish boxed set of Patton's recordings.

Fahey was a character. On his first album he invented a mythical blues guitarist named Blind Joe Death, a blues singer whom John claimed to have rediscovered. Of course Fahey *was* Blind Joe Death. Fahey recorded some albums of his fingerstyle guitar playing and started Takoma Records, which recorded Leo Kottke and Peter Lang, among other guitarists. Although a good deal of Fahey's music goes far afield from the blues, it is certainly an ingredient of much of his work.

fiddle

The fiddle is one of the most important instruments in classical music, although it is generally called the violin. There is no difference between the fiddle and the violin, the term "fiddle" usually referring to the use of the instrument in such nonclassical music styles as blues, country, or Celtic music. The fiddle is usually tuned G D A E, although a number of other tunings are used by folk musicians.

The fiddle is played with a bow, which requires a more complex technique than, for example, playing the banjo. Many fiddle players also play mandolin, because the tuning is the same.

The presence of the fiddle on blues records goes back to about the same period when PAPA CHARLIE JACKSON was recording. In 1926 "PEG LEG" HOWELL recorded blues selections for Columbia Records, but he also recorded some rags and country string band numbers with fiddler Eddie Anthony. A number of black fiddlers recorded with various jug and string bands like the famous MISSISSIPPI SHEIKS.

Slave fiddlers have been documented as early as the late 17th century, and as explained in the article on banjos, slave fiddlers entertained both their owners and their fellow slaves. Some of the fiddles were the standard European instruments, while others were homemade. As was the case with the banjo, some African instruments were similar to the fiddle. In the 19th century the fiddle and the banjo were the dominant instruments among African Americans.

The fiddle was especially popular in New Orleans, where early jazz bands used fiddle players. One of the most important musicians in the history of the blues was talented guitarist Lonnie Johnson, who also played fiddle. Johnson was born in New Orleans and played with his family's string band there, but all of them died during the influenza epidemic of 1918, except for one brother, James "Steady Roll" Johnson. James was a fiddler and pianist, and the two of them moved to St. Louis. Lonnie is well known among blues fans and scholars as a prolific guitarist, composer, singer, and studio musician, but his first record deal came about when he won a contest at the Booker T. Washington theater in St. Louis, where he sang and played the fiddle. An excellent example of his violin work appears on the CD anthology *Violin, Sing the Blues for Me.* Johnson's selection is called "Violin Blues." He also played violin on several recordings of the duo Hayes and Prater, who are discussed in the entry on mandolin.

Early violin players utilized the instrument in several ways. Some simply played the same melody as the singer was singing. A second technique was to play rhythmically, and not to emphasize the melody. Sometimes the player would play a repetitious figure as a response to the melody, rather than a mirror of it. The most advanced players, like Johnson, would improvise different choruses in the same way that a guitarist would do.

As with the banjo, some African-American fiddle players played a repertoire that included a substantial number of white country dance tunes. HOWARD ARMSTRONG, who used the nickname "Louie Bluie," not only played country tunes but developed a repertoire of tunes in a variety of languages. Originally from Tennessee, Armstrong ended up in

CHICAGO, playing in a trio called Martin, Bogan, and Armstrong, that included GUITAR and MANDOLIN.

The violin has also been used in jazz, with such players as Joe Venuti and Stuff Smith recording with swing bands during the 1930s and 1940s. In more recent years such players as Leroy Jenkins and Jean Luc Ponty have achieved notoriety as jazz violinists.

In recent years fiddle players, like many other musicians, have begun to play electric instruments. Some have used electronic pickups on their instruments, and solid-body electric violins are also currently available. Papa John Creach played on a number of recordings by folk-rock group Jefferson Airplane and also toured with them. Another blues violinist of some renown is CLARENCE "GATEMOUTH" BROWN, a multi-instrumentalist whose repertoire varies from country fiddle "breakdown" tunes to electric blues.

field hollers

The closest musical relative to the blues was the field holler, an unaccompanied song sung while working in the fields. It seems logical that the vocal style preceded any performance of blues that included a musical instrument, but there is no absolute evidence of that. What is documented is W. C. HANDY's oft-cited report of seeing a black man beside a railroad crossing in Mississippi, playing guitar with a knife and singing about the railroad, in 1903. There is also MA RAINEY's report of a young woman coming backstage and singing an unaccompanied blues to her in 1902 or 1903.

Fleetwood Mac

Of all the popular rock and roll bands, Fleetwood Mac has probably gone through the most musical transformations. The bedrock of the band has always been drummer Mick Fleetwood and bass player John McVie, but its musical styles have varied greatly over the years. The original group was a blues band featuring two guitarists—Peter Green and slide guitarist Jeremy Spencer. The band recorded a

Peter Green of Fleetwood Mac (Bruce Polonsky Photography)

boards and vocals, and wispy singer-songwriter Stevie Nicks and guitarist-vocalist Lindsay Buckingham. Their 1977 album *Rumours* marked the crest of the band's career, selling over 17 million copies in the United States alone. The combination of three songwriters—McVie, Buckingham, and Nicks—and the distinctive vocals of Nicks and McVie produced numerous hit songs. By this time the band had largely abandoned the blues and had become a popular rock band.

After the *Rumours* album, Nicks, Buckingham, and McVie left, and various others filtered in and out of the band. During the last few years the band re-formed, with Nicks and Buckingham returning but without McVie.

Flower, Mary (b. 1949) *singer, songwriter, and guitarist*

An original and inventive guitar and dobro player and singer, Mary Flower moved to Denver from Indiana in the 1970s. She sings folk music, country tunes, and blues, and was in several bands, one with country-folk singer Katy Moffatt, and another one an amalgamation of various female folk-oriented performers in Denver called The Motherfolkers. She also played on a number of other recordings by Denver artists.

By the mid-1990s Flower developed a concert program called Women in the Blues, and her career expanded to include several solo recordings, national and international tours, and teaching blues guitar privately and at various prestigious guitar workshops. In addition to playing and singing traditional blues, Flower is an accomplished songwriter, who writes instrumental pieces as well. She is now based in Portland, Oregon.

Foley, Sue (b. 1968) *blues guitarist and recording artist*

Sue Foley left her native Ottawa, Canada, and moved to Austin, Texas, in 1992. She had sent a demo tape to Antone's Records in Austin, which

blues album in CHICAGO in 1968 with WILLIE DIXON and pianist OTIS SPANN on bass and piano. At that time the band included guitarist Danny Kirwan. Fleetwood himself had also backed up various touring American blues musicians in England. Various personal problems caused all three guitarists to leave the group, although Green reemerged in the 1990s, and has recorded two albums in tribute to ROBERT JOHNSON. He also wrote the song "Black Magic Woman," a huge hit by the rock band Santana.

During the mid-1970s the band moved to California, adding Christine Perfect McVie, formerly of Chicken Shack, and then John's wife, on key-

agreed to record her. She is an excellent electric lead blues guitarist, touring Europe and Japan and performing on national television in Canada. Foley is a particularly strong blues player, but she also has played country and rhythm and blues guitar as well. In addition to covering blues by such well-known performers as Willie Dixon, Memphis Minnie, Buddy Guy and Howlin' Wolf, she has recorded songs by less famous artists and her own compositions.

Folkways Records

Folkways Records, founded in 1949, was MOE ASCH's successor company to Disc Records, his earlier label. Unlike other record company founders, Asch never desired to achieve commercial success but wished to use the recording medium to document musical life. Although the label is probably best known for recording music from many nations and ethnic groups, Asch also was interested in documenting all sorts of traditional music. He did not let commercial considerations interfere with his objectives, issuing long-playing albums of obscure performers like holy blues artist BLIND WILLIE JOHNSON.

Producers would propose projects to Asch, and he would advance them minimal sums to put albums together. In the blues idiom, the Folkways albums produced by blues scholars SAMUEL CHARTERS and Frederick Ramsey formed important cornerstones for the blues revival. So did Harry Smith's six-album set, *The Anthology of American Folk Music,* released in 1952. Smith obtained obscure 78 RPM recordings of artists like MISSISSIPPI JOHN HURT and dubbed them onto long-playing records. These six albums in particular formed the musical influences on most of the young white folk and blues revivalists.

Asch also issued many recordings of LEAD BELLY, and the first recordings of the pioneering white blues revivalist DAVE VAN RONK. When Asch was ill in 1986 he looked for a way of keeping all his records in print. That was another unique aspect of his company—once he issued a record, it

Mary Flower (Nicholas de Sciasse)

remained in print forever. Asch brokered a deal with the help of Ralph Rinzler, who was a folk musician and scholar who worked for the Smithsonian Institution. Today the legacy continues, and in addition to the original recordings, most of which are available on CD through special orders, many other albums have been issued or reissued.

Ford, Robben (b. 1951) *multi-instrumentalist*

Robben Ford has had a long and colorful career marked by changes of musical direction. He started playing in the Charles Ford Band with two of his brothers in San Francisco in a jazz-oriented blues band. Later Ford accompanied blues shouter JIMMY WITHERSPOON and singer-songwriter Joni Mitchell, and he played with studio saxophone player Tom Scott in the L.A. Express. He now tours with a trio called Robben Ford & the Blues Line.

He is also a founding member of the Yellowjackets, from 1977 to 1983, playing with major jazz-fusion artist Miles Davis and ex-Beatle George Harrison, and doing studio work with various artists.

Forest City Joe (Joe Bennie Pugh)
(1926–1960) *harmonicist and songwriter*
Forrest City Joe was an ARKANSAS harmonica player who worked with BIG JOE WILLIAMS, recorded for CHESS RECORDS' predecessor, Aristocrat Records, played on the radio in West Memphis, and worked with OTIS SPANN. Joe wrote a tribute song to SONNY BOY WILLIAMSON called "Memory of Sonny Boy," and ALAN LOMAX recorded Joe. Yet largely today Forest City Joe is forgotten.

See also MEMPHIS.

Foster, Ruthie *singer and guitarist*
Ruthie Foster is a singer who performs with Cyd Cassone. Foster took up guitar after playing piano as a child. She led an eight-piece funk band in the navy, and her music is a blend of blues, gospel, and soul music. She is an active performer, and after an early record deal at Atlantic Records has her own label. Foster is one of a handful of black women singer-musicians active today.

Fuller, Blind Boy (Fulton Allen) (1907–1941)
Piedmont singer and songwriter
Blind Boy Fuller is possibly the musician most identified with Piedmont blues. His music showed the influence of ragtime and pop music as well as blues. He was also an important songwriter, and his composition "Rag Mama" has often been played and sometimes recorded by blues revivalists. "Step It Up & Go" and "Truckin' My Blues Away" are some of his other compositions still performed today.

Fuller started as a street singer in North Carolina in the early 1930s and moved to Durham, where he got his record deal through record store owner J. B. Long. He recorded 135 songs during his six-year recording career, and he was quite popular during the 1930s. Fuller recorded many solo pieces and used Bull City Red (George Washington) on washboard, SONNY TERRY on harmonica, and GARY DAVIS on guitar. Fuller was a strong singer and capable guitar player, playing slide guitar as well as excelling at fingerpicking.

Fuller's songs varied from party music that celebrated romantic encounters to sensitive love songs like his "Weepin' Willow Blues" with the lyric "That weeping willow, and that moanin' dove, I got a gal called Corrinne, boy that I sure do love," accompanied by a soulful guitar part. Long also got BROWNIE MCGHEE his first recording contract. Fuller was so popular that McGhee recorded under the name Blind Boy Fuller #2, and one of his first recordings, made after Fuller died, was "The Death of Blind Boy Fuller."

Fuller, Jesse (1896–1976) *multi-instrumentalist and singer*
Georgia-born Jesse Fuller wandered around the United States. Among his various occupations was working in anonymous roles as a film extra in Los Angeles in the 1920s. He moved to the San Francisco Bay area but did not work as a full-time musician until 1951. In 1954 he wrote the song "San Francisco Bay Blues," which became a blues and folk revival standard, performed by dozens of revivalist artists, and on ERIC CLAPTON's *Unplugged* album.

Fuller was a one-man band, playing 12-STRING GUITAR, HARMONICA, kazoo, cymbal, and a homemade bass made of piano strings that he called a fotdella and played with his feet. The harmonica and kazoo were in a rack that he wore around his neck. It made for a spectacular sight, and Fuller always seemed to be in control of his one-man orchestra. An excellent fingerpicking guitarist, he played everything from blues to religious songs, ragtime, and blues. He appeared in Europe, played the 1964 Newport Folk festival, and performed on the concert and coffeehouse circuit.

Fulson, Lowell (b. 1921) *guitarist and songwriter*

Tulsa-born Lowell Fulson became a fixture on the West Coast blues scene in the 1940s and 1950s. Raised by black and Choctaw Indian parents, Fulson had a fiddler grandfather, and his father played guitar with him. He also had an uncle who played guitar and another who played mandolin. Fulson performed in an Oklahoma string band, played guitar for blues singer TEXAS ALEXANDER in 1940, and moved to Oakland, California, in 1945. Fulson's first solo recordings were made by blues producer-impresario BOB GEDDINS in California. His song "3 O'clock Blues" became a hit by B. B. KING, but Fulson had his own taste of success with the 1954 R&B tune "Reconsider Baby." It was recorded on the Checker Records subsidiary of CHESS RECORDS. In 1967 Fulson hit number five on the R&B charts with his recording of "Tramp." During the 1970s and 1980s he played blues clubs and festivals. Folson plays the electric guitar and is a strong singer. He continues to record and perform today, in his eighties.

Funderburgh, Anson (b. 1954) *musician and bandleader*

Anson Funderburgh is a Texas blues revivalist who grew up in Dallas at about the same time as the guitar-playing Vaughan Brothers (Stevie Ray and Jimmie). He played in black and white clubs around Dallas when he was a teenager and formed a band called Anson Funderburgh & the Rockets. In 1986 he added veteran Chicago bluesman Sam Myers on harmonica and vocals, making this band unusual in its blend of black Chicago blues and Texas electric styles as played by a white blues revivalist.

Gallagher, Rory (1949–1995) *singer and guitarist*

Rory Gallagher was a British rock-blues guitarist and singer. He played in several British blues bands including one called Taste before starting his solo career. Gallagher recorded with MUDDY WATERS on Waters's *London Sessions,* and he also made a live recording with guitarist Albert King. Gallagher was known as a dynamic slide guitarist and singer who enjoyed performing lengthy shows. Although his career was cut short by illness and premature death, he left behind a large body of recordings. He wrote most of the material that he recorded.

Geddins, Bob (1913–1991) *record producer and record company owner*

Bob Geddins was a fixture on the San Francisco Bay area blues scene as songwriter, record producer, and record company owner. He had owned a record shop in Los Angeles in 1933, and in 1939 he started Big Town Records in Oakland. Swing Time was the first of many labels that Geddins owned, and he also produced records for other West Coast companies, including Specialty, Modern, Aladdin, and Imperial Records. Although Geddins himself never became fabulously successful, he recorded such important artists as LOWELL FULSON, JIMMY MCCRACKLIN, Juke Boy Bonner, ETTA JAMES, and BIG MAMA THORNTON.

Gellert, Lawrence (1898–1979) *folklorist*

Lawrence Gellert had a long and unusual career. He was born in Budapest, Hungary, and came to the United States in 1905, growing up in New York City. A political radical, Gellert advocated the rights of African Americans. Sometime during the 1920s his doctor advised him to move south because of a medical condition. He moved to the Carolinas, living with a black woman. This was considered shocking at the time, but Gellert used it as a springboard to gain the trust of the black community. From 1933 to 1937 he recorded singers and musicians in the Carolinas and Georgia. Although most of the blues and folksong collectors remarked on how few songs they found that protested racial injustice, Gellert found and recorded dozens of such songs in his travels. He published two collections of these songs, starting in 1936, and after a limited release of one album in 1940 by Timely Records, Rounder Records eventually released two long-playing albums from Gellert's collection in the 1980s. Unfortunately none of them has been rereleased on CD. The songs he recorded and the ones published in his books included work songs and blues. Gellert was mostly interested in songs of social protest and did not care what musical category a song fit into.

Gellert was a controversial figure in folklore circles, and initially some folklorists believed that he had written the songs himself. To protect his artists against retaliation for singing these songs, Gellert kept no records of the names of the singers, or even much information about where the songs were recorded. Blues singer JOSH WHITE recorded some of the songs that Gellert had collected, but mostly they were not widely performed. The University of

Indiana has archived all of Gellert's collection, including recordings and folk tales.

Geremia, Paul (b. 1944) *Piedmont songwriter, singer, and guitarist*

Paul Geremia is an outstanding songwriter, singer, and fingerpicking blues guitarist who plays mostly in the Piedmont style. His first recording was made for Folkways in 1968; since then he has recorded a half dozen albums and played in blues clubs and folk festivals. Geremia's subtle approach has never attained the popularity that his talents deserve.

Gerlach, Fred (b. 1930?) *12-string guitarist*

Although LEAD BELLY had a strong influence on the New York folk and blues scene, Fred Gerlach was virtually the only musician who devoted his musical life to playing the 12-STRING GUITAR. Gerlach recorded an album of Lead Belly songs, then moved to California, where he recorded an album of his own more free-form guitar work. Gerlach has worked as a draftsman, and has not toured widely. His nephew, Jesse Kincaid, also a musician, was one of the members of the Rising Sons with RY COODER and TAJ MAHAL.

Although Gerlach could imitate Lead Belly almost exactly, he generally did not do this, but recorded his own variations on Lead Belly's songs. Jimmy Page of LED ZEPPELIN has acknowledged that their version of the song "Gallows Pole" came about after he heard Gerlach's recording of it.

Gillum, Jazz (William Mc Kinley Gillum) (1904–1966) *harmonicist and recording artist*

Recording a hundred tracks for the RCA/Bluebird record label in the 1930s and 1940s, Jazz Gillum was a popular figure in the Chicago blues world. Gillum originally learned to play the harmonica as a boy, growing up in Indianola, Mississippi. He moved to Chicago in 1923, working with BIG BILL BROONZY and WASHBOARD SAM. Although he was popular in

the 1930s and 1940s, his career was somewhat overshadowed by the work of SONNY BOY WILLIAMSON, who was also in Chicago at that time.

Guitar Gabriel (Robert Lewis Jones) (1925–1996) *guitarist*

Guitar Gabriel's father was Sonny Jones, who had played with SONNY TERRY and BLIND BOY FULLER. Gabriel had a large repertoire of musical styles, drawing from ragtime, Dixieland jazz, and blues. As a teenager he played in old-time medicine shows. After a stint in the army in World War II, Gabriel played with Houston bluesman LIGHTNIN' HOPKINS, R&B sax player King Curtis, and other musicians. He lived in Pittsburgh during the mid-1960s, then returned to his native Winston-Salem, North Carolina.

In 1991, Tim Duffy found Gabriel. Duffy was a blues fan who started a foundation and a record label called Music Maker. The label was intended to provide a recording outlet for older musicians, especially blues artists. Duffy recorded Gabriel and also published a book that contains a chapter and photos of Guitar Gabriel.

Guitar Slim (Eddie Jones) (1926–1959) *songwriter and guitarist*

Guitar Slim was a spectacular performer who used a 50-foot-long electric guitar cord. He could move from a club into the street, into the audience, the parking lot of a club, or the kitchen, playing guitar all the while. Slim was born in Greenwood, Mississippi, but after he learned how to play the guitar he moved to New Orleans. He wrote and recorded a major hit song, "The Things I Used to Do," which stayed on the R&B record charts for 14 weeks in 1954. Slim continued to record with some success, but nothing approaching what had happened in 1954. He was one of the first electric guitarists to use distortion, deliberately overdriving the guitar amplifier, a technique later perfected by JIMI HENDRIX.

Guralnick, Peter (b. 1940?) *music writer*

One of the best writers about American popular music, Guralnick has written a huge two-volume biography of Elvis Presley, two books of essays on blues and country music, a book on soul music, a short biography of Robert Johnson, and a novel about a bluesman. He has also edited and contributed to numerous other books, written magazine articles, and produced records and written the liner notes for records.

Guy, Buddy (b. 1936) *recording artist and guitarist*

Only in recent years has Buddy Guy achieved the sort of career success that many observers long expected of him. Born in Louisiana, Guy began playing in Baton Rouge in the early 1950s, moving to Chicago in 1957. A victory in a battle of the blues live contest led to a recording contract with the Cobra Record Company. Cobra went bankrupt shortly after Guy's two singles were released, and he moved on to Chess Records. Besides recording for Chess as an artist, Guy played guitar on many Chess releases during the 1960s, including records by Muddy Waters, Little Walter, Koko Taylor, and Sonny Boy Williamson No. 2 (Rice Miller). He also had a blues duo with harmonica player Junior Wells in the late 1960s and early 1970s.

In 1989 Guy opened a blues club called Legends, and in 1991 he recorded an album called *Damn Right I've Got the Blues.* English rock stars Eric Clapton and Mark Knopfler made guest appearances on the record, and it won a Grammy Award, bringing Guy's career to the level that so many observers had anticipated years earlier. Today Guy continues to perform and record, settling into playing at his club in the month of January.

Hammond, John, Jr. (John Paul Hammond)
(b. 1942) *composer and blues revivalist*

John Hammond, son of talent scout JOHN HAMMOND SR., was one of the first white blues revivalists. He fell in love with the blues when he heard Chicago bluesman JIMMY REED at New York's Apollo Theater. Hammond spent one year at Antioch College in Ohio, then left to become a bluesman, singing and playing guitar and harmonica. During the 1960s he lived in New York's Greenwich Village and played at many of the area's clubs. Over the years Hammond has made many recordings, and he has recorded with a number of distinguished musicians, including DUANE ALLMAN, DR. JOHN, MIKE BLOOMFIELD, and David Bromberg. Hammond composed the soundtrack for the movie *Little Big Man* and appeared in the video *The Search for Robert Johnson,* performing and narrating the story. Most recently he departed from his blues work to record an album of songs by singer-songwriter Tom Waits. Hammond has played some excellent electric guitar on a few of his recordings, but his specialty is interpreting the prewar blues. Unlike many of the revivalists, Hammond is not a songwriter.

Hammond, John, Sr. (1910–1987) *talent scout and producer*

John Hammond Sr. was the father of his blues artist son, John Hammond Jr. Hammond grew up in a wealthy family in New York, and sometimes after his violin lessons he would go to Harlem's Apollo Theater to hear BESSIE SMITH. Hammond's primary music role was to scout talent to be recorded. He brought those he found to Columbia Records and turned them over to another record producer, or produced their records himself. In 1938 and 1939 he presented a history of black popular music at New York's Carnegie Hall, which he called From Spirituals to Swing. These concert presentations did a great deal to bring black music to the attention of white music fans in New York.

In his role as a talent finder, Hammond "discovered" Billie Holiday, Benny Goodman, BOB DYLAN, Leonard Cohen, Bruce Springsteen, and STEVIE RAY VAUGHAN. He also was partly responsible for the original Columbia LP reissues of ROBERT JOHNSON. Hammond worked for many years at Columbia Records. He also produced the last records of Bessie Smith, partly funding them himself because Columbia had long since lost interest in her.

Handy, W. C. (1873–1958) *songwriter and musician*

W. C. Handy has been called the "father of the blues," not because he invented them, but because he was the first person to develop his compositions around folk blues, and to make them available in a more accessible style to a wide audience. Handy was born in Florence, Alabama. As a teenager he saved up enough money to buy a guitar, but his parents were unimpressed and made him take it back and trade it for a dictionary. Later he learned how to play cornet. He had several jobs as a bandleader and teacher, ending up in Clarksdale, Mississippi, leading a band called The Knights of Pythias from 1903 to 1909. He then took the band to MEMPHIS, where he composed his first famous song, "The Memphis Blues." In 1912, Handy sold the rights to the song for $100. Realizing later that he had given up thousands of dollars in royalties, from that time on he vowed to publish his own music. In 1914 he wrote one of the most famous blues of all time, "The St. Louis Blues." Handy's blues were not folk blues but popular music adaptations of blues songs. Handy had heard folk blues musicians playing slide guitar in the early part of the 20th century, and he had also heard early string bands. It was his goal to make this relatively raw music accessible to the casual listener. Handy later moved to New York, was a partner in the short-lived Black Swan record label, and ran his own music publishing company for many years. His autobiography *Father of the Blues* was published in 1941.

harmonica

The harmonica, also known popularly as the harp, is the cheapest and most portable of all musical instruments, so it is only natural that blues artists wanted to adapt it to suit the blues. The diatonic harmonica is a small 10-holed instrument suitable for playing in a specific key. The most common models are made for the keys of C, G, D, E, and A.

One of the earliest blues harmonica players was DeFord Bailey. Oddly enough, his major claim to fame was that he was a regular member of the cast of the country music radio show *Grand Ole Opry.* This show was broadcast every Saturday night from Nashville. Bailey had appeared on radio station WDAD in Nashville as early as 1925, and through meeting a white country player, Dr. Humphrey Bate, Bailey got a job on WSM, the station that broadcast the Opry. Bailey was the only person on the show who always played alone, and he was also the only black performer on the show at the time. He appeared almost every week from 1926 until 1941. He was noted for his imitation of train sounds in such tunes as the "Pan American Blues." Bailey

was fired from the program in 1941 for a complex set of reasons, some involving racism and others involving the disputes that were going on about the disposition of performance rights, centering on the radio station's desire to fight against the American Society of Composers, Authors, and Publishers (ASCAP), the older performing rights group and to favor Broadcast Music, Inc. (BMI), the new one. Bailey was asked not to play his old favorites, but only new songs that BMI controlled, and he was unwilling or unable to do this.

One of the early important harmonica players was Noah Lewis, who played with Gus Cannon's Cannon's Jug Stompers. Like Bailey, Lewis was noted for his train imitations. This was also a feature of the playing of many white country harmonica artists as well. Both also shared in attempting musical portraits of fox chases and in exploring the harmonica as a way of mimicking speech. The latter technique was used by white harmonica player Lonnie Glosson and also by black blues artist SONNY TERRY. Glosson was widely known through his broadcasts on Chicago's WLS *Barn Dance* show. He was the first harmonica player that LITTLE WALTER ever heard, according to the book *Blues with a Feeling,* by Tony Glover, Scott Dirks, and Ward Gaines.

Glosson, like some of the early black players, played so-called cross harp. In this technique the player used a harmonica in a key an interval of a fourth above the key designated on the harmonica. In this way a harmonica player could use an F harp to play in the key of C, a G harp to play in the key of D, and so forth. Cross harp also helped the player bend notes to get the so-called blue notes, the flatted third and seventh of the scale. Cross harp was sometimes referred to as playing in second position.

Two of the best-known blues harmonica artists of the 1940s were SONNY BOY WILLIAMSON I (JOHN WILLIAMSON) and SONNY BOY WILLIAMSON II (RICE MILLER). Many blues singers use ALIASES or named themselves after existing artists. For example, BROWNIE MCGHEE initially recorded under the name BLIND BOY FULLER #2. Rice Miller may be the only one who comes to mind who deliberately appropriated another artist's name. At the time, Sonny Boy I was extremely popular in CHICAGO. Miller was playing on the KFFA radio in Helena, Arkansas. Supposedly renaming Miller was a scheme concocted by the sponsor of the show, who wanted to capitalize on the real-life Sonny Boy to sell more of his product, King Biscuit Flour. The original Sonny Boy was murdered on the streets of Chicago in 1948, leaving the field to Rice Miller. In 1964 Miller toured Europe and recorded with the British rock band YARDBIRDS.

Little Walter (Jacobs) was probably the most influential harmonica player of all time. He was one of the first harp players to use amplification, with cheap microphones and playing through public address (P.A.) systems in clubs in the 1940s. This enabled Walter to realize his vision of playing the equivalent of horn lines on his modest instrument, and he could also play louder or softer, using his amplifier to adjust the volume. Walter's other innovations included playing behind the beat, changing the accent of the beat in the middle of a solo, writing numerous instrumental pieces for his instrument, and developing the ability to play two notes an octave apart by blocking the intervening notes with his tongue. Walter also devised ways of playing in other keys. Like other blues artists, he sometimes played in second position. He also mastered third position, where the player uses a harmonica tuned a whole tone below the other musicians (a B-flat harp in the key of C). In 1953 Walter also started to play a chromatic harmonica. The chromatic instrument was set up with a lever that enabled the player to access easily sharps or flats, instead of having to find them through tonguing the notes. It also was a larger instrument, with a range a full octave below the diatonic harmonica.

Little Walter played with MUDDY WATERS's band, continuing to play on some of Waters's records after leaving him to start his own group. Walter had several major hit records, including the instrumental "Juke" and WILLIE DIXON's song "My Babe." Walter Horton, known as "Big Walter," was also one of the early players to amplify the harp, but he did not

want to be a bandleader, so most of his working life was spent playing with other bandleaders.

By the end of the 1950s Little Walter's health had started to decline, and the novelty of the harmonica as a lead instrument had worn off. Harmonica players and Chicagoans Billy Boy Arnold and CAREY BELL started to pick up the bass to keep working. Several talented white players emerged during the blues revival of the 1960s, especially PAUL BUTTERFIELD and CHARLIE MUSSELWHITE. A number of Walter's disciples, like JAMES COTTON and JUNIOR WELLS, managed to continue their long careers, and another group of younger white players like William Clark, Jerry Portnoy, PAUL OSCHER, Kim Wilson, and ROD PIAZZA emerged on the scene. Oscher was the first white musician whom Waters hired, and he was followed by Portnoy. Other black harmonica players of some notoriety include Hammie Nixon, who played with SLEEPY JOHN ESTES; JAZZ GILLUM, who played on dozens of recordings during the 1930s and 1940s; and the Louisiana swamp artist SLIM HARPO, and JIMMY REED, who played guitar and harmonica together by mounting the harmonica on a rack. JOHN HAMMOND and BOB DYLAN did this as well.

Two other blues harmonica players of importance are SONNY TERRY (Saunders Terrell) and Phil Wiggins. Sonny was a contemporary of BLIND BOY FULLER. Terry then teamed up with Brownie McGhee, recording and touring all over the world, and also recording on his own. They stayed together from 1941 until the mid-1970s. One of Sonny's recordings was a blues harmonica instruction album. Terry's style was rough and to the point, and he would alternately play the harp and whoop or sing. Like Lonnie Glosson he also got a good deal of mileage by making the harp "talk," saying "I want my mama."

Wiggins plays with guitarist JOHN CEPHAS in a duo that has taken over McGhee and Terry's mantle of spreading the Piedmont sound. They have been playing together since 1984, and, like McGhee and Terry, have toured widely and recorded a number of albums. Besides their repertoire of Piedmont blues, the duo play originals and covers of other folk, gospel, and R&B material. Wiggins was born in 1954, so he is roughly contemporary with some of the mid-1990s black blues revivalists. In addition to the duo's recordings, Wiggins acted in and appeared on the soundtrack of a John Sayles film, *Matewan*.

Harpo, Slim (1924–1970) *swamp blues style singer and songwriter*

Slim Harpo was one of the founders of the so-called swamp blues sound. Harpo was a rhythm and blues singer and stylist who performed a pop version of the blues. He began his recording career accompanying LIGHTNIN' SLIM for J. D. Miller's Excello label. He achieved a good run of hit songs of his own with "I'm a King Bee," (1957) "Rainin' in My Heart" (1961), and "Baby Scratch My Back" (1961). These hits allowed him to play rock venues in New York, including the Electric Circus, the Fillmore East, and the Scene, as well as the Whiskey A-Go-Go.

Harris, Corey (b. 1969) *singer, songwriter, and guitarist*

One of the younger generation of black bluesmen, Corey Harris was a schoolteacher in New Orleans when he began playing on the streets. He traveled to Africa and was inspired to seek out the relationship between African music and the blues. Filmmaker Martin Scorsese's documentary series *The Legacy of the Blues* shows Harris in Africa jamming with several important African artists. Harris is a specialist in the blues before 1940 and records many blues popularized by artists of that period, also writing some of his own songs and showing gospel and rhythm and blues influences in his later recordings. Starting his recording career in 1995, he has a half dozen albums to his credit.

Harris, Wynonie (Mr. Blues) (1915–1969) *singer*

Wynonie Harris was a blues shouter and R&B singer. He started out as a jump-blues singer, singing blues with an up-tempo swing feel with the

Lucky Millinder jazz orchestra in 1944 in CHICAGO. He then recorded for Apollo Records, before settling in for most of his major hits at King Records in Cincinnati, Ohio. His biggest hit was "Good Rocking Tonight," written by Roy Brown and later covered by ELVIS PRESLEY.

Hart, Alvin Youngblood (Gregory Edward Hart) (b. 1963) *multi-instrumentalist*

Another of the new generation of younger black urban bluesmen, Alvin Hart was born in Oakland, California, but his musical roots were nurtured during trips to his grandparents and relatives in Carroll County, Mississippi. His uncle played guitar and his grandmother was a piano player. When his family moved to Schaumberg, Illinois, Hart took to hanging out at the Sunday market on Chicago's Maxwell Street, where he encountered many blues artists. In 1986 he served in the Coast Guard, first in Natchez, Mississippi, and later was stationed in Berkeley, California. Opening for TAJ MAHAL in Oakland, California, created opportunities for Alvin, and he got a management deal and a recording contract. Hart plays six- and 12-STRING GUITAR, banjo, and tenor guitar, specializing in Delta blues but including influences from black string band music.

Hawkins, Ernie (b. 1941) *guitarist*

One of the many white blues guitarists who studied with GARY DAVIS, Hawkins gave up a career in psychology for the blues. He has stayed in Pittsburgh, Pennsylvania, for most of his musical career, playing 10 years with an R&B band called Gary Bellow & the Blues Bombers. Since then he has recorded several solo albums, toured, taught, and made instructional recordings and videos.

Hawkins, Ted (1936–1995) *singer and guitarist*

Ted Hawkins's life was like a blues song. As a teenager he was sent to reform school for shoplifting, then transferred to the notoriously brutal Parchman

Prison Farm in Texas. Most of Hawkins's musical career was spent singing for tips on the beaches of Southern California, especially Venice Beach. He had a light and airy vocal style, resembling the style of gospel-trained pop singer Sam Cooke, although Hawkins accompanied himself on guitar, which Cooke did not. His repertoire was a blend of cover songs from various musical styles and original tunes. A number of deals with small record labels gained him a small cult following. Hawkins finally seemed headed for financial success when he signed with Geffen Records, but he suffered a stroke and died shortly after his Geffen album, *The Next Hundred Years,* was released.

Hemphill, Jessie Mae (b. 1934) *guitarist and multi-instrumentalist*

MISSISSIPPI native Jessie Mae Hemphill played in her family's fife and drum band, picking up guitar at the age of eight. She often played guitar in open tunings, where the guitar is tuned to a chord rather than the standard tuning. Hemphill was one of the few black women blues artists who wrote her own songs and accompanied herself on the guitar. Hemphill won the W. C. HANDY Best Traditional Female Artist awards in 1987 and 1988, and she played an electric guitar while playing leg bells and a tambourine with her feet. Unfortunately she suffered a stroke in 1994 and today is confined to a wheelchair.

Hendrix, Jimi (1942–1976) *electric guitarist*

Many people feel that Jimi Hendrix was the greatest rock guitarist who ever lived. Hendrix grew up in Seattle, Washington, and played with several rhythm and blues bands before drifting to New York. He played in basket coffee houses in Greenwich Village, clubs where most of a musician's income came from passing a basket around for tips. While playing in New York, Hendrix met Chas Chandler of the Animals, who became Hendrix's manager, taking him back to England.

Hendrix was a dynamic electric guitarist who experimented with feedback at high volumes on the guitar, used wah wah pedals, dressed in wild clothes, and had a colorful stage act. His group, the Jimi Hendrix Experience, made some successful records, and rock artists still perform his tunes, like "Purple Haze," and others that are identified with him, like "Hey Joe," or his dramatic version of Bob Dylan's "All Along the Watchtower." Possibly the climax of Hendrix's career came at the Monterey Pop Festival in 1967, when in the midst of an atmosphere filled with peace, love, and flowers Hendrix literally set his guitar on fire. He followed this up with an amazing performance of "The Star Spangled Banner" at the Woodstock Festival in 1969.

It is difficult to overestimate the influence of Jimi Hendrix on electric guitar players of all descriptions. BUDDY GUY recently recorded an album of Hendrix songs, and the Kronos String Quartet has "translated" his work into classical music. The Experience Music Project in Seattle was originally intended by founder Paul Allen as a museum that would pay tribute to Hendrix, but Allen and Hendrix's parents were unable to reach a financial agreement. Hendrix's estate has earned millions of dollars since his death by the release of many recordings of varied quality.

Highway 61

This highway is the main route through the MISSISSIPPI Delta. Many blues artists, and even BOB DYLAN, memorialized it in song. The Mississippi section of the highway runs from MEMPHIS to Clarksdale, forming a veritable tableau of the state's blues history. Extending north from Memphis, the road goes through St. Louis and north to Illinois and Iowa. Richard Knight has written an entire book, *Blues Highway,* detailing clubs, record shops, museums, gravestones, and historical points of interest to the blues fan on highways 61 and 55, or as he puts it, "New Orleans to Chicago."

Hill, Bertha "Chippie" (1905–1962) *singer*

One of the classic blues singers of the 1920s, Hill had a vaudeville background, but her singing style was earthier than many of her classic blues sisters. She started her career as a dancer and toured with MA RAINEY's troupe. She recorded with such outstanding jazz accompanists as cornet-trumpet player King Oliver and clarinetist Jimmie Noone. In 1946 jazz critic Rudi Blesh rediscovered Hill and brought her to the famous Village Vanguard club in New York, as well as Carnegie Hall. He also brought her back to the recording studio.

Hill, Z. Z. (1935–1984) *singer and guitarist*

A TEXAS bluesman, Z. Z. Hill never found a white audience. His 1981 album *Down Home Blues* was on the R&B charts for more than 100 weeks. Before making that album Hill had recorded for a number of different record labels, moving to the West Coast in 1964. In 1980 he began to record for Malaco, a label based in Jackson, MISSISSIPPI, that recorded music for an older black audience. Once again he hit the R&B charts, and he followed up with several successful albums and singles. He died when his career was flourishing.

Hogg, Smokey (Andrew Hogg) (1914–1960) *recording artist*

During the period of his recording career extending from 1947 to 1954, this TEXAS electric blues artist recorded over 200 tracks. Hogg was a cousin of Houston blues artist LIGHTNIN' HOPKINS. Hogg's father taught him to play guitar, and in the course of his extensive recording career Hogg had several R&B hits such as, "Long Tall Mama" and "Little School Girl." Hogg recorded for half a dozen different labels and worked both in Texas and on the West Coast.

Holiday, Billie (1915–1959) *legendary singer*

Billie Holiday was a jazz singer steeped in the blues, but preferred to take a more modern approach to her music. She recorded with many famous jazz musicians, notably tenor saxophone player Lester Young. Holiday was noted for her unique, identifiable sound and the emotional quality of her vocal style. She had a tragic life, continually fighting off heroin addiction, and was later banned from New York nightclubs because of her drug addiction and arrests. Her own song "God Bless the Child" has endured in her recorded performances, and the work of other singers. Holiday's trademark song was "Strange Fruit," a song protesting a racist lynching, written by New York songwriter Lewis Allen (Able Merropol). Holiday originally resisted performing this emotional and depressing song, but ultimately it became her trademark. Decca Records, the company Holiday recorded for, would not issue "Strange Fruit" because they thought it was too controversial. Milt Gabler, Holiday's record producer at the time, then convinced Decca to allow him to release the song on Commodore Records, his own small jazz label.

Several dozen reissue albums of Holiday are available today, several biographies, and an autobiography. The film *Lady Day Sings the Blues* is about her tragic life.

holy blues

Blues scholars are fond of categorizing the music of African Americans into two categories; religious music and secular (nonreligious) music. They point out that religious people tended to see blues as the "devil's music," and associate it with drinking, wild dancing, and outrageous sexual behavior. The same authorities like to make the case that blues singers scorned the church, and had a cynical view of the role of the black preacher, whom they viewed as making a living off the backs of their economically deprived parishioners.

The truth is that there was not that clear a separation between the blues and religious music. In the biographical listings of this book, the reader encounters holy blues in the work of BLIND GARY DAVIS and BLIND WILLIE JOHNSON. Both these artists sang religious words with guitar accompaniments that were quite similar to what blues guitarists were playing. In Davis's case his guitar playing was the Piedmont ragtime-influence style of guitar, and Johnson's music was TEXAS blues, often played with a slide in open tuning.

But there is more to this story than the fact that some religious artists played guitar in a fashion similar to what blues artists were doing. In his early days, Davis had recorded some blues as well as his more typical religious songs. Later in life Davis occasionally played and recorded some of these songs and other blues as well, along with instrumental music that sounded like turn-of-the-century brass band or ragtime piano music.

There were also many instances of blues musicians who also recorded religious songs, sometimes using pseudonyms to avoid annoying what their record companies believed to be separate audiences. Early in his career, JOSH WHITE recorded both styles of music under other names. His blues songs were recorded by "Pinewood Tom," and for his religious material he used the name "The Singing Christian." In Alan Young's book *Woke Up This Morning: Black Gospel Singers and the Gospel Life,* Young points out that BLIND LEMON JEFFERSON recorded religious material using two different names. His first religious recordings use the name Deacon L. J. Bates, but later he recorded religious songs under his own name.

Delta songster and blues artist CHARLEY PATTON used the name Elder J. J. Hadley for his sacred songs, although he later dropped that name and recorded everything under his real name. BLIND BOY FULLER called himself Brother George and His Sanctified Singers. When BROWNIE MCGHEE borrowed Fuller's name for his first recordings after Fuller's death, he also recorded some religious songs, this time borrowing Fuller's alias.

BARBECUE BOB reversed the process, recording religious songs under his real name, Robert Hicks, and blues under the name Barbecue Bob. Other artists simply recorded whatever songs they wished, not bothering with the subterfuge of attempting to hide their identities. On this list can be placed FRED MCDOWELL, Brownie McGhee (later in his career), BLIND WILLIE MCTELL, SON HOUSE, SLEEPY JOHN ESTES, SARA MARTIN, and MEMPHIS MINNIE (unless one believes that Minnie's "other" name, Gospel Minnie, hid her identity).

Many blues singers, ranging from SKIP JAMES to B. B. KING, began their musical careers singing in church. In addition, quite a few blues artists abandoned their careers in blues toward the end of their lives and became ministers or church deacons, or at least sang in the church. ROBERT WILKINS refused to play blues music after he became a minister. Other artists went back and forth between the different musical genres. Skip James's early career in blues did not result in much success for him, so he returned to the church. When he was rediscovered in the 1960s he did not hesitate to go back to singing the blues, performing before thousands at the Newport Folk Festival and resuming his recording career. Similarly a long-retired SIPPIE WALLACE resumed her career in the blues after her rediscovery.

A brief discussion of the holy blues may provide perspective here. African-American music of the mid- and late-19th century was divided into spirituals—religious music sung in church—and a variety of nonreligious musical styles. The latter included work songs, unaccompanied field hollers, ring shouts, and other early ancestors of the blues. Similar to spirituals, field hollers followed the "call and response" model. One of the more respected field hands would lead the workers in a song, while others responded in sync with the rhythmic tone of the call. The task at hand determined the tempo and work pace. A ring shout is a shuffling circle dance that involves clapping. It was performed with lively spirituals.

Spirituals were a congregational form of music, usually sung in a church with a song leader, sometimes the minister calling out the words, with the congregation singing choruses or repeating the phrases sung by the song leader. This was a call-and-response pattern, with the song leader singing a line and the rest of the singers responding to the leader.

By the 1870s spirituals became much more formalized, largely because of the work of choral groups at Fisk University in Nashville and the Hampton Institute in Virginia, two leading black colleges of the day. Both these institutions used vocal groups to tour and raise money for their institutions. The singers not only toured throughout the United States but performed in Europe, Australia, and New Zealand. To raise money from largely white audiences it was necessary to smooth out any rough edges in the music. The singers were college students—educated, literate young adults, much more apt to work on their diction and pronunciation in a way that white audiences could easily relate to. Other colleges and professional singers imitated the sound of these choirs, and the Dinwoodie Colored Quartet recorded cylinders in 1902.

As the years went by, spirituals were relegated to the concert hall, and trained musicians like John W. Work and Nathaniel Dett wrote concert-style piano arrangements. It seemed to become obligatory for all trained black singers to include spirituals in their performances, even for operatic and art singers like Marian Anderson.

Negro spirituals were then taken away from the folk and turned into a concert hall presentation. Perhaps holy blues offered a reassertion of the importance of religious music in that community. Many of the early singers of holy blues, like Blind Man Arnold, who employed a young JOSH WHITE as his "lead boy," and Reverend Louis Pinson, never recorded, and we know about them only through other artists who heard or saw them. There were a whole group of artists, mostly obscure today, who did get to record. An extraordinary number of them were blind, including BLIND JOE TAGGART, "The Singing Evangelist;" Blind Roosevelt Graves; Blind Mamie Forehand; and blind pianist-singer Arizona Dranes. Some other holy blues artists include Sister Cally Francis, Reverend Edward Clayborn, and the Georgia Peach.

Another outlet for religious sentiment was supplied by recorded sermons. The format for these recordings was an impassioned sermon by a minister, with spoken or shouted encouragement from the congregation. Blues scholar Mark A. Humphrey, in his article "Holy Blues: The Gospel Tradition" (in Lawrence Cohn's anthology of descriptive articles about the blues, *Nothing But the Blues*), describes the development of the sermon genre. Humphrey traces its beginnings to a 1925 recording by Calvin Dixon, "As an Eagle Stirreth Up Her Nest." A year later Reverend J. C. Burnett's "The Downfall of Nebuchadnezzar" sold more than 80,000 copies, but the real superstar of the genre was Rev. J. M. Gates. He recorded about 200 titles between 1926 and 1941. His topics ranged from discussing the hellfire that awaited sinners to complaints about the economy during the Great Depression.

The success of these recorded sermons inevitably led to sermons accompanied by musical instruments, such as piano, tambourines, mandolin and guitar, harmonicas, jugs, washboards, and brass. Besides the male evangelists powerful women artists were also strong singers. These recordings were the direct predecessors of the emotional performances found in gospel music.

Many of the holy blues performers did not simply deal with religious issues, although there was always a religious component to their lyrics. They used wars as a symbol for human sinfulness, warning political leaders that a "greater power" looking down upon them would punish the unjust. Just how passionate these artists could be is indicated by the arrest of Blind Willie Johnson in New Orleans. He was delivering an impassioned performance of the song "If I Had My Way I Would Tear the Building Down," performing in front of a courthouse in New Orleans. Supposedly he was arrested when a policeman interpreted the song as being a literal plea to destroy the courthouse. Johnson also wrote songs that referred to contemporary events, such as the great influenza epidemic of 1918–19, which he saw as a warning from God to destroy his enemies. Another song referred to President

Woodrow Wilson, never popular among African Americans, as "sitting' on his throne, makin' laws for everyone."

The strangest Willie Johnson recording of all is his "Dark Was the Night." Although this song has lyrics, instead of singing them, Johnson recorded the entire song with hummed moans and a few vocal interjections. His emotional slide guitar playing sets the mood for the performance, which years later was used by composer-musician RY COODER as one of the central themes in his film score for the movie *Paris, Texas*.

Eventually holy blues evolved into modern gospel music. Certain performers were essentially the human bridge to gospel music. SISTER ROSETTA THARPE sang both religious and secular music and played excellent and rhythmic guitar. Roebuck "Pop" Staples's simple but effective Mississippi-style guitar playing derived from the playing of Charley Patton in Drew, Mississippi. Staples formed a band with his family, with his daughter Mavis singing lead and the Staple Singers enjoyed some of the first pop-gospel hits.

Another key figure in the popularity of gospel music was T. A. DORSEY. Dorsey had been a blues songwriter, composer, and arranger who turned to gospel music because of the death of his wife and newly born child, and because he was experiencing depression and despair despite his financial success as a blues artist. After a busy career as MA RAINEY's bandleader and in a duo with TAMPA RED, Dorsey turned to songwriting and music publishing. His music was much more formally arranged than the music of the holy blues artists and had a foot in popular music, as well as the gospel field. He worked with various singers, initially Sallie Martin and later the singer Mahalia Jackson.

Some of the success of gospel was due to the use of microphones and public address systems that had not been available when spirituals were in their heyday. In addition to impassioned male and female soloists, there were many male quartets and quintets. They often used two lead singers and close harmony vocals. Without the use of a public address system, the harmonies would never have been heard in the increasingly larger churches and auditoriums where the music was presented. The vocal soloists exploited low bass notes and high, lightly sung falsetto parts that also would have been nearly inaudible without amplification. A style of piano playing developed that became referred to as gospel piano, where piano players like Mildred Falls, who played for Mahalia Jackson, could rock an entire auditorium as though the piano alone were a complete orchestra. Some of the groups, like the Staple Singers and the Dixie Hummingbirds, used electric guitars instead, and bass, drums, and organs started to enter the gospel music scene as well.

Many soul music singers started out singing gospel music, including Sam Cooke, who had become the lead singer of the Soul Stirrers, and Aretha Franklin, who was the daughter of a famous Detroit minister, Reverend E. L. Franklin. As was the case for blues music, soul and pop-rock artists like Al Green (later the Reverend Al Green) and the colorful rock and roller Little Richard, bounced back and forth between religious and rock music.

Although periodically raw holy blues artists emerged through the 1960s and into the 1970s, gospel music basically eclipsed the holy blues as a musical style.

Homesick James (James Williamson) (b. 1910)
guitarist

Tennessee-born Williamson played with SLEEPY JOHN ESTES and BLIND BOY FULLER during the early years of the Great Depression (1929–32), but by 1935 he had migrated to CHICAGO, where he played with bottleneck guitarist ELMORE JAMES. James was self-taught, starting to play at the age of 10. He was one of the earliest bluesmen to play electric guitar, purchasing an electric Gibson Guitar in the mid-1930s.

Homesick James recorded a half dozen albums and did some European tours with harmonica player Snooky Pryor. His most recent recording was in 1997, at the age of 87.

Hooker, Earl (1930–1970) *slide guitarist and composer*

Earl Hooker was a versatile and superb guitarist, thought by many critics to be the best slide guitarist. Born in Clarksdale, Mississippi, Hooker moved to CHICAGO in the 1940s, and studied music at the Lyons & Healy Music School. He mastered the BANJO, MANDOLIN, PIANO and drums. Hooker did not sing much and recorded primarily as a sideman or a composer of instrumental music. Among the artists with whom he recorded were JUNIOR WELLS, MUDDY WATERS, and IKE TURNER. He also worked with blues shouter JIMMY WITHERSPOON. A biography of Hooker, Sebastian Danchin's *Earl Hooker: Blues Master,* is available.

Hooker, John Lee (1917–2001) *recording artist and guitarist*

John Lee Hooker may be the most recorded blues artist who has ever lived. A trip to a well-stocked record store reveals dozens of his recordings. Although it is customary for artists to be under contract to one record label at a time, Hooker recorded for many labels simultaneously, often using other names. Hooker had a background in gospel music in his native MISSISSIPPI, where his stepfather taught him guitar. John Lee then moved first to Cincinnati, then to DETROIT, where he began his recording career.

Hooker was an emotional singer and an interesting songwriter whose guitar style was primitive and eccentric. He would often play an entire song with one chord or use chord fragments or partial chords. He set up rhythmic grooves, sometimes tapping his foot like a primitive drum to create an infectious rhythm. Periodically he had rhythm and

John Lee Hooker (Neal Preston/Corbis)

blues hits with such songs as "Boogie Chillen," "Boom Boom" and "I'm in the Mood." The British rock band YARDBIRDS recorded Hooker's song "Louise," and the ANIMALS recorded three of his songs on their first album.

By the 1970s Hooker's career started to slow down, but he came roaring back with a Grammy-winning album, *The Healer,* released in 1989. *The Healer,* which had guest appearances by BONNIE RAITT, Carlos Santana, ROBERT CRAY, and GEORGE THOROGOOD, revived Hooker's career. Tribute concerts, induction into the Rock and Roll Hall of Fame, and more recordings followed. According to the *All Music Guide to the Blues,* John Lee Hooker recorded 70 CDs. Some of these albums duplicate performances on other albums, but it is still an extraordinary legacy.

Hopkins, Lightnin' (Sam) (1912–1982)
guitarist and performer

Lightnin' Hopkins, who spent most of his music career around Houston, Texas, was a prolific blues recording artist. Hopkins's listings in the *All Music Guide to the Blues* number only 58 albums. Hopkins had a dual career. On the one hand he was an electric guitarist who played blues and boogie-woogie at black clubs in Houston, and on the other hand he played down-home folk acoustic blues for white audiences. Hopkins did not like to fly, which prevented him from playing in Europe or far-flung venues that were open to most blues artists. Hopkins was a fine guitarist and songwriter whose song subjects varied among his time in jail, space explorations, and romance. In the late 1920s he played with singer TEXAS ALEXANDER, and he got to play with BLIND LEMON JEFFERSON, later acting as his guide. Hopkins's brothers also sang and played guitar. In the late 1940s Hopkins had a series of R&B hits for West Coast label Aladdin, and in 1954 folklorists-blues scholars SAM CHARTERS and Mack McCormick discovered Hopkins and recorded him extensively for a number of folk labels. For the rest of his life Hopkins went back and forth between his role as a "folk blues artist" and an electric guitar player playing in rowdy black clubs for dancers. The electric blues artist recorded fast, raucous boogie-woogie music and the folk artist played slow, thoughtful, down-home blues.

Horton, Big Walter (Shakey Horton)
(1918–1981) *harmonicist and composer*

Big Walter Horton may have been the first person who started to play amplified harmonica on the CHICAGO blues scene. Because he was not a singer, Horton never got the attention or notoriety that SONNY BOY WILLIAMSON and LITTLE WALTER (Jacobs) received. As a young boy Horton worked with the legendary MEMPHIS JUG BAND, and after moving to CHICAGO from MEMPHIS in 1953 he played and recorded with MUDDY WATERS. This led to working with guitarists OTIS RUSH, JOHNNY SHINES, and JIMMY ROGERS. During the 1960s he backed up TAMPA RED and BIG MAMA THORNTON, and toured with WILLIE DIXON's Blues All Stars. Harmonica player CAREY BELL was a student of Horton's. Besides his work as a sideman for other artists, Horton also wrote blues instrumentals.

Hot Tuna

Guitarist Jorma Kaukonen and bass player Jack Casady are lifelong friends, and both were original members of the psychedelic-rock band Jefferson Airplane. Hot Tuna started as a side project for the two musicians but turned into their full-time band. Jorma is a skillful fingerpicking guitarist, and Casady has been regarded as one of the most creative electric bass players in rock music. The combination of the two makes for interesting improvisational music. At times the band included Papa John Creach on violin and Will Scarlett on harmonica, and it briefly turned into an electric blues band in the early 1970s. In the late 1970s the band dissolved, resuming in the late 1980s. Kaukonen also runs a guitar school in Ohio, where he offers guitar instruction workshops.

House, Son (Eddie James House Sr.)
(1902–1988) *singer and guitarist*

Son House was one of the most important figures in the blues of the MISSISSIPPI Delta. By the time he had turned 20, Son had become a Baptist minister. He moved to Louisiana in the early 1920s, and returned to Mississippi in 1926. By that time he had learned how to play guitar and worked locally. House shot and killed a man in 1928, allegedly in self defense, and was sent to Parchman Farm (Mississippi State Penitentiary).

A year later a judge released him, apparently accepting House's story that he had acted in self-defense. Son was a friend and associate of

CHARLEY PATTON, and especially WILLIE BROWN, who recorded in the 1930s for Paramount Records. In 1941 ALAN LOMAX recorded House for the Library of Congress, and a year later he recorded him again. House then moved to Rochester, New York, and disappeared from the blues scene until his rediscovery. Blues musician Alan Wilson, a future member of Canned Heat, helped House to remember the songs he had played 30 years earlier, and House played at the Newport Folk Festival in 1964 and at Carnegie Hall in 1960, recorded for Columbia Records, and played American and European blues festivals. House was a powerful singer and guitarist who often strummed across the strings with an intensity captured in several videos. To convey the level of that intensity, in his *Encyclopedia of the Blues* Gerard Herzhaft describes a Parisian festival where the microphones lost power. According to Herzhaft, House continued performing his "Preaching Blues" without even noticing the loss of power. At the end of the performance a stunned audience gave him a standing ovation exceeding anything received by a blues artist in Europe. A number of House's tunes have been transcribed by Stefan Grossman, and RORY BLOCK has made an excellent set of tapes and a video showing his guitar technique.

Howell, Peg Leg (Joshua Barnes Howell)
(1888–1966) *guitarist and recording artist*
Peg Leg Howell was one of the first Atlanta bluesmen to record, starting his recording career in 1926. He fingerpicked the guitar and also played slide. Most of his music was country dance and string band music, mixed with rags and straight blues. Howell recorded as a soloist and also with a trio called Peg Leg Howell & His Gang. The other members of the trio were violinist Eddie Anthony and second guitarist Henry Williams. After Howell's recording career ended the trio continued to play for tips on the streets of Atlanta. In 1963 blues record label owner Pete Welding rediscovered

Howell, and he recorded an album for Welding's Testament label.

Howlin' Wolf (Chester Arthur Burnett)
(1910–1976) *soulful performer and harmonicist*
Besides MUDDY WATERS, the other CHICAGO blues giant of the 1950s was Howlin' Wolf. At 300 pounds, the Wolf cut an imposing figure, and his performances were not only dynamic but, by some accounts, downright frightening. Wolf was born in West Point, MISSISSIPPI, where he met and was influenced by CHARLEY PATTON and his brand of showmanship. Wolf played harmonica and sang with a powerful growl. He had a radio show in West Memphis early in his career, and he was recorded by Sam Phillips, the discoverer of ELVIS PRESLEY. Phillips produced Wolf's records for the CHESS label. In Chicago Wolf hooked up with lead guitarist Hubert Sumlin and cut some hit R&B records. He recorded mostly WILLIE DIXON's songs for some years, such as "Little Red Rooster" and "Back Door Man," then turned to his own repertoire.

His songs have been covered by many rock artists, including the Doors, CREAM, the Electric Flag, and the BLUES PROJECT. Sam Phillips thought that Wolf was the deepest artist he ever recorded.

"How Long, How Long Blues" (1928) *blues hit written by Leroy Carr*
LEROY CARR was one of the most popular songwriters and blues artists of the early 1930s. He wrote this song in 1928, and it became one of his biggest hits. It was so successful that he recorded it with new verses. Most blues songs simply have verses, but "How Long" has a repeated refrain, of "How long, how long, baby how long." This probably contributed to the song's popularity.

In addition to Carr's own recording, the many other recordings of "How Long" include performances by KOKOMO ARNOLD, three different records by Count Basie, British skiffle star Lonnie Donegan, BERTHA "CHIPPIE" HILL, JOHN LEE HOOKER, Howlin'

Wolf, BLIND LEMON JEFFERSON, vibes player Milt Jackson with RAY CHARLES, Lead Belly, MEADE LUX LEWIS, TAMPA RED, JOE TURNER, and JIMMY YANCEY. And this is not a complete list.

The song tells the story of a traveling man who has lost his woman, has no money, and keeps asking "How long?"

Humes, Helen (1913–1981) *singer and member of the Count Basie Orchestra*

Humes was a versatile singer, capable of singing blues, jazz, and pop music. In the late 1930s and early 1940s, she shared the singing chores in the Count Basie Orchestra with blues shouter JIMMY RUSHING. Humes's background included childhood piano and vocal lessons, and her first recording was made when she was 14, in 1927, accompanied by guitarist LONNIE JOHNSON. She traveled to NEW YORK in 1938 and was advised by jazz record producer JOHN HAMMOND to join the Basie band. She replaced BILLIE HOLIDAY, who had decided to pursue a solo career. She had turned Basie down a year earlier, but this time she joined the band.

In 1942 Humes left the Basie band and in 1944 she moved to California, recording several movie soundtracks. After recording with Red Norvo's band in the mid 1950s, Humes resumed her blues career, traveling to Europe with the American Folk Blues Festival package. She performed in Australia from 1964 to 1967, but returned to care for her sick mother. After several years away from the music business, she sang at the Newport Jazz Festival in 1973, and she continued to make appearances and to record until her death in 1981.

Hunter, Alberta (1895–1984) *singer and composer*

During her long life, Alberta Hunter had a varied musical career. She was one of the classic blues singers of the 1920s, recording with such jazz greats as Sidney Bechet and LOUIS ARMSTRONG. During the 1920s she performed in London in the musical *Showboat,* with actor and singer Paul Robeson, and later sang in Paris. She then entertained American troops during World War II and again in the Korean War.

Hunter became a nurse in 1956 and mostly retired from music, until she retired from nursing in 1977. In 1977, when she was 82, New York impresario Barney Josephson coaxed her out of retirement to appear at his Cookery restaurant. Her performances received a great deal of publicity and drew large audiences. This led to further engagements and a Columbia Records recording contract. Hunter's music was not pure blues, but included show tunes and jazz standards. She was the co-composer of BESSIE SMITH's biggest hit, "Downhearted Blues," with bandleader LOVIE AUSTIN. Hunter was a savvy enough business woman to contact Smith's producer, FRANK WALKER, to suggest that they record her song.

Hurt, Mississippi John (1893–1966) *singer*

In 1964, John Hurt was found in Avalon, MISSISSIPPI, where he had lived during and after his short 1920s record career. Blues revivalists were familiar with Hurt because his song "Spike Driver Blues" was one of the highlights of the 1952 reissue LPs *The Anthology of American Folk Music,* compiled by Harry Smith. Hurt was rediscovered by Tom Hoskins a blues aficionado, who one day while listening to an old Hurt record of "Avalon Blues" and heard the lyric "Avalon, that's my home." Hoskins looked up Hurt in the Avalon phone directory, and found him there.

Hurt had originally recorded only 13 songs, but when he was rediscovered he was in good physical and mental shape, and for the first time in his life he had time to practice extensively. His appearance at the 1964 Newport Folk festival was a sensational success. This rather small, unimposing man sat in a chair and played for thousands of cheering fans, many of whom had never heard of him.

John Hurt influenced many of the young blues fans and folk revivalists, with his subtle fingerpicking guitar style and his warm, almost spoken vocals.

Many of his songs were folk ballads rather than blues, so that some folklorists thought of him as a songster, rather than a blues artist. HAPPY TRAUM and Tom Paxton, two influential folksingers, have both written songs about Hurt, and a number of his guitar solos have been written out for those wanting to learn them. A tribute album, *Avalon Blues,* was released in 2001.

Hutchison, Frank (1897–1945) *slide guitarist*

Frank Hutchison was one of the first white musicians to record blues. Hutchison, originally a coal miner, was basically a country artist, but he loved blues and played slide guitar with a knife. A good fingerpicking guitarist, he played much more convincingly than he sang, with his high nasal quality.

Ichiban Records

This label was founded in 1985 in Atlanta to record all genres of popular African-American music, including blues, gospel, R&B, and rap. Some of the blues artists on the label include Cleveland Fats, JIMMIE DAWKINS, Theodis Ealey, and Little Mike & the Tornados.

Iglauer, Bruce (b. 1947) *record company owner*

Starting his record company in his CHICAGO apartment, Bruce Iglauer now has the largest blues record company, with 19 full-time employees. Iglauer started out working in the shipping room at BOB KOESTER'S DELMARK RECORDS and started his own ALLIGATOR RECORDS in 1971 when Koester refused to record HOUND DOG TAYLOR. Today Koester has released over 200 albums. Many of his records have won Grammy or W. C. HANDY Blues Awards. Among the artists Alligator has recorded are ALBERT COLLINS, KOKO TAYLOR, COREY HARRIS, LONNIE MACK, JOHNNY WINTER, and SAFFIRE—THE UPPITY BLUES WOMEN.

improvisation

Improvisation occurs when a musician invents musical parts that vary from one performance to another, or even during a performance of a single song. For example, if a song has a chorus, the musician will play it differently each time. Improvisation is a fundamental part of jazz, but it is found in varying degrees in the blues.

Peter Silvester, in his book on boogie-woogie, *A Left Hand Like God,* points out that in some of JIMMY YANCEY's pieces, he incorporates entire sections from some of his earlier compositions. This brings up the point that many apparent improvisations are actually based on or even consist entirely of passages that a musician has previously played.

Many musicians have identifiable styles that use particular devices. An example of this is B. B. KING's particular way of bending strings or using left-hand vibrato. These are some of the techniques that make his particular guitar sound so identifiable. The improvisational elements in his playing would come in his choice of notes for the guitar solos.

Improvisation can also be rhythmic or harmonic. In rhythmic improvisation the musician may subtly change a rhythm pattern or go into a completely different rhythm or meter. To get a sense of how this works, one can play a familiar, simple tune in a different meter. A tune in 4/4 time, for example sounds very different when played as a waltz, in 3/4 time. Changing the pattern used in accompanying the song will change the rhythm but not the meter. If, four quarter notes are generally played in each bar of music, playing eight eighth notes or two quarter notes and four eighth notes will alter the sound. Singers not accustomed to varying their accompaniment patterns in this way may have trouble singing the song.

In harmonic improvisation a musician utilizes substitute chords to reharmonize a song. The substitutions may be an extension of the original chord—change C to C6, for example, by adding an

A note to the chord—or adding chords that are not in the usual progression. For example, if a song goes from C to F, play C, then follow it with a D minor and an E minor chord on the way to an F.

In jazz the harmonic substitutions are much more complex and use more elaborate alterations of the chord. For example, take a C7 chord, C E G B-flat, and change the chord to a C7-flat/5, which is C E G-flat B-flat. When complex chord substitutions are utilized, the entire shape of a melody may shift to the point where the average person no longer recognizes the original tune.

As record companies have begun to reissue alternate takes of recordings, listeners are now in a position to hear exactly how much some musicians improvised. The ROBERT JOHNSON box set reveals that Johnson's recorded music consisted essentially of set pieces that he arranged and changed very little from one take of a song to another. Whether his live performances featured more efforts at improvisation may never be determined, although few players interviewed who performed with him indicated that they did.

A creative blues or jazz musician improvises on a regular basis, but even the most talented musicians may resort to stock phrases or rhythmic patterns when stuck, or when they play with musicians they do not know. A great deal of improvisation occurs in a group context when creative musicians who do not usually play together arrange a performance or recording session. The recording environment has changed so much during the last 50 years that yet another level of improvisation occurs when a musician adds a part to what has already been recorded on a multitrack tape recorder. This is quite a different challenge from playing with live musicians, where each part may be influenced by what each musician plays.

Indiana

INDIANAPOLIS

Indianapolis, Indiana, was an important blues town in the 1930s because pianist-composers LEROY CARR and SCRAPPER BLACKWELL lived there and made many influential and commercially successful blues recordings. Carr was one of the earliest performers to bring an urban sophistication to the blues by his relatively smooth vocal style and songwriting skills.

RICHMOND

Richmond, in the western part of the state, was the headquarters of Gennett Records. During the 1920s Gennett was an important label in jazz, blues, and country music. Among the blues artists who recorded for Gennett were BIG BILL BROONZY, COW COW DAVENPORT, and ROOSEVELT SYKES. Oddly, at the same time that Gennett was recording the blues, the company also pressed records for the racist Ku Klux Klan.

instruments

Blues instrumental styles have changed greatly during the years that the blues have been in existence. In 1890–1900, blues was folk music, rooted in its own community and performed in informal situations. No one knows when or where the first blues was actually written or performed, but the form likely developed loosely through the experimentation of many different musicians. When the music started to be performed publicly, the venues available were local dances, parties, and "juke joints," small, informal southern clubs.

African-American slaves played FIDDLES and BANJOS, for their own entertainment and for the entertainment of their masters. This can be observed in paintings of slaves playing musical instruments, comments by historical figures like Thomas Jefferson, observations of travelers writing in journals, and ads for runaway slaves describing the musical prowess of the slaves. The guitar seems to have been introduced much later. HARMONICAS were available to people with limited funds, because they were exceptionally cheap and portable. For the same reasons jug bands used homemade instruments like jugs and combs. Like harmonicas, kazoos, also a wind instrument, were inexpensive and portable. Homemade basses, usually consisting of a single string mounted on some sort of bucket, were also part of the jug band sound. Various sorts of banjos were used in these bands, and the MANDOLIN was also present, although less popular. PIANOS were found in saloons and the rough barrelhouses in lumber and turpentine camps.

The classic blues singers of the 1920s were polished female performers, who appeared in larger venues, such as theaters and traveling shows. Although a few classic blues singers, like SARA MARTIN, used a relatively country-folk type of accompaniment, many of the classic singers relied on a piano-playing bandleader like T. A. DORSEY, and a small orchestra that usually included one or two horn players. On recordings these small combos were sometimes augmented by other musicians who did not tour with the artist. As already pointed out, many of the horn players were jazz musicians playing the blues because it was a paying job, not their musical preference. Meanwhile some Delta blues artists used resonator guitars to achieve higher levels of volume, and also because they were well suited to slide guitar playing.

The introduction of public address systems and portable microphones during the 1920s made it much easier for singers to be heard over the sound of their accompanists. During the 1920s the banjo became less and less an instrument in the blues and was largely replaced by the guitar.

The CHICAGO "Bluebird beat" of the mid-late 1930s included upright basses and drum sets, and sometimes a saxophone. By the late 1930s the ELECTRIC GUITAR started to become relatively common, and the rhythm and blues bands of the 1940s often included loud tenor saxophone players, and piano or organ.

The post–World War II bands included solid-body electric guitars, and gradually electric basses were introduced. Drummers were considered a regular part of the scene instead of a novelty. As sound technology improved, solid-body electric guitars and larger, more powerful guitar amplifiers allowed guitarists to play at much higher volumes, and to develop techniques specific to the nature of the electric instruments. Rock and roll started to play a prominent part in the music of the mid-1950s, and blues-rock developed. Blues-rock involved the use of pop-rock songs accompanied by blues guitar techniques and vocal styles that were part gospel, part blues, and part rock.

Today's blues encompasses a large variety of contrasting styles. The Chicago blues continues to be strong, as it has been since the 1950s. A number of white and black blues revivalists perform in the older musical styles, and some artists like RY COODER, Harry Manx, BOB BROZMAN and Corky Siegel have integrated everything from world music styles to chamber music with the language of the blues.

Jackson, Jim (1890–1937) *songster*

Jim Jackson's recording of "Kansas City Blues" was one of the most successful blues records of the 1920s, selling almost a million copies. Jackson worked in minstrel and medicine shows— shows in which a troupe of performers, often in blackface, sang songs and performed—early in his career and moved to MEMPHIS in the 1920s. Jackson was a songster whose music reflected a combination of blues and minstrel songs. Over the years many other artists have recorded "Kansas City Blues," albeit in a partially rewritten version, including JAMES BROWN and Wilbert Harrison, but none of them credited Jackson for it. After his big hit in 1927, he continued to record until 1930, cutting over 30 songs. He often worked the Memphis streets with singers and guitarists FURRY LEWIS and Will Shade, and country blues performer ROBERT WILKINS, and in 1929 he appeared in the film *Hallelujah.* He also was the first artist to record "Old Dog Blue," a song that became very popular during the folk revival.

Jackson, John (1924–2002) *guitarist and banjoist*

A guitar and BANJO player, John Jackson spent many years playing music part-time. He was a songster with a broad repertoire, influenced by BLIND WILLIE WALKER, BLIND BOY FULLER, BLIND BLAKE, and country artist JIMMIE RODGERS. He met Walker, who visited Jackson's father at his house. His songs included rags, folk ballads, and dance tunes, as well as blues.

In 1951 Jackson worked as a gravedigger, but the sixties blues and folk revival enabled him to get more music jobs, and he became quite popular in the Washington, D.C., area. He also toured and recorded a half dozen albums, the last ones in 1999.

Jackson, Papa Charlie (1890–1938) *folk blues singer*

Jackson was the first successful folk blues artist, beginning his recording career in 1924. Born in New Orleans, he moved to CHICAGO around 1920. He usually played the six-string banjo, which was strung and tuned like a guitar but sounded like a BANJO because it had a skin head. He also occasionally played the ukulele. Jackson was a talented player who could both fingerpick and strum, according to the needs of a song. In addition to his own recordings Jackson accompanied some of the classic blues singers like MA RAINEY and IDA COX when they chose to frame their music with more of a down-home and less of a jazz feeling. Many of the songs that Jackson recorded are still sung today, like "Salty Dog" and "Spoonful." Jackson's recording career lasted until 1934, during which time he recorded about 70 songs. Toward the end of his career he started to play guitar. One of the highlights of his career was recording with the Chicago guitarist BLIND BLAKE in 1929. Some of their recordings had a minstrel show flavor, with the two playing ragtime figures and kidding each other. They were not singing but talking to each other.

James, Elmore (1918–1963) *guitarist and singer*
Another product of the MISSISSIPPI Delta, Elmore James built much of his career around one song. He recorded the ROBERT JOHNSON song "I Believe I'll Dust My Broom," retitling it "DUST MY BROOM." James had met Johnson in 1937, a year before Johnson's death. James, a former radio repairman, tinkered with guitar amplifiers, trying to get more volume out of them. Elmore was an aggressive guitarist and singer who basically took Delta blues and turned it into a rhythm and blues style. James's band included his cousin Homesick James on guitar, plus piano, drums, and one, sometimes two, saxophones. Their loud dance music became popular in the black clubs on the South Side of CHICAGO.

Elmore had been a protégé of SONNY BOY WILLIAMSON, and his first recording of "Dust My Broom" was made on LILLIAN MCMURRY's Trumpet label, during the last few minutes of a Williamson session. It was done so quickly that McMurry had to use another artist for the other side of the record, because James did not record anything else. The record turned out to be a top-10 R&B hit in 1951. Elmore played as a guest star on the blues radio program King Biscuit Radio Show on station KFFA in Helena, Arkansas. Later he performed on other radio shows as well.

Throughout his career Elmore kept rerecording "Dust My Broom," but he also came up with interesting songs of his own, like "The Sky Is Crying." Another of his songs, "Shake Your Moneymaker," has been recorded and performed by other artists, and is a blues standard.

James, Etta (Jamsetta Hawkins) (b. 1938) *songstress*
Etta James is a powerful and emotional singer whose repertoire covers blues and rhythm and blues selections. As a child James had been a gospel prodigy, singing in the Baptist choir in her native Los Angeles. She then worked with R&B bandleader JOHNNY OTIS, and by 1960 she was recording for CHESS. In 1967 James recorded an album in Muscle Shoals, Alabama, at Rick Hall's Fame recording studio, which featured a house band of white players who grew up on blues and rhythm and blues, and who also played for R&B singer Aretha Franklin, among others. The sessions resulted in James's big hit "Tell Mama."

During the 1970s James overcame drug addiction and other personal problems outlined in her autobiography *Rage to Survive*. She recorded a number of albums in the 1990s, including her 1994 album *Mystery Lady*, a tribute album to jazz singer BILLIE HOLIDAY.

James, Skip (Nehemiah Curtis James) (1902–1969) *guitarist and singer*
Skip James is a unique figure in MISSISSIPPI blues. He had a high and haunting voice, often moving into the falsetto range. He had a unique style, not only on the guitar but also on the piano. He took piano lessons in high school and learned guitar from his friend Henry Stuckey. James spent times as a laborer, sharecropper, bootlegger, and gambler. He recorded 18 songs for Paramount Records in the late 1920s and early 1930s, none of which sold well. He then disappeared from the music scene for 30 years. He became a gospel singer and was ordained as a Baptist minister in 1932, and a Methodist minister in 1946. He does not seem to have actually worked as a minister.

In 1964 blues scholar–recording artist JOHN FAHEY and his friends Bill Barth and Ed Denson found James and brought him to the Newport Folk Festival. Although James was not in good health, during the last five years of his life, he recorded a half dozen albums and played at various folk festivals and in concerts. Cream recorded James's "I'm So Glad," and the royalties helped James pay his medical bills. James often played in open E minor tuning, which is E G E G B E, an unusual guitar tuning rarely used by anyone else. A biography of James, by Stephen Calt, *I'd Rather Be the Devil: Skip James and the Blues*, is a bit condescending in its evaluation of his talents and character.

Etta James (Bruce Polonsky Photography)

James, Steve (b. 1950) *guitarist and mandolinist*
Steve James is a white blues enthusiast who plays guitar and MANDOLIN, and sings and write songs. He particularly favors the ragtime-oriented blues, and he studied with MEMPHIS songster FURRY LEWIS and the white country guitarist Sam McGee. James also studied guitar making for a year, and has been active as a teacher, making instructional albums, teaching at guitar workshops, and serving as a contributing editor for *Acoustic Guitar*.

jazz and the blues
Jazz as a musical style arose roughly at the same time as the blues. Although they are related, there are more differences between them than similarities.

The similarities between the styles revolve around the use of blue notes—flatting third and seventh of the musical scale. On the piano these notes are E-flat and B-flat in the key of C, but other instruments play notes that are between the pitches—higher than Eb-flat, for example, but lower than E. The same techniques are used by jazz vocalists.

As for the differences between the two musical forms, jazz historically has focused on horns, initially trumpets and clarinets, and later saxophones. The guitar was most often found in jazz as a member of the rhythm section, rather than as a solo instrument. During the late 1930s the invention of the ELECTRIC GUITAR and the musical innovations of guitarist Charlie Christian changed all of this, but this was well into the development period of the blues. The guitar, and to a lesser extent the PIANO, have always been the instruments most closely identified with the blues. Not until the development of rhythm and blues, beginning around 1940, were horns commonly used in blues music.

The classic blues singers often used jazz musicians as accompanists. BESSIE SMITH, for example, used cornet player Joe Smith, and occasionally LOUIS ARMSTRONG, as well as trombonist Charley Green. Some jazz players were better blues players than others. Jazz tends to use more elaborate chords than blues utilize, and jazz players often play complicated melodic lines that are out of context for the blues. Some jazz players did not especially care for the blues. Pianist Sam Wooding even joked that Bessie Smith dragged the beat by holding notes out so long that he could go to the bathroom and when he came back she was still singing the same line.

Part of the reason that classic blues singers used band musicians was because a good deal of their repertoire included pop and vaudeville music in addition to blues. A number of these singers did cabaret shows or appeared on Broadway. HARMONICAS and guitars were not readily suitable in those situations, although the more sophisticated guitarists managed to fit in successfully to a variety of musical styles. Certainly one of the reasons that jazz musicians played on blues records was that freelance recording was a welcome source of income for them.

A similar situation occurred in rhythm and blues, and soul music, where many of the singers, like B. B. KING, JAMES BROWN, BOBBY BLUE BLAND, and RAY CHARLES, liked to use fairly large orchestras to "fatten up" their sound in large venues. Many of the musicians who played in these bands were jazz musicians.

The importance of the blues changed as various jazz styles appeared. In the earliest jazz, some of the musicians, like Louis Armstrong, would occasionally sing blues as part of their show. During the late 1920s and throughout the 1930s the musical style called swing appeared. Dixieland jazz used small combos of five to seven musicians. The typical instrumentation was trumpet, clarinet, and trombone, together with a rhythm section that used a simple drum set, tuba or string bass, piano, and BANJO. Most of the music was not written down in musical notation, and the horn players mostly used their ears to avoid playing notes that duplicated or conflicted with one another. Swing used much larger orchestras, with three or four trumpets, about the same number of saxophones, two or three trombones, and a rhythm section of guitar, bass drums, and piano. Because of the large number of brass and reed instruments it was necessary for the parts to be written out. This role was assumed by music arrangers, who had a thorough knowledge of orchestration. There was relatively little improvisation, and it was usually limited to solos, where one musician would invent a lead line, while the orchestra played written chordal patterns or figures behind the soloist. Most swing bands carried one or two singers in addition to the instrumentalists. A few of the bands, like Count Basie, would utilize singers like JIMMY RUSHING or BIG JOE TURNER, who could sing pop or jazz tunes, but could also shout the blues. Most swing bands used crooners, singers hired for their sex appeal who were strongly influenced by pop music. Many of these singers, like Frank Sinatra and Jo Stafford, went on to become stars as solo singers.

By the mid-1940s black musicians developed a new style of jazz called bebop. They had largely been frozen out of the richest financial rewards that were attained by such white swing musicians as Artie Shaw, Benny Goodman, and Glenn Miller. A group of young virtuoso jazz musicians, especially alto saxophonist Charlie Parker and trumpet player Dizzy Gillespie, started to play increasingly complicated chord progressions and tunes. Bebop, with some rare exceptions, restored the importance of combo music to jazz. Even though the music was much more complicated than swing had been, some of the bebop players, notably Charlie Parker, prided themselves on their ability to play the blues. Because they rarely used the relatively simple blues chords, many of these tunes were barely recognizable as being rooted in the blues.

Later jazz included the development of funk, music more rooted in the blues, as well as other musical styles like third-stream jazz, integrating elements of classical music into jazz. Third-stream jazz and the "cool" sounds of West Coast jazz were even further afield from blues than swing had been. Many jazz musicians grew up schooled in the blues, so that a musician like vibes player Milt Jackson actually recorded some blues playing relatively simple guitar. In the late 1950s white musician-composer-arranger Jimmy Giuffre formed a trio with clarinet, guitar, and bass, and recorded what became known as "chamber jazz," because he did not use a drummer. Some of Giuffre's compositions, especially "The Train and the River," featured instrumental parts close to the folk blues.

Although many of the current jazz players have some familiarity with the blues, their playing does not integrate many musical elements that would be readily familiar to blues fans.

Jefferson, Blind Lemon (1893–1929) *singer and guitarist*

One of the most successful of the male country blues guitarists, Blind Lemon Jefferson recorded nearly 100 sides between 1925 and 1929. Jefferson is to TEXAS blues what CHARLEY PATTON was to MISSISSIPPI blues: a primary source for those who followed him.

Despite his popularity, very little is known about Jefferson's life. His birthdate, is thought to be 1893, and it is not known whether he was partially sighted or whether he was born blind. (The well-known photograph of him in a Paramount Records advertisement shows him wearing clear glasses.) He was born to a cotton-farming family in Coucham, near Wortham in east Texas. He taught himself guitar, and his singing and playing style was influenced not only by black music styles but also by the Spanish guitar playing of Mexican farmworkers.

In his late teens, Jefferson began playing on the streets, traveling to other east Texas towns and on to Dallas, where he joined LEAD BELLY, who was a few years older. The two probably influenced each other. Lead Belly later recorded a song called "Blind Lemon," with a spoken portion that described the two of them riding on passenger trains and playing guitars in place of paying any fare. Jefferson traveled around the Mississippi Delta and MEMPHIS regions during the decade before 1920, and he married around 1922 or 1923 and had at least one son. T-BONE WALKER served as his lead boy in Dallas around 1920, guiding him through the streets and collecting money from those who listened to him perform.

Jefferson had an unusual guitar style, in the sense that he did not have a single recognizable way of playing. Rather, he tailored his accompaniment to the particular song. He was capable of playing quick runs, but at other times he was content to play churning rhythms and let his singing do the work. Often he used the guitar almost like another singing voice, commenting on what the voice had sung, or what the lyric of the song was saying. The songs varied from telling a story with a beginning, middle, and end, to songs that were collections of verses found in other songs.

In 1925 a Texas talent scout sent a demonstration recording of Jefferson to producer J. Mayo Williams at Paramount Records in CHICAGO. Paramount gave him a contract, and the first two songs recorded were gospel songs. Except for two songs recorded for Okeh, all of Jefferson's recordings were for Paramount, and almost all of them were blues. Oddly, the two songs recorded for Okeh were his second recording of "Black Snake Blues" and "Match Box Blues." The primary verse of "Match Box"—"sittin' here wondering, would a matchbox hold my clothes?"—was later used in recordings by CARL PERKINS, Jerry Lee Lewis, and the Beatles.

There were over 40 record releases, and they sold a remarkable average of 100,000 copies apiece. The Paramount photograph shows a well-dressed, seemingly successful man. Jefferson performed throughout the South and in St. Louis. In the winter of 1929 he went to Chicago to record and was caught in a severe snow storm. He left a party that he was attending and either froze to death or suffered a heart attack and died, or some combination of the two. He was at first buried in an unmarked grave in Wortham, Mississippi. This was ironic, considering that one of his most famous songs was titled "See That My Grave Is Kept Clean." All Jefferson's recordings have been reissued in a boxed set.

J. Geils Band

J. Jerome Geils was the lead guitarist in this Boston blues-rock band, Peter Wolf was the lead vocalist, and Magic Dick was a featured instrumentalist on HARMONICA and saxophone. Seth Justman was the principal songwriter and played keyboards. The band, known as a raucous party band, became enormously popular when it recorded the album *Freeze Frame* with its number one hit, "Centerfold." The wild antics of the group made them popular on MTV, but the band broke up in the mid-1980s. Although Wolf continued to work as a soloist, and Geils and Magic Dick formed a band together, none of these acts achieved the popularity that the J. Geils Band had enjoyed.

Johnson, Big Jack (b. 1940) *songwriter and guitarist*

Not all blues artists wanted to travel to the big urban centers of the North and Midwest. Jack Johnson learned guitar from his father in Lambert, MISSISSIPPI. He plays country acoustic blues but has also performed electric blues in a trio with HARMONICA-PIANO-guitarist Frank Frost and Sam Carr, and as the leader of his own band. Besides performing, Johnson writes songs about today's world, whether involving social commentary or romantic situations. Although he has toured nationally and internationally, he chooses to live in his native Mississippi.

Johnson, Blind Willie (1902–1947) *"holy blues" singer*

Willie Johnson was an impassioned singer with a growling quality to his voice. He sang on the streets, supporting himself by playing for tips. Johnson was born in a small Texas town and was blinded at the age of seven. He became a Baptist preacher, and after he married he performed on the streets with his wife, Willie B. Harris.

The music that Johnson performed is "holy blues," religious lyrics with blues melodies. One of his most famous songs, "Dark Was the Night," is a stark guitar figure accompanied by wordless moaning. RY COODER used it as the theme in his film score for the movie *Paris, Texas*. BOB DYLAN and ERIC CLAPTON have also recorded some of Johnson's songs. All in all, Johnson recorded 30 songs. His songs "I Just Can't Keep from Cryin'" and "John the Revelator" have also retained some popularity among blues revivalist artists.

Johnson and his wife are depicted fictionally in the Wim Wenders–directed video in the Blues Legacy television series. The narrator correctly states that Johnson's "Dark Was the Night" was beamed into space on the *Voyager* space shuttle. Other selections chosen included CHUCK BERRY and Ludwig van Beethoven.

Johnson, Johnnie (1924–2005) *pianist*

Johnnie Johnson played PIANO for CHUCK BERRY from 1955 to 1973. He eventually left, feeling that he never received songwriting credits for songs that he participated in writing. Since Berry's records sold in the millions and generated considerable income, this was a serious problem. Johnson is a self-taught piano player who grew up in West Virginia and moved to DETROIT to work in defense factories during World War II. After serving in the marines in 1943 he moved to CHICAGO, then to Detroit, where he met Berry. A documentary film about Chuck Berry called *Hail! Hail! Rock'n'Roll* featured Johnson and resulted in several albums under Johnson's name, one of which included guest appearances by ERIC CLAPTON and ROLLING STONES guitarist Keith Richards.

Johnson, Larry (b. 1938) *guitarist*

During the 1960s, Larry Johnson was a young black student of the Reverend Gary Davis in New York City. Johnson's father was a preacher in Georgia, and the son often traveled with him, going from town to town. He encountered the recordings of BLIND BOY FULLER and decided to learn to play guitar. After serving in the navy from 1955 to 1959, Johnson moved to New York. He fell in with the New York blues artists BROWNIE MCGHEE and his brother Sticks, and guitarist ALEC SEWARD. Johnson played on recordings by Big Joe Williams and Seward, and sometimes performed with BLIND GARY DAVIS. Johnson started to record solo albums in 1970, and has recorded on and off since then. He still favors the Piedmont fingerpicking guitar style.

Johnson, Lonnie (1899–1970) *singer, songwriter, and guitarist*

Blues singer, guitarist, songwriter, and jazz guitarist Lonnie Johnson had enough different careers in his lifetime, for a half dozen musicians. Johnson played violin in his father's string band, then

Lonnie Johnson (left) (Library of Congress Films and Photographs Division)

picked up the guitar. In 1917 he went to London to perform in a musical revue. He stayed two years, and when he returned in 1919, he found that his entire family, except for one brother, had died in the influenza epidemic.

Lonnie's first recordings were made in 1925 for Okeh records. He also played and recorded with LOUIS ARMSTRONG's Hot Seven, one of the most influential New Orleans bands of all time. Some of his guitar solos on these records still sound surprisingly modern. In 1928–29 he hooked up with white jazz guitarist Eddie Lang to form a band they called Blind Willie Dunn's Gin Bottle Four. Even 75-years later the music sounds as though it could have been recorded in the 21st century. The two players alternate solos, and each of them wrote some of the tunes.

Johnson also had a career as an accompanist, particularly with singer TEXAS ALEXANDER. The two of them made dozens of recordings together, and Johnson also recorded with numerous other artists, including VICTORIA SPIVEY. Somehow Johnson had time to record with famed jazz composer and bandleader Duke Ellington as well. Johnson is considered to be one of the fathers of jazz guitar. He could play fast and accurate patterns of single notes, and he also had a knowledge of chords that went beyond what just about any other blues guitarist was capable of.

During the 1930s Johnson lived in Cleveland, Ohio. This was the period of the Great Depression, and work was hard to find. Johnson worked in factories, as well as playing music jobs. By 1937 he moved to Chicago, and he recorded 34 sides for Bluebird between 1937 and 1944. In 1947 Johnson was transformed into an R&B ballad singer, and had a major hit with the song "Tomorrow Night." He disappeared from the music scene but was found by his friend guitarist-banjoist Elmer Snowden working at the Ben Franklin Hotel in Philadelphia as a bellhop. Snowden encouraged him to play, and Johnson's career started up again. He made recordings and moved to Toronto, Canada, where he performed with a Dixieland band, and remained popular until his death.

Johnson, Pete (1904–1967) *pianist*

Pete Johnson was a rhythmically powerful boogie-woogie pianist who often accompanied blues shouter BIG JOE TURNER. Around 1940 boogie-woogie became very popular, and Johnson formed a trio with pianists MEADE LUX LEWIS and Albert Ammons that continued into the early 1940s. They performed at the John Hammond From Spirituals to Swing Carnegie Hall concert. Later Johnson performed in a piano duo with Ammons. Johnson's most famous tune was "Roll 'Em Pete," which is still played by most boogie-woogie pianists.

Johnson, Robert (1911–1938) *folk blues artist*

Robert Johnson is probably the single most famous folk blues artist. Strangely, during his lifetime only one of Johnson's recordings could have been described as even a moderate success. "Terraplane Blues," a song about a new automobile model, recorded in November 1936, sold 5,000 copies at the most. There are more questions than answers about the life and career of Robert Johnson. No one has ever explained exactly why his record company, American Record Company, even bothered to call him back to do more recording. Did they sense that he was capable of making a better-selling record? Did someone at the company feel that he had a musical potential that the first record failed to capture? At Johnson's first recording session in San Antonio he recorded 16 songs during a three-day period. At his second session, only seven months later in June 1937, he recorded another 13 songs. Why did ARC want to record that much material in 1937 from an unknown artist, and in giving him a second chance, why would they record that much material from someone who had not proven that his recordings could sell?

This is only one of the many Robert Johnson mysteries. Johnson was an illegitimate child conceived when his father was forced to leave his Mississippi Delta home because of a dispute with a white man. Johnson's father went to MEMPHIS, but his mother stayed at home. While they were separated, his mother took up with another man and became pregnant. After Robert was born, he stayed with his mother but later moved in with his stepfather in Memphis, who accepted the boy as a son but never forgave his mother. This set the tone for Johnson's adult life, which was one of constant and sometimes aimless travel. Bluesmen JOHNNY SHINES and ROBERT LOCKWOOD, JR., both of whom were associated with Johnson, describe his never wanting to stay in one place and disappearing at a moment's notice, not to be seen again for months.

Johnson's musical development also holds its share of unanswered questions. As a young boy Robert played harmonica and wanted to play guitar. SON HOUSE and WILLIE BROWN, together with CHARLEY PATTON, were the leading Delta blues artists in the early 1930s. House recalls Johnson sitting in with them and playing the guitar when they took a break. He played so badly that the audience begged House and Brown to take the guitar away from Johnson. Around 1931, Robert disappeared for, depending upon which Son House story is believed, from six months to two years. When he came back he once again went to one of the performances by House and Brown, and asked if he could play the guitar. The two were prepared for another poor performance and were astounded that the Robert Johnson they were now listening to not only had become an excellent guitarist but had even surpassed their own abilities. How did this happen?

Here is where the legend of Robert Johnson begins. The story spread in the 1960s that Johnson had gone to a crossroads and made a deal with the Devil. Under the terms of the deal the Devil would turn Johnson into a phenomenal guitar player, but the guitarist would surrender possession of his immortal soul to Satan. This story is a recurring legend in world folklore. The same tale is spun about blues artist TOMMY JOHNSON (not a relative of Robert.) To believe this story, the reader needs to believe in voodoo. Most blues writers have taken the story to be a metaphor, probably for the

fact that Johnson gave up every other part of his life in his quest to become the greatest blues guitarist who ever lived.

The real story of Johnson's transformation from a bad amateur into a great guitarist was probably a year spent studying with unrecorded bluesman Ike Zinneman, combined with his continued travels and careful listening to such guitar greats as LONNIE JOHNSON, SKIP JAMES, and KOKOMO ARNOLD. Zinneman may have had a role in the legend about the Devil, because he was known to enjoy practicing a guitar while sitting on tombstones in the cemetery. In any case, by 1933 Robert Johnson had established himself as the equal or superior of any Delta guitarist.

Rumors of his abilities spread, and Ernie Oertle, a salesmen for the American Record Company, contacted him and arranged a contract. Johnson's recordings were produced by Don Law. The first group of sessions were done at a makeshift studio in a San Antonio hotel room. Johnson's first record, "Terraplane Blues," was considered to be a minor success, selling about 5,000 copies. The record company asked Johnson to return to the studio a few months after the first record was released.

After those recordings were made, Johnson continued his endless travels, doing one more session some months later. In 1938 he played at a party in Greenwood, MISSISSIPPI, and was poisoned to death by a jealous husband. As if there are not enough legends about Johnson, some of the stories told about his death report that it took him three days to die, and that he crawled on his hands and knees and howled like a dog. This was just another tangled thread in a life that never seems to have worked out very well. Johnson had been married as a teenager, and his wife and child had died while she was in childbirth. For the rest of his life he never seemed able to have a long-lasting relationship with a woman, although he did marry again. His fellow blues singers report that he was always on the lookout for women, and he never seemed to care whether they had boyfriends or husbands that might object to his presence.

JOHN HAMMOND wanted to use Robert Johnson for his 1938 Spirituals to Swing concert at Carnegie Hall, but Oertle reported that Johnson had died. Hammond took the unusual step of playing recordings of two of Johnson's songs at the concert, while praising his work. The records themselves were soon out of print, although ELMORE JAMES carried the guitarist's song "I Believe I'll Dust My Broom" to success on the rhythm and blues charts.

Hammond never forgot Robert Johnson. When the long-playing record was introduced in the late 1940s, record companies looked at their catalogs and started to reissue recordings that had been out of print for years. Hammond was working at Columbia Records, which had acquired the American Record Company. He convinced producer Frank Driggs to put together an album called *King of the Delta Blues Singers* in 1961. The album did reasonably well and also was sold in England, where the young Keith Richards, the future guitarist of the ROLLING STONES, and ERIC CLAPTON heard it. Several years later Columbia released the rest of Johnson's recordings on another LP. So an unknown artist who never had an album of his own during his lifetime now had two albums in release, some 30 years after his death.

This is where the Robert Johnson legend catches fire. Most of the English rockers, and quite a few American rock and blues artists, had become familiar with the work of Robert Johnson. Scholars interviewed his former associate Son House, and they talked to Johnny Shines, who had traveled with Johnson. Two valuable sources of information were Robert Lockwood, Jr. who actually took guitar lessons from Johnson because he was hanging around with Lockwood's mother, and St. Louis bluesman Henry Townsend, who had worked with Johnson and spent time with him in St. Louis. Young blues revivalists, especially JOHN HAMMOND JR., started to perform some of Johnson's songs. In the late 1980s the compact disc format was introduced, and Columbia reissued all of Johnson's songs, including alternate takes of the same songs, in a double CD boxed set. Clapton and Richards wrote short essays about the guitarist's importance to the blues, and all the lyrics to the songs were enclosed in the notes. Sales were anticipated to be around 20,000, but in fact by 2004 the sales were close to two million.

During the last 20 years five biographies have been written about Robert Johnson, two videos devoted to him, an unfilmed screenplay published about his life, and a movie, *Crossroads,* was made. The movie is a version of the deal with the Devil at the crossroads legend, although it does not specifically deal with Johnson's life. Two more biographies are reported to be being written. There have been tribute albums of others recording Johnson's songs and other albums where individual artists have recorded particular songs, or even entire CDs of his songs. All his music has been transcribed, and anyone who wants to learn his guitar parts can turn to several instruction books. Why has Johnson's life gained so much attention more than 60 years after his death?

First, there is the music. The listener can hear the power of his voice and guitar, and the intensity of his performances. Many of the instrumental performances are extremely well executed, possibly reflecting Johnson's interest in adapting piano techniques to guitar and his admiration of Lonnie Johnson. Although many of Johnson's songs were derived partly or closely from the work of other blues artists like Skip James and Kokomo Arnold, the intensity of his performances and the quality of his lyrics is often better than the work of the people whose songs he adapted. Phrases like "hellhound on my trail" and "I'm standing at the crossroads and I believe I'm sinking down" definitely get the attention of even the casual listener. There is also the matter of his influence on other Delta musicians, like Elmore James, Johnny Shines, and Robert Lockwood, Jr., and to a lesser extent, MUDDY WATERS. Johnson's music, or at least the recordings of it, seems to have been set arrangements that did not involve much improvisation. The variations between the alternate takes on the CD package are very small. This conflicts with some of the stories about Johnson's ability to take songs out of the air and put them together at a moment's notice, but possibly he simply wanted to focus on carefully recording his best material. We will never know the whole story, and that may be part of Robert Johnson's appeal today.

Johnson, Tommy (1896–1956) *singer and guitarist*

Like ROBERT JOHNSON, Tommy Johnson did not do a lot of recording, cutting only 17 songs. In Tommy's case his persistent alcoholism was the enemy of his musical career. His career was the opposite of Robert's in that Tommy was popular among other MISSISSIPPI singers during his lifetime but has been somewhat neglected since his death. Tommy learned how to play guitar from his brother Le Dell, who spread the story about Tommy's making a deal with the Devil at midnight. Unlike Robert, Tommy had a hand in spreading the story, telling his friends about the supposed deal. It seems odd that the same story would appear about these two unrelated Mississippi artists. Tommy was known as a show-man, and he played the guitar behind his back and neck, just as CHARLEY PATTON was known to do. Johnson worked with Charley Patton and WILLIE BROWN at dances and juke joints in the Delta. HOWLIN' WOLF saw Tommy and picked up some of his own showmanship skills from watching him.

Several of Tommy Johnson's songs have entered the standard blues repertoire. One song, "CANNED HEAT," became the name of a successful 1960s blues-rock group. Canned heat refers to Johnson's habit of drinking Sterno, canned alcohol intended for fuel use. Two other Johnson songs, "Big Road Blues" and "Maggie Campbell," were covered by Howlin' Wolf, ROBERT NIGHTHAWK, and other blues artists.

Johnson was considered to be an outstanding singer and a creative guitarist, but his continual problems with alcohol interfered with his career. Other than a short trip to Chicago in 1930, Johnson spent his whole life in Mississippi, playing on the streets, at parties, and at juke joints. Along the way he performed with such blues artists as the MISSISSIPPI SHEIKS, ISHMON BRACEY, and CHARLEY MCCOY. Ethnomusicologist DAVID EVANS has con-ducted extensive interviews with Johnson's rela-tives, especially Le Dell, and has written a short biography of him, as well as a section of his book *Big Road Blues.*

Jones, Curtis (1906–1971) *guitarist, pianist, and composer*

Curtis Jones wrote and recorded one song, "Lonesome Bedroom," that became his blues calling card. He played guitar as a boy but switched to PIANO. During the 1930s he played in Dallas, Kansas City, and CHICAGO. From 1937 to 1940 he recorded 100 titles, most of them forgotten today. In 1962 Jones moved to Europe, where he spent time and in North Africa. His career was hindered by his shy-ness, and for some reason in Europe he insisted on playing the guitar. His piano playing was far more interesting, and Curtis did not experience the suc-cess that his fellow piano players Memphis Slim and CHAMPION JACK DUPREE found in Europe.

Jon Spencer Blues Explosion

The Jon Spencer Blues Explosion is not exactly a blues band, but it plays music that stems from the blues. It is more of a garage rock band, although singer Jon Spencer recorded with Delta blues veteran R. L. BURNSIDE. Spencer's records feature a good deal of shouting, repeated phrases, and sarcasm. Lacking a better description, one might call the group a "punk" blues band.

Joplin, Janis Lyn (1943–1970) *singer*

Janis Joplin grew up in Port Arthur, Texas, where she sang both blues and country songs. She was a fixture on the Austin music scene until she moved to San Francisco during the mid-1960s. There she hooked up with the band Big Brother and the Holding Company. Joplin was a very emotional singer who had no hesitation in screaming the blues. The band did one album for Mainstream Records, a small record label, then attracted tremendous record company interest after they performed at the Monterey Pop Festival in 1967. Columbia Records then bought out their contract, and Joplin hired Albert Grossman as her personal manager. Grossman was managing BOB DYLAN and Peter, Paul & Mary at the time.

Big Brother and the Holding Company's first record for Columbia was *Cheap Thrills;* it featured Joplin's tortured performance of the song "Ball & Chain." It became apparent to Joplin and to Grossman that the Big Brother band was not anywhere near as dynamic as Joplin herself, so she left the group, taking only guitarist Sam Andrew with her for her next recording, *I Got Dem Old Kosmic Blues.* This led to yet another change in bands, and her final recording *Pearl,* which was released after her death. It contained Joplin's only hit single, "Me and Bobby McGee," written by Kris Kristoffersen. Ironically, this was not a blues song but a sing-along country-folk song that was probably closer to what Joplin had been singing in the early days of her career when she lived in Austin.

Janis Joplin, like JIMI HENDRIX, is another artist whose death did not end her career. There have been a number of biographies written about her, many of them playing up her personal problems and drug abuse. Her sister Laura has compiled a book of letters that Joplin wrote to her in a book called, *Love, Janis.* This book was also made into a play that ran on Broadway.

Joplin was a powerful singer who influenced many young white women to sing the blues. There are a half dozen reissue albums of her music, together with an album based on the *Love, Janis* play. There are supposedly two movies about Joplin in production.

Jordan, Louis (1908–1973) *singer, songwriter, and saxophonist*

Louis Jordan is one of the founding fathers of rhythm and blues music. Jordan was a singer, song-writer, and alto saxophone player who had a talent for writing happy songs.

Jordan got his start as a saxophone player, moving from the Charley Gaines band to drummer Chick Webb's orchestra. When Webb began to feature Ella Fitzgerald, his other singer, more than Jordan, Jordan quit the band and began his solo career. He formed a band called the Tympany Five and had dozens of hit songs. During the period 1941–57 he had 54 R&B hits, second only to JAMES BROWN's 57 hits. Some of the humorous tunes that he recorded include "Caldonia," "Choo Choo Ch'Boogie," and "Saturday Night Fish Fry." His music has often been called jump blues, up-tempo blues with a strong beat. It included loud vocals and playful lyrics that focused on parties, women, and drinking. After World War II several Los Angeles saxophone players , notably Illinois Jacquet, and Big Jay McNeely, added "honking" saxophone to the jump blues stew. T-BONE WALKER is also sometimes considered to be a jump blues artist, often featuring large orchestral arrangements showcased alongside his spectacular and showy electric guitar playing.

Jordan recorded 219 songs for Decca Records between 1938 and 1954. Not only was he extremely successful, but his music influenced CHUCK BERRY and RAY CHARLES, among many others. During the 1990s a successful Broadway show was built around Jordan's music. It was named after one of his songs, "Five Guys Named Moe."

jug bands

Jug bands had a varied instrumentation that included homemade or simple instruments like jugs, combs, washboard basses, washboards, rattles, cowbells, kazoos, and HARMONICAS, and such stringed instruments as BANJOS, FIDDLES, MANDOLINS, banjo mandolins, and guitars. The washtub bass is a washtub turned upside down with a broom handle and a single string. Sometimes even the stringed instruments, like the cigar-box fiddle, were homemade.

The jug player would blow into the jug, using a combination of singing and spitting, producing a sound much like a tuba. The music of the jug bands was loose and informal, and the songs were generally light-hearted and amusing. Cincinnati, Birmingham, Louisville, and MEMPHIS all boasted jug bands, and in MISSISSIPPI Sid Hemphill had a jug band that included the quills, a panpipe with three quills made from cane. Phillip's Louisville Jug Band included a flute and alto saxophone player, and they mostly played instrumental music. Clifford Hayes's band the Louisville Jug Band had two banjoists, and Will Shade's MEMPHIS JUG BAND included a bass made from a garbage can. Jack Kelly's Jug Busters and GUS CANNON's Jug Stompers were also jug bands. Cannon's five-string banjo was featured, a somewhat unusual instrument for the style. When jug bands did perform blues, as Cannon, for one, did, there was a light, nostalgic sadness to the songs, rather than the sort of intense outpouring of emotion found in Delta blues.

The folk revival saw several jug bands form in the 1960s, including the Even Dozen Jug Band and Jim Kweskin & His Jug Band. Although they were not literally a jug band, the LOVIN' SPOONFUL, which featured Even Dozen veteran John Sebastian, wrote rock songs in the late 1960s that had a jug band feeling to them. In one of their biggest hits, "Do You Believe in Magic," Sebastian refers to jug band music in the lyric of the song.

Some of the white jazz-oriented bands like The Mound City Blues Blowers or The Hoosier Hotshots used jugs and kazoos, and their music had a feeling similar to the jug band genre.

jump blues and rhythm and blues

Alto SAXOPHONE player, singer, and bandleader LOUIS JORDAN was tremendously successful with his "jump blues." His style featured up-tempo, often humorous tunes, and Jordan had 57 R&B hits from 1942 until 1951. The audience would dance to the so-called shuffle rhythms, with strong rhythmic accents, and they would laugh at the playful lyrics of the songs. By the late 1940s a number of independent record companies were in the R&B business in the New York area, especially ATLANTIC and Savoy. Artists like RUTH BROWN, DINAH WASHINGTON, the Coasters, the Drifters, and many others enjoyed R&B and crossover hits.

Los Angeles was an important place in the evolution of rhythm and blues, starting during World War II. Nat "King" Cole was a model for the more pop, softer R&B artists, like Charles Brown. Cole was basically a jazz piano player who turned himself into a pop singer. He had an excellent trio, with guitarist Oscar Moore and bassist Wesley Prince. Although Cole was not really a rhythm and blues singer, he occasionally recorded songs in or close to that style, like his 1943 recording "Straighten Up and Fly Right." Other important R&B and blues artists working out of Los Angeles were early electric guitarist T-BONE WALKER, AMOS MILBURN, and PEE WEE CRAYTON.

New Orleans had its own fun-loving exponents of R&B, notably Fats Domino, whose records crossed over into pop. Domino sold millions of records, but Little Richard, PROFESSOR LONGHAIR, the NEVILLE BROTHERS, HUEY "PIANO" SMITH, and many others were also recording and performing.

"Kansas City Blues" (and "Gonna Move to Kansas City") (1928) *blues hit later transformed into a pop hit*

These are actually two different songs, but the second song illustrates the way that various composers took traditional material and turned it into pop music. "Kansas City Blues" was a big hit, as sung by its composer JIM JACKSON in 1928. Some authorities believe it to have been the first blues recording to sell a million copies. The song became a blues standard and was recorded by ROBERT NIGHTHAWK, by an odd white songster named Harmonica Frank Floyd, and in more recent days by BROWNIE MCGHEE, SONNY TERRY, and DAVE VAN RONK. Like so many of the most popular blues songs, this one has a chorus. The verses are only loosely connected to one another and do not have repeated lines, but the catchy chorus makes the song stand out.

In 1952 Jerry Leiber and Mike Stoller, two white teenagers, took the basic theme of Jackson's song, removed the choruses, used repeating lines in the verses, and added a catchy bridge and an additional musical section to the song. It was recorded by Wilbert Harrison and became a major hit record.

To further complicate matters, JANIS JOPLIN recorded yet another song called "Kansas City Blues." In it she refers to Jim Jackson, saying in two verses that she will "bring Jim Jackson home."

Another example of a folk blues being transformed into a pop song occurred with the traditional folk ballad about a bad man named Stackolee. As a folksong, this ballad told the tale of a saloon shooting that happened in 1895. R&B singer Lloyd Price was familiar with the story and, changing the melody entirely, he wrote a tune called "Stagger Lee" that became an enormous pop hit in 1959. There have been over 200 recorded versions of the two songs.

Kelly, Jo Ann (1944–1990) *singer and guitarist*
Several critics have called Jo Ann Kelly the greatest female British blues singer. Kelly was a powerful guitar player and singer who learned how to play from her brother David. She toured the United States and England, and recorded with American guitar legend JOHN FAHEY in 1970. The band CANNED HEAT offered her a job, but Kelly never wanted her own band and preferred to remain independent, touring whenever she chose. She also turned down an offer from blues-rock guitarist JOHNNY WINTER. Occasionally she would sit in with bands run by her friends, but she preferred to work alone. Her specialty was Delta blues, but she also made recordings that included rhythm and blues songs. More than a half dozen Kelly recordings are still available. Kelly was an artist who never gained a large audience but still influenced other musicians.

"Key to the Highway" (1941) *classic blues song written by Big Bill Broonzy and Chas. Segar*
If any one song typifies the life of the blues singer—walking the lonesome highway, hitching a ride, bumming freight trains, riding a Greyhound Bus—

this is it. Written in 1941, the song was composed by BIG BILL BROONZY and Chas. Segar. It was recorded four times by Broonzy and covered by JAZZ GILLUM, Little Walter, Joe Williams with the Count Basie Orchestra, B. B. KING, BROWNIE MCGHEE, ERIC CLAPTON's band Derek & the Dominos, The Band, and the Steve Miller Band.

The lyric talks about wanderlust and walking the highway "until the break of day." Many of the artists who have recorded the song added a verse or two of their own. The melody is also a bit unusual for the blues, changing from the I chord (E in the key of E) to the V7 chord (B7) and then going to the IV (A) chord. This device is used now and again in country and western music.

Kimbrough, Junior (David Kimbrough) (1930–1998) *singer and guitarist*

Junior Kimbrough was not well known outside his native MISSISSIPPI until he was featured in musicologist Robert Palmer's film *Deep Blues*. He had mostly played Mississippi juke joints in the 1970s and 1980s, and even owned one. Palmer found him performing at one of these clubs. The film led to an English tour and a recording contract with Mississippi's Fat Possum Records. Sometimes Kimbrough played alone; on other occasions he performed with bass and drum accompaniment.

King, Albert (Albert Nelson) (1923–1991) *singer and guitarist*

Albert King's unique guitar style was partly based on his playing the guitar upside down because he was left-handed. Most left-handed guitar players either re-string the guitar so that their left hand picks the bass notes with the thumb, just as a right-handed player does, or they play exactly as if they were right-handed. When King played, his thumb played the treble notes and his fingers played the bass notes. This is the opposite of what 99 percent of guitar players do. King was also an imposing figure at six feet five inches and 250 pounds. His pow-

erful hands enabled him to bend the strings more than other guitarists could do.

King was born in Indianola, MISSISSIPPI, the same as B. B. KING. He moved to Gary, Indiana, in 1953, then to St. Louis in 1956. King was also noted for playing the Gibson Flying V Guitar, a guitar shaped like a V. After cutting several records for Bobbin and King Records from 1959 to 1963, King went on to record for MEMPHIS label Stax Records. Things picked up when he recorded an album in 1966 that featured Booker T and the MG's, the Stax rhythm section, and was produced by their drummer, Al Jackson. Stax recorded three live albums with King at the Fillmore West club in San Francisco. The Stax recordings allowed King to perform blues in his own style, but he modernized the sound by adding the tight rhythm section and the Memphis Horns as well. King's guitar work was a major influence on rock guitarists ERIC CLAPTON, JIMI HENDRIX, and STEVIE RAY VAUGHAN.

King, B. B. (Riley B. King) (b. 1925) *legendary guitarist*

If one artist comes to mind for most people when blues guitar is mentioned, it is probably B. B. King. King has recorded dozens of albums, has done commercials, owns night clubs, and, approaching his eighties, still performs many times a year. King's career can be divided into three periods. The first period was learning the guitar in his native MISSISSIPPI, becoming a disc jockey in MEMPHIS in 1949, and making his first records. During the second period, starting around 1949, the beginning of his Memphis radio career, King began to make hit R&B records, and his 1964 *Live at the Regal* album is still regarded as a landmark in his career. In 1966, toward the end of this period, ethnomusicologist Charles Keil wrote a book called *Urban Blues*. Keil regarded King as possibly the best blues artist around, and he complained that King's audience seemed to be almost entirely black. The next part of King's career made him a worldwide star.

B. B. King (Bruce Polonsky Photography)

In 1969 a young record producer named Bill Szymsyck recorded King singing "The Thrill Is Gone." The song became a major hit record on the pop charts and brought King the white audience that he had previously lacked. This was followed by an appearance at Fillmore West, the San Francisco rock club run by Bill Graham. When King first arrived at the neighborhood of the club, all he saw was white faces. He told his bus driver that he must be in the wrong place. Graham introduced King to the audience very simply by saying he was the "chairman of the board." The crowd gave King a standing ovation even before he had sung or played a note. He was so moved that tears streamed down his face as he performed. He received another standing ovation at the end of his set. B. B. King had arrived to a whole new audience.

For many years King played 300 dates a year. He toured widely and continued to record albums. His ELECTRIC GUITAR, which he named Lucille, became a household word, and the Gibson Guitar Company designed a model after it. King, whose nickname was taken from Memphis's Beale St.—Beale Street Blues Boy—opened a club in Memphis on Beale Street, and King toured all over the world.

A number of things set King apart from other blues artists. First was his powerful singing, which reflects his gospel roots. He sang in local churches from the age of four, and a school spiritual quartet when he was in grade school. As a teenager he occasionally sang in a church choir, and he formed a gospel group called the Elkhorn Singers, performing in local churches from 1940 to 1943. King's cousin BUKKA WHITE gave him his first guitar when he was nine years old. He absorbed the guitar techniques of LONNIE JOHNSON and T-BONE WALKER, and he also listened to such jazz guitarists as Charlie Christian.

King developed an original guitar technique that worked beautifully on the electric guitar. Instead of playing guitar with a slide, he used two left-hand techniques to get a similar but smoother effect. He bent the notes with his left hand, pulling them off the fingerboard. This has the effect of raising the pitch of a note, but just as the use of a slide almost imitates the sound of a person crying, string bends have a similar effect. King's other left-hand technique was vibrato. He would take a left-hand finger and move it on a particular fret with the left hand, making a shaking motion. This makes the note ring longer and provides an emotional effect on the audience.

King took the folk blues to the city. Many middle-class blacks had scorned the blues as raw and unsophisticated. King was a star, even before his Fillmore West debut. He dressed well and present-ed the blues as music that young people could enjoy and relate to. When he developed a white audience, he had crossed the last barrier to stardom. Today he is a household name, and he continues to perform and to record. B. B. King has recorded more than any other living blues artist, with 71 CDs in the *All Music Guide* list. It appears that as long as he wants to perform and record he will have an audience.

King, Freddie (1934–1976) *guitarist*

Texas-born Freddie King was taught the guitar by his mother at the age of six, and he also took more lessons from his uncle. At the age of 16 he moved to CHICAGO, where he worked at nonmusical jobs, sitting in with local musicians. Soon he began to work with various Chicago bands, making his first records for the short-lived Cobra label in 1956. These recordings were never released. Throughout the 1960s he played clubs and blues festivals, traveling to Los Angeles, San Francisco, and other cities. By 1960 he was recording for Federal-King Records, where he cut more than 100 songs. In the late 1960s King recorded two albums for Atlantic/Cotillion Records that were produced by R&B SAXOPHONE player KING CURTIS. He was one of the first blues artists to appear at the Fillmore East club in New York . The bill also included ALBERT KING. During the early 1970s Freddie recorded for rock PIANO player Leon Russell's Shelter Records, hoping to cross over into rock success. Later he recorded several albums with ERIC CLAPTON, who was heavily influenced by King. He then toured Australia, Europe, and the United States.

King was six foot seven inches tall, and he played loudly. His rhythm section, consisting of guitar, bass, and drums, also played at what one critic described as "room-rattling volume." He recorded instrumentals as well as vocals, and during his recording career with Federal he often put out singles that had a vocal on one side and an instrumental on the other. King may have been the only artist to use this approach consistently. His career was cut short by heart disease.

King Curtis (Curtis Ousley) (1934–1971) *studio saxophonist*

King Curtis was possibly the most popular R&B studio SAXOPHONE player during the 1960s. Born in Fort Worth, Texas, Curtis had moved to New York by the mid-1950s. He made albums under his own name and even had a few hit R&B singles, but he was best known for his studio records, playing on many for Atlantic Records, as well as dozens of other labels. He played on recordings by Wilson Pickett and Aretha Franklin, among many others. His musical talents extended into pop music, jazz, and soul. He became a session leader and musical contractor, calling the other musicians for Atlantic sessions. He also coproduced records with famed Atlantic producer Jerry Wexler.

King Records

King was basically the vision of a single man. Syd Nathan founded the company in 1943. Nathan's vision was to establish a label that would entirely control its own destiny. He had a recording studio, he pressed his own records at his pressing plant, and he controlled his own distribution. Distribution has always been the biggest problem for independent labels. The major labels also have distribution companies that deliver their records to stores and to radio stations. Historically the independent labels have used a set of independent record distributors located in various American cities. These independent distributors often have dozens of labels on their shelves, and they generally do not waste much time promoting product that they feel will not be profitable. Thus it is difficult for a new company to break into the system. Worse yet, independent record distributors are notoriously slow in paying their bills. A record company can have thousands of records that are selling, but there is a lag between when the record stores pay the distributors and when the distributors pay the record companies. It is also not unusual for independent record distributors to go into bankruptcy; then the record companies not only do not get paid for the records that have been sold, but the assets of the distributors are frozen, and the record company cannot even get their own records back. Nathan's answer to the problem was to bypass it and hire his own distribution staff. He had 32 sales branches throughout the United States for this purpose.

Nathan had another ace up his sleeve. He knew that music publishing was an important potential source of revenue. He decided to take the same songs that his country artists were recording and to record R&B versions of them. In other cases he did the reverse. An artist would write and record an R&B song, and Nathan would get his record producer to record a country version of the song. Nathan owned the publishing rights and usually bought the songwriting rights as well, to virtually everything he recorded.

King maintained its own studio band, which included Kenneth (Jethro) Burns on MANDOLIN, fiddler Tommy Jackson, and guitar players Billy Grammer and Hank (Sugarfoot) Garland. King's key record producer was Henry Glover. Glover was black, and King, whose staff consisted of about one-fifth African Americans, used him to produce both country and R&B records.

In 1956 R&B performer JAMES BROWN walked into this musical stew of country and R&B music. Nathan was thoroughly bewildered by Brown's music, but he let Glover record him. As a result of this judgment call, King became one of the hottest R&B companies in the United States. King recorded "Tomorrow Night," a major R&B hit with veteran blues artist LONNIE JOHNSON in 1947. Other blues and R&B artists who appeared on King, or its Federal subsidiary label, included FREDDIE KING, ETTA JAMES, JIMMY WITHERSPOON, STICKS MCGHEE, JOHN LEE HOOKER, Charles Brown, and instrumentalists sax player Earl Bostic and organist Bill Doggett.

Syd Nathan died in 1968, and his company was sold several times in the next few years. He left a legacy of over 10,000 recordings in his 25 years in the music business.

Kinsey, Lester (Big Daddy Kinsey)
(1927–2001) *slide guitarist and harmonicist*
Lester Kinsey was born in MISSISSIPPI but moved with his family to Gary, INDIANA. He spent many years working in the Gary steel mills, while playing SLIDE GUITAR and HARMONICA in clubs on the weekends. When his sons grew up, he founded a band called The Kinsey Report, which featured them playing bass, guitar, and drums. Big Daddy's music ranged from covers of MUDDY WATERS's songs to more aggressive rock-blues. His songs brought a more modern rock and even reggae feel to the music.

Kirkland, Eddie (b. 1928) *recording artist*
Born in Jamaica, Eddie Kirkland is one of the few West Indian–born bluesmen. He is best known for his recordings with JOHN LEE HOOKER, whom he met in DETROIT. Kirkland had moved to Detroit after World War II to work in the auto factories. He also recorded and toured with R&B performer Otis Redding. Kirkland began to record his own albums in 1961 and continues to record and tour today. His music is a mixture of blues and soul.

Koda, Cub (1948–2000) *musician and journalist*
Cub Koda was a guitar and HARMONICA player and vocalist, songwriter, and blues journalist. He was the leader of the blues-rock band Brownsville Station and wrote their hit "Smokin' in the Boy's Room." Koda was an avid record collector, and he wrote columns for the record collector's magazine *Goldmine*, and later for *DISCoveries*. He also wrote the book *Blues for Dummies*, and edited the original *All Music Guide to the Blues*. The guide was a huge undertaking, reviewing hundreds of records and including articles about the blues. For the rest of his life Koda went back and forth between writing about the blues and writing and recording music.

Koerner, Ray, and Glover

Koerner, Ray, and Glover were among the first white blues revival bands. All three were students attending college at the University of Minnesota in the Minneapolis area. They became deeply immersed in playing and singing the blues. Their 1963 album for Elektra attracted many young people to the blues. John (Spider) Koerner is a songwriter and storyteller who specializes in lighthearted blues, Tony (Little Sun) Glover is a blues HARMONICA player, and David Ray was a 12-string guitarist who was a big LEAD BELLY fan.

Chicago blues revivalists like MIKE BLOOMFIELD had studied at the feet of such blues masters as MUDDY WATERS, but Koerner, Ray, and Glover played more in the direction of revivalist folk music than Chicago blues. In addition to their trio work, they all had solo performing and recording careers.

John "Spider" Koerner (Art Thieme)

Glover wrote one of the most important instruction books for blues harmonica and liner notes for albums by JOHN LEE HOOKER and the country-folk-rock group the Jayhawks. The three played together from time to time until Ray's death in 2002.

Koester, Bob (b. 1932) *record label and record store owner*

Bob Koester is the founder and owner of DELMARK RECORDS and owns a large independent record store in CHICAGO called the Jazz Record Mart. Koester started producing records while he was a student at St. Louis University. He moved to Chicago in 1955, working for a jazz record store called Seymour's Record Mart, which left in 1961 to start his own store and also found Delmark Records. Delmark records blues and jazz music and has developed a large catalog of recordings ranging from traditional blues artists like SLEEPY JOHN ESTES and Chicago electric blues artists like LUTHER ALLISON to a variety of jazz artists. Blues revivalists MIKE BLOOMFIELD and CHARLIE MUSSELWHITE both worked at Koester's record store. The store has a huge collection of vinyl, cassettes, and CDs, especially in jazz and blues.

Korner, Alexis (1928–1984) *British blues artist*

Alexis Korner was one of the most active blues artists on the early British blues scene. He was a singer and guitarist who started out on PIANO. In 1949 he began working with bandleader Chris Barber in his jazz and skiffle (music featuring vocals along with nonstandard instruments such as a jug or washboard) bands, and in 1952 he was part of the larger Ken Colyer band that absorbed the Barber group. Korner became friendly with guitarist Cyril Davies, and together they opened a blues club where the duo performed and brought in visiting American blues artists. Korner and Davies started their band, Blues Incorporated, in 1961. For six years Korner served as the mentor to such future stars as Robert Plant, the lead singer of LED ZEPPELIN, and Steve Marriott of Humble Pie. Among those who passed through Blues Incorporated were Charlie Watts, the future drummer of the ROLLING STONES; Jack Bruce, future bass player of CREAM; and singer LONG JOHN BALDRY. Many of the British blues-rock stars, like Mick Jagger of the Stones and John Paul Jones of Led Zeppelin, hung out at yet another club that the band started.

Blues Incorporated recorded their first album in 1962—the first complete album made by a British blues band. They included several WILLIE DIXON songs and a few originals.

Korner had little success recording hits, but some of his bandmates went on to major pop careers. Later Korner became a music journalist and hosted a children's TV show. He continued to record, and his performances were more popular in Scandinavia than in England, where he had been overshadowed by his own successors. During the 1970s Korner had his one British record hit, a big band version of Led Zeppelin's "Whole Lotta Love." A dozen of Korner's albums are still in print.

Kubek, Smokin' Joe (b. 1956) *singer and guitarist*

Texas-based bluesman Smokin' Joe Kubek has recorded for the Bullseye Blues record label since 1991. As a teenager Kubek backed up bluesmen FREDDIE KING and Al "TNT" Braggs in Texas music clubs. He teamed up with the more jazz-oriented Bnois King, who sings and plays rhythm guitar, while Kubek sings and plays lead guitar. They continue to record and tour. Their more recent albums feature fewer covers and more original songs.

Landreth, Sonny (b. 1951) *guitarist*

Sonny Landreth is a talented guitarist who also plays dobro and SLIDE GUITAR. His first professional job was with zydeco accordion player and singer CLIFTON CHENIER. Landreth has recorded with singer-songwriter John Hiatt and has also played on recording sessions for rock band Leslie West & Mountain. Landreth has spent most of his life in Lafayette, Louisiana, and his music is a blend of swamp blues and cajun music. He sings and writes songs but is best known for his slide guitar technique. He has developed a technique whereby he uses his left-hand fingers and the slide at the same time.

Lang, Jonny (b. 1981) *musician*

Jonny Lang started playing professionally as a teenager. Lang comes from the unlikely blues town of Fargo, North Dakota. He played SAXOPHONE in junior high school and recorded his first album at the age of 15, singing and playing guitar. Lang is an impressive guitarist who has brought blues to younger rock fans.

La Salle, Denise (b. 1935) *vocalist and songwriter*

MISSISSIPPI-born vocalist Denise La Salle has a background in gospel and country music. She moved to Chicago at the age of 13, where she sang with an all-girl gospel group called the Sacred Five. La Salle has recorded more than a dozen albums for several different labels. Most of her recordings are combinations of blues and soul music, although she has also recorded gospel music. Her greatest success came when she wrote the song "Married but Not to Each Other," which became a hit country record for Barbara Mandrell.

Lay, Sam (b. 1935) *drummer and singer*

For years Sam Lay has been one of the major drummers on the CHICAGO blues scene. He is noted for creating a drum sound that imitates gospel handclaps. He played drums and recorded with MUDDY WATERS, JIMMY REED, HOWLIN' WOLF, and OTIS SPANN, and he was in one of the first interracial blues bands, playing with the PAUL BUTTERFIELD BLUES BAND, the band that played for BOB DYLAN's electric debut at the 1965 Newport Folk Festival. Also a singer, Lay splits his time between his own band and the SIEGEL-SCHWALL BAND.

Lazy Lester (Leslie Johnson) (b. 1933) *songwriter and multi-instrumentalist*

Lazy Lester was part of the J. D. Miller swamp blues crew based in Crowley, Louisiana. Lester is a songwriter who sings and plays HARMONICA, washboard, and guitar. Lester's songs have been recorded by the Kinks and the Fabulous Thunderbirds, and his music combines elements of blues, cajun, and country. In addition to his solo recordings, Lester has played on records by LIGHTNIN' SLIM, LONESOME SUNDOWN, and KATIE WEBSTER. From 1972 to 1987, Lester left the music field, but in 1987 he resumed his career, recording and touring in Europe.

Lead Belly (Huddie Ledbetter) (1888–1949)
songster and multi-instrumentalist

Lead Belly was a songster who played a number of instruments and sang country songs, old pop songs, and folksongs in addition to his blues repertoire. Born about 30 miles from Shreveport, Louisiana, Lead Belly played at country dances. He sang and played concertina, piano, and six- and 12-STRING GUITARS, but the 12-string was his trademark instrument.

Lead Belly served two prison terms for murders, allegedly committed in self-defense, in Texas and Louisiana, and continued singing and playing while in prison. He persuaded Texas governor Pat Neff to pardon him by singing a song that had the lines in it "Governor Neff, if I had you where you have me, on Monday morning I'd set you free." Neff had promised never to pardon any murderer while he was in office, and he solved that problem by pardoning Lead Belly at the very end of his term as governor, when someone else had been elected and was about to take office.

Lead Belly became better known when JOHN LOMAX recorded him at the Angola Prison in Louisiana in 1934. Once again, Lead Belly was able to get a pardon from prison and traveled with Lomax as a kind of personal valet and associate song collector. Lead Belly could break the ice with other imprisoned singers, persuading them to sing for Lomax. Lomax also became Lead Belly's manager, and he arranged a variety of concerts and radio appearances for him, including a performance at Harvard University. Eventually the two feuded and Lead Belly stayed in New York City, where he became a popular performer, particularly for radical political causes. He wrote several protest songs, including one about the Scottsboro Boys, and another called "The Bourgeois Blues." "The Bourgeois Blues" described how he and his wife could not find a place to stay in Washington, D.C., because "it's a bourgeois town." The word "bourgeois," popular in left-wing political circles, was associated with racism and uptight behavior. Lead Belly became friendly with folk artists Pete Seeger

Lead Belly (Bettmann/Corbis)

and Woody Guthrie and would sometimes perform with them and with fellow blues artists JOSH WHITE, SONNY TERRY, and BROWNIE MCGHEE.

Lead Belly met and befriended BLIND LEMON JEFFERSON in 1912, and Jefferson taught him how to play SLIDE GUITAR. The two of them would ride trains together, playing their guitars in place of paying the fare. Later Lead Belly wrote a song recalling those days, "Blind Lemon." A number of the songs that he wrote or rearranged have become hits, including "Goodnight Irene," "Cotton Fields," and "The Rock Island Line." "Goodnight Irene" became a number-one hit, recorded by Lead Belly's friend Seeger with his group, the Weavers. Unfortunately this happened one year after Lead Belly's death in 1949.

There were several unique qualities about Lead Belly's music. When he found that white audiences had trouble understanding his accent or the subject matter of many of his songs, he started inserting spoken stories into the songs. Some of the stories were longer than the songs themselves. Musically Lead Belly often began his songs on the I7 chord. In the key of C, this is a C7 chord, containing the notes C E G B-flat. By starting with a seventh chord, a certain feeling of uncertainty is created and is particularly effective with the heavy sound of the 12-string guitar. Lead Belly became sufficiently popular that a number of folk revivalist artists started to play it. Even Seeger, better known for his BANJO playing, took up the 12-string.

Lead Belly recorded for many record labels and was extensively recorded by the Library of Congress. Many of these recordings remain available today. A movie was made about his life, the Lomaxes wrote a combination songbook and biography about him, and a more recent biography has also appeared. There are also instructional books that teach Lead Belly's guitar style, and several additional songbooks have been published since his death.

Lead Belly had a powerful influence on the folk and blues revivals, not only through his own work but because of his influence on Seeger, who dedicated himself to mentioning Lead Belly in his concert appearances, playing 12-string guitar, and performing and recording his music.

Led Zeppelin

Led Zeppelin is one of the most successful and influential rock bands of all time. The band was formed when studio musician guitarist Jimmy Page (b. 1944) and keyboard and bass player John Paul Jones (b. 1946) decided to form a rock band. They added a young Robert Plant (b. 1948) as their lead singer and the ferocious drummer John Bonham (1948–80) to the group. Page had a background as a versatile guitarist who had done considerable studio work and played guitar in the YARDBIRDS, while Jones, who was a well-trained musician, was also a studio veteran.

The band's early records included a large dose of blues, including WILLIE DIXON's "I Can't Quit You

Baby." Plant could scream and shriek with the best of the rock singers, and Page provided the exciting ELECTRIC GUITAR accompaniments. As the band continued to record, it emerged as a founding father of heavy metal music, and the members began writing many of their own songs. When they recorded blues they tended to grab as much of the writer's credit as possible, so that on paper, at least, they cowrote Memphis Minnie's "When the Levee Breaks." In 1985 Dixon sued them for reworking his song "You Need Love" into one of their most successful songs, "Whole Lotta Love." Not until 1987 did the band settle by giving Dixon a "substantial sum." The band continued its experimentation by turning to world music and also writing their version of an art song, "Stairway to Heaven."

Led Zeppelin were legendary party boys, and the band broke up when John Bonham died following an all-day drinking binge. The band vowed never to tour again as Led Zeppelin, a promise they kept. Since the break-up of the group both Plant and Page have made solo albums, and Jones has written film scores. In the late 1990s Page and Plant toured without asking Jones to join them.

Leigh, Kerri (b. 1969) *singer and writer*

Kerri Leigh is a blues singer who also has produced records and written about the blues. She works with her husband and collaborator, Mark Lyon. The duo moved to Austin, Texas, from Oklahoma in 1990, and frequently played Antone's Night Club. They write songs together, and Leigh is the lead singer. Her band's performances include a Delta blues set featuring just the two of them. They do rhythm and blues covers and originals and rock-flavored music as well. At the age of 18, Leigh founded the Oklahoma Blues Society, and in 1993 she wrote a biography of STEVIE RAY VAUGHAN, *Soul to Soul*.

Leigh's vocals are often compared with those of JANIS JOPLIN. Her band works over 150 nights a year, partly due to the Leigh's promotional and writing skills. .

Lenoir, J. B. (1924–1967) *songwriter and singer*

J. B. Lenoir was a spectacular showman who dressed in a variety of outrageous outfits, including one with zebra stripes. He moved to CHICAGO from his native MISSISSIPPI in 1949 and was befriended by BIG BILL BROONZY. Lenoir's band included two SAXOPHONE players.

In 1963 Lenoir toured Europe. WILLIE DIXON advised him to play ACOUSTIC GUITAR on the tour, in the same way that Broonzy had done some 10 years earlier. Lenoir wrote a number of songs about social conditions that went over especially well in Europe. Some of these titles were "Eisenhower Blues," "Alabama Blues," "Korea Blues," and "Viet Nam Blues."

Recently Lenoir resurfaced in the Wim Winders–directed film in the Martin Scorsese series of Blues Legacy documentaries. It seems that a young couple made two films about him that were intended to be shown on Swedish television but never aired. Winders interviewed the couple and also included portions of their work in his own film. In the films we see a relaxed Lenoir, performing and talking with his friends, and insisting that the male filmmaker sit in with him on guitar.

Lenoir was just beginning to become known to American audiences when he died in an automobile accident.

Lewis, Furry (Walter Lewis) (1893–1981) *recording artist*

Furry Lewis started his musical career playing in medicine and minstrel shows. He was born in MISSISSIPPI but moved to MEMPHIS when he was a young boy. Furry was a showman, and he told funny stories and played fingerpicking and bottleneck guitar. He was very involved with the Memphis music scene, which included the MEMPHIS JUG BAND, GUS CANNON, JIM JACKSON, and MEMPHIS MINNIE. Lewis was a songster who sang ballads about folk heroes like John Henry and Casey Jones, as well as blues songs.

In 1927 Furry's friend Jim Jackson took him to CHICAGO to record. He recorded 23 titles during the period 1927–29, then returned to Memphis, where he owned an antique shop. He worked for the city of Memphis as a street cleaner and played guitar mostly for himself and his friends. In 1959 blues scholar and fan SAMUEL CHARTERS found Lewis, and his recording career resumed. Not only did he record again, but he was in the film *W. W. and the Dixie Dancekings,* appeared on several TV shows, and was the subject of a song by well-known singer-songwriter Joni Mitchell, called "Furry Sings the Blues." The song describes Mitchell embarking to Furry's house in her limousine, and captures the irony of a successful pop artist listening to a blues artist who lived a modest existence. Reportedly Lewis was not fond of the song, which he felt exploited his reputation without any compensation to him.

Almost a dozen of Furry's records have been reissued on CD. He is a very fine guitarist. His relaxed vocal style is halfway between speaking and singing.

Lewis, Meade Lux (1905–1964) *pianist and composer*

Meade Lewis was one of the principal boogie-woogie PIANO players during the boogie-woogie craze of the late 1930s and into the 1940s. He was especially known for his composition, "Honky Tonk Train Blues." Lewis, a taxi driver in Chicago, teamed up with a fellow taxi driver named Albert Ammons. They lived together in a building where PINETOP SMITH, one the pioneers of boogie-woogie, also lived and Lewis learned this piano style from Smith.

Lewis recorded with Ammons, and the two played and recorded with PETE JOHNSON in the Boogie Woogie Trio. After the boogie-woogie craze died down, Lewis played not only piano but celeste and even harpsichord, recording with such famous jazz players as guitarist Charlie Christian and clarinetist Edmond Hall. Lewis continued to play cocktail and jazz piano at various venues until his death.

Lewis, Noah (1895–1961) *harmonicist*

Noah Lewis was a fixture on the MEMPHIS scene in the 1920s and 1930s. Blues critics regard him as one of the most important pre-1940 HARMONICA players. He had a soulful, melodic playing style. Lewis played and recorded with GUS CANNON's Jug Stompers and also made records of his own in the late 1920s, singing as well as playing the harmonica. He also recorded with SLEEPY JOHN ESTES.

Lewis was a street performer who could often be found playing for tips in Memphis. One of his entertainment features was performing with two harmonicas at the same time, playing one with his nose.

Lightnin' Slim (Otis Hicks) (1913–1976) *guitarist and singer*

A guitarist and singer, Lightnin' Slim was the father of the so-called swamp blues style. He was the first black artist recorded by record producer J. D. MILLER, and he influenced a number of Louisiana blues artists, including SLIM HARPO, LAZY LESTER, and Silas Hogan. The swamp blues sound featured a relatively simple ELECTRIC GUITAR and usually had HARMONICA accompaniment. Slim was influenced by the success of Houston blues artist LIGHTNIN' HOPKINS, and he began to work in Baton Rouge, Louisiana, bars, using a drummer or a harmonica player to accompany him.

Slim began recording for Miller in 1954. Blues scholar and critic Robert Santelli compares Slim's influence in Louisiana to the importance of MUDDY WATERS's effect on the CHICAGO scene. Both men, trendsetters and bandleaders, influenced many younger musicians. Many of these musicians played in Waters's or Slim's bands. Slim's biggest record, "Rooster Blues," got to number 23 on the R&B charts in 1959. Slim wrote many of his own songs, and two of them were recorded by Hopkins. He recorded about 80 songs between 1954 and 1966. He then moved to DETROIT, where he resumed his career in 1972, recording again and touring Europe.

Lipscomb, Mance (1895–1976) *fingerpicking guitarist*

Mance Lipscomb was a farmer who in earlier years had worked as a sharecropper, starting his musical career late in life. His first instrument was the FIDDLE, but he took up the guitar at the age of 10. Lipscomb performed around his hometown of Navasota, TEXAS, on weekends, singing blues, spirituals, and folksongs. In 1959 Texas blues scholar and playwright Mack McCormick found Lipscomb and brought San Francisco area blues fan CHRIS STRACHWITZ to see him. Strachwitz started the ARHOOLIE record label in 1960 to record Lipscomb.

Lipscomb was a talented fingerpicking guitarist whose style was closer to such artists as MISSISSIPPI JOHN HURT and FURRY LEWIS than to Texas blues artists. Arhoolie issued a half dozen albums of

Mance Lipscomb (Larry Shirkey)

Lipscomb, and another one was recorded for Reprise, a subsidiary of Warner Brothers. Lipscomb was also the subject of several documentary films, notably Les Blank's biographical *A Well Spent Life.*

Little Milton (Milton Campbell) (b. 1934)
recording artist
MISSISSIPPI-born Little Milton has been a staple on the so-called chitlin' circuit for many years. He has never achieved the broad audience that B. B. KING tapped into, but Milton remains quite popular among black blues fans, especially in the South. Milton is an excellent electric blues player, somewhat in the King mode, but he has never crossed over into the pop music area. Milton learned to play guitar by listening to the radio and recordings, and besides his blues interests, he was influenced by country music.

SAM PHILLIPS, who first introduced the music world to ELVIS PRESLEY, Johnny Cash, and Jerry Lee Lewis, recorded blues artists in the early days of his Sun Records label in MEMPHIS. Phillips met Milton through pianist-guitarist IKE TURNER, and Phillips recorded Milton in 1953 and 1954. The records did not attract much attention, but by 1961 Milton was a CHESS RECORDS artist. He hit paydirt with his number one R&B recording "We're Gonna Make It," in 1965.

Starting in the 1980s, Milton recorded for Malaco and has done well enough to record more than a dozen albums. His performing and recording career continues, and he is especially active in the South.

Little Walter (Marion Walter Jacobs)
(1930–1968) *harmonicist*
Little Walter was probably the most influential blues HARMONICA player of all time. Born in Louisiana, Walter played on the streets of New Orleans at the age of 12. During World War II he moved to CHICAGO, but stopped off in Helena, ARKANSAS, and St. Louis to study harmonica with BIG WALTER HORTON and SONNY BOY WILLIAMSON (Rice Miller.) In Chicago

Walter played harmonica and guitar on the streets for tips in his early teenage years.

Walter made his first real impact playing in MUDDY WATERS's band in 1948. Even after he stopped performing with Waters, Walter continued to record with him. The tune "Juke" was Walter's first hit, and between 1952 and 1958 he recorded 14 songs that reached the top 10 on the R&B charts. One of them, "My Babe," became a number one hit.

As a harmonica player Walter made two major contributions to the blues. He was one of the first players to amplify the instrument, which allowed him to play single notes in a style similar to that of a trumpet or SAXOPHONE. He could also play much louder because of the amplification. Walter's other calling card was that he often played the chromatic harmonica. There are two kinds of harmonica. The smaller instrument, which in 1940 cost 25 cents or less, cannot readily play sharps or flats. The chromatic harmonica is larger and has a button on the side that enables the player to play sharps and flats easily, and to play in multiple keys.

Walter was a demanding bandleader and required his musicians to do much rehearsing. Louis and David Myers played in his band, and then ROBERT LOCKWOOD JR. replaced Louis. Toward the end of the 1950s the blues suffered a decline in popularity among younger black audiences, although Walter did tour Europe and Great Britain in 1962, and was part of an American tour by the ROLLING STONES in 1964. Walter developed a drinking problem and sometimes got into fights. One of these street brawls resulted in his death.

Lockwood, Robert, Jr. (b. 1915) *guitarist*
Robert Lockwood Jr. got his start in the blues when his mother kept company with ROBERT JOHNSON. Lockwood is the only person known to have taken guitar lessons from Johnson.

Lockwood traveled with SONNY BOY WILLIAMSON in MISSISSIPPI and ARKANSAS, then going on to

Robert Lockwood Jr. (Bruce Polonsky Photography)

MEMPHIS and St. Louis, and landing in CHICAGO in 1941. He then went back south for a couple of years, performing regularly on the King Biscuit Radio Show on station KFFA in Helena, Arkansas.

Lockwood came to Chicago in 1950, doing studio work at CHESS RECORDS, then moved to Cleveland, Ohio, in 1961. During the 1980s he recorded with JOHNNY SHINES, another associate of Johnson.

Lockwood is more jazz-oriented than most blues players, and he has used that influence in his playing. In recent years he has often played acoustic 12-STRING GUITAR. With over a dozen albums to his name, Lockwood is one of the last links to the Delta blues of Robert Johnson and his predecessors, but he has interpreted their music in his own unique way.

Lofton, Cripple Clarence (Albert Clemens)
(1887–1957) *pianist and performer*

Although Cripple Clarence Lofton had a limp, his dancing career belied his nickname. Lofton was a blues PIANO player and singer in CHICAGO during the early 1920s. His early career included dancing, whistling, and playing the piano while standing up. He owned his own nightclub in Chicago and played at many rent parties (gatherings where the person living in an apartment charged a small admission fee and provided musical entertainment to help pay the rent). These parties were popular in New York as well as Chicago.

Lofton was one of the pioneers of boogie-woogie piano. During his songs he was fond of throwing in spoken phrases, as though he were having a conversation with the piano. His song "I Don't

Know" was later recorded by Willie Mabon and by the Blues Brothers.

Lomax, Alan (1915–2002) *ethnomusicologist, record producer, and archivist*

Alan Lomax's father, John, was a white southerner who retained some of the prejudices that came with his upbringing. Son Alan, a different sort of person, was a blues fanatic from the beginning. Alan traveled with his father collecting songs when he was only a teenager. Alan seemed to have a better relationship with many of the artists they encountered, especially LEAD BELLY.

During the 1930s Alan Lomax became involved in left-wing politics, and he had radio shows and produced records. He promoted the career of country-folk artist Woody Guthrie and other artists who he thought were good representatives of folk and blues music. For an untrained musician he possessed a remarkable ear, and many of his recordings remain among the most interesting examples of blues and folk songs ever made. Besides assisting his

Unidentified blues artist photographed by Alan Lomax (Library of Congress Films and Photographs Division)

Unidentified blues artists photographed by Alan Lomax (Library of Congress Films and Photographs Division)

father with several collections of songs, Alan wrote a novel, a biography of jazz pianist JELLY ROLL MORTON, and a hefty book about the blues, *The Land Where the Blues Began.*

During the 1950s the United States turned politically conservative, and Lomax moved to England, afraid he might be branded as a communist or a communist sympathizer. He recorded an extensive series of albums documenting the folk music of such far-flung areas as East Africa, as well as recording folk music from various parts of Europe. Lomax returned to the United States in the late 1950s, presented bluegrass and rock and roll music at Carnegie Hall, and resumed his career by recording music from all over the United States. He also created a controversial theory, called cantometrics, which attempted to divide the entire world into two singing styles—open-throat singing and closed-throat singing. Lomax claimed that each of these styles was not just a musical style, but was related to the social world that the singers inhabited. This included everything from family structure to the political organization of a culture. Lomax wrote a book on the subject, *Folk Song Style and Culture,* and after his death, Ronald Cohen of the University of Indiana at Gary edited Lomax's *Collected Writings, 1939–1997.*

In terms of his involvement with the blues, Lomax was the first to record MUDDY WATERS, and in 1946 he recorded an album with BIG BILL BROONZY, Memphis Slim, and SONNY BOY WILLIAMSON, on which they discussed racism in the South. The album, issued many years later by United Artists Records, is currently available on a Rykodisc CD. It is called *Blues in the Mississippi Night.* When the album was first issued it was considered so controversial that the artist's names were not listed.

Lomax's lasting influence on the blues and on world folk music in general will remain strong for years, because ROUNDER RECORDS is currently issuing some 150 CDs of the music that Lomax collected.

Lomax, John (1867–1948) *folklorist*

John Lomax was one of the earliest collectors of American folksong. His career started when he began to collect cowboy songs in the early part of the 20th century. He published a collection of cowboy songs in 1910. Later Lomax collected songs for years for the Library of Congress. He sought out places where he thought older songs would be preserved. This led him to record in many southern

Alan Lomax (Bettmann/Corbis)

prisons, on rice and cotton plantations, and in isolated workplaces, like lumber camps.

Many of the songs Lomax collected were African American in origin, including work songs, spirituals, and blues. One of the many people that Lomax encountered was Lead Belly, after whose release from prison Lomax used him as a chauffeur to collect songs from other singers. Lomax also served as Lead Belly's manager and introduced him at concert performances, until the two had a falling out. Lomax compiled a book about Lead Belly that included his songs and stories about his life. Later Lomax edited several other collections of songs and wrote his autobiography.

John Lomax was a major figure in folk music collecting and scholarship, but some of his practices were controversial. The song collections that Lomax and his son Alan put together combined many different versions of a song, usually without giving specific information about the origins of these versions. Lomax then copyrighted the songs in his own name. In the case of Lead Belly, Lomax's name and that of his son appear as coauthors of the song "Goodnight Irene," although it is not clear that they made any contributions to writing it. It is also the case that some of the verses of the song were collected by folklorists long before Lead Belly recorded his version, which he first heard from his uncle. When the song became a number one pop hit by the Weavers in 1950, it became a valuable property.

Lomax worked for several years at the University of Texas and later as a banker. He also worked for the Library of Congress for many years at a salary of $1 a year. He supported himself through sales of his songbooks and grants from various foundations.

In recent years a lengthy biography of Lomax entitled *Last Cavalier: The Life and Times of John A. Lomax, 1867–1948,* by Nolan Porterfield, was published.

Lonesome Sundown (Cornelius Green)
(1928–1995) *guitarist and pianist*
Lonesome Sundown played PIANO as a child, taking up the guitar at the age of 15. He played guitar for

zydeco master CLIFTON CHENIER, then was recorded by JAY MILLER from 1956 to 1965. Although he showed more popular music influences than many of the artists that Miller recorded, his work is still classified as part of the swamp pop Louisiana blues style. He also crossed over into the world of rock and roll.

Sundown stopped recording blues in 1956, when he joined the Church of the Lord Jesus Christ. In 1977 he was persuaded to make another blues album, but it was not commercially successful. Sundown then retired from music and became a construction worker in his native Louisiana.

Long, J. B. (James Baxter Long) (b. 1903)
talent scout
Many of the folk blues artists of the 1920s and 1930s obtained their recording deals through talent scouts who acted as middlemen between artists and record company. J. B. Long was one of these "middlemen." Long ran a store for a company called United Dollar Stores in Kinston, North Carolina, where he began to sell records alongside the other merchandise. The store did so well that Long was transferred to a more profitable store in Durham, North Carolina.

Long observed that black music recordings did well at his store, and he started holding contests for talent that he hoped to present to record companies. When he moved to Durham, he met BLIND BOY FULLER and presented him to the American Record Company. Fuller became an extremely successful artist, and Long signed him to a lifetime recording contract after Decca Records managed to record a few Fuller songs without Long's knowledge or participation.

Other artists whom Long was involved in recording include BUDDY MOSS, SONNY TERRY, BLIND GARY DAVIS, and BROWNIE MCGHEE. Long often accompanied his artists to recording sessions, although he did not personally produce the records. Long managed to get Moss paroled out of jail in his custody, in return for which Long worked on his farm, receiving $30 a week and room and board.

There is some controversy about whether Long was fair to his artists. Sonny Terry, Blind Gary Davis, and Fuller claimed that he did not pay them money that was due them, while Long countered that he never made any money from his artists, but simply recorded them because he liked their music. McGhee had only positive memories about Long, who, he felt, started him in the music business. Blues scholar SAM CHARTERS, writing in the *Bluesmen,* seems to feel that Long purposely kept Buddy Moss at his farm because he did not want him to compete with Fuller, who was selling very well.

It is hard to determine exactly how fair Long was to his artists. There were no writing or publishing credits given on many of Fuller's early records, so that Long could not possibly have collected royalties for them. Blues researcher BRUCE BASTIN points out in his book, *Red River Blues,* that Terry, Davis, and Fuller were all blind black men in the South. It would have been natural for them to expect to be cheated by a white man, and many white business-people did indeed cheat African Americans. Whether Long himself did this is something we will probably never know.

Louisiana

LAFAYETTE
Lafayette, about 60 miles west of Baton Rouge, is the world headquarters for cajun and zydeco music. The most important musicians in these genres live around Lafayette, which is also home to Savoy's Music Center, operated by musician Marv Savoy. Savoy is one of a group of younger Louisiana musicians who have successfully sparked interest in a musical style that was threatening to disappear by 1960. He holds regular weekend jam sessions at his music store.

NEW ORLEANS
New Orleans is famous as the nurturing source for early jazz. It was also the home of the young LONNIE JOHNSON, the talented guitarist and singer who played with LOUIS ARMSTRONG and jazz composer and musician Duke Ellington, accompanied numerous blues singers, and also had a solo career that included several post–World War II rhythm and blues hits.

New Orleans was extremely influential in the growth of rhythm and blues. During the 1950s it spawned numerous hit records by various artists, especially Fats Domino, almost all recorded by a single engineer named Cosimo Matassa. Over the years New Orleans has also developed a rich tradition of blues PIANO, featuring such artists as JAMES BOOKER, PROFESSOR LONGHAIR, and DR. JOHN.

Louisiana Red (Iverson Miller) (b. 1936)
multi-instrumentalist
Louisiana Red sings and plays HARMONICA and guitar. Red had a difficult childhood. His mother died shortly after he was born and his father was lynched by the Ku Klux Klan. Red taught himself to play harmonica and guitar and moved to Pittsburgh, Pennsylvania, around 1945. He went to CHICAGO in 1949 and recorded for the Checker label subsidiary of CHESS RECORDS. He spent most of the 1950s in the Air Force and, since the 1960s has recorded numerous albums. He worked with blues producer Henry Glover and Herb Abramson, one of the founders of ATLANTIC RECORDS, and recorded an album in Woodstock with several members of The Band accompanying him.

Red is known for his autobiographical songs, such as "I Am Louisiana Red," and his songs of social commentary, including "Antinuclear Blues," "Reagan Is for the Rich Man," and "Starving in Detroit." He has lived in Germany for many years.

Lovin' Spoonful (1965–1968)
The leader of the Spoonful was John Sebastian, a harmonica player whose father was a virtuoso classical HARMONICA player. Sebastian went in a different

musical direction, immersing himself in the blues. He started the Spoonful in 1965, with guitarist Zal Yanofsky, bass player Steve Boone, and drummer Joe Butler. The band had many pop hits, including "Do You Believe in Magic" and "Daydream." Sebastian sang most of the lead parts, played guitar and harmonica, and wrote all the songs. The band also recorded blues tunes like "Wild About My Lovin'," "On the Road Again," and "Fishing Blues." Sebastian had a unique vocal sound and is a talented harmonica player.

After the band broke up in 1969, Sebastian had a solo career and has also recorded with a jug band. Before the Spoonful started he had been in the New York group Even Dozen Jug Band. The Spoonful has re-formed and now tours, but Sebastian is not in the group, and Yanovsky died in 2002.

Lutcher, Nellie (b. 1915) *pianist and singer*

Nellie Lutcher, born in Lake Charles, Louisiana, was a PIANO player and singer. At the age of 14 she was good enough to accompany MA RAINEY at a local performance. Lutcher's father was a bass player, and her brother played SAXOPHONE.

Lutcher moved to LOS ANGELES in 1935, working as an accompanist for singers. In 1947 a Capitol Records producer discovered her, and she went on to record several hit R&B records, like "Hurry On Down," and "He's a Real Gone Guy." These records were also successful on the pop charts. Lutcher's career at Capitol was over by 1952, and she then recorded less successfully for other labels.

Nellie Lutcher was like a female LOUIS JORDAN, who sang in a style halfway between blues and jazz, and played good swing piano.

Mack, Lonnie (Lonnie McIntosh) (b. 1941)
guitarist

Harrison, Indiana–born Lonnie Mack bought a Gibson Flying V guitar (a guitar in the shape of a V). He then bought a Maganatone amplifier, after seeing local bluesman ROBERT WARD using it. Mack thus developed his trademark guitar sound. He went on to hold recording sessions as a guitarist at nearby KING RECORDS in Cincinnati, Ohio, playing on JAMES BROWN and FREDDIE KING records. Sometime later he also played on a Doors rock album.

In 1963 Mack had a number five pop hit with his instrumental remake of CHUCK BERRY's "Memphis." On some of Mack's other recordings his singing was so convincing that R&B stations played his music, until they discovered that he was white. Mack recorded for Elektra and Epic Records but was not able to recapture national popularity. During the 1980s he moved to Austin, TEXAS. He continues to perform and record today.

Magic Sam (Samuel Maghett) (1937–1969)
West Side sound pioneer

CHICAGO blues started out on the South Side of Chicago. After World War II, the bands went electric, with MUDDY WATERS, HOWLIN' WOLF, and LITTLE WALTER dominating proceedings. The next generation of blues artists represented the West Side. Magic Sam was one of the founders of the style, along with BUDDY GUY, FREDDIE KING, and the less well-known OTIS RUSH. Magic Sam, like so many of the Chicago bluesmen, was born in the MISSISSIPPI Delta where he made his own guitar and listened to the local players. He moved to Chicago specifically to further his ambitions as a blues guitarist.

Sam's version of the West Side sound was to adapt B. B. KING's guitar style to Chicago blues and throw in gospel vocal elements as well. After he moved to Chicago Sam played in slide guitarist HOMESICK JAMES's band. His first recordings were made for the short-lived Cobra label in Chicago; then he moved to the Chief label. Sam finally found a home on BOB KOESTER's DELMARK label, where he cut two albums, in 1967 and 1968. After a sensational performance at the Ann Arbor (Michigan) Blues Festival in 1969, it looked as though Sam's career would finally take off, but he died of a heart attack several months later.

Mahal, Taj (Henry St. Claire Fredericks) (b. 1941) *singer and multi-instrumentalist*

Taj Mahal was one of the few young black blues artists to emerge in the folk music revival of the 1960s. His father was a jazz musician, and his mother sang gospel music; Taj was playing in coffeehouses at the age of 14. He continued to play and sing in 1956 while he was a student at the University of Massachusetts at Amherst, breaking into the Boston folk scene. He then moved to the West Coast, hooking up with guitarist RY COODER in a band called the Rising Sons. The band got a recording contract with Columbia Records, but it broke up after completing one album. The album was released years

Taj Mahal (Larry Shirkey)

later, in 1992 as *Rising Sons featuring Taj Mahal and Ry Cooder,* when both Cooder and Mahal had become salable commodities, in the record company's opinion.

Mahal has had a long recording and performing career, and in addition to singing and playing guitar and SLIDE GUITAR, he also played PIANO, bass, and the BANJO. Few black musicians had much interest in taking up the banjo, because they identified it with the minstrel era and racial stereotypes, but Mahal did not care. Unlike many of the older CHICAGO musicians, Mahal developed a good following among white folk fans.

Mahal branched out into other areas of music, like world music and reggae, and for a while he toured and recorded with a tuba section. He wrote the music for the films *Sounder* and *Brothers,* as well

as the 1991 Broadway show *Mule Bone,* and also recorded two critically acclaimed children's albums.

With over 38 albums to his credit, Mahal continues to tour and record.

Malaco Records

Malaco was founded by Tommy Couch in 1962. He went from running a booking agency to operating a nightclub, to operating a four-track recording studio. The label records R&B, blues, and gospel music, and has also acquired the Savoy Records gospel music catalog.

Initially the operation was a production company that leased product to other labels, but in 1975 they started to issue their own product. In 1985 they acquired the renowned Muscle Shoals Sound recording studio, where R&B artist Aretha Franklin and many other artists recorded hit songs. It closed in 2005.

Some of the artists who have recorded for the label include BOBBY "BLUE" BLAND, LITTLE MILTON, Z. Z. HILL, and Johnnie Taylor. Many of these artists had R&B hits for major labels, and Malaco has reconstructed their careers by selling smaller numbers of records with less money spent on production and promotion. Many of these recordings sell to a primarily older African-American audience.

Mandel, Harvey (b. 1945) *guitarist*

Like guitarist Roy Buchanan, Harvey Mandel is better known to musicians than to the general public. Part of the reason for this is that Mandel does very little singing and has never found a powerful singer with whom to start a band. Mandel is a spectacular lead guitarist who has roots in the blues but also crosses over into rock and country music and jazz. Harvey has played with HARMONICA player CHARLIE MUSSELWHITE, was the lead guitarist for the rock band CANNED HEAT from 1969 to 1970, has played with British blues pioneer JOHN MAYALL, played on two songs recorded by the ROLLING STONES, and had a band called Pure Food & Drug Act with violinist

Don "Sugarcane" Harris. Mandel has also recorded solo albums. He was one of the first guitarists to use the ELECTRIC GUITAR technique called tapping, a means of playing notes without strumming or picking by tapping the fingers of both hands against the strings over the fretboard.

mandolin

Of all the instruments played in the blues style mandolin was among the least common. Many of the artists who played the mandolin, like KANSAS JOE MCCOY, also played the guitar. Even mandolin soloists like YANK RACHELL played guitar as well.

Like the SLIDE GUITAR, the mandolin entered the blues scene from foreign shores. It was a popular instrument among immigrants from eastern and southern Europe, especially Italians. The CHICAGO musical instrument manufacturer Lyon and Healy produced 7,000 mandolins a year by 1894. The instrument was popular as a parlor instrument, and all sorts of pop tunes as well as rags were played on it. Mandolins were available through mail-order catalogs in the same way that guitars were sold.

The traditional mandolin had a somewhat awkward shape for playing, with a bowl back. During the 1920s the flat-backed mandolin replaced the bowl-back models. The Gibson Company of Nashville, Tennessee, in particular, made other design changes that improved the volume and playability of the instrument. Like the HARMONICA, the mandolin achieved popularity in the white country string bands, as well as their black equivalent and in jug bands as well. Blues performer Coley Jones played with the Dallas Jug Band during the early 1920s, and their big hit, "Dallas Rag," sold over 10,000 copies. The King David Jug Band from Cincinnati with a little-known mandolin player named Dude recorded in 1930. Will Shade's popular MEMPHIS JUG BAND utilized Vol Stevens on mandolin and banjo-mandolin, a mandolin with a banjo head, and they made a number of recordings from 1927 to 1934.

The mandolin had two basic musical roles. The instrument had four sets of paired strings, tuned GG DD AA EE. It could be used to play rhythm, and the double strings and small body seemed to emphasize the higher notes of the instrument. It could also play lead lines, which were always doubled, because the player was hitting two strings at once. The instrument is virtually always played with a flat pick. Another common technique was the use of the tremolo, where a musician plays rapidly across a pair of strings to get the effect of playing a continuous stream of notes. This is often done in Italian music.

Gibson A-9 mandolin (Gibson Guitars)

At the same time as the instrument was being utilized in the blues, white country players were using mandolin, first in the mountain string bands with players like Ted Hawkins playing with the Skillet Lickers and Charley Hunt with the Blue Ridge Ramblers and a bit later in bluegrass music. Mandolin was used frequently in white country bands, often in duos with guitarists. Often the duos consisted of two brothers, like the Monroe, Shelton, and Callahan Brothers. Black musicians Nap Hayes and Matthew Prater played guitar and mandolin, and they recorded several of Ragtime composer and pianist Scott Joplin's rags.

Mandolin player Bill Monroe was largely responsible for the evolution of mountain music from string band music to bluegrass. Bluegrass was played much faster, and generally featured FIDDLE or banjo playing the lead parts, although in Monroe's band the mandolin often played that role. As with the harmonica, country players picked up blues to a greater or lesser degree. Monroe was particularly interested in adapting blues on the mandolin, and he acknowledged the early influence of black musicians on his playing. The band Jim and Jesse (McReynolds), who started recording in the early 1950s, was another bluegrass band that featured lots of mandolin leads.

None of the famous blues artists were mandolin players, although CHARLIE MCCOY, who played both mandolin and guitar, did considerable recording, playing with Delta artists ISHMON BRACEY and TOMMY JOHNSON. Several musicians were best known as mandolin players, particularly Yank Rachell and JOHNNY YOUNG. Rachell played with SLEEPY JOHN ESTES, and it was the mandolin that played the lead parts. Between 1938 and 1941 he had several hits, playing with SONNY BOY WILLIAMSON I. As a result of Sleepy John Estes's rediscovery in the 1960s, Rachell was discovered as well, and he resumed his musical career.

JOHNNY YOUNG was another blues mandolin player. Born in Vicksburg, MISSISSIPPI, in 1917, he took up harmonica and then guitar before settling on mandolin. He moved to Chicago in 1940 and performed with his cousin Henry Williams, each of them playing guitar and mandolin alternately. He also made recordings with SNOOKY PRYOR, but by 1956 he had given up music as a full-time occupation, although he played at a number of blues and folk festivals during the 1960s.

HOWARD ARMSTRONG (Louie Bluie) played mandolin, as well as fiddle and a number of other instruments. Armstrong was not strictly a blues player but a well-rounded musician who knew no musical borders, playing pop tunes, rags, blues, and ethnic music.

Although the mandolin has now been amplified and is available in a solid-body model, the instrument has never caught on in blues bands. Since the black string bands declined, the mandolin has mostly been taken up by bluegrass musicians and by jazz-oriented enthusiasts like David Grisman, a veteran of the white revivalist Even Dozen Jug Band.

Margolin, Bob (b. 1949) *guitarist*

Bob Margolin is best known for the seven years he spent playing guitar with MUDDY WATERS. Margolin was born in Boston and got his start in music playing in local bands. He played with Luther "Georgia Boy" Johnson. Johnson had played with Waters, and Margolin met Waters through Johnson. Margolin is a talented guitarist and songwriter, and his primary musical goal is to keep CHICAGO blues alive, especially the music of Waters. A Boston disc jockey gave Margolin his rhyming nickname, "Steady Rollin' Bob Margolin," a tribute to his faithfulness to the blues.

Martin, Sara (1884–1955) *singer*

Born in Louisville, Kentucky, Sara Martin was a classic blues singers of the 1920s. Like many of these artists she had a background as a vaudeville performer, touring on the Theater Owners' Booking Association (TOBA) circuit and then singing in the South and on the East Coast. Like many of the blues performers who came out of a theatrical background, Martin specialized in wearing fancy jewelry and unusual costumes. She was often accompanied on records by pianist-entrepreneur CLARENCE WILLIAMS, and some gifted jazz musicians, like King Oliver, Sidney Bechet, and Fats Waller appeared on her recordings. Martin retired in the early 1930s, ran a nursing home, and did gospel singing.

Mayall, John (b. 1933) *harmonicist and vocalist*

HARMONICA player–vocalist John Mayall was one of the founding fathers of the British blues. Mayall's father was a jazz musician, and in 1950 Mayall formed his first band, the Powerhouse Four. The band he formed in 1963 the Bluesbreakers, was important both for its influence on the British blues and rock scene and because many famous musicians at one time or another played with the group. Among them were guitarist Mick Taylor, who later played with The ROLLING STONES; John McVie, Mick Fleetwood, and Peter Green, who were the founders of FLEETWOOD MAC; Jack Bruce, later a member of CREAM; and ERIC CLAPTON. More than three dozen Mayall albums are available, and Mayall continues to tour today.

Mayfield, Curtis (1942–1999) *songwriter and record producer*

Curtis Mayfield appears in this book because of his tremendous influence on black popular music during the 1960s and 1970s. Mayfield was a consistent and active songwriter and record producer, and his bluesy guitar figures heavily influenced soul music. During the 1960s he was the leader of the Impressions, who had many hit pop and R&B records. Possibly Mayfield's major contribution to black music was his lyrics, many of which discuss civil rights issues. During the civil rights movement of the 1960s, Mayfield gave permission for his lyrics to be rewritten to reflect specific issues, and civil rights workers called him a "movement man."

In the early 1990s Mayfield, seriously injured in an accident, was paralyzed for the rest of his life, but he recorded the album *New World Order* while lying in bed in 1996.

Mayfield, Percy (1920–1984) *songwriter*

Percy Mayfield was known as an outstanding songwriter and as "the poet of the blues." Several of his songs, such as "River's Invitation" and "Please Send Me Someone to Love," have become rhythm and blues standards. During the 1950s Mayfield wrote songs for RAY CHARLES, including the number one pop song "Hit the Road, Jack."

McClennan, Tommy (1908–1962) *singer and guitarist*

MISSISSIPPI-born Tommy McClennan had a rough, growling vocal sound, accompanied by his insistent-rhythm guitar. As a young man McClennan picked cotton and played for tips on the street. He was recorded by LESTER MELROSE in the late 1930s. McClennan often played with ROBERT PETWAY, who sounded like him.

Between 1939 and 1942 McClennan moved between CHICAGO and the Delta. The song most identified with him, "Bottle Up and Go," was controversial, and many black people did not care for it because it used the word "nigger." In BIG BILL BROONZY's autobiography, Broonzy tells of warning McClennan not to use that word when singing at a house party. McClennan did it anyway, and his guitar was demolished by unhappy listeners.

McClinton, Delbert (b. 1940) *singer, songwriter, and harmonicist*

Delbert McClinton is a singer, songwriter, and HARMONICA player who has strong roots in both the blues and country music. He cut his professional teeth playing in TEXAS honky-tonks. His songs have been recorded by country artists Emmylou Harris, Martina McBride, and Vince Gill, and by the blues variety act of the Blues Brothers. He sang with BONNIE RAITT on her hit album *Luck of the Draw*.

McClinton, who continues to perform and record, has some 25 CDs currently available on numerous record labels. McClinton is an artist honored more by other musicians than by the general public.

McCoy, Charles (Papa Charlie) (1909–1950), and Joseph McCoy (Kansas Joe McCoy) (1905–1950) *musicians*

The McCoy Brothers played guitar and MANDOLIN, and sang. They sometimes performed together, and each also performed with a number of other musicians. Charley worked with delta guitarists TOMMY JOHNSON and ISHMON BRACEY, and went to CHICAGO in the 1920s. He recorded with Bo Chatmon, BIG BILL BROONZY, and the original SONNY BOY WILLIAMSON (John Lee Williamson.)

Joe McCoy was married to MEMPHIS MINNIE between 1929 and 1935, and made many successful recordings with her. Among these recordings were the influential "When the Levee Breaks" and "Bumble Bee." Joe was particularly known for his SLIDE GUITAR work. When their marriage broke up, they stopped working together.

From 1936 to 1939 the brothers formed a band called the Harlem Hamfats, a combo that played jazz and blues. Kansas Joe went on to play with other bands, but Charley's musical career ended with World War II.

McCracklin, Jimmy (b. 1921) *singer, pianist, and harmonicist*

Jimmy McCracklin sings and plays PIANO and HARMONICA. Pianist and singer WALTER DAVIS was the main influence on his piano playing. McCracklin was one of the important figures in the CALIFORNIA post–World War II rhythm and blues scene, with his smooth crooning vocals and piano work. He has had a long and versatile recording career, moving from one musical style to another. He has recorded traditional blues and rhythm and blues that featured big bands and written musical arrangements. Like a number of other blues singers, such as WILLIE

DIXON, McCracklin worked as a professional boxer before he began his musical career.

During the middle 1940s into the 1960s McCracklin recorded for Bay Area independent producer and small record company owner BOB GEDDINS. His biggest hit was "The Walk," recorded for CHESS RECORDS in 1958. It crossed over into the pop market and reached number seven on the national charts. A few of his other songs also made it to the pop charts. He may be best known as the writer of Lowell Fulson's big R&B hit "Tramp." He continued to record into the mid-1990s.

McDowell, Mississippi Fred (1905–1972) *singer and songwriter*

Many excellent blues musicians did not turn professional until relatively late in life. Fred McDowell was one of them. He bought his first guitar at the age of 35 and for years played for his own amusement and for occasional Saturday night dances. Most of his life was spent farming. McDowell sang and played bottleneck guitar, and adapted and rearranged traditional songs rather than writing new material. In 1959 ALAN LOMAX recorded McDowell for a series of albums that he was producing for ATLANTIC RECORDS, which led to McDowell's discovery during the folk-blues revival of the 1960s. He made two albums for ARHOOLIE RECORDS, played the Newport Folk Festival in 1964, and toured Europe the following year.

The ROLLING STONES recorded McDowell's song "You Got to Move," which brought considerable royalties for McDowell. BONNIE RAITT also recorded some of his songs. Fred McDowell was one of the few older bluesmen discovered during the 60s folk-blues revival, not one of the artists resuming a career after years of silence.

McGhee, Brownie (Walter Brown McGhee) (1915–1996) *singer, guitarist, and songwriter*

Although to most people Brownie McGhee is always identified with his musical partner SONNY TERRY, each of them had quite a few career credits separate from the other. McGhee was in a gospel group at a young age, and he met HARMONICA player Terry in 1939. Each got his recording start through furniture store owner J. B. LONG. Long arranged for each of them to go to New York with his most successful artist, BLIND BOY FULLER. When Fuller died in early 1941, McGhee recorded for a while using the name Blind Boy Fuller #2. He played guitar in a style that was similar to Fuller's and he wrote and recorded a song called "The Death of Blind Boy Fuller," even using Fuller's guitar. The song praises Fuller and ends with the idea that now that Fuller is gone, Brownie will "carry his business on."

In the early 1940s McGhee and Terry teamed up and had a 30-year career together. They played at folk festivals and concerts, and made a large number of recordings together. They settled in New York and frequently performed as a duo and with other musicians. During the early part of their career they had two different audiences. McGhee wrote many songs, recorded for a number of labels, had a guitar school in Harlem, and the two of them had a black audience in Harlem. They also played at hootenannies, gatherings of mostly white musicians who played for politically radical audiences in New York. McGhee and Terry performed with such artists as LEAD BELLY, JOSH WHITE, Pete Seeger, and Woody Guthrie, and McGhee also worked with his brother STICK MCGHEE.

During the late 1940s McGhee made an excellent album for MOE ASCH, later issued on Folkways Records. It featured him without Terry. McGhee wrote all the songs and came up with very original guitar arrangements for such tunes as "The Way I Feel" and "Me and My Dog."

The duo also became popular among the artistic set in New York, and they had parts in the long-running Tennessee Williams play *Cat on a Hot Tin Roof* and Langston Hughes's play *Simply Heavenly*. Later McGhee appeared in several films. When the folk music revival hit during the early 1960s, McGhee and Terry became popular among folk fans. Their audience by now had become primarily the white

folk audience, and they toured more than ever. Some blues critics believe that by this time much of their music had become dull and repetitious; moreover, the two of them were not getting along well. They finally broke up in the mid-1970s, and although McGhee continued to do solo work, by the early 1980s he had mostly retired. His last appearance was at the Chicago Blues Festival in 1995, and he died a year later.

Brownie McGhee deserves more credit than he has received for his contributions to the blues, as a writer, singer, and guitarist. He had a very original guitar style, adapting the Piedmont style to a more contemporary setting by using a thumb pick and metal fingerpicks. He may have been one of the first black bluesmen to do this. Although, his tune "Walk On" has been recorded by other artists, some of his other songs, like "Born with the Blues," will probably be recorded by other artists eventually.

One of McGhee's guitar students, HAPPY TRAUM, compiled a book of McGhee's songs that teaches his guitar style.

McGhee, Stick (Granville McGhee) (1917–1961)
singer and songwriter

Stick McGhee was BROWNIE MCGHEE's younger brother. He is best known for writing and performing the hit song "Drinkin' Wine Spo-Dee-o-Dee." This was the first hit recording made for ATLANTIC RECORDS. Stick recorded for several other labels but never had that kind of success again. He sometimes performed with his brother, and occasionally he also played with SONNY TERRY.

McMurry, Lillian (1921–1999) *record company owner*

Among all the bad stories about white businesspeople taking advantage of black blues artists, Lillian McMurry represents the exception to the rule. McMurry loved blues and started her career in the music business at her husband's furniture store in Jackson, MISSISSIPPI. She noticed that her black customers wanted to buy blues and gospel records, so she started carrying them. By 1950 she had started the Trumpet Record Company.

Her first recordings were of gospel artists, but she soon branched out to the blues. She produced a major hit record with ELMORE JAMES's "Dust My Broom." She also recorded important records with SONNY BOY WILLIAMSON #II (Rice Miller), particularly "9 Below Zero."

McMurry had originally been a bookkeeper in her husband's furniture store, and she kept accurate records of what money was owed to her artists. She went to great lengths to find artists who had disappeared in order to pay them their royalties. McMurry left the music business by 1955, because she was unable to collect money from the independent record distributors that were selling her recordings to stores. She then returned to her husband's business and lived the rest of her life in Jackson. A book entitled *Trumpet Records: Diamonds on Farish Street* by Marc Ryan about her label and her contributions to the blues was published in 2004.

McShann, Jay (James McShann) (b. 1916)
bandleader

Jay McShann is most famous for being a bandleader in Kansas City. Blues singer JIMMY WITHERSPOON and the incredible alto saxophone player Charlie Parker are among the musicians who were in McShann's big band. McShann was also a talented PIANO player and singer, and he cowrote the hit song "Confessin' the Blues" with singer Walter Brown. In his late 80s, McShann is still performing.

McTell, Blind Willie (William Samuel McTell)
(1901–1959) *guitarist and singer*

Willie McTell had an amazing life story. He taught himself to read and write music in Braille, and he played for years on the streets of Atlanta. McTell developed a unique style on the 12-STRING GUITAR,

his favorite instrument, fingerpicking the guitar, rather than strumming it. Because the 12-string has six pairs of strings, this is difficult to do.

McTell's repertoire included folk ballads, ragtime pieces, pop songs, gospel music, and blues. He started to record in 1927, for Decca, Victor, and Columbia at different times. In 1940 JOHN LOMAX ran across McTell on one of his song-collecting trips. Lomax was amazed that McTell seemed to carry a map of the streets of Atlanta in his head. As they were driving around town, whenever Lomax wanted to go anywhere McTell would quickly tell him what street to turn on and how far to go. McTell had a clear falsetto voice, and besides his fingerpicking he also played bottleneck guitar, and sometimes played the six-string instrument as well.

One of McTell's most memorable songs, "Statesboro Blues," was recorded in 1969 by the Allman Brothers, shortly after McTell died. After years of playing on the streets of Atlanta, often with his friend guitarist CURLY WEAVER, McTell recorded an album for ATLANTIC RECORDS in 1949 and another album recorded for Atlanta Record store owner Ed Rhodes was entitled *Blind Willie McTell's Last Session* album. Both these albums were released after McTell's death. A dozen CDs of McTell's work are available, including the two albums that were never released during his lifetime.

Melrose, Lester (1891–1968) *record producer and talent scout*

Lester Melrose was a white businessman responsible for the so-called Bluebird beat sound, coming out of CHICAGO during the middle to late 1930s. This was blues played with small combos, like BIG BILL BROONZY's Chicago Five. During the course of his career Melrose also produced recordings for Columbia, Victor, and Vocalion Records.

Melrose's business practices were the opposite of those of LILLIAN MCMURRY. Melrose signed the artist directly to himself, and *he* then signed a contract with the record company. He paid his artists a flat fee with no royalties, and he received the artists' royalties from the record company. He also listed himself as the songwriter and publisher of the songs, so he received those royalties as well.

Many blues critics have criticized Melrose not only for his business practices, but because the music that he recorded tended to sound the same. He encouraged his artists to stay with whatever style was popular at the time. In a sense he was one of the first people to develop the concept of a studio band, later used by Sam Phillips at Sun Records, Leonard Chess at CHESS RECORDS, and Berry Gordy at Motown, among others.

Melrose began his career in music by owning a record store in Chicago. When he met jazz pianist and singer JELLY ROLL MORTON in 1923, Melrose decided that he wanted to get into the record business. Among the artists whom he recorded were Broonzy, TAMPA RED, SONNY BOY WILLIAMSON II (Rice Miller), MEMPHIS MINNIE, and BUKKA WHITE. By the mid-1950s Melrose's sound had become old-fashioned, and the electric sound of Chess Records dominated the Chicago blues scene.

Memphis, Tennessee

Memphis, Tennessee, is just north of the MISSISSIPPI Delta on HIGHWAY 61. When musicians left the Delta, they tended to gravitate either to Memphis or to CHICAGO, both of which became major blues centers. Composer W. C. HANDY was one of the first influential individuals connected to the blues who came to Memphis. He arrived in 1908 and wrote his "Memphis Blues." The original version of the song was the theme song commissioned by E. H. Crump, who became the longtime mayor of the town. Capitalizing on his Memphis connection, Handy then wrote "Beale Street Blues" before moving to New York.

Memphis during the 1920s under Mayor Crump had a similar environment to Kansas City, MISSOURI, during the 1930s under Tom Pendergast.

Beale Street was full of bars and theaters and music flourished everywhere. There were jug bands, like GUS CANNON's Jug Stompers, and musicians like FURRY LEWIS and MEMPHIS MINNIE.

In 1949 B. B. KING became a disc jockey after several trips to the city from his Mississippi home, and he and BOBBY "BLUE" BLAND, who had also come to Memphis, played a major role in modernizing the blues for an urban audience.

By the 1950s Crump was still mayor but, under pressure from the reform movement, had cracked down on the widespread gambling and prostitution in town, causing a drastic decline in the Beale Street entertainment area.

Around the same time as Crump was forced into these reforms, a young white record producer named Sam Phillips started a recording studio. Initially he recorded black blues artists, including B. B. King and HOWLIN' WOLF, producing records for a variety of record labels. Frustrated at receiving little compensation for his work, Phillips started his own record label, SUN RECORDS. Phillips concluded that he would never make a good living recording authentic blues, the music that he genuinely loved. He began a search for a "white boy who could sing the blues." The search eventually led to ELVIS PRESLEY, and later to Jerry Lee Lewis, Johnny Cash, Roy Orbison, CARL PERKINS, and Charley Rich. Phillips and his artists developed a whole new kind of music that was referred to as rockabilly. Rockabilly was a fusion of country music and blues, with a simple rock beat.

Many of Phillips's records were major hits in the early 1950s. He sold Elvis's contract to RCA, then his other hit artists started to leave him for better-paying major label recording deals. Phillips then left the record business.

A similar if more complicated story evolved 10 years later with Stax-Volt Records. The company was started in 1960 by Estelle Axton and her brother Jim Stewart. Axton and Stewart were white but had a real feel for R&B music. They used an integrated rhythm section who themselves recorded under the name

Booker T. and the MGs. (Booker T. Jones was the keyboard player.) Under their own name and as the rhythm section for such artists as Sam and Dave, and Otis Redding, they played on dozens of hit records. Stax developed a distribution deal with ATLANTIC RECORDS, and Jerry Wexler came from New York with artists like Wilson Pickett, who utilized the Stax rhythm section. ALBERT KING was the Stax artist most closely connected with the blues.

During the 1960s Stax successfully competed with Motown Records as the rhythm and blues powerhouse. Both companies had house rhythm sections and a group of artists who doubled as record producers and songwriters. Eventually Stax was strangled by overexpansion and some bad business judgments, and in 1975 it went into bankruptcy.

Beale Street has been redeveloped and today it is a thriving magnet for tourists. B. B. King, for example, has one of several blues club on Beale Street. This is fitting enough, given that King's nickname was originally "Beale Street Blues Boy." There is also a W. C. Handy Museum, which displays his sheet music and photographs.

Visitors to Memphis will find a number of worthwhile blues sites to visit. It is possible to visit Sam Phillips's Sun Studios, and there is a Stax Museum on the site where the record company used to be located. On the second floor of the Gibson Guitar factory is the Memphis Rock 'n Soul Museum, with an exhibit that celebrates Memphis soul and the early Memphis rock scene. Rock and roll enthusiasts will want to check out Elvis's mansion, Graceland.

Serious blues scholars will want to visit the Center for Southern Folklore. The center documents the blues and other forms of African-American music through a collection of films, records, books, and oral histories. It also sponsors blues concerts and occasional screenings of movies and has an art gallery.

The flavor of the Memphis music scene is beautifully depicted in singer-songwriter Mark Cohn's song "Walking in Memphis," which describes everything from the ghost of Elvis to a real person who was a gospel music singer and pianist.

The University of Memphis has a doctoral program in Southern Regional Music Studies, presided over by blues scholar and musician DAVID EVANS. The university also runs a record label called High Water Records, specializing in Memphis blues and gospel music.

Memphis Jug Band

Will Shade (also known as Son Brimmer) sang, played jug, guitar, and HARMONICA, and was the leader of the Memphis Jug Band. A number of other singers and musicians like BIG WALTER HORTON and FURRY LEWIS wandered through the group, playing guitars, BANJO, kazoo, PIANO, and FIDDLE. Sometimes singer-guitarists Laura Dukes and MEMPHIS MINNIE played in the band, as did guitarists and singers Bo Chatmon and Casey Bill Weldon.

The band's music varied from pop to blues, waltzes, and vaudeville tunes. They recorded about 60 songs for Victor Records, starting in 1927. Most of their recordings were made from 1927 to 1930. The music was light party music, as compared with the heavy and serious music of the Delta.

Memphis Minnie (Lizzie Douglas)
(1896–1973) *singer, songwriter, and guitarist*
There were very few prominent female guitarists in the folk blues of the 1920s and 1930s. Memphis Minnie was the most famous blues player among the women artists of the period. Minnie sang and wrote songs, and she usually performed with her second husband, KANSAS JOE MCCOY, or her third husband, Little Son Joe (Ernest Lawlar.) Minnie played the lead guitar parts, and her husband would play rhythm guitar.

Minnie started to record in 1929 with Joe McCoy, and in 1930 she recorded with the MEMPHIS

JUG BAND. During the early 1930s she and McCoy moved to CHICAGO, where she worked in clubs and recorded for the Okeh label. She won a famous blues contest, competing against BIG BILL BROONZY and TAMPA RED, with the prize a bottle of liquor. Broonzy admitted that he ran off with the bottle before Minnie could get her hands on it. It is doubtful that any other woman artist at that time could have competed with, let alone defeated, such well-known blues guitarists as Broonzy and Tampa Red.

Besides playing the blues, Minnie performed spirituals and old-time dances, as well as writing some original songs. Her songs "Bumble Bee" and "Memphis Minnie-Jitis Blues" sold well. Minnie could play bottle-neck guitar and lead guitar, and her rhythm guitar playing was advanced for its time. The music that Minnie played with Little Son Joe had a harder edge, more like the Chicago blues styles of the early 1950s than her previous, more folk-style records. LED ZEPPELIN recorded her "When the Levee Breaks," giving her only partial composer credit. Altogether Minnie recorded over 150 songs.

After her third husband died in 1957, Minnie left the music business. She became paralyzed and was placed in a nursing home in MEMPHIS. She had no idea that anyone was still interested in her music until British blues artist JO ANN KELLY came to visit her shortly before Minnie's death.

migration

As the blues developed, the geographic profile of the African-American population changed in several ways. First, there was a consistent movement from farms to cities. Second, the population originally centered in the southern states moved to the north and western United States. There were a number of reasons for this transformation. Over the years farms became less dependent on maintaining a large labor force that did most of its work by hand. Tractors replaced individual workers using horses and mules, and mechanical devices like the mechanical cotton picker replaced other workers.

During the 20th century America was transformed into a giant industrial power, and the auto factories in DETROIT, and the packing houses and stockyards in CHICAGO and Kansas City required thousands of workers to function. The wages paid in these factories were much higher than what a southern farmer could make, so they represented an attractive option to the southern African-American worker. The situation was accelerated during World War I (1914–18) and World War II, (1939–45), when immigration dropped severely, and many other jobs were available because so many American workers were serving in the armed forces. Although wages at the northern factories seemed generous to southern blacks, the giant factories saw these workers as a constant and steady supplier of cheap labor.

Another important aspect of northern migration was a difference in social conditions. The northern migrants felt that their children would have a better chance to get a good education, and that the political and social restrictions of the North were less discriminatory than conditions in the southern states. This was especially true in the more oppressive states like MISSISSIPPI, where lynchings and police brutality were common.

One of the earliest large migrations took place during the period 1865–80, when 40,000 blacks, known as "Exodusters," moved to Kansas. Leon F. Litwack, in his book *Trouble in Mind: Black Southerners in the Age of Jim Crow*, maintains that the exodusters were fleeing poverty and terrorism. They came from rural TEXAS, LOUISIANA, Mississippi, and Tennessee, and some of them created towns that had no white residents. It is also significant that this migration coincided with the end of slavery. African Americans were now free to travel around the country without worrying about being returned to their masters.

The next migration was much larger. Between 1916 and 1919 about half a million black southerners left the South, and almost a million more followed during the decade of the 1920s. Some southern states, like Louisiana and Mississippi, suffered a decline in their black population.

In 1919 the price of cotton reached a high point of one dollar a pound, but by 1920 the price had fallen to 10 cents a pound. Although scholars generally date the beginning of the Great Depression as starting in 1929, the farm depression began in 1920. With work scarce and wages low, there was a strong motivation for African Americans to leave the South.

The *Chicago Defender* was the most prestigious and widely circulated black newspaper, and it launched a propaganda campaign to convince African Americans to leave the South. Nicholas Lemann's book, *The Promised Land,* describes this campaign as using biblical images and spirituals in an attempt to convince black southerners to move to Chicago. The newspaper even negotiated with railroad companies to offer reduced prices for train tickets to Chicago. Black pullman porters on the trains passed out copies of the *Defender* at train stops in Mississippi.

As a result of these efforts, the black population in Chicago grew from 44,000 in 1910 to 109,000 in 1920, and 234,000 in 1930. By 1940 the black population had grown to 492,000, and during he 1950s it reached 813,000. By 1980 the population had reached 1,197,000.

A similar population shift occurred in other northern and western cities. Washington, D.C., had 86,000 African Americans in 1900, and 189,000 by 1940. New York had over 50,000 blacks in 1900, and in 1940 477,000. Philadelphia's black population grew from over 50,000 to 253,000 during the same period.

The growth of the black population in the southern states also was in urban centers. New Orleans's black populations grew from 77,000 in 1900 to 150,000 in 1940, for example. Large-scale migration to the West Coast occurred somewhat later. LOS ANGELES's black population increased from 98,000 in 1940 to 505,000 in 1980, and during the same period Oakland's black population went from 14,000 to 159,000.

Even with all this urban growth, as late as 1940 77 percent of black Americans lived in the South,

and 49 percent were still living in the rural South. Lemann reports that between 1910 and 1970 six and a half million black southerners moved north. Five million of these migrants moved after 1940, the period when cotton farming became mechanized. By 1970 49 percent of African Americans lived in the South, and less than 25 percent of that population was rural.

In considering the migration patterns and thinking of the development of the blues, it is significant that much of the migration to Chicago came from the Mississippi Delta. Artists who followed this path include MUDDY WATERS, ELMORE JAMES, HOWLIN' WOLF, and BUDDY GUY. Piedmont artists, like SONNY TERRY, BROWNIE MCGHEE, and BLIND GARY DAVIS, like their nonmusical brothers and sisters, tended to go to New York. This was not invariably true, because BLIND BLAKE and TAMPA RED were Piedmont-born, but they ended up in Chicago. The development of Chicago electric blues can be traced almost entirely to Delta-born artists.

During the early migrations, white southerners opposed the mass migration of blacks. They feared that they would lose the basis of their rural economy—a consistent and large supply of cheap labor. They attempted to slow the northern migration by making northern factory agents who were recruiting southern blacks pay heavy labor fees. In some instances blacks seen near railroad stations were arrested for vagrancy. They were even pulled off trains going north and jailed.

When soldiers and sailors came home from the war in 1918, the demand for laborers declined, and migration also slowed down. The Great Depression had a similar effect, because jobs for migrants were not available.

Later migration patterns indicated different social forces at work. Southern planters and newspapers opposed black mass migration in the early twentieth century, and they tried to convince black southerners that the South offered them a better environment. When the civil rights movement developed during the 1950s and 1960s, some of the racist southern organizations encouraged migration, feeling that it would help their cause to rid the South of "troublemakers." Of course, they also were influenced by the South's greatly diminished demand for a large supply of cheap labor.

Although much of the motivation for migration was based on political as well as economic considerations, the migrants did not always find what they were looking for. In 1919, following the end of World War I, there were race riots in a number of American cities, including Longview, Texas; Chicago; Knoxville; Elaine, Arkansas, and Omaha. A virtual race war erupted in Tulsa, Oklahoma, in 1921. Black soldiers returning from fighting for their country during World War I began to demand more rights than they had enjoyed before the war. The resistance to these demands occurred in the North as well as the South, but despite these nationwide patterns of discrimination, blacks still received a better education and higher wages, and they began to participate in politics in the northern states.

Milburn, Amos (1927–1980) *songwriter and recording artist*

Milburn is an artist who played boogie-woogie, blues, and rhythm and blues. He was born in Houston, TEXAS, and migrated to the West Coast in the late 1940s, where he became one of the founders of West Coast rhythm and blues. Milburn's song "Chicken Shack Boogie" reached the top of the R&B charts in 1948, and Milburn followed it up with "Bewildered." He had a number of major hits in the early 1950s, many of which were songs about drinking. "Bad Bad Whiskey" reached number one on the R&B charts. "One Scotch, One Bourbon, One Beer" reached the second position, and some of his other recordings on the same subject reached numbers three and five. Milburn never crossed over into the rock and roll market, although he continued to perform through the 1960s, recording unsuccessfully for the Motown label.

Miles, Lizzie (Elizabeth Mary Inee Landreaux Pajaud) (1895–1963) *singer*

Lizzie Miles, a New Orleans native, became nationally known during the era of the classic blues singers. She became a band singer and performed with such well-known New Orleans musicians as King Oliver, Kid Ory, Bunk Johnson, and the great clarinetist Alphonse Picou. She later moved to CHICAGO and successfully auditioned for Oliver's band, which had previously relocated there. In that band was the great Louis Armstrong.

For two or three years Miles worked in NEW YORK, and in 1924 she went to Paris. Miles was fluent in French so she sang in English and French. By 1926 she returned to New York, moving back to New Orleans in 1938 to take care of her mother.

Besides singing the blues, Miles performed pop songs, especially those associated with white vaudeville performer Sophie Tucker. During the last few years of her life Miles turned to the Catholic Church and gave up her singing career. More than half a dozen CDs of Lizzie Miles are currently available.

Miller, J. D. (1922–1996) *songwriter and record producer*

J. D. Miller was the father of swamp rock, recording LONESOME SUNDOWN, LIGHTNIN' SLIM, LAZY LESTER, and SLIM HARPO at his Crowley, LOUISIANA, studio. He entered the music business as a record store owner, built his studio, then leased his recordings to Excello Records in Nashville. Miller was also a songwriter who wrote many songs for his artists.

Oddly, for someone so involved with the blues and black artists, Miller also ran Rebel Records, a racist and pro-segregation label that operated out of his studio.

minstrel shows

The early minstrel shows were based on observations by white actors of African American musicians and dancers. The most famous of these early characterizations was Thomas D. Rice's depiction of a slave "jumping Jim Crow." Rice had seen an old black slave whose shoulder and left leg were deformed, and Rice's depiction of the old man's performances created a sensation on the NEW YORK stage in 1832. This led to a proliferation of minstrel companies, some of which enjoyed lengthy runs in urban theaters, particularly Ordaway's Aeolian Group in Boston, and E. P. Christy's Minstrels in New York City.

The early minstrels were white men who blackened their faces to look like African Americans. They caricatured African-American behavior through "comedic" stereotypes, exaggerating black singing, dancing, and playing styles. The format of the shows included stand-up comedy, with a character called the interlocutor. The music consisted of FIDDLE and/or BANJO players. Although many of the songs depicted a fun-loving happy slave, some anti-slavery sentiments appeared in minstrel songs, even before 1850.

Inevitably black entertainers grasped a possible economic opportunity, and black minstrel companies began to appear in the 1850s. Many of the black companies were white-owned. By the 1870s some of these companies, like Callender's Colored Minstrels, had become so popular that they sent out three different touring companies under the same name in 1882.

The most prolific black songwriter of the minstrel era was James Bland, who wrote "Carry Me Back to Old Virginny," "In the Evening by the Moonlight," and over 700 other songs. Minstrel shows offered a decent career option to black performers, and according to Robert C. Toll, in his book *Blacking Up: The Minstrel Show in Nineteenth Century America,* by 1882 black minstrels made "pretty good salaries." The black shows added religious songs to the minstrel show repertoire in the late 1870s, and these songs were performed in a relatively informal style, similarly to the way they were performed in rural African-American communities. This contrasted with the formal, highly-arranged performances of these songs by such

groups as the Fisk Jubilee Singers. Most black minstrels did not wear burnt cork, but their style of performance and the script of the shows was quite similar to the material presented by the white minstrel companies.

By the 1870s minstrel show songs presented a sort of nostalgic, pastoral image of the African American. Some songs utilized formats similar to traditional spirituals, and some involved pleas for racial tolerance, like Frank Howard's "Pass Down de Centre," written in 1879. This song contained the lyrics:

Times are hard for de darkie,
Way down in Tennessee;
Mister Ku Klux can't you let me be.

During the 1880s and 1890s numerous songs used the derogatory racist term "coon" to refer to African Americans, and blacks were depicted as mildly dangerous razor-toting, watermelon-eating clowns. Ernest Hogan, who was an African American, wrote a song called "All Coons Look Alike to Me" in 1896. This song was quite popular and was instrumental in perpetuating such unfortunate stereotypes. The song was sufficiently obnoxious that if a white person whistled it in the presence of blacks, it was considered a serious insult and could lead to trouble. Other black composers, like J. Rosamund Johnson and his brother James Weldon Johnson, wrote less obnoxious songs, but even some of those reinforced racial stereotypes. One example was "Underneath the Bamboo Tree," which had a fake African Zulu motif.

By the 1890s the popularity of the minstrel companies had declined, but the goofy image of the happy colored man, the so-called Black Sambo image, remained. For many years it remained the way that Hollywood depicted African Americans in the movies. A few minstrel shows continued to tour until World War II.

If the minstrel show created unfortunate stereotypes of African Americans, it still performed a positive function in showing that the black entertainer was a creative artist who had instrumental, vocal, and dancing talent. Minstrels even introduced the notion of black performers as capable entertainers. In the period 1890–1915 black entertainers could be found performing in black theaters all over the country, even on the Broadway stage. Performer and producer Billy McClain produced a show called *Black America,* with a cast of over 500 performers. They played in Ambrose Park in Brooklyn, New York, in 1895. Theater company owners and performers Bob Cole and J. Rosamund Johnson wrote over 150 songs for more than a dozen shows, and piano wizard Eubie Blake and his writing partner Noble Sissle wrote a number of successful shows, such as *Shuffle Along.* By 1922, 360 black theaters employed 600 acts.

The shows of the late 19th century used some of the "coon" stereotypes from the minstrel era, but they included all sorts of other material, such as nonsense songs, humorous sketches, and commentaries on the battle between the sexes. They also included ethnic stereotypes about other groups. This was a common device in songs and shows of the late 19th and early 20th centuries, and Irish, Italians, German, and Jews were among the groups lampooned. Nevertheless, the coon image was the most prevalent one, and over 600 coon songs were written during the period 1895–1900.

Mississippi

Of all the places where the blues represented an important part of African-American culture, Mississippi has the most museums and grave sites and in general seems to have devoted more attention to celebrating the blues as an art form. With a history as the nation's most racially oppressive environment, there is a certain irony to the blues being turned into a tourist attraction by a society that in the past was contemptuous of anything African-American. A recent issue of *Living Blues* contained a full-page letter-advertisement from Ross Barbour, the governor of Mississippi. The letter was designed to welcome "blues tourists." A group known as the

Mississippi Blues Highway Association has even begun to place signs on prominent blues sites that read "MS Delta Blues Trail."

AVALON
The burial place of songster MISSISSIPPI JOHN HURT, who was rediscovered in 1963 through his recording "Avalon Blues," which mentioned that Avalon was his home. Hurt's house was moved from its original site and has been restored and reopened as a museum.

BENTONIA
Located at the southern tip of the Delta, Bentonia was the home of SKIP JAMES, who had a unique vocal and instrumental style that was not widely influential but survived because of his rediscovery during the 1960s and through the performances of JACK OWENS. Owens claims to have taught James, but another guitarist, Henry Stuckey, apparently influenced both of them. Although Bentonia is in the Delta, Bentonia blues is fingerpicked on the guitar and utilizes a light falsetto vocal style. It does not sound anything like the classic Delta blues. It is interesting to speculate on how many other pockets of local music style that existed in the Delta have been lost because they were never recorded.

CLARKSDALE
Clarksdale was the place where ALAN LOMAX and folklorist John Work came in 1941–42 on the blues collecting trip that turned up a young MUDDY WATERS. The town was also the birthplace for R&B artist-producer IKE TURNER and gospel-pop-soul singer Sam Cooke. Delta blues artists Wade Walton, Henry "Son" Sims, and Jackie Brenston, who made the "Rocket 88" record that many regard as the first rock and roll record, are all buried here. The hospital room where BESSIE SMITH died after her tragic automobile accident is now part of the Riverside Hotel. There are numerous nightclubs, record shops, and recording studios in town, but the most important site is the Delta Blues Museum.

The museum contains a variety of blues exhibits, and it is the home of the famous Muddywood guitar, an instrument commissioned by rock band ZZ Top and made out of wood that came from Waters's house in Mississippi. Various works of art and blues memorabilia are housed here, and the museum also sponsors an arts and education program. In this program, various veteran Clarksdale blues musicians teach classes to educate young people about the history and traditions of the Delta blues.

CLEVELAND
W. C. HANDY was playing a dance in Cleveland in 1905 when he discovered during an intermission for his band that the audience was more enthusiastic in supporting a ragged string band with generous tips than in paying attention to his well-rehearsed band. This celebrated incident led Handy to turn to the blues as a source of inspiration for his musical compositions.

Halfway between Cleveland and Ruleville is Dockery's Plantation, home of Delta blues pioneer Charley Patton. Here Patton's students Son House and Howlin' Wolf studied with him.

North of Cleveland is the famous Parchman Penitentiary. Among the blues artists who spent time in jail at Parchman farm were SON HOUSE, SONNY BOY WILLIAMSON, and BUKKA WHITE. Mississippi-born white jazz and blues artist MOSE ALLISON wrote a well-known song about Parchman Farm that starts with the lyric, "I'm standin' here on Number 9, and all I did was drink my wine."

FRIARS POINT
The North Delta Museum here has a small display devoted to Robert Johnson.

GREENVILLE
Greenville has a Blues Walk of Fame, which honors a number of blues musicians with stones carved in the sidewalk. Some of the musicians honored include B. B. KING and Sam Chatmon, and other stones are planned for CHARLEY PATTON, BO CARTER, Sam and Lonnie Chatmon, and WALTER VINSON.

Many blues artists have lived in Greenville, including JIMMY REED, Johnny and Edgar Winter, LITTLE MILTON, SONNY BOY WILLIAMSON II, and Willie Nix.

GREENWOOD
ROBERT JOHNSON died here, and FURRY LEWIS, GUITAR SLIM, Tommy McLennan, ROBERT PETWAY, and HUBERT SUMLIN all lived in the area. Sylvester Hoover offers Delta Blues Legend Tours that allow the visitor to trace Johnson's footsteps through the back streets and juke joints of Greenwood.

Steve LaVere, who administers Johnson's estate, bought a house in Greenwood and has opened the Greenwood Blues Heritage Museum and Gallery. The museum includes his collection of Robert Johnson artifacts. Another museum located in Greenwood is the Delta Gallery Blues Museum.

HOLLY RIDGE
The grave of CHARLEY PATTON, marked with a headstone mostly financed by rock star John Fogerty, of Creedence Clearwater Revival, is located here.

INDIANOLA
Birthplace of blues superstars ALBERT and B. B. KING (they were not related to each other.) B. B.'s handprints and footprints are placed in cement, and there is a street named after him. B. B. makes an annual trip to Mississippi to play at a festival remembering civil rights leader Medgar Evers and plays at a small club here called the Club Ebony. He also gives a free concert in Fletcher Park on this pilgrimage.

JACKSON
Farish Street was the location for H. C. Speir's record shop, where he auditioned talent. Speir was the catalyst for recording a number of major Delta musicians, including ROBERT JOHNSON, Charley Patton, Skip James, and TOMMY JOHNSON, and for their receiving recording contracts. Some of the musicians who lived in Jackson include Tommy Johnson, Skip James, the MISSISSIPPI SHEIKS, Otis Spann, Sonny Boy Williamson II (Rice Miller),

ELMORE JAMES, and Sam Myers. Tommy Johnson and ISHMON BRACEY are buried here, and Tommy Johnson is buried in nearby Crystal Springs. Also on Farish Street was LILLIAN MCMURRY's furniture store and record shop, and later the offices of her record label, Trumpet, which recorded Elmore James's "Dust My Broom."

Johnny Vincent founded rhythm and blues label Ace Records here in 1954.

Blues researcher Gayle Dean Wardlow is establishing a Farish Street Blues Museum, and the city of Jackson has signed a long-term lease with Performa Entertainment, the group that renovated Memphis's Beale Street. The plan is to develop retail, restaurant, and entertainment space to promote the blues as a tourist attraction, just as this group has done with Beale Street. Part of the plan is the renovation of the Alamo Theater and the development of a regular blues concert series.

Jackson is the home of Malaco Records, a company that has been very successful in marketing soul-blues records to a black audience. Some of their most successful artists include Dorothy Moore and Z. Z. HILL, and they have also picked up older artists, including BOBBY "BLUE" BLAND, Denise La Salle, Tyrone Davis, Johnny Taylor, and LITTLE MILTON, who had been abandoned by their previous labels.

MERIDIAN

Meridian's favorite son was blues yodeler JIMMIE RODGERS. The Jimmie Rodgers Museum honors him, and his gravesite is nearby. An annual music festival pays tribute to him during the first week of May, and many country music stars usually come down to perform at it.

MORGAN CITY

No one is entirely certain where Robert Johnson is buried, but there is a monument here at the Mt. Zion M. B. Church, with inscriptions on all four sides. Columbia Records donated the funds for the monument, presumably partly as a result of the unexpectedly heavy sales of its Robert Johnson

reissue boxed set. There were at least two Zion churches at the time of Johnson's death, and some believe that the tombstone is in the wrong one. Although Johnson's birth certificate specifies the church as his burial site, some who knew Johnson claim that his body was moved to another cemetery, at the Payne Chapel M. B. Church in Quito. There is another Johnson tombstone at that site. Some say Johnson died behind the Three Forks Store, which is believed to have also been located near Quito.

OXFORD

The University of Mississippi is located in Oxford, in northern Mississippi. It is the publisher of *Living Blues,* the most significant periodical devoted exclusively to the blues. The university also boasts a blues archive, with over 50,000 recordings, and many photos, posters, and magazines. The archive is housed in the J. D. Williams Library. The university also operates a press that in recent years has published a number of books about the blues. Twelve miles south of Oxford in Water Valley, Fat Possum Records operates a recording studio in its offices.

ROBBINSVILLE

A large repository of blues memorabilia can be found at the Blues & Legends Hall of Fame Museum.

SENATOBIA

This area is the center of northern Mississippi fife and drum music that focused around the late Sid Hemphill, Napoleon Strickland, OTHA TURNER, Ed Lonnie, and Cag Young. Their traditions are maintained by the Rising Star Fife & Drum Band. The late guitarist and singer Fred McDowell also lived in this area.

TUNICA

Yet another museum offers a tribute to local residents one-man band Dr. Ross and harmonica great James Cotton.

TUTWILER

In 1903 W. C. HANDY heard a black man playing guitar with a knife at the railroad station here. He was singing about going where the southern crosses the yellow dog (the Yazoo & Mississippi Valley Railroads.) This incident made an unforgettable impression on Handy, which he recounted in his autobiography, *W. C. Handy: Father of the Blues.*

WALLS

MEMPHIS MINNIE grew up here, and she is buried at the New Hope Baptist Church Cemetery. In nearby Pritchard is the grave of her first husband, guitarist WILLIE BROWN. Willie Brown and HOWLIN' WOLF both lived on nearby plantations.

WEST POINT

Howlin' Wolf (Chester Burnett) was born here. A museum in his honor is planned as a separate building in the West Point/Clay County Museum.

Mississippi Sheiks

The Chatmon family had 11 brothers and sisters and a father, all of whom played music in their native MISSISSIPPI in the early 1900's. The Sheiks grew out of their family band, and their recordings featured fiddler Lonnie Chatmon and guitarist WALTER VINSON, an adopted brother. Sam Chatmon and Bo Carter, whose real name was Armenter Chatmon, sometimes participated. In 1930 the Sheiks recorded "Sittin' on Top of the World," which was their big hit song. In addition to that successful recording, the song was later recorded by HOWLIN' WOLF, CREAM, the Grateful Dead, and BOB DYLAN, among others. The band had a huge repertoire that included pop songs, blues, rags, and anything else their audience wanted to hear.

The Sheiks were popular enough to cut almost 100 songs between 1927 and 1936. They briefly reunited after World War II, and Vinson made recordings under his own name after the Sheiks broke up.

Missouri

KANSAS CITY

During the years of the Great Depression (1929–40) Kansas City was a great town for working musicians. Thanks to a politician named Tom Pendergast, the city was filled with bars, many of them open all night. There were over 160 jazz clubs and music venues in town, and many of the clubs featured blues shouters like JIMMY RUSHING and JOE TURNER. Julia Lee was another popular singer during that time, singing music that was a blend of swing, blues, and novelty tunes. Rushing and Turner could rock a club without the benefit of a microphone. Musicians played music all night and there were "breakfast shows," early-morning shows complete with music. In 1938 Pendergast was indicted and convicted by the federal government on charges of income tax evasion. A reform political movement developed, the clubs started to close down, and the musicians left town.

Jay McShann is a veteran bandleader from that period. In recent years he has recorded and toured as a solo act, singing the blues and playing piano.

ST. LOUIS

St. Louis is most famous musically for its role as the birthplace, or at least one of the centers, of ragtime music. Two of the most popular blues songs, "Stackolee" and "Frankie and Johnny," were supposedly based on events that occurred in St. Louis. A number of blues artists stayed here either en route to or from Chicago, and Henry Townsend lives there to this day. LONNIE JOHNSON lived in the city for some years, as did Big Joe Williams and PEETIE "The Devil's Son-in Law" WHEATSTRAW. Rock and roll star CHUCK BERRY is originally from St. Louis, and still lives there. Tina Turner is a native daughter, and she and her ex-husband Ike lived in the city when they were first married. It is possible to visit the house of ragtime composer Scott Joplin. The building is now part of the Missouri State Parks system.

A recent article in the magazine *Music & Sound Retailer* stated that there are currently more than 60 blues clubs in the area. Many of them are across the river in East St. Louis, Illinois. That town is almost entirely populated by African Americans.

Mo', Keb (Kevin Moore) (b. 1951) *songwriter and entertainer*

'Keb Mo' is a contemporary blues entertainer, story-teller, and songwriter who sings and plays guitar, SLIDE GUITAR, and BANJO. He has a background in R&B music from his younger days, and he gradually became fascinated by the blues. In 1990 he played the role of a bluesman in the film *Rabbit Foot,* and later he portrayed blues guitarist and performer ROBERT JOHNSON in the documentary video *Can't You Hear the Wind Howl?* Keb is an active songwriter who writes much of the material that he performs and records. He has a pop music side to him and has cowritten songs with jazz performer Bobby McFerrin and singer-songwriter Melissa Manchester. Keb Mo' has won two Grammy Awards.

Montgomery, Little Brother (Eurreal Montgomery) (1906–1985) *pianist*

Little Brother Montgomery was a versatile PIANO player who played Dixieland jazz and blues equally well. He also played boogie-woogie and ragtime, and could play hymns and any sort of pop music as well. Montgomery learned how to play at his father's club in Kent, LOUISIANA. He played with a New Orleans jazz band at the age of 18, then moved to CHICAGO in 1928. He played Chicago rent parties and began his recording career in 1930. Montgomery then split his time between Chicago and the South. In addition to his own recordings he accompanied classic blues singer SIPPIE WALLACE and other singers.

The last 40 years of his life were spent in Chicago, where he played clubs, toured at festivals, and did session work for such musicians as OTIS RUSH and Magic Sam. He started his own record label with his second wife. During his lifetime he made 30 albums, nine of them still available. His songs "Vicksburg Blues" and "No Special Rider" have become blues standards.

Mooney, John (b. 1955) *guitarist*

John Mooney, from Rochester, New York, was inspired to take up the blues because he met SON HOUSE there. This was his introduction to MISSISSIPPI blues, and he accompanied House on several occasions. By 1976 Mooney had moved to New Orleans, where he integrated that tradition into his music. Starting out as an acoustic musician, Mooney became the leader of a blues-rock band, playing ELECTRIC GUITAR.

Moore, Whistlin' Alex (1899–1989) *blues pianist*

One of the founders of TEXAS blues PIANO, Whistlin' Alex Moore also played boogie-woogie and ragtime. He made a few recordings in 1929 and 1937, and in 1960 he recorded for the ARHOOLIE label. This enabled him to tour Europe. In 1987 he received a Lifetime Achievement Award from the National Endowment for the Arts. His final recording was made in 1988, at the age of 89. He was still playing and singing the Texas blues at that late date.

Morton, Jelly Roll (Ferdinand Joseph Morton) (1890–1941) *songwriter, composer, and performer*

One of the biggest figures in jazz, Jelly Roll Morton's work crossed over into pop music, and blues. ALAN LOMAX recorded Morton in an extensive series of sessions for the Library of Congress. On these recordings pianist Morton played and occasionally sang some blues and reminisced about the New Orleans jazz scene. Morton was an extremely talented songwriter and composer, who was fond of claiming, "I invented jazz." Lomax wrote an informative biography of Morton.

Moss, Buddy (Eugene Moss) (1914–1984)
harmonicist and guitarist

Buddy Moss was never able to achieve the level of success that his talent merited. As a child he taught himself to play HARMONICA, and he played at local parties in Augusta, Georgia. Moss then worked on the streets of Atlanta, where he met CURLEY WEAVER and BARBECUE BOB. At the age of 16 he recorded with their group, the Georgia Cotton Pickers.

Barbecue Bob helped Moss learn to play the guitar, and later Moss performed with BLIND WILLIE McTELL. From 1933 until 1935 Moss did several recording sessions, and played with JOSH WHITE on the streets of Atlanta. Moss was arrested in 1935, accused of murdering his wife. He denied this and was finally paroled in 1940. By that time BLIND BOY FULLER had pretty much surpassed Moss's popularity, but Fuller died in 1941, and Moss went to NEW YORK to record with BROWNIE McGHEE and SONNY TERRY. These sessions did not prove successful for Moss, and he went back to performing, first in North Carolina and then in Atlanta. He often played with his old friend Curley Weaver.

Buddy Moss was rediscovered in 1965 during the blues revival. He recorded a little and performed at several folk festivals, but his career was not destined to take off again.

Muldaur, Geoff (b. 1945) *vocalist and musician*

Geoff Muldaur is a bit of a mystery man in blues history. He is well known to his fellow musicians, but his name does not appear in any of the half dozen books that list blues recordings, except for his work with his ex-wife Maria. Muldaur was a member of the Jim Kweskin Jug Band, one of the important blues revivalist groups of the 1960s, playing MANDOLIN, and guitar and singing. He later played in one of PAUL BUTTERFIELD's various bands. In midcareer he went to the Berklee College of Music in Boston and got a degree in arranging—the art of writing music for various instruments. He left the music field during the 1980s, but returned, stronger than ever, in the 1990s. Since that time he has made

a number of solo records, the latest one being an album that contains his arrangements of legendary trumpet player Bix Beiderbecke's piano pieces.

Muldaur is a unique artist, one of the few white blues artists with his own vocal sound. Richard Thompson, the superb British songwriter, singer, and guitarist, has said "there are only three white blues singers; Geoff Muldaur is at least two of them." Muldaur has a very light, high vocal sound that bears a slight resemblance to the work of SKIP JAMES.

Muldaur, Maria (Maria D'Amato) (b. 1943)
singer

Maria Muldaur was a member of NEW YORK's Even Dozen Jug Band and of Jim Kweskin's Boston-based group, the Jim Kweskin Jug Band. While singing with Kweskin she married GEOFF MULDAUR, and after the Kweskin band broke up, the two of them performed together. During the 1970s she had a major pop hit with the quirky "Midnight at the Oasis," something totally unrelated to her previous work. During the 1980s she became a born-again Christian but returned to the blues and to touring during the 1990s.

Murphy, Matt "Guitar" (b. 1929) *guitarist*

MISSISSIPPI-born Matt Murphy moved to MEMPHIS in the 1940s. He played with pianist Memphis Slim during the 1950s, and, later, with HARMONICA player JAMES COTTON. He recorded as a guitarist for CHESS RECORDS during the late 1950s, playing on records by CHUCK BERRY, OTIS RUSH, and ETTA JAMES. Although Murphy has done little recording as a bandleader, he did appear in the *Blues Brothers* movie as a band member and played on the related records.

See also LEONARD CHESS.

music business and the blues

In the early days of the blues, at the turn of the 20th century, an artist's financial horizons were limited. Many musicians played on the streets for tips, while others were paid small amounts for performing at juke joints, barrelhouses, rent parties, bars, or restaurants. Other performing income came from touring with medicine shows and in musical reviews that played in urban theaters. Medicine shows were put together with the object of selling patent medicines of dubious use that claimed to cure various illnesses or afflictions. The income from theater shows varied greatly, depending upon whether the performer headlined the show, as MA RAINEY did, or was hired by the producer of the show. The most enterprising artists not only headlined but owned their own shows, and traveled in private railroad cars. Naturally the artists who sold the most records, like BESSIE SMITH, commanded the most money in personal appearances.

Over the years talent agents and managers developed as intermediaries between the artist and owners of nightclubs or promoters of concerts. These intermediaries took a percentage of the artist's income, in return for which they fulfilled various business functions for the artist. Booking agencies acted as an employment service, obtaining jobs for the artists, while another group, called personal managers, acted as overseers of an artist's entire career. Managers negotiated deals with record companies, made sure that booking agencies were doing a good job for the artist, and sought other financial and career opportunities for the artists whom they represented; for example, both B. B. KING and RAY CHARLES filmed a fair number of television commercials for various products.

When British rock bands started to sell millions of records, beginning in the 1960s, a certain amount of success spilled over to blues artists. Some of this income came from writing songs, and some of it represented an increased demand for blues artists to tour in the United States and also in Europe and Asia. The 1990 reissue of Delta blues artist ROBERT JOHNSON was enormously successful, selling something like two million copies to date. By the beginning of the 21st century, the demand for blues had created a specific musical niche of some importance. The blues were featured at major music festivals, drawing hundreds of thousands of people, and a group of clubs called the House of Blues opened in a number of American cities in the 1990s, including LOS ANGELES, Las Vegas, New Orleans, and CHICAGO. The clubs featured a slick version of the blues, selling sweatshirts and old guitars, and presenting various kinds of music, including the blues.

Hollywood jumped into the scene in the early 2000s when director and producer Martin Scorsese produced a series of documentaries about the blues, and acted as executive producer of a number of CDs of artists who were featured in the videos. The series in turn led to a book about the blues. National Public Radio (NPR) produced a radio series about the blues, and dozens of blues CDs were reissued, other videos were produced and marketed, and dozens of books about the blues were published.

Much of the income generated from all these events went to Hollywood producers and directors, record companies, and nightclub owners. As has always seemed to be the case, outside of a few superstars like B. B. King, the income that came to blues artists was a much more diluted stream. A closer examination of how and when the artist gets paid may clarify this situation.

Apart from income generated by actual performances, artists earn royalties from two primary sources. One is the royalties that come from performing on recordings, and the other is from songwriting. Artists who do not write songs receive income only from record royalties.

MUSIC PUBLISHING

The literal meaning of the words "music publishing" is the actual printing of sheet music. Up until the mid-20th century, it was the printing of sheet music that constituted the most important financial aspect of songwriting. The biggest sheet music hits, like recorded hit songs today, could sell millions of copies.

The royalties from sheet music sales went to the music publisher, and the publisher had a contract with the songwriter, paying the songwriter a portion of these proceeds. Another source of income for songwriters and publishers came from the sales of records. This income was two cents a copy, to be shared between the publisher and the songwriter. This amount was stipulated in the copyright act of 1909, which remained in effect through 1977.

For these royalties to be generated a song had to be copyrighted. Copies of a lead sheet were sent to the Copyright Office in Washington, D.C. A lead sheet consisted of the melody line of the song along with the chord symbols and lyrics of the song.

Several problems quickly surfaced in the way blues songs were copyrighted. Many of the verses of early blues songs were basically folk song lyrics. Their original author or authors were unknown, and the songs were widely circulated by word of mouth, and from one musician to another. It was not unusual for different folk-blues singers of the 1920s and 1930s to sing songs that contained lyrics found in songs that had been previously recorded by other artists, or themselves, and copyrighted by other music publishers. The problem was also aggravated by the fact that blues melodies tended to derive similarly from a common stock, and were often similar to one another. Furthermore, many of the early blues were recorded without songwriting credits listed. If there were no credits on a record, and another artist recorded the same song, the second artist, or his music publisher, might copyright the song. Although the second artist had not written the song, the attitude that prevailed was that since the song had folk roots or origins anyway, the second company might as well attempt to derive some revenue from it.

Unfortunately it was quite common for record companies to induce songwriters to give up their songwriting royalties by either paying them very small sums or simply signing away the rights. Songwriting royalties have increased with the years and this practice has become particularly damaging to the early songwriters.

When two companies both claim to own the copyright of a song, two elements determine whether one song is a copy of the other one. First, similarity must be established between the two songs. If the matter comes to trial, trained musicians are brought in to establish similarities in the melody or lyrics. However, similarity alone is not enough to win the lawsuit. The publisher must also prove that the other publisher had access to the original version of the song. Access can be proven by establishing that the second songwriter attended a performance where the first writer sang the song, by the fact that there was radio play of a song in the area where the second writer lived, that the two had mutual friends or acquaintances who might have performed the song or played a recording of it, or any other logical form of access. An example of the sort of conflict over authorship of a song that could and did develop was "Black Snake Moan." Both VICTORIA SPIVEY and BLIND LEMON JEFFERSON claimed to have composed the song. Another example is the song "Milk Cow Blues," which was copyrighted by a dozen different artists. The title itself of a song cannot be copyrighted. There are dozens of songs in the Copyright Office with the title "I Love You," for example.

During the 1920s none of this appeared to be terribly significant, because record sales were usually comparatively small (a 5,000–10,000 sale of a record was considered reasonable), and so the amount involved was not great. However, when American folksingers and, even more important, British rock stars started recording old blues songs in the 1960s, the sums involved greatly escalated. Artists like CREAM, the ROLLING STONES, and the Beatles sold millions of records, so a considerable amount of revenue was generated from the rights to those songs. These artists and their record companies varied in their approach to the question of songwriting credits. Over the years ERIC CLAPTON developed a particularly honorable reputation for crediting original songwriters and making sure they received the proper credits and royalties. On the other hand, LED ZEPPELIN listed themselves as cowriters on MEMPHIS MINNIE's "When the Levee Breaks," and they gave no credit to WILLIE DIXON for revamping his work into their huge radio hit "Whole Lotta Love."

When the new copyright law took effect in 1978, royalties on record sales were raised to 2.75 cents, and gradually increased, so that in 2004 they were up to 8.5 cents, and in 2006 they will increase to 9.1 cents. Some of the CD blues reissues, notably the 2 million–selling Robert Johnson boxed set, brought in a great deal of revenue to the company. Blues researcher Steve La Vere negotiated the rights to the songs with Johnson's estate and received considerable income from Johnson's recorded legacy.

Starting in the 1980s record companies began to revolt against paying full royalties to music publishers on the sale of recordings. They created a new monetary model, called controlled composition clauses. Under these clauses, a record company would arbitrarily limit the amount of money that it would pay to music publishers on the sale of records. Part of the reason for this new development was the arrival of CDs. A compact disc could have as many as 70 minutes of music, which might include 25 songs or more. At an eight-cent royalty this would cost the record company two dollars an album, while a 10-song long-playing record would cost the company only 80 cents. Record companies did not bother to mention that long-playing records sold for prices like $5.98, while compact disc were priced at $15–$20. Controlled composition clauses might state that the record company would pay a specified rate to music publishers for an album, regardless of how many songs were on the album. The record companies also started to negotiate what was called a 3/4 rate. This reduced their cost for each song by 25 percent. An eight-cent royalty then became a six-cent royalty.

Other songwriting and music publishing royalties come from songs played on the radio and used on television. Radio and television play comes under the category of performing rights, and these rights are administered in the United States by three organizations, the American Society of Composers, Authors and Publishers (ASCAP), Broadcast Music, Inc. (BMI), and SESAC. The three organizations use various sampling techniques, not unlike those used in political polling, and television networks report all music used on their shows. Writers and publishers are paid a variety of fees based on the number of times a song is played on the radio, how many times it is used in a television show, and so on. Performance income is highest when a song crosses over from one style of music (and radio station) to another. A crossover blues song, like ROBERT CRAY's "Because of Me," might start out being played on rhythm and blues stations and blues shows, but it generates the most income when it also achieves airplay on pop-rock radio.

When a song is used in a movie, the amount paid for the publishing rights is negotiable. It will depend partly upon whether the song is used one or more times in the film, and whether the song is used as an integral part of the film or as background music. Fees for all the songs in the Blues Brothers' movies, for example, had to be negotiated between the music publishers involved and the films' producers. In the United States music publishers and songwriters do not receive royalties for films that play in movie theaters. However, when the movies appear on television, then royalties are paid. This is not true in European countries, where royalties are paid for the use of songs in movie theaters.

Other income can be derived from the use of songs in commercials, any reprints of a song, telephone ring tones, greeting cards, and the like. These rates are highly negotiable. K. C. Douglas's song "Mercury Blues," has been used as a Ford truck commercial, sung by country star Alan Jackson. The commercial has generated a good deal of income for Douglas's estate and for the publisher, CHRIS STRACHWITZ of ARHOOLIE RECORDS. Sheet music remains a source of income, although its importance is nothing like it was in 1925, when sheet music for a hit song sold as many as hundreds of thousands copies. Any reprints of a song in collections of lyrics, books, or magazines also generate income to the songwriter and music publisher.

Songs used in plays receive a totally different form of payment. These rights are known as grand rights. The author of the play (known as the book), the composer, and the lyricist all split a percentage of the gross receipts of the play, usually 6 percent. (On Broadway the lyricist and composer are generally two different people, with a few exceptions, like Stephen Sondheim. Some lyricists also write the book.) If a play runs for a long time, this can generate an enormous amount of income. When the play goes on a road tour, or when high schools, colleges, or dinner theaters perform it, fees must be negotiated that go to the same three creative groups. Outside of a few plays like *Nothing But the Blues* or *Love, Janis,* not too many blues songs get to Broadway, although the 1990s saw a number of shows that celebrated rhythm and blues artists and songwriters.

One myth widely circulated among musicians is that it is permissible to "borrow" a small portion of a tune, such as four bars or fewer. There is nothing in the copyright law that suggests that this is true. The key concept is "substantial similarity," and that might stem from a very short repeated musical or lyric phrase in a song. Another unfortunate myth is that a songwriter can copyright a song by mailing it to him- or herself. This is usually called a "poor man's copyright," or an "Oklahoma copyright," although no one seems to know where these terms originated. A mail copyright will not hold up in a court of law, because it is considered that the writer might have steamed open an envelope and replaced it with another one, actually sent at a later date. A valid copyright can be established only by registering a song with the Library of Congress in Washington, D.C. This can be done by sending a copy of the melody and lyrics, written out in music notation, or by sending a taped copy of the song. The importance of registering a copyright is that although the very act of writing a song establishes ownership, proving authorship at a particular time is a trickier business. Registration also entitles the writer to extensive damages in addition to any royalties due, if the writer can prove that someone has infringed the original copyright. The current fee to copyright a song or collection of songs is $30, as the U.S. copyright office charges the fee for each submission.

Detailed information about songwriting and music publishing income is found in several books, especially Jeffrey and Todd Brabec's *Music, Money And Success,* published by Schirmer Trade Books.

RECORD ROYALTIES
Very few recording artists would record today without a contract that guarantees them royalties based on record sales. Typically in the 21st century these royalties might start at 10–12 percent of the retail selling price of a record. Even in the early days of the record business, royalties were not unknown. Enrico Caruso, for example, one of the early classical recording artists, received royalties, and his estate continued to receive them after his death.

Blues artists, and country music artists as well, were considered to be in a different category. In some instances they were never offered royalties. In other cases they were told to choose between royalty deals and fees paid for each song recorded. Bessie Smith, for example, started her recording career with her record company paying her $125 for each song that she recorded. When her records sold in the hundreds of thousands, the rate was changed to $200 a side. She never received royalties for any of her recorded performances. The situation was also complicated by the fact that Frank Walker, who produced her records, was also her manager. If Smith had used an entertainment attorney, it is doubtful that he would have allowed her to sign such a contract, because Walker's dual role—representing her and the record company—was a clear conflict of interest. Neither Smith nor her estate received artist royalties for her recordings, for the long-playing or the CD reissues that appeared years later.

Some blues singers accept flat fees rather than royalties, for several reasons. First, they did not think that their records would sell that well. Second, they did not trust the white-owned record companies to pay them royalties. Finally, they relied on the notion that a bird in the hand was worth two in the bush, believing that receiving cash enabled them to use the money immediately, while a royalty agreement meant that they would have to wait for months until the record was actually issued, and the sales receipts were accounted for.

A further impediment to artists' receiving royalties was that often the person at the record company who signed the artist had that artist sign over her royalties to the record company executive. This was particularly significant with publishing rights, because royalties for songwriting can come not only from the artist's performances but from future performances by other artists.

Blues artists also fought the system in a less legal or ethical way. Artists like JOHN LEE HOOKER recorded for numerous record companies, using pseudonyms. They could then receive multiple cash payments. In many cases the artists made little or no attempt to disguise their identities, and often the record companies were well aware that they had no legal right to record the artists.

Another example of this process was jazz composer-pianist Fats Waller's habit of making the rounds of NEW YORK music publishing companies and selling the same song on a given day to several different companies. He then could obtain three or four advances from the various companies for the identical song.

Another reason why recording artists often ended up receiving no royalties, even if the contract specified that they would get such payments, was that record company contracts became increasingly complicated (120-page recording contracts are not uncommon today). The contracts contain many deductions from the actual royalty percentages; for example, the record company might agree to pay a royalty of 10 percent of the retail selling price of a record, a fairly typical amount today. Before the artist receives any royalties, the expenses of the record company must be met. The cost of using musical arrangers, studio musicians, and the rental costs for the use of the studio are all part of these charges. So are any monetary advances given to artists. These days the deductions also usually include 50 percent of the cost of making any videos. If independent record promoters are hired, these costs also come out of the artist's royalties, as do the

monies paid to record producers. Other deductions from the artist's royalties include breakage fees, even though the era of breakable 78 rpm records is long gone, and lower royalties on the sale of compact discs. The latter custom dates from the late 1980s, when all record companies spent considerable amounts of money building CD factories. The artist is also charged a packaging fee, which has to do with the creation of album artwork, and whatever form of packaging that the album is placed in, like a CD jewel box.

Finally, record companies created another contractual monster, called cross collateralization, which means that the charges for one record are deducted from the income from the next record; for example, if an album cost $50,000 to produce, and the earnings from the sales of the album were $35,000, the $15,000 deficit is charged against the artist's next recording. Since a typical recording contract specifies the delivery of five to seven albums, the artist may well go through the entire contract period without earning any actual royalty income, despite the fact that the payment of royalties is specified in the contract.

Over the years, the music industry has become aware that record companies have not always paid royalties that are due in a timely or accurate way, particularly to blues and rhythm and blues artists. The matter came to a head in 1987 when rhythm and blues artist RUTH BROWN met a corporate lawyer named Howell Begle at a dinner. Begle was a long-time Brown fan, from the days of her many hit recordings for ATLANTIC RECORDS during the 1950s. He noticed that Brown was somewhat shabbily dressed and did not appear to be in good health. Further conversation revealed that she had never received any royalties from Atlantic Records, a highly regarded rhythm and blues record company that had come under the ownership of the Warner Brothers Record conglomerate. Begle then undertook an extensive investigation of why Brown had never received royalties, and he came to represent an additional 16 artists who had recorded for Atlantic. After considerable stalling and resistance on the part of the company, Atlantic eventually allowed him to inspect their books, where he discovered that, in some instances, they did not even have written records of Brown's sales.

Eventually Begle got Atlantic to contribute to an organization called the Rhythm & Blues Foundation, which provides financial aid to sick or impoverished musicians. The initial funding of the organization came from a $1.5 million contribution from Atlantic, followed by monies contributed by other major labels. Atlantic then "zeroed out" the royalty accounts of the early rhythm and blues artists. They paid the artists whom Begle represented an undisclosed settlement, removed any monies that the artists owed to the company from their business ledgers, and agreed to pay the artists royalties on any new reissue projects. Blues singer-songwriter BONNIE RAITT was then at the peak of her popularity, and she induced EMI, the parent company of Capitol Records, to tear up all their contracts with artists dated before 1970, and to agree to pay these artists a 10 percent of retail selling price royalty on any reissues. This was an important step because Capitol had acquired the catalogs of other companies, such as Aladdin, that had recorded numerous blues and rhythm and blues artists during the 1950s and 1960s. Universal Records agreed to a similar procedure with any of the companies that they acquired but, oddly, did not agree to pay royalties to the artists whom they had originally recorded on their own Decca Records label.

To this day the majority of artists who make records do not receive royalties on their sale. Though the royalties are specified in the contract, the monies charged against the artist's royalties usually exceed any income from the sales of their records. This is not true for industry superstars, but it is true of the majority of recording artists. Many artists have now begun to form their own record labels to receive all the profits from their sales. Although the Internet holds eventual promise for such endeavors, major record companies still control the sales and distribution of most recordings. A number of writers, including this author, have estimated that less than 10 percent of records released break even.

Music Maker

Music Maker has one of the most unusual origins of any record label. In the 1980s Tim Duffy was a folklore student at the University of North Carolina. He was disturbed that older musicians in both the mountain music and blues communities were living in poverty, and that their music was disappearing, as they died off or became infirm.

Duffy initiated the Music Maker Foundation to help these musicians, and he started the record label to promote their music. He has provided financial assistance to more than 100 musicians and has recorded many of them. A few of these musicians, like GUITAR GABRIEL, were known at one time but had disappeared into obscurity. Many of the artists whom Duffy unearthed had never had the opportunity to be recorded until he found them.

Musselwhite, Charlie (b. 1944) *harmonicist*

Charlie Musselwhite learned how to play HARMONICA from Will Shade, of the MEMPHIS JUG BAND. He played HARMONICA for HOMESICK JAMES, ROBERT NIGHTHAWK, and JOHNNY YOUNG, performing at the Maxwell Street market in CHICAGO, and later with BIG JOE WILLIAMS. Musselwhite relocated to the West Coast during the 1970s, and has recorded more than 30 albums, including some with blues guitarist ROBBEN FORD. He has also written a blues harmonica instruction book and recorded an instructional album.

Myers, David (b. 1926) *guitarist and bassist*

With his brother Louis, David Myers was a member of the CHICAGO blues group the Aces. Myers was brought up in MISSISSIPPI, where he learned guitar. His family moved to Chicago in 1941. The Aces began as a group that included the Myers Brothers and HARMONICA player JUNIOR WELLS, then added drummer FRED BELOW. Junior Wells left to play with MUDDY WATERS, and was replaced by LITTLE WALTER, who became the front man for the band, renamed the Jukes, after one of Walter's hits. In 1955 the brothers joined another band led by guitarist OTIS RUSH. In 1958 Myers became one of the first blues players to play electric bass. Myers still works as a freelance guitarist and bass player.

Myers, Louis (1929–1994) *guitarist and harmonicist*

Louis Myers played guitar and HARMONICA. He left the Aces, to play with MUDDY WATERS; he later performed with pianist OTIS SPANN and several other CHICAGO blues artists, including EARL HOOKER. During the 1970s Myers re-formed the Aces and toured Europe. He continued to perform and record until suffering a stroke in 1991.

Naftalin, Mark (b. 1944) *musical arranger and keyboardist*

Naftalin is one of many fine players who passed through PAUL BUTTERFIELD's band, playing keyboards with Butterfield's original band from 1965 to 1968. This band also featured MIKE BLOOMFIELD; it played everything from blues to jazz and raga-rock. Naftalin not only played keyboard but did the musical arrangements for the band. Later he played on recordings by such artists as JOHN LEE HOOKER, PERCY MAYFIELD, LOWELL FULSON, and BIG JOE TURNER, among others. Besides playing PIANO, his talents extend to the guitar, vibraphone, and organ. He hosted a long-running blues radio show during the late 1960s, and he did several TV specials. He has worked at the business end of things, producing the Marin County Blues Festival, and the blues portion of the Monterey Jazz Festival. Naftalin also has a long-running radio show called Mark Naftalin's Blues Power Hour, and he performs in the San Francisco Bay Area, usually with an old friend, slide guitarist Ron Thompson.

Neal, Kenny (b. 1957) *songwriter and multi-instrumentalist*

Kenny Neal started his music career by playing bass in his father's band in Baton Rouge, LOUISIANA. Neal sings, plays HARMONICA and guitar, and writes songs. He was influenced by the Louisiana swamp blues sound. He also played bass with BUDDY GUY, and was in a band with four of his brothers, the Neal Brothers Blues band. Neal played the lead in the 1991 Broadway production of the Langston Hughes musical *Mulebone*. Since that time he has released a half dozen albums under his name, and he continues to perform and tour.

Nelson, Tracy (b. 1944) *recording artist*

Tracy Nelson has recorded for a number of labels, and her records have been well reviewed, but she remains little known to the general public. Nelson emerged during the folk-blues revival of the 1960s and was often, although unjustly, compared to JANIS JOPLIN. Nelson is a much subtler singer, rather than a blues shouter. She also plays PIANO. Because Nelson is just as good at singing country and soul music as she is at performing the blues, her albums have not followed a consistent musical pattern, which may be confusing to some. Nelson had a band called Mother Earth in San Francisco, and they moved to Nashville in the late 1960s. Since then she has recorded blues and country albums as a soloist, and has recorded albums with other singers as well.

Neville Brothers

As soloists or performing together, the Neville Brothers have been an important ingredient in the New Orleans rhythm and blues sound. The four brothers—Aaron, Arthur, Charles, and Cyril—have recorded in various combinations. Aaron had a major pop hit in 1966 with "Tell It Like It Is," then he formed a band that included Arthur and Charles. New Orleans producer ALLEN TOUSSAINT hired

Arthur and Cyril as part of his house rhythm section that backed various artists, and they then recorded on their own as the Meters. The brothers were in still another band when they played behind their uncle George Landry's Wild Tchoupitoulas. The brothers have a distinctive and recognizable vocal sound using a strong vocal vibrato.

From 1977 the Nevilles began to perform as a unit and made several records, none of which was very successful. Aaron has had success in recent years as a soloist, and the brothers continue to perform for their fans. Aaron's son Ivan has played for Keith Richards of the ROLLING STONES, and has also released and recorded four albums of his own.

New York

The Apollo Theater on West 125th Street in New York City's Harlem has featured performances by virtually every major black nonclassical music artist. Among them have been blues artists BESSIE SMITH, BROWNIE MCGHEE, and SONNY TERRY; JIMMY REED; R&B stars RAY CHARLES and JAMES BROWN; and many famous jazz artists. The theater was built in 1913 and still operates today.

W. C. HANDY lived in New York for many years, moving there from MEMPHIS in 1919. Handy operated his own successful music publishing company in New York until his death in 1938.

Carnegie Hall, on West 57th Street, was the site of JOHN HAMMOND's From Spirituals to Swing concerts in 1938 and 1939. Café Society in Greenwich Village featured performances by JOSH WHITE and LEAD BELLY, and ALBERTA HUNTER performed at the Cookery near Greenwich Village after resuming her career in 1977. Brownie McGhee and Sonny Terry lived here for many years, appearing in Broadway shows, recording, and doing shows all over the world. McGhee also operated the School of the Blues on 125th Street in Harlem, where he taught blues guitar. GARY DAVIS taught guitar to many of the white blues revivalists during the 1950s and 1960s, and promoter BOBBY ROBINSON operated a number of record labels, recording blues and R&B musicians.

New York was an important center for the development of stride piano techniques, combining blues, ragtime, and jazz and featuring such outstanding musicians as JAMES P. JOHNSON, LUCKY ROBERTS, WILLIE "THE LION" SMITH, and Fats Waller. All these musicians played at various clubs and at rent parties in Harlem, the historically African-American neighborhood in uptown Manhattan. Eubie Blake, ragtime pianist and composer, lived here for many years, and Scott Joplin experienced his final frustrations while living in New York unsuccessfully attempting to produce his opera *Treemonisha*. His protégé, white pianist-composer Joseph Lamb, lived in obscurity in Brooklyn for many years before being rediscovered toward the end of his life.

Stefan Grossman (Larry Sandberg)

A number of important figures in the blues revival lived in New York during the 1960s and some stayed on. DAVE VAN RONK lived in the same apartment building in the west part of Greenwich Village for about 40 years. Van Ronk recorded prolifically over a long period of time, performed widely, and also taught other guitarists. Another revivalist who lived here is Stefan Grossman, who has probably written more blues instruction books than any other author. Grossman's first musical partner was RORY BLOCK, who grew up in Greenwich Village and herself has had a long and distinguished career as a blues musician and songwriter. Grossman was also in a jug band with several other New York revivalists, including harmonica player John Sebastian, later the leader of the LOVIN' SPOONFUL; guitarist Steve Katz, later a member of the BLUES PROJECT and Blood, Sweat & Tears; and mandolin virtuoso David Grisman, who went on to play his own new acoustic music on a number of successful recordings and in concert. JOHN HAMMOND JR. began his recording career in New York and continues to play and sing the blues.

ATLANTIC RECORDS recorded most of their early R&B successes in their own studio in midtown Manhattan, with artists like STICKS MCGHEE, RUTH BROWN, the Coasters, and the Drifters. There were dozens of independent recording studios in Manhattan, and all the major labels had their own studios as well. MOSES ASCH operated Disc Records and later Folkways in Midtown. Asch recorded Brownie McGhee, LONNIE JOHNSON, Sonny Terry, Lead Belly, and many other blues and folk artists. Riverside Records was a jazz label that also released a number of blues albums. Some of them were reissues of out-of-print records by artists like MA RAINEY and BLIND LEMON JEFFERSON, and some were releases by artists active during the 1960s, like GARY DAVIS. Folklorist Kenneth Goldstein supervised or licensed many of these recordings, first for Riverside and later for Prestige Records. Prestige's headquarters was just across the river in New Jersey. The Riverside and Prestige albums were important because they introduced the music of obscure or deceased blues artists to the young revivalists. The revivalists later rerecorded many of these songs. Nick Perls, a blues fan, started Yazoo Records, mostly to reissue obscure blues artists. He originated the label in the late 1960s and just before his death in 1987 sold it to his friend Richard Nevins. Nevins owns Shanachie Records in New Jersey. He has kept Yazoo's recordings in print and added additional titles.

McGhee and Terry, along with many other folk and blues artists, performed at Gerde's Folk City near Greenwich Village. Brother John Sellers, who sang both blues and gospel music, was a frequent performer there. Vanguard Records, also based in Manhattan, recorded a set of influential albums of CHICAGO blues, and they recorded a number of blues artists at the Newport Folk Festival and in their own studios. Elektra Records, which started in New York, recorded a number of albums in the 1960s with JOSH WHITE.

JIMI HENDRIX performed as Jimmy James in the Night Owl, the same coffeehouse where the LOVIN' SPOONFUL started their career. In the case of Hendrix, it was not until he moved to England that much interest developed in his music.

Along with ALBERTA HUNTER, other classic blues artists surfaced in the 1960s and 1970s. VICTORIA SPIVEY not only resumed her performing career but started her own record label to record herself and her friends.

These days the blues can be found at several New York clubs, especially Chicago B.L.U.E.S. There are several other downtown blues clubs and a B. B. KING facility, which, oddly, does not feature much in the way of blues. All the older New York black blues artists have either died or moved away.

Nighthawk, Robert (1909–1967)
multi-instrumentalist and radio host
Slide guitarist Robert Nighthawk was one of the architects of the CHICAGO blues sound. As a young man he played HARMONICA on pianist PEETIE WHEATSTRAW's records. Later his cousin Houston

Stackhouse taught him to play guitar, and they toured the South. Nighthawk made solo records from time to time, but considering his influence on other Chicago musicians, he is not well represented on records, although his song "Black Angel Blues," recorded in 1949, was fairly successful. Nighthawk influenced such important blues musicians as MUDDY WATERS and EARL HOOKER, played on the streets of Chicago, and in 1965 took over the King Biscuit Radio Show in his hometown of Helena, ARKANSAS, after the death of SONNY BOY WILLIAMSON. Nighthawk's radio tenure was cut short by his death in 1967.

"Nobody Knows You When You're Down and Out" (1922) *popular blues song written by Jimmie Cox*

This song was written by Jimmie Cox, about whom little is known. It was copyrighted in 1922 and recorded by BESSIE SMITH, La Vern Baker, LOUIS JORDAN, Sammy Price, Nina Simone, and JOSH WHITE. More recent artists who have recorded it include ERIC CLAPTON, Otis Redding, and Rod Stewart. The music to this song is close to ragtime, using the chords E7, A7 in the key of C, as well as the D minor chord. The theme of the lyrics is that when you are on top of the world you have lots of friends, but "nobody knows you when you're down and out."

North Mississippi All Stars

One of the spark plugs of the MEMPHIS music scene is musician and record producer James Dickinson. The All Stars is a band that includes his sons guitarist Luther and drummer Cody, along with bass player Chris Chew. Like their father, the sons are dedicated blues fans who played at juke joints and blues festivals in the South. Their performance and recordings feature some of MISSISSIPPI FRED MCDOWELL's songs, and more recently some of their own music. The All Stars do extended jams, which has earned the group an audience that enjoys rock jam bands like the Grateful Dead and Phish.

Oden, Jimmy (St. Louis Jimmy) (1903–1977)
pianist, singer, and songwriter
St. Louis Jimmy was a PIANO player, singer, and songwriter whose most famous song was "Going Down Slow." This blues standard has been recorded by HOWLIN' WOLF and WILLIE DIXON, among others. Some of his other compositions have been recorded by OTIS SPANN, JAMES COTTON, and Little Walter. Oden recorded for a number of labels and had his own record company for a while.

During the 1930s and 1940s Oden performed with ROOSEVELT SYKES at CHICAGO rent parties, as well as with other blues artists.

Oscher, Paul (b. 1950) *harmonicist*
A talented HARMONICA player, Paul Oscher may have been the first white sideman in a black blues band. He played in the MUDDY WATERS band between 1968 and 1974, and also recorded with them. Oscher was sitting in at black blues clubs by the time he was 15 years old. He disappeared from the music scene during the 1980s but reemerged with a solo album in 1996, entitled *Knockin' on the Devil's Door.* The album was produced by Foghat band member Dave Perverett.

Otis, Johnny (John Veliotes) (b. 1921) *musician*
Johnny Otis has worn many different musical hats during his long career. He has been a drummer, bandleader, record producer, label owner, concert promoter, author, and disc jockey. Otis, who is Greek, chose to live in the African-American section of Los Angeles, because he considers himself to be "black by persuasion." He got his start playing drums in swing bands, and he and his partner Bardu Ali opened a successful club in the Watts section of Los Angeles. Otis discovered a number of R&B artists, including the Robins (later called the Coasters), Little Esther Phillip, ETTA JAMES, and Jackie Wilson. Otis had some R&B hits of his own, recording for a number of different record companies starting in 1949. In 1955 he briefly ran his own label, ending up on Capitol in 1957 with the Johnny Otis Review.

Otis moved to northern California in the early 1990s, opened his own deli-night club, made radio broadcasts, and became an ordained minister. He has written two books about his life and the music scene entitled *Upside Your Head! Rhythm and Blues on Central Avenue* and *Red Beans and Rice and other Rock & Roll Recipes.* His son Shuggie is a well-known guitarist who has recorded under his own name.

Owens, Jack (1904–1997) *musician*
Jack Owens came from SKIP JAMES's hometown, Bentonia, MISSISSIPPI. Over the years he was a farmer and a bootlegger, and operated a juke joint. He came to the attention of the music world because of folklorist DAVID EVANS, from the University of Memphis. Owens played some folk festivals in the United States and Europe, particularly after the death of his wife in the 1980s.

Like Skip James, Owens often played in minor keys and in open tunings. Both of them had light, high-register voices. One album of Owens's music is currently available, entitled *It Must Have Been the Devil.*

Parker, Junior (Herman Parker Jr.) (1932–1971)
songwriter and recording artist
Junior Parker was a country blues HARMONICA play-er who had some successful R&B recordings for Sam Phillips's SUN RECORDS in MEMPHIS. However, it was ELVIS PRESLEY's cover record of Parker's song "Mystery Train" that became a pop music hit. Later Parker tasted some success recording for the Duke label in Houston, TEXAS, touring with label-mate soul singer BOBBY "BLUE" BLAND.

Patton, Charley (1891–1934) *guitarist and singer*
Charley Patton was the original king of the Delta blues, making his reputation when ROBERT JOHNSON was just a baby. Like Johnson, Patton played with SON HOUSE and WILLIE BROWN, but it was he who taught them some of his tricks. Patton was a flashy entertainer, playing the guitar between his knees and behind his back. Despite the intensity of his blues performances, Patton was known as a song-ster, playing ballads, folk tunes, rags, and gospel music, as well as blues. Record store owner H. C. SPEIR found Patton and arranged for him to record for Paramount Records. Patton's biggest hit was "Pony Blues," recorded in 1929.

Patton was difficult to deal with. He was only five foot five and weighed 135 pounds, but he had a reputation as ill-tempered and sometimes violent. He could not read or write but was an excellent guitarist. He was the first guitarist on record to thump the bass strings in a way that resembles what rap and funk bass players do today. According to

guitarist JOHN FAHEY's book *Charley Patton,* 28 of Patton's 46 recorded titles are in open G tuning. Patton was one of the pioneers of the Delta SLIDE GUITAR sound. Despite his small size, Patton had a huge voice and could supposedly be heard 500 yards away without a microphone. SLEEPY JOHN ESTES said that Patton was the loudest blues singer he ever heard.

Some of Patton's recordings included FIDDLE player Son Sims, showing the string band influence in Patton's music. In 1929 Patton was supposedly the best-selling blues artist around. He recorded more than 60 songs. Fahey compiled a boxed set of all the recordings that he could locate.

Patton may never achieve Robert Johnson's pop-ularity, but an entire conference was held about his music at the University of Liege, Belgium in 1984. One of the problems in listening to Patton is that the records are poorly recorded, so it is difficult to understand the words.

Peacock
Not until Don Robey established Peacock Records in Houston, TEXAS, in 1949 was there a significant black-owned label. Most of Robey's artists were either R&B singers like BOBBY "BLUE" BLAND or gospel singers, like the Spirits of Memphis.

Robey was a shrewd businessman who owned nightclubs, a booking agency, a record shop, a music publishing operation, and a number of busi-nesses outside the music industry. He even put his name down as the composer of a number of songs actually composed by his artists, using the pseudonym Deadric Malone.

Robey's closest dealings with the blues came from his recordings of CLARENCE "GATEMOUTH" BROWN, who played both country hoedowns on the FIDDLE and electric blues on the guitar. Future rock and roller Little Richard (Penniman) was also a Robey artist, as were BIG MAMA THORNTON and Johnny Ace.

Robey, a bit of a thug, did not mind threatening his artists with a gun if things failed to go his way or if an artist were so rash as to complain about royalties. In 1973 Robey sold his company to ABC-Dunhill Records, and he worked on his ranch until his death in 1975.

Peer, Ralph (R. Sylvester Peer) (1892–1959)
record producer
Ralph Peer holds the twin distinction of having produced the first commercially successful country record, recorded by Fiddlin' John Carson, and one of the first blues, recorded by MAMIE SMITH. Peer was a record producer for Columbia Records who moved over to RCA. Peer's deal with RCA specified that he would not receive any money from the company, but that he could own the music publishing rights to anything that he recorded that was not already published. This proved to be a gold mine for Peer, who started the Southern Music Company, now Peer-Southern, to house his copyrights. Peer discovered country singer JIMMIE RODGERS, one of country music's first big stars, and he also published music by such jazz artists as LOUIS ARMSTRONG and JELLY ROLL MORTON. Because the only way that Peer made money was for him to own the copyrights to his artists' songs, he discouraged them from singing traditional songs, encouraging them to write their own music instead.

Perkins, Carl (1932–1998) *guitarist and recording artist*
Like his fellow SUN RECORDS artist Johnny Cash, Perkins was brought up poor, living with his sharecropper parents and two brothers in a one-room country shack. Like many black blues artists, Perkins started playing on a homemade guitar made from a cigar box and baling wire. When his father gave him a real guitar, Perkins took lessons from a sharecropper. Even before he started to play, even though he was white, he had listened to the music of black sharecroppers working in the fields.

Perkins recorded for Sun Records in 1954, making his big hit record with his own song, "Blue Suede Shoes," a year later. Perkins played in a family band. When an automobile accident killed one of his brothers and hospitalized Carl, this prevented him from following up with the record. In fact, while Perkins was in the hospital, ELVIS PRESLEY started performing his song.

The musical style that Sam Phillips recorded at Sun Records in MEMPHIS was known as rockabilly. It combined musical elements of rhythm and blues and country music. Of all the Sun artists, Perkins was the best guitar player, playing fluid lead guitar lines that were often imitated by other guitarists. Perkins also adapted BLIND LEMON JEFFERSON's song "Matchbox Blues." Ten years later the Beatles recorded it, and Perkins performed and recorded some with Beatles George Harrison and Paul McCartney. Later he returned to country music, touring with Johnny Cash, then returned to rock in the 1980s in a band that featured him performing with his sons.

Perkins, Pinetop (Joe Willie Perkins) (b. 1913)
pianist and member of the Legendary Blues Band
A singer and PIANO player, Perkins took up guitar early in his career. A run-in with an angry chorus girl resulted in her cutting some tendons in his left arm, so he turned to the piano. He was playing guitar with SONNY BOY WILLIAMSON II at the time. Perkins spent five years playing with Williamson on radio station KFFA's famous *King Biscuit Time* radio program.

He recorded Pinetop Smith's "Pinetop's Boogie," then took that name for himself. Perkins replaced OTIS SPANN as the piano player in the MUDDY

Pinetop Perkins (Bruce Polonsky Photography)

WATERS band, and he stayed with Waters for 10 years. He also played with ROBERT NIGHTHAWK, EARL HOOKER, and B. B. KING. In 1980 Perkins joined several other alumni of the Waters bands, including drummer WILLIE SMITH, bass player CALVIN JONES, and harmonicist Jerry Portnoy to form the Legendary Blues Band.

Petway, Robert (dates unknown) *recording artist*
Little is known about Robert Petway, except that he was a close friend of MISSISSIPPI guitarist TOMMY MCCLENNAN. Petway had only two recording sessions in CHICAGO in 1941 and 1942, recording 16 songs. MUDDY WATERS took Petway's song "Catfish Blues" and changed it into the song "Rollin' Stone." This song inspired the name of the English rock band ROLLING STONES.

Phelps, Kelly Joe (b. 1959) *slide guitarist*
Kelly Joe Phelps is an incredible slide guitarist whose father taught him country and folk songs, and how to play drums and PIANO. Phelps started to play modern jazz during the 1970s but became fascinated with blues during the 1980s. He is both a fingerpicker and a slide guitarist, and his more recent recordings include an increasing number of original songs.

Phelps is a very original artist who uses the slide as a form of self-expression rooted in the blues, but includes other musical territory as well.

piano (acoustic and electric)
The piano and the guitar are among the most suitable instruments for playing without additional instrumental accompaniment. Both instruments enable the musician to play full, rich chords. Chords

are playable on both the BANJO and the MANDOLIN, but neither instrument has much of a bass register. Therefore mandolin and banjo players usually need other musicians to perform with them. In the early days of the blues, from 1890 to 1920, there was not much money to be made playing music, so this was an economic inconvenience.

The piano, with 88 keys, gives the player more musical range than any other instrument but the organ. And because the player cannot carry it, he or she can travel without worrying about caring for an instrument. But pianists must sometimes have to cope with playing pianos that are out of tune or those that have been so badly treated that some of the keys stick and make no sound.

A group of pianists known as the Santa Fe School traveled to many of the towns served by the Santa Fe Railroad, usually bumming rides by hopping freight trains. These towns included Shreveport, LOUISIANA, and the TEXAS towns of Dallas, Abilene, San Antonio, Corpus Christi, Houston, and Beaumont. The musicians would get off the trains and find the nearest place that had a piano to play, though it was usually an old piano in poor condition. Another group of pianists played in the rough lumber and turpentine camps of southern Mississippi and southeast Louisiana, during the 1920s.

The Santa Fe School musicians and the lumber camp players are obscure figures today, mostly known through the reminiscences of the few people whose careers brought them more notoriety, like EURREAL "LITTLE BROTHER" MONTGOMERY and ROOSEVELT SYKES. Both these musicians had extensive recording careers, but most of the other pianists either recorded only a few sides or never recorded at all. The names of a few of these obscure figures convey the atmosphere in which they must have worked. A few of the players lost in musical history are Big Boy Knox, Black Ivory King, and Pinetop Burks.

Many of these players had only a rudimentary technique, using devices like major chords with only occasionally added sixths and sevenths of the chord. Many used a walking bass line, a series of bass notes, usually a quarter note in length. Another common device was to omit the third, or middle, note of a chord; that is, a C chord would be played with only the notes C and G, omitting the E. Pianists who sang often used the piano in a way similar to singing guitarists. They would play very simply during the vocals and use melodic decorations or answers to the vocal between the vocal phrases. Other players used a left-hand pattern that alternated between a single note and a chord.

Sometimes the piano player would change the sound of the piano by mechanical means, rather than his own technique; for example, tacks might be placed in the piano or newspapers placed behind the piano strings. Triplets were often played with the left hand. (Triplets occur when three notes are played in the time allowed for two.) Piano keys cannot be bent to get pitches between the notes, so instead piano players sometimes play rapid combinations of two adjacent notes, like E and E-flat in the key of C. When the notes are repeatedly played rapidly back and forth, the effect is almost like bending a guitar string. Pianists also use tremolo effects that mirror what mandolin players do—playing one or two notes repeatedly in rapid succession.

It is a characteristic for the left hand to keep a steady rhythm and for the right hand to wander in front of and behind the beat, producing an attractive musical tension for the listener, who begins to wonder if the two hands will ever get back together on the beat. Piano players also often use grace notes, played with the right hand. Grace notes are notes of such short duration that no musical length is assigned to them in printed music. Although the piano is also capable of sustaining notes for long periods by using the foot pedals, most blues players used this device sparingly if at all. The reason for this may have been that the sort of abused pianos found in barrelhouses and rough saloons often had malfunctioning pedals.

Although there are dozens of blues guitar transcriptions of even the most obscure blues guitarists of the 1920s and 1930s, there are relatively few piano transcriptions of the blues pianists. Similarly, although a number of blues piano recordings have been reissued on CD, the number pales compared with the massive number of available guitar recordings. The appendix discusses those piano transcriptions that are available, mostly the work of blues scholar and pianist Eric Kriss. Blues piano recordings are also listed. The piano does not seem to have captured the imagination of blues fans in the same way as the guitar.

Just as certain cities became gathering places for particular guitarists—Atlanta and Durham North Carolina, for the Piedmont players, for example— pianist seemed to have settled around certain cities. Many of these musicians were migrants, like the guitarists who left the Deep South. CHICAGO, St. Louis, and DETROIT were the main cities where they went. In Detroit's African-American enclave of Hastings Street were piano players Tupelo Slim, "Fishtail," James Hemingway, Rufus (Speckled Red) Perryman, CHARLEY SPAND, and Will Ezell. St. Louis seemed to offer musicians who played guitar and piano with almost equal facility. Among them were veteran Henry Townsend, and William Bunch (better known as Peetie WHEATSTRAW "The Devil's Son-in-Law", also known as "the High Sheriff from Hell"). Other piano players included Wesley Wallace, St. Louis Henry, Barrelhouse Buck McFarland, and the colorful CRIPPLE CLARENCE LOFTON. The influential Roosevelt Sykes commuted between CHICAGO and St. Louis; in addition to his own recordings, he played piano for the popular blues singer WALTER DAVIS. Davis soon picked up a simplified version of Sykes's piano work and began to play on his own records.

Chicago has always been a mecca for blues artists, and the resident piano players included BLIND JOHN DAVIS, Black Bob, Joshua Altheimer, who often performed with guitarist BIG BILL BROONZY, Eurreal "Little Brother" Montgomery, Jimmy Blythe, BIG MACEO (MERRIWEATHER), and MEMPHIS SLIM. T. A. Dorsey ("Georgia Tom") was an important figure, until he abandoned the blues for gospel music. Sykes was often on the scene, and so was Pinetop Smith, one of the fathers of boogie-woogie piano. Doug Suggs and the much better-

known JIMMY YANCEY both worked at the Chicago White Sox park during the day and played piano at night and on weekends. Yancey was a particularly influential blues and boogie pianist, adept at playing soulfully at slow tempos.

Just as MEMPHIS MINNIE proved that women were perfectly capable of playing excellent blues guitar, LOVIE AUSTIN (CORA CALHOUN) was an accomplished jazz and blues pianist who accompanied many blues singers, including MA RAINEY, IDA COX, Ethel Waters, and ALBERTA HUNTER. Austin had studied music in college and had her own jazz band. During the 1920s she worked with such outstanding jazz musicians as Louis Armstrong and Johnny Dodds. Austin also cowrote the song "Down Hearted Blues" with Hunter. It became Bessie Smith's biggest hit. By the mid-1920s Austin was a session player for Paramount Records who functioned in much the same way that WILLIE DIXON did for CHESS RECORDS 30 years later. She often supervised the musical arrangements for blues singers. Memphis Slim (Peter Chatman) was another important Chicago player, who often teamed up with Dixon. He left Chicago in 1962 to move to Paris.

Indianapolis was an important blues town from the mid-1920s to the mid-1930s. The major figure was LEROY CARR, who had a tremendous influence with his lighter-textured vocals, and his own piano work teamed with the tasteful single-string guitar playing of SCRAPPER BLACKWELL. Carr was enormously popular during the mid-1930s, his music striking a chord with a more sophisticated urban audience. Arthur Taylor was another Indianapolis blues piano artist.

Despite the extensive northward migration of blues artists, a number of piano players never left the South. Birmingham, Alabama, was the original home of PINE TOP SMITH, but other local musicians include Walter Roland, who played for blues singers Lucille Bogan and JOSH WHITE, and ROBERT MCCOY, who recorded again during the 1960s. JELLY ROLL MORTON, who played ragtime and blues and was a great jazz bandleader, held forth in his native New Orleans, which was also the home of composer-pianist Richard M. Jones and Eurreal "Little Brother," Montgomery. Morton mentioned other early New Orleans players Rip Top, Papa Lord God, and No Leg Kenny, who literally had no legs. Later New Orleans piano players like PROFESSOR LONGHAIR, JAMES BOOKER, and ALLAN TOUSSAINT were major figures in early R&B music, and their influence carries on in the music of white blues revivalists DR. JOHN and MARCIA BALL.

Morton, who recorded a series of albums for ALAN LOMAX at the Library of Congress that included an extensive history of his musical roots, mentioned another group of pianists who played in such Gulf Coast cities as Mobile, Alabama, and Pensacola, Florida.

In Dallas, WHISTLING ALEX MOORE, George W. Thomas, and his younger brother Hersal, K. D. Johnson, and Willie Tyson were on the scene, and in Houston Rob Cooper and Andy Boy were in residence. Regional styles reflected either local preferences or the influence of one or more musicians on other players. The Texas players tended to be more interested in chords and played a bit more softly than the barrelhouse players. Curtis Jones went from Dallas to Chicago, then like Memphis Slim moved to Europe in 1962. Another later group of Texas players, including Ivory Joe Hunter, CHARLES BROWN, and AMOS MILBURN, moved to LOS ANGELES and were important figures in the early years of rhythm and blues music.

New York was home to pianists Montana Taylor, Dan Burley, Romeo Nelson, and "Mr. Freddie" Shayne. A school of extremely sophisticated blues-jazz players also developed, including Willie "The Lion" Smith, Lucky Roberts, James P. Johnson, and Thomas "Fats" Waller. These monster piano players delighted in lengthy "cutting contests," where each person would play until the various contestants finally admitted defeat. All these musicians were composers and jazz musicians, as well as playing on many recording sessions featuring blues singers. Waller was also renowned as a singer of happy-go-lucky, amusing songs, of which he recorded dozens. Eubie Blake was a great ragtime and pop player, and

Fletcher Henderson was a jazz musician and arranger who also played piano on many blues singers' records. Clarence Williams was a songwriter and musical entrepreneur who played piano on some of Bessie Smith's records, and always seemed to be hustling some sort of record deal for someone. Perry Bradford, who was responsible for MAMIE SMITH's recording debut, was a similar personality—a composer, arranger, producer, pianist, and musical entrepreneur.

The electric piano is most common in the arsenal of blues-rock musicians. The early electric pianos were particularly troublesome to traditional pianists, because the touch of the keyboard was so different from the feel of the acoustic keyboard. Over the years electric keyboards have greatly improved, and it is possible to find electric pianos with a touch much closer to the acoustic instrument. The main advantage of electric pianos is that they do not have to be tuned, so that the musician can travel with an instrument that is reliable and consistently in tune. These days the term "keyboard" generally refers to an electric piano, and these instruments are often equipped with all sorts of gear that resemble guitar effects. One example is a device called pitch bend. By pulling this lever, the pianist can bend notes in the same way that a guitarist can accomplish this feat. Most modern keyboards are also equipped with MIDI attachments, devices that control two or three keyboards simultaneously from a single keyboard, enabling the musician to get organ effects, for example, out of one keyboard, and piano effects out of the other. This is why one may see two or three keyboards piled on top of one another at a performance of a rock-blues band. It is also possible to simulate bass lines on the keyboard, removing the need for a bass player. Other on-board effects enable the keyboard to imitate the sounds of strings, horns, and percussion.

Many rock bands utilize players like Chuck Leavell or the late Ian Stewart, talented piano players who can make the instrument sound like an entire orchestra. Edgar Winter is one of the rock-blues artists whose main instrument is keyboards, and Greg Allman is another.

Electronic keyboards do not lend themselves as well as acoustic pianos to the work of solo blues artists or traditionally-oriented blues bands. But they have the virtue of being able to use the many colorful effects that keyboards feature, plus the ability to play at high volumes through the use of amplifiers. The player can also rest secure in the thought that the keyboard will have a consistent sound from one job to another and will always play in tune, assuming no electrical glitches develop and the piano is not damaged during its travels.

In rock blues bands, electronic keyboards can blend better than acoustic pianos with ELECTRIC GUITARS. This is partly because comparable volumes can be achieved through the use of electronics and partly because of the similarity of the tone colors of the sound. It takes negotiation for guitarist and pianist to play well together. A mediocre pianist is apt to add all sorts of extra notes to chords. For the two instruments to function well together, it is necessary for the piano player to simplify the piano parts, or for the guitar to develop a good knowledge of chord inversions. This difficult task for guitarists involves developing a thorough knowledge of the guitar fingerboard.

Piano Red (William Lee Perryman) (1911–1985) *pianist and singer*

Piano Red was the younger brother of Speckled Red, and his rollicking PIANO playing and vocals brought him two different careers. He played piano at the age of 12, and he recorded with BLIND WILLIE MCTELL. His 1950 RCA record "Rockin' with Red" became a number five R&B record. "Red's Boogie" also turned out to be a hit.

In 1961 Red created a new identity for himself with the band Dr. Feelgood and the Interns. His song "Doctor Feelgood," made it to the pop charts, as well as being an R&B hit. Another hit followed, when Perryman rerecorded an old song of his, "The Right String but the Wrong Yo Yo." Red enjoyed a 10

year engagement at an Atlanta club from 1969 to 1979, taking some time off to tour in Europe.

Piazza, Rod (b. 1947) *harmonicist and singer*

Rod Piazza has been in a succession of bands, starting with the Dirty Blues Band, and continuing in Bacon Fat. He played with his idol, George "Harmonica" Smith, in the band Hamfat. Next came the Night Flyers, his current band, which includes his wife, Honey Alexander, on keyboards. Piazza is a harmonicist and singer who has also played on records by other artists, including Michelle Shocked and PEE WEE CRAYTON.

Pitchford, Lonnie (1955–1998) *diddley bow player*

Lonnie Pitchford was one of the few musicians who specialized in the diddley bow, a one-stringed instrument mounted on a platform or attached to a wall. Many Delta guitarists used a diddley bow when they first learned how to play guitar. Pitchford may be the only one who ever performed on the instrument. ROBERT LOCKWOOD JR. taught Pitchford some ROBERT JOHNSON tunes, which he arranged for the diddley bow. Pitchford did not tour much during his brief life, but ALAN LOMAX captured his playing on video.

Pleasant Joe (Cousin Joe Pleasant) (1907–1989) *singer and multi-instrumentalist*

Pleasant Joe was a LOUISIANA PIANO, guitar, and ukulele player and a singer. He began his career singing in church, then began to play piano in New Orleans clubs. He played jazz in NEW YORK during the 1940s with BILLIE HOLIDAY, Charlie Parker, and many other musicians. Along the way he made a number of recordings for various small labels. He made several trips to Europe during the 1960s and 1970s. In 1987 he wrote his autobiography, *Cousin Joe: Blues from New Orleans*, which was published by the University of Chicago Press.

Pomus, Doc (1925–1991) *songwriter*

Doc Pomus was a NEW YORK songwriter. A childhood bout with polio put him on crutches, and at the age of 40 a fall left him in a wheelchair for the rest of his life. Pomus wrote many hit songs. Some of them were pop-rock songs, and some were in the rhythm and blues style that Pomus particularly loved. He wrote "Lonely Avenue" for RAY CHARLES, "Save the Last Dance for Me" recorded by the Drifters, "There Must Be a Better World Somewhere," which won a Grammy for B. B. KING in 1982, and "Boogie Woogie Country Girl" for BIG JOE TURNER. He also wrote a number of songs that were recorded by ELVIS PRESLEY. Pomus cowrote his songs, many of them with Mort Schuman, and later with a number of other writers, including DR. JOHN. Doc Pomus was dedicated to the cause of making sure that the pioneer R&B songwriters, so many of whom had been cheated by record companies and music publishers, received their proper royalty payments.

"Pony Blues" (1929) *influential folk-blues song by Charley Patton*

CHARLEY PATTON was one of the earliest and most influential Delta blues guitarists. He recorded his song "Pony Blues" in 1929. What stands out in Patton's performance is his creative use of the guitar. Sometimes he doubled the melody with the guitar, sometimes he commented on it, and sometimes he thumped the bass with his right thumb to emphasize the lyrics. This song is very much a folk blues, in the sense that the verses are loosely connected and presented as a group of disconnected thoughts on the singer's mind. These thoughts vary from looking for his woman, directions on riding his horse, and stating that he does not want to marry his woman but to be her man. Other artists who have recorded "Pony Blues" include ERIC CLAPTON, Duke Robillard, SON HOUSE, Stefan Grossman, and ALVIN YOUNGBLOOD-HART.

Presley, Elvis (1935–1977) *legendary singer and performer*

A large library of information has been published about Elvis Presley and his musical career. Presley was a white southern boy who grew up with a love for black blues and gospel music. His career began when he made a record at Sam Phillips's SUN RECORDS studio, renting the facility to make one copy of a song he recorded as a gift for his mother. Phillips had been seeking a "white boy who could sing the blues," and over time Presley developed into that boy. Many of Presley's early songs were covers of R&B songs, such as ARTHUR CRUDUP's "That's All Right Mama," and Junior Parker's "Mystery Train."

In 1955 Phillips sold RCA Presley's contract for $35,000. This was considered a risky deal at the time. Presley then became a superstar, appearing in numerous movies, starring in television specials, and appearing in Las Vegas. His hip-shaking dancing was a sensation at the time and got him a tremendous amount of publicity. As he became more popular, his records became less and less like what he had been singing when he recorded for Phillips and further removed from the blues, becoming more commercial and smooth than the rougher recordings made by Phillips.

Price, Lloyd (b. 1933) *songwriter and multi-instrumentalist*

Louisiana-born Lloyd Price was a talented R&B artist who wrote some very successful songs. He played PIANO and trumpet in high school, and also sang in Sunday School choir. His 1952 recording of "Lawdy Miss Clawdy" became a huge pop music hit. Price served in the military in Korea in the early 1950s, and when he came back he started his own record label. He hit paydirt once again in 1958 with a rewritten version of the folk ballad "Stackolee," called "Stagger Lee." He later owned another record label and operated his own nightclub in New York City.

During the 1970s Price went to Africa, after his business partner was murdered in NEW YORK. He did some boxing promotion in Africa, together with American promoter Don King. A 1993 oldies tour led to further television and touring work.

Price, Sammy (1908–1992) *pianist*

A blues and boogie-woogie PIANO player, Sammy Price played with the Alphonse Trent band in Dallas, TEXAS, in 1927. He played piano for blues singer Trixie Smith and gospel singer Sister Rosetta Tharpe, had a jazz band in NEW YORK during the 1940s, and spent 10 years performing with trumpet player Henry "Red" Allen. A number of his dozens of albums are still available.

Professor Longhair (Henry Roelin Byrd) (1918–1980) *recording artist and pianist*

One of the founding fathers of New Orleans rhythm and blues, Professor Longhair influenced the playing of Fats Domino, HUEY "PIANO" SMITH ALLEN TOUSSAINT, and DR. JOHN. Longhair grew up in New Orleans, tap dancing on the streets for tips. He learned how to play from such early obscure New Orleans piano players as Kid Stormy Weather. He could also play guitar and drums.

Longhair, who had little interest in touring, finally made his recording debut in 1949. In 1950 he made his only hit record, "Baldhead," which reached 35 on the R&B charts. Much more recording for many labels followed, but without much commercial success. A famous New Orleans nightclub, Tipitina's, is named after a Professor Longhair song.

At different times in his life Professor Longhair worked outside of music. Early in his career he was a gambler, and when he was not doing well as a musician during the 1960s he became a janitor. By the 1970s things had picked up, particularly after a performance at the 1971 New Orleans Jazz & Heritage Festival. His performance was so well received that he toured Europe, becoming a big star

there. He also made more recording. After 1971, Longhair played the New Orleans festival every year until his death.

protest songs

Protest songs object to some particular set of social conditions or individuals that the singer is complaining about.

Unlike previous or subsequent folksong collectors, LAWRENCE GELLERT assembled a large body of protest songs. The collection became so large that some folklorists accused him of writing the songs himself. Even though Gellert was a political leftist, it seems a stretch to believe that he could write 500 songs, teach them to singers, then record them. The entire collection is currently housed at the University of Indiana. According to Guido Van Rijn's book *Roosevelt Blues,* between 1924 and 1937 Gellert recorded 500 songs, of which half included outspoken protests against the social condition of African Americans. Forty-eight of the songs were published in two now out-of-print collections: *Me and My Captain,* published in 1936, and *Negro Songs of Protest,* published in 1939.

In reading blues histories one encounters the assertion that blues are almost entirely about romance, and that political issues are rarely mentioned. In his book *The Poetry of the Blues,* for example, SAMUEL CHARTERS writes, "There is little social protest in the blues. There is often a note of anger and frustration; sometimes the poverty and the rootlessness in which the singer has lived his life is evident in a word or phrase, but there is little open protest at the social conditions under which a Negro in the United States is forced to live. There is complaint, but protest has been stifled." Not all the songs in Gellert's books are blues, although some are specifically blues, and others fall between the categories of blues and work songs. In song after song the anonymous singers threaten revenge against mean bosses, lynchings, and other injustices. For example, in "Out in de Rain," the singer complains that if you ask the Captain (chain gang boss) for money, he will kill you, but he says that Russell better not "mess wit' me no mo', Ah's ready dis time wit mah foh'ty 'fo." Other songs in these collections refer to unjust prison terms, and the song "Way Down South" maintains that "if you don't get lynched, you sho' get pinched in Atlanta." There is a protest song about the Scottsboro case, in which eight black men were framed for the "rape" of two white prostitutes, and there is a reference to the bossman as "the meanest dog I ever did see." In "Work Ox" there is an assertion that I "ain't gonna be your old work ox no more," and in "Told My Captain," the singer says that if he had his weight in lime, he'd whip his captain " 'till he went stone blind." In a note to the song, Gellert explains that the singer means that if the fight were even, if the singer was a white man, that is what he would do.

Gellert did almost all his recording in Georgia and the Carolinas although he did do some recording in Mississippi. Social conditions for African Americans were relatively favorable in the Piedmont region compared with what blacks were experiencing in the MISSISSIPPI Delta. One can only imagine what Gellert might have turned up if he had recorded in Mississippi or ARKANSAS.

Although the Gellert collection included the largest concentrated body of protest songs, there are quite a few others that have been recorded over the years. A large percentage of these songs were written and recorded during 1929–40, the period known as the Great Depression. During this time there was severe unemployment all over the United States, and it was at its worst among the minority populations, who are traditionally known as the "last hired, and the first fired." Black unemployment in CHICAGO, for example, was 43.5 percent in 1935, and fell to the still considerable 16.7 percent in 1940.

Republican Herbert Hoover was president at the beginning of the depression, but in 1932 the democratic candidate, Franklin Delano Roosevelt, was elected to the presidency. Roosevelt remained in office until his death in 1945, winning reelection three times. Roosevelt instituted a number of public works projects to create employment. They ranged from the WPA (Works Project or Progress Administration) to the Civilian Conservation Corps (CCC), and others. People were put to work doing everything from building roads, rehabilitating national parks and forests, and engaging in the arts. A number of the recorded blues of the 1930s refer to "working on the project," and some of these songs protest budget cuts that ended or reduced the size of the projects.

One of the most popular and often-recorded blues protest songs was "Red Cross Store." It refers to the Red Cross's role as a relief agency in the drought of 1930–31. Versions of this song were recorded by Lucille Bogan, Walter Roland, BROWNIE MCGHEE, LEAD BELLY, the Mobile Washboard Band, SONNY BOY WILLIAMSON, FOREST CITY JOE, Thomas Shaw, Boogie Bill Webb, and Henry "Bubba' Brown."

According to blues scholar Guido van Rijn, WALTER ROLAND is thought to have been the original composer, although relatives of a deceased blues artist named Marshall Owens disputed his authorship. Roland's recording that the Red Cross people "treat you mean, don't want to give you nothing but two-three cans of beans" has a refrain that asserts, "I don't want to go." He then turns the lyric in another direction, stating that he has a new girlfriend who is going to get a job and "take care of me now, when the time is bad." Roland recorded a sequel on the same day, which indicates that his record company recognized the commercial potential of the song. The second version complains about the food that the Red Cross gives out at their store but admits that he will probably have to go anyway because "my wife and children is hungry." Bogan's version, which Roland accompanied on piano, uses the twist that if her man had listened to her in the first place "he wouldn't had to go to the Red Cross store."

Lead Belly takes still another point of view, and much of his lyric is a complaint from the singer's woman that he needs to go down to the Red Cross store and assert himself so that they can get some food. Brownie McGhee's version specifically refers to Herbert Hoover and the hardships of 1929.

McGhee also ends the song by finding a woman who will support him.

A number of other protest songs from the Great Depression era are printed in *Hard Hitting Songs for Hard-Hit People*. This book is a collaboration between ALAN LOMAX, the compiler-editor, Woody Guthrie who wrote notes about the songs in his impressionistic style, and Pete Seeger, who transcribed and edited the music. It was originally supposed to be published in 1941, but World War II created a 25-year interruption in the publication process.

Many of the songs are not blues, but those that are merit discussion. "Collector Man Blues," another song by Walter Roland, is about a poor man who cannot pay his bills and is being harassed by "that collector man." The singer advises others never to buy anything on the installment plan, so that they will never have to deal with the collector man. Of course, avoiding the installment plan is difficult for a person who has no credit and insufficient funds to pay the bills. Roland then tells us that he is going to leave this "no-good town" and return to Florida.

BIG BILL BROONZY in his "Unemployment Stomp" has a different set of complaints. He says that he is a "law-abiding citizen," that he is trying to pay his debts, that he does not steal, and that his family is breaking up because he cannot get a job and they are starving. He is also worried that his job will end because a war will start, and he will be drafted, and therefore will not be able to continue paying his debts.

Ramblin' Thomas's "No Job Blues" complains that he cannot get a job, his woman, who was working, has quit him, and the police have arrested him for "vag" (vagrancy). His solution is to try to find another "meal ticket woman" so that he will not have to find a job.

BLIND BLAKE's "No Dough Blues" complains that he cannot find a job, and nothing he can do satisfies his woman. He anticipates that she will leave him to get herself a job. His only hope is that if things change, maybe he can get a job, and she will change her ways. Finally he resorts to pleading, begging her not to quit him, because "the dirt you done to me is comin' back to you."

There is some truth to Charters's point of view in the sense that in many of the depression songs the singer portrays himself as a pitiful figure. KOKOMO ARNOLD's "Down and Out" complains that he cannot afford to buy a decent meal, that he has no car or airplane(!), that he now guesses he will have to rob and steal, and that he cannot get any help from his "women." BLIND LEMON JEFFERSON's "One Dime Blues" starts out complaining about his bad luck and hard times, then throws the outlaw Jesse James into the song. Jefferson says that if you want your friend to be "bad like Jesse James, just give 'im a six shooter and highway some passenger train."

It is necessary to understand the pressure on protest songs not to be too inflammatory. Most of the songs were released on white-owned record labels, and white record producers might lack enthusiasm for major complaints against the existing social system. Some of the expressions of self-pity, like TAMPA RED and Georgia Tom's "New Stranger Blues," express a longing for the singer's southern home. In this case Tampa Red sings that he is headed back south where "I know I'll be welcome and I won't have the stranger's blues."

As the depression wore on and Roosevelt was reelected in 1936, some of the budgets for his social programs were cut, and blues singers protested that they voted for him but were disappointed that he was cutting the programs. Jimmie Gordon's "Don't Take Away My PWA" concerned yet another Roosevelt-era social program, the Public Works Administration. Gordon congratulates Roosevelt on his reelection, then exhorts the president "you can take away all of the alphabets, but please leave the PWA." Washboard Sam, in his "CCC Blues," takes a more sarcastic approach. He begs the secretary for a job, and when he tells her that his rent is due, she "sent me a can of beef." She then follows up by indeed giving him a job. What she comes up with is "takin' care of the dead in a funeral home," which Sam describes as "everything was nice and warm."

PEETIE WHEATSTRAW's "Working on the Project" registers another sort of complaint. Since he will have to wait "three or four weeks" until payday, he cannot pay the grocer or his landlord.

Broonzy's "Starvation Blues" is probably the most pathetic of all, with the singer maintaining that he is starving, his house has a for rent sign on the door, he has no job, and his woman has left him.

Other depression-era blues include FURRY LEWIS's "The Panic Is On," Samson Pittman's "Welfare Blues," where the singer threatens to use his gun if the relief people will not help him, Carl Martin's "Let's Have a New Deal," and another song by Peetie Wheatstraw, "New Working on the Project," in which the singer complains about getting his #304 dismissal form, which will keep him from paying the furniture man or his landlord.

If the folk-blues singers tended to protest in general rather than specific terms, another set of singers set out on another path. The folk song movement in NEW YORK during the 1930s and 1940s was tied in to left-wing politics and calls for social change. A loose confederation known as the Almanac Singers centered around folksingers Woody Guthrie and Pete Seeger, and also included Lee Hays and Millard Lampell. They lived in a house in Greenwich Village on MacDougal Street and worked together in everything from larger groups of singers to soloists. Blues artists Lead Belly, JOSH WHITE, Brownie McGhee and SONNY TERRY were loosely associated with the group, especially White. All these artists wrote songs about political events, ranging from peace, war, and the economy to racial discrimination. New York had an audience for protest songs, particularly in the union movement and two political parties—the left-wing American Labor Party (ALP) and the Communist Party. These groups were heavily committed to fighting for racial equality, and they hired radical singers for parties and political rallies. Another source of jobs was Alan Lomax, who as a record producer, folksong collector, and radio program host provided economic opportunities for White, Lead Belly, Guthrie, and Seeger. He encouraged

Lead Belly and White to write and perform songs that were much more direct protest songs than the depression-era songs discussed above. Guthrie and Seeger were also involved in writing and performing these songs, although neither was a blues artist.

Lead Belly wrote and recorded a song called "The Bourgeois Blues" that detailed an experience he had in Washington, D.C., when he and his wife, Martha, and Alan Lomax and his wife were unable to find a restaurant that would serve a black and a white couple that wanted to dine together and to rent a room. Lead Belly included the verse "land of the brave, home of the free, I don't want to be mistreated by no bourgeoisie." The word "bourgeoisie" was in common use among political radicals; it referred to members of the comfortable, self-important middle class who never stooped to do anything as difficult as physical labor. Other Lead Belly protest songs included one about the Scottsboro case; nine black men falsely accused of rape in Alabama; an anti-Nazi song called "Mr. Hitler"; "One Dollar Bill, Baby," a song about being broke; and "Jim Crow," from an expression used to indicate racial discrimination that stems from minstrel days and a dance called Jump Jim Crow.

White sang many songs besides the blues, but he tended to be identified with his largely white audience as a blues artist, partly because of his unique guitar style. White invented a number of guitar strums, and also had a very smooth technique of bending the strings with his left hand. His protest songs were probably the most explicit ever written and performed on the subject of racial discrimination and oppression. In 1940 White recorded an album called *Chain Gang*, which featured the vocal arrangements of choral conductor Leonard De Paur. According to Elijah Wald, writing in *Society Blues*, his biography of White, all seven of the songs on the album were taken from Lawrence Gellert's two books of protest songs. Wald correctly points out that in a number of the songs the melodies were extensively altered, and in at least one case, almost entirely changed. White did not acknowledge Gellert's copyright claims, believing that the songs

Prisoners playing the blues (Library of Congress Films and Photographs Division)

were in the public domain, although Columbia Records apparently paid him royalties on the songs. These songs were strong medicine; for example, in "Jerry" the singer talks about a mule who is so overworked that he eventually kicks the boss man in the head. In "Troubled," the singer maintains that they "say he beat a white man, and they locked him in the can." The offender receives no trial and gets a sentence of 40 years "on the hard rock pile."

But White's protest songs were not confined to the Gellert collection. He followed up the Chain Gang album with a 1941 collection called *Southern Exposure: An Album of Jim Crow Blues.* These songs were cowritten by black poet Waring Cuney and White himself. In the song "Bad Housing Blues," White asserts that he is going all the way to the White House lawn, and he warns the president that he had "better wipe out these slums, been this way since I was born." In "Hard Times Blues" the singer takes a trip down South and finds burnt crops, empty barrels, and children with pellagra; when he asks the boss for mercy, the landlord kicks him off the land. "Uncle Sam Says" details discrimination in the armed services, pointing out that African Americans are not allowed to fly airplanes, their navy jobs are as mess boys, and when the black soldier returns home he faces the same discrimination.

In 1950 the U.S. Congress began investigating entertainers accused of having connections with communism. White appeared voluntarily before the House Committee on Un-American Activities, where he issued a statement that tried to separate his antiracist activities from any association with communism, or his old friend Paul Robeson. He did not name any of his associates as communists or former communists, and, as Elijah Wald indicates, the fact that he was black probably made the committee treat him with kid gloves. In any case White continued to perform but did not write any more directly political songs.

Big Bill Broonzy was a long-term resident of Chicago, and his audience turned from one where he performed almost entirely for African Americans to his "re-creation" as a country blues artist, playing for white folk fans. Along the way he met a number of people involved in left-wing political causes, like author and radio station host Studs Terkel. Broonzy recorded several songs that were strongly political. "I Wonder When I Will Get to Be Called a Man" is a protest against southerners calling adult black males "boys." "Black, Brown and White Blues" is about racial discrimination, with the key phrase, "if you're white, you're right, if you're brown, hang around, but if you're black, buddy get back, get back." Broonzy also wrote and recorded hundreds of other songs that had absolutely nothing to do with politics.

J. B. LENOIR, who was younger than the artists mentioned above, lived through the Korean War and into the Vietnam conflict, dying in 1967. Lenoir wrote several songs about the Korean War, such as "Korea Blues" and "I'm in Korea." These songs are not so much protests as expressions of his fears of death and of losing his woman friend while he is away. Lenoir did not serve in Korea, so he was obviously speaking for others. His 1954 song "Eisenhower Blues" complains about a lack of money, detailing his inability to pay the rent or buy clothes for his woman.

Lenoir became quite popular in Europe, and he wrote even more explicit songs, particularly "Alabama Blues," one of the rare songs to mention lynchings, "Mississippi Blues," "Viet Nam Blues," and "Shot on James Meredith," a song about the young African American who integrated the University of Mississippi. No one has directly connected Lenoir and radical political organizations, so it is reasonable to assume that his songs came from his personal beliefs. Certainly he was aware that there was more of an audience for such songs in Europe.

Although many blues do not openly suggest political issues, a considerable body of blues songs point out social injustices and often complain about them. The work of Lawrence Gellert suggests that many more such songs may have existed than were discovered by folklorists or produced by record companies. Even without Gellert's work, a considerable number of blues songs complain about racial discrimination and inequality, though they often do not present solutions for these problems. If one considers the number of songs about prison experiences, which are often more descriptive than political, the number of political songs rises even further. Blues scholar Van Rijn, having detailed blues and gospel songs about Presidents Franklin Roosevelt, Harry Truman, and Dwight Eisenhower, is now working on a book that covers up through the Kennedy period.

Pryor, Snooky (James Edward Pryor)
(b. 1921) *Chicago harmonicist*

A drummer, HARMONICA player, and singer, Snooky Pryor claimed to be the first CHICAGO harmonica player to amplify the instrument. He did this by running it through a public address (PA) system. Pryor played harmonica at the age of eight in MISSISSIPPI. He got the idea of amplifying the harmonica from playing through amplified sound systems while serving in the army. Pryor worked with HOMESICK JAMES, and recorded for a number of small record companies. He moved from Chicago to downstate Illinois in 1967 but was rediscovered and made several more albums, starting in 1987.

Quattlebaum, Doug (Douglas Elijah)
(1927–1959) *guitarist*
Doug Quattlebaum was from South Carolina. He moved with his mother to Philadelphia when he was seven years old. He learned how to play guitar and performed with various gospel groups, touring the southeastern states. He left home and rode freight trains to ARKANSAS and worked with BIG JOE WILLIAMS in Philadelphia. He worked in MEMPHIS, St. Louis, and CHICAGO before returning to Philadelphia. Blues record producer Pete Welding recorded one Quattlebaum album, issued on the Prestige label. Called *Softee Man Blues,* it showed Quattlebaum in the uniform of an ice cream truck driver.

See also MEMPHIS.

Rachell, Yank (James) (1910–1997)
mandolinist

Although Yank Rachell also sang and played guitar, his most important contribution to the blues is MANDOLIN playing. What few mandolin players there were often used the instrument to play rhythm, as did Rachell, but he was also among those who used it like a lead guitar. He started playing mandolin at the age of eight, and by the late 1920s he had hooked up with guitarist SLEEPY JOHN ESTES. They formed a trio with pianist Jab Jones. They recorded 14 songs for RCA and played on the streets and in clubs in MEMPHIS.

Although the band was successful at first, as the Great Depression continued, they broke up. Rachell had a family, and he farmed in Tennessee and later worked on the railroad. Rachell continued to do occasional recording, with SONNY BOY WILLIAMSON I, Dan Smith, and other artists. In 1958 Yank moved to Indianapolis, and when his wife died in 1961, he resumed his performing career. He reunited with Sleepy John Estes and another longtime friend, HARMONICA player Hammie Nixon. They recorded and toured Europe. After Estes died in 1977, Rachell cut down on his performances, although he was supposedly working on a new album at the time of his death.

Rachell made important contributions as a songwriter. His "Hobo Blues" was later covered by JOHN LEE HOOKER. Other artists who covered some of his other songs include BIG JOE WILLIAMS and JIMMY ROGERS.

radio and the blues

Over the years, radio has played several roles in the history of the blues. It has been a vehicle for musicians to play live, it has provided jobs for musicians as disc jockeys, and it serves as a means of introducing new recordings to the public. In 1948 WDIA in MEMPHIS became the first radio station to adopt an all-black music format. B. B. KING became a disc jockey at this station.

Playing live on the radio created opportunities for musicians to promote their live performances. KFFA in Helena, ARKANSAS, had the *King Biscuit Radio Show,* which still exists today on the station. In rhythm and blues music, some of the stations like WLAC in Nashville not only featured white disc jockeys who adopted black speech patterns, but also helped to promote black music through their advertisers, such as Randy's Record Shop in Nashville, which sold records by mail. Both WLAC and WDIA had powerful signals and were 50,000 watt stations that could be heard all over the South when the smaller daytime stations went off the air at sunset. CHESS RECORDS bought radio station WVON ("The Voice of the Negro") and used it as a vehicle for promoting the company's recordings.

Many public radio stations either play blues as part of their mix of music or devote shows specifically to the blues. Folklorist Nick Spitzer has a current radio show called *American Routes,* which often focuses on blues artists.

See also LEONARD CHESS.

ragtime and the blues

Ragtime had its roots in the vaudeville and music hall songs of the minstrel era. Minstrelsy originally consisted of white performers-singers, BANJO and FIDDLE players, and dancers and comedians imitating black musicians. Then came professional black performers following the same formula. Ragtime was an attempt to turn black popular music styles into more formal musical compositions and arrangements. Ragtime developed out of the so-called coon songs of the 1890s. These songs generally made fun of African Americans, using the derogatory term "coon" to describe them.

Scott Joplin (1868–1917) was the most famous ragtime musician, and his PIANO pieces are generally identified with ragtime. The style developed in MISSOURI in the period 1890–1910 and became popular among middle-class musicians in NEW YORK and New Orleans.

Many of the pieces were based on folk or folklike melodies, but they were transformed into a much more complex form. Ragtime piano pieces had as many as four separate sections, and they often changed key from one section to another. Syncopated melodies were juxtaposed against march music forms. There were many original compositions, and many of the best players were also composers. Ragtime existed in a sort of friendly opposition to jazz, which was developing at about the same time. Jazz was more of a working-class style of music, and many of the early jazz players did not rely on musical notation but developed their music from the blues.

Joplin and his students James Scott and the white pianist-composer Joseph Lamb did very little improvising. Their music was circulated through sheet music publications by a white music publisher, John Stark, whose music publishing company was based in St. Louis. The other way that ragtime made its way into the American musical picture was through piano rolls, often recorded by ragtime composers and purchased by owners of player pianos. A player piano functioned like a record player—the listener inserted the roll into the piano, pumped the pedals, then the piano roll played itself.

Ragtime piano became so popular that a number of instructional methods were published.

By the 1920s New York piano wizards James P. Johnson, Fats Waller, and Luckey Roberts had assimilated ragtime piano technique into their jazz stylings, adding improvisation to the mix. Joplin and Johnson also had greater composing ambitions, and Johnson wrote orchestral pieces, while Joplin spent the last part of his life unsuccessfully attempting to get his opera, *Treemonisha,* on the stage. (Many years after Joplin's death the opera was performed in Houston, Texas, and later in New York.)

The biggest influence of ragtime on the blues took place in the Piedmont area of the South, where Carolina guitarists WILLIE WALKER, BLIND GARY DAVIS, and BLIND BOY FULLER adapted ragtime piano styles to the guitar. They also utilized ragtime chord progressions, especially the progression I VI7 II7 V7I (C A7 D7 G7 C in the key of C). Several white musicians, notably Fred Van Eps and Vess Ossman, adapted rags to the five-string banjo in exceedingly complex musical arrangements that were well beyond the scope of the blues.

Ragtime was adapted into American popular music by New York Tin Pan Alley composers, like Irving Berlin. The instrumental style had virtually disappeared by the 1920s, but it was revived by a number of white musicians. Some were associated with the Dixieland jazz revival of the 1950s, and classical performer-musicologist Joshua Rifkin made a best-selling long-playing record of Joplin's music in 1970; the movie *The Sting* featured more of his music.

In the 1970s and 1980s white blues revivalists, including Stefan Grossman, David Laibman, Eric Schoenberg, and English guitarist John James, arranged and recorded rags for the guitar.

Rainey, Ma (Gertrude Pridgett) (1886–1939)
singer and songwriter
Of all the classic blues singers of the 1920s, Ma Rainey was the most rooted in the blues tradition. Although she shared the usual background of the

classic blues singers in minstrel shows and touring companies, Rainey came to the blues in the early years of the 20th century, when a young woman came backstage and sang her the blues. From then on Rainey started to perform the blues in her shows. Rainey informally taught BESSIE SMITH when they were both touring with the Rabbit's Foot Minstrels.

Rainey, a heavyset woman, dressed in flashy costumes, headbands, and gowns and wore large, expensive jewelry. From 1923 to 1928 Ma Rainey recorded about 100 songs, many of which have been reissued on CD. She wrote a large number of her own songs, which was unusual for most classic blues singers. Some of the songs that became well known include "C.C. Rider" (also called "Easy Rider"), "Bo Weevil Blues," and the humorous "Ma Rainey's Black Bottom." Rainey used two sorts of accompaniment for her records. Sometimes she recorded with famous jazzmen like LOUIS ARMSTRONG or Tommy Ladnier; at other times she went for more of a folk-blues sound, recording with guitarist TAMPA RED, pianist T. A. DORSEY (then called Georgia Tom), and homemade instruments like a trombone-kazoo and a one-string bass. This down-home approach appealed to many of her southern fans.

By 1933 classic blues and touring shows had become less popular, and Rainey retired to her native Columbus, Georgia, where she operated two theaters until her death.

Raitt, Bonnie (b. 1949) *singer and slide guitarist*

Bonnie Raitt's father, John, was a musical comedy star on Broadway and in film, and she was exposed to music at an early age. She started to play guitar when she was 12. She attended prestigious Radcliffe College, dropping out to participate in the Boston folk and blues scene. Besides being a talented singer, Raitt was a powerful slide guitarist, a style that few women, especially white women, had attempted at the time. She signed with manager Dick Waterman, and he sent her to tour with such blues masters as

Fred McDowell and HOWLIN' WOLF. Raitt recorded a number of albums for Warner Brothers during the 1970s and even recorded and toured with classic blues singer SIPPIE WALLACE, one of her idols.

By the end of the 1970s Warner Brothers had dropped her, and although she continued to tour, her career seemed to have come to a stop. In 1989 she got a new deal with Capitol Records, hooking up with producer Don Was. Her first album, *The Nick of Time*, sold in the millions and won six Grammy awards. More success came with her follow-up album, 1991's *Luck of the Draw*. By this time Raitt still performed blues in concert and played SLIDE GUITAR on her records, but her records featured more of her own songs and other pop-rock songs written by other songwriters.

For some years Bonnie Raitt has been involved with the Rhythm & Blues Foundation in Washington, D.C., which attempts to recover royalties for older rhythm and blues musicians, and to help those in financial need.

recording vs. live performance

There is quite a difference between performing and recording. In live performances acrobatic instrumental tricks and dance steps can bring an audience to a frenzy. In a recording situation, it is possible to play subtle instrumental passages or background vocal parts that the average listener would never be able to pick out.

Blues histories often discuss the limitations of the early recording medium. The songs had to last less than three minutes, for example. It is assumed that most songs were much longer in live performances. Yet most of what we know about the blues comes from listening to recordings. Another factor was that many of the early record producers were white men with little knowledge of the blues. Who knows how many great songs were dismissed by these producers as too innovative or odd. How many artists were rejected at auditions for similar reasons? Some of our current opinions are influenced by technology as well. MA RAINEY, for instance, never had the opportunity to make records on decent equipment; consequently, the reissues of her music are difficult to listen to. This has undoubtedly affected her place in blues history.

record labels

EARLY RECORD LABELS

A handful of labels have always dominated the market for recordings. In the days of the classic blues singers, these labels were RCA and Columbia. Over the years new labels have formed, and the big labels have bought out many of the smaller, independent labels. This continues today.

Traditionally the smaller labels made inroads in the marketplace by recording music that the major labels did not think was salable to a mass audience or did not know about. This principle has held throughout the history of the blues on record. In the 1920s, the major labels assumed that the black population of the United States was not large enough to make it worth their while to issue records of black music. Several companies jumped into the void. A black-owned record company, Black Swan, had a brief foray into the record business in 1921. The company was owned by songwriter-band-leader-music publisher W. C. HANDY and his publishing partner Harry Pace. Black Swan was primarily interested in recording music by black operatic and classical artists, although they issued a few blues recordings, including some by classic blues singer ALBERTA HUNTER.

The first company that issued black blues recordings was Okeh Records, an independent label that recorded Mamie Smith. When Smith's recordings proved to be successful, Paramount and Gennett Records started their own searches for blues artists. Paramount made its way into the blues by buying the bankrupt Black Swan and soon was recording MA RAINEY and BLIND LEMON JEFFERSON. Gennett recorded COW COW DAVENPORT, BIG BILL BROONZY, and Delta artists Cryin' Sam Collins and William Harris.

Gennett was owned by the Starr Piano Company, whose offices and recording studio were located in Richmond, INDIANA. Paramount was a division of the Wisconsin Chair Company in Grafton, Wisconsin.

Although the people who ran these companies were not particularly knowledgeable about black music, they were aware that it represented an untapped market. Paramount hired a black executive, J. Mayo Williams, to handle their blues endeavors, because they realized that they had little contact with the blues community for finding talent or determining what records were commercially viable. Williams operated out of a CHICAGO office, and he was instructed not to have anything to do with the label's white performers.

RECORD LABELS IN THE DEPRESSION

Gradually the independent labels went out of business. Okeh was acquired by Columbia Records in 1926, and the Great Depression, which started in 1929, led to the demise of Paramount and Gennett. Record sales plummeted from 150 million in 1929 to 10 million in 1933. In 1942 Chicago music fan John Steiner bought the rights to all Paramount recordings for $2,000. During the 1950s and 1960s many of these recordings were reissued on long-playing records by such labels as Riverside, Folkways, Origin Jazz Library, and Yazoo Records. These reissued albums were the catalyst for the work of the young white blues revivalists.

During the 1930s new record labels appeared on the scene. A new label called Decca, a division of the English Decca Company Limited, was established in 1934. Meanwhile, Columbia Records was bought by Consolidated Film Laboratories, which also acquired Brunswick and Vocalion Records.

RECORD LABELS DURING AND AFTER WORLD WAR II

During World War II the record business was affected by two different problems. The number of records pressed was limited because the government needed shellac for the war effort, and the American Federation of Musicians (AFM) issued a recording ban that lasted from August 1942 until September 1943. The union had decided that recordings were destroying opportunities for musicians to play live music, and it forbade musicians to play in recording sessions.

While the major labels were temporarily out of the business of making new recordings, a number of small labels opened their doors in or near New York City. Among them were Savoy (in New Jersey,) Alert, MOE ASCH's Disc, Sittin' In With, Jax, Derby, Harlem, Old Town, Red Robin, Gramercy, and Jackson. NEW YORK–based bluesmen BROWNIE MCGHEE and his brother Sticks and McGhee's playing partner SONNY TERRY seemed to be recording for virtually all of them.

TECHNOLOGICAL ADVANCES IN RECORDING

In 1948 Columbia Records introduced the long-playing (33 1/3 rpm) record, and RCA introduced the smaller 45 rpm format in 1949. After considerable bickering among the various companies, the industry adopted the standard long-playing record for albums and the seven-inch 45 rpm format for the release of double-sided singles. These new formats also used sturdier records, so that it now became feasible to ship records through the mail.

The other technological innovation that shook the recording business was the introduction of recording tape. Before 1947 all recordings were done "direct to disc." This meant that all artists would record with any accompanying instruments onto a wax master record. If there was a single mistake in the recording, the record would be scrapped, and the artist would record the selection again. The first tape recorders were brought back by American soldiers from Germany after World War II. Recording on tape was cheaper and easier than the old direct to disc format. The artist could record the same song repeatedly on the same piece of recording tape.

What happened next was of even greater significance. Guitarist Les Paul, record producer Mitch Miller, and a few others started to experiment with the process of over-dubbing, originally called sound on sound, where they would record on one tape recorder, then play that tape into another recorder while adding additional instrumental or vocal parts.

The first tape recorders were monaural machines—they had only a single track to record on. By the 1960s two-track tape recorders were in use in recording studios. With a two-track machine, it became possible to record a band on one track and the vocals on another. The process accelerated, and three-track, four-track, and eight-track machines were successively introduced, and ultimately 16- and 24-track recorders appeared; later even more tracks could be recorded.

The improved technology had little effect on the recording of, for example, folk-blues artists. However, it did affect the recording of rhythm and blues, which involved four, five, or more instruments, and often included background vocals as well as the lead vocal parts. Recording studios started to appear in all major cities and in many smaller ones as well. With them grew an ever-increasing number of record labels. Although part of this growth undoubtedly could be attributed to technology, much of it evolved from the somewhat unexpected commercial success of the music.

RECORD COMPANIES AND THE BLUES REVIVAL

Just as the larger record labels did not initially comprehend the existence of a market for African-American music, in 1950 the major record labels were primarily caught up in the marketing of white "middle of the road" music. Once again they sought a mass audience, and the white population of the United States was considerably larger than the black. A group of young entrepreneurs saw a void in the marketplace for black music and they decided to fill it. In New York two jazz fans, brothers Nesuhi and Ahmet Ertegun, partnered with Herb Abramson to start ATLANTIC RECORDS. The company quickly evolved from a jazz label to a rhythm and blues company interested in selling black popular music to white audiences as well as black. By the mid-1950s, CHESS RECORDS in Chicago, and SUN RECORDS in Memphis had begun their colorful odysseys. Cobra and Vee Jay operated in Chicago, Trumpet Records and Ace in Jackson, MISSISSIPPI, PEACOCK in Houston, TEXAS, and DELMARK RECORDS in St. Louis, later moving to Chicago. Folkways, Moe Asch's revival of his bankrupt Disc label, and Vanguard Records both opened their doors in New York.

A string of companies that either specialized in or often recorded rhythm and blues labels appeared in LOS ANGELES and San Francisco during this period. Among them were Big Town, Downtown, Aladdin, Modern, Specialty, Black & White, Imperial, and Exclusive. Capitol Records started in 1943, and it quickly became one of the major labels and the only one headquartered on the West Coast. By 1950 the major American labels were RCA, Columbia, Decca, and Capitol.

BLUES RECORD COMPANIES TODAY

The independent labels of the 1950s ran the gamut from short-lived companies that released a handful of records to companies that still have a presence in today's record business. Atlantic Records is the outstanding example of a survivor, albeit no longer as an independent label, but as a part of the WEA conglomerate that includes Warner Brothers and Elektra Records, among others. Many of the smaller companies were established by a single person, or a family who felt that they understood a particular musical style.

Many other blues labels operate today, including Antone's, Biograph, Bullseye, Burnside, Earwig, Fat Possum, High Tone, House of Blues, Canadian label Northern Blues, and Telarc. There are other, smaller labels. Most labels can be found with a Google search on the internet.

See also LEONARD CHESS; MEMPHIS; MISSISSIPPI.

Vee-Jay (1952)   Another black-owned label was started in Chicago in 1952 by husband-and-wife team Vivian and James Bracken. Vivian was a disc jockey in Chicago, and the couple owned a record shop in nearby Gary, INDIANA. During its early years, the label, called Vee-Jay, was quite a success, scoring R&B hits with Betty Everett and Gene Chandler, and

signing a white quartet from New Jersey, the Four Seasons. The white group was enormously successful, and Vee-Jay also released the Beatles' first American single when Capitol Records initially turned the band down, despite the entreaties of its English-owned EMI label.

The label's closest connection to the blues was its successful recordings of blues artist Jimmy Reed. Reed had a knack for writing simple, catchy songs, and he played guitar and HARMONICA at the same time, in the manner later popularized by BOB DYLAN, with the harmonica mounted on a rack around his neck. By 1965 the company had overexpanded and it went out of business.

Stax Records (1959)   During the 1960s Stax Records became one of the most successful independent record labels. Originally called Satellite Records, it was founded in 1959 in Memphis by Jim Stewart, a former country FIDDLE player, and his sister Estelle Axton. Stax did not record much blues, but they had dozens of successful rhythm and blues records. Some of their hit artists were Sam & Dave, Carla and RUFUS THOMAS, Otis Redding, the Staples Singers, Johnnie Taylor, ALBERT KING, and Isaac Hayes.

The success of the label was largely built on its rhythm section, Booker T. and the M.G.s, who played on most Stax Records but were also hit artists in their own right. In highly segregated Memphis, this rhythm section had two white and two black musicians playing together. Guitarist Steve Cropper and keyboard player Booker T. Jones also functioned as songwriters and producers for the label.

Overexpansion and poor business decisions brought the label into bankruptcy in 1975, and in 1977 all its product was sold. Today it is distributed by West Coast label Fantasy Records.

Motown Records (1960)   After some forays into songwriting for Jackie Wilson, Detroit entrepreneur Berry Gordy came to the conclusion that the only way he could make any real money was to own his own company. He started Motown Records in 1960, supposedly borrowing $600 from his family, and he was successful beyond his wildest dreams.

Motown's label used the logo "the sound of young America." From the very beginning it was Gordy's intention to go after the mass marketplace. Although many Motown Records did make their way onto the R&B charts, groups like The Supremes, Smokey Robinson & the Miracles, Martha & the Vandellas, and artists like Marvin Gaye and Little Stevie Wonder had numerous pop hits as well.

Motown operated like a well-oiled machine. Gordy hired a choreographer, owned the publishing rights on most of what was recorded, and employed staff songwriters and record producers. The instrumental tracks were recorded first, then various singers or vocal groups would sing over the instrumentals, until the producers and Gordy determined who performed the song the best. It was not an artist-friendly way to operate, but for many years it seemed to work perfectly. Motown had a separate division that managed their artists, and many of their artists were on allowances.

There are many books about Motown that detail Gordy's tight-fisted business practices and the iron rein that he held over the company. By 1971 Gordy had become more interested in the movie and theater aspects of show business than in records. He moved the entire company to Los Angeles.

Motown used independent record distributors until 1983, when cash flow problems led Gordy to make a distribution deal with MCA (the company that had evolved out of Decca Records). In 1988 Gordy sold the company to MCA, retaining his publishing company for some years.

Other Black Record Companies BOB GEDDINS operated a dozen record labels in the San Francisco area from 1944 until the mid-1960s. Geddins had some successful records and wrote a number of songs that became hits in performances by black and white artists that were not on his own label. He

was often forced to lease his productions to larger companies, because he did not have the ability to distribute his recordings effectively. Geddins was originally from Texas, but he moved to the San Francisco Bay Area in 1945. He owned his own studio and had his own pressing plant, and found many of his artists, like JIMMY MCCRACKLIN and LOWELL FULSON, singing in Bay Area clubs.

New York businessman Bobby Robinson operated a number of small labels, starting in the 1950s. Among them were Red Robin and Fire. Robinson recorded some 1950s unaccompanied vocal groups and occasionally issued records by such New York blues artists as Brownie McGhee. Never adequately financed or distributed, none of his labels ever caught on.

Today there are many black-owned rap record labels, but that goes beyond the scope of this book.

Other Independent Labels This brief survey shows only the tip of the iceberg. There were hundreds of independent labels. Trumpet Records was in Jackson, Mississippi, from 1951 to 1956 by LILLIAN MCMURRY, a white woman who worked in a hardware store that she and her husband owned. They began to sell records, and soon she was in the record business. At the time women operated few record companies and no other blues labels, especially in the Deep South. McMurry left the business in 1956, frustrated by her inability to collect bills from independent record distributors.

Other Labels Before 1965 Listing all the record labels of the period would take up many pages. Vanguard was active in the folk revival of the 1960s, issuing important Chicago blues albums. Elektra issued a number of Josh White albums during the later part of his career. Both these companies started in New York and exist today, but under different ownership.

The rhythm and blues labels include Ace in Jackson, Mississippi, Los Angeles–based Imperial, with its many hit R&B recordings by Fats Domino that crossed over into pop. Los Angeles–based

Aladdin, which recorded LIGHTNIN' HOPKINS among others, and such companies as Black & White, Galaxy, Chicago's Cobra, Modern, National, Satellite, Savoy, Specialty and Swingtime. All are gone now, and much of their product has disappeared from the marketplace.

Reed, Jimmy (James Mathis Reed) (1925–1976)
recording artist and harmonicist
Jimmy Reed recorded more hit records than any other bluesman. He had a genius for writing simple, easy-to-remember songs that listeners could quickly learn and other musicians could easily play. Not only were his songs successful on the R&B record charts, they also did well on the pop charts. Reed's audience was an unusual combination of older African Americans and young white fans.

Reed learned how to play HARMONICA and guitar from his boyhood friend EDDIE TAYLOR in his native MISSISSIPPI. Reed played both instruments together, placing the harmonica in a rack held around his neck. Some of his big hits include the classic "Big Boss Man" and "Bright Lights, Big City." They were recorded for CHICAGO's Vee-Jay Records, but when the company went bankrupt in 1965, Reed never recaptured his magic touch. Reed had 14 R&B hits and 11 songs that made the pop charts.

Unfortunately Reed was both a diabetic and an alcoholic, and the combination put an early end to his life.

rhythm and blues combos
Rhythm and blues evolved through "jump blues" combos like LOUIS JORDAN's Tympany Five, and by the end of World War II there were various genres of R&B. On the West Coast, Nat King Cole's sophisticated King Cole Trio influenced the work of soft blues crooning of such artists as CHARLES BROWN and even RAY CHARLES's early records. New Orleans featured a small-combo jazz-inflected R&B that climaxed in the million-selling records of pianist-singer Fats Domino, and in NEW YORK ATLANTIC

RECORDS and other companies were exploring marketing R&B to white teenagers.

The music featured either guitar or "honking" SAXOPHONE leads, and in short order New York saxophone player King Curtis became one of the primary recording saxophone players. While in LOS ANGELES saxophonist Plas Johnson played on dozens of recordings. The blues, especially the MISSISSIPPI blues, had always emphasized the second and fourth beats of the songs. Rhythm and blues accentuated this rhythmic feel, and the drummers were pounding these beats. In white country music it had been traditional to place the emphasis on the first and third beats of a bar in 4/4 time.

Certain rhythm section musicians, like drummers Pretty Purdie, Panama Francis, and Jimmy Johnson in New York; Los Angeles–based drummer Earl Palmer (originally from New Orleans); and New York bass players Jerry Jemmott and Chuck Rainey played on dozens of records, and stable rhythm sections developed in Muscle Shoals, Alabama; Motown Records in DETROIT; Stax Records in MEMPHIS; and in Los Angeles recording studios. These musicians could be counted on to do a quick and professional job of recording, and on their best days they could even be awe-inspiring. A movie and video, *Standing in the Shadows of Motown,* details the contributions of the Motown studio rhythm players, who were virtually never credited in the notes of the many Motown hits and albums that they played on.

In the 21st century record producers have inherited this mantle, creating rhythm grooves for hundreds of rap recordings. These days much of this work is done electronically, with the drums being programmed electronically instead of played live in the studio.

Ricks, Jerry (Philadelphia Jerry Ricks)
(b. 1945) *guitarist*
Jerry Ricks learned how to play guitar while working as a dishwasher and then as manager of the Second Fret folk club in downtown Philadelphia. Many great guitarists, including SKIP JAMES,

MISSISSIPPI JOHN HURT, and Doc Watson, stayed at Rick's house, which was located close to the club. As a result Ricks developed an encyclopedic knowledge of blues, and of American folk and country guitar styles. During the early 1960s, TAJ MAHAL and LARRY JOHNSON were virtually the only other young black artists interested in the blues. Ricks taught guitar to a bunch of aspiring blues guitarists in Philadelphia, and briefly in Denver, where he studied jazz guitar with Dale Bruning. Ricks also was a tour manager for an African tour with BUDDY GUY and SAXOPHONE player A. C. Reed.

Ricks spent most of the 1970s and 1980s living, touring, and recording in Europe. At one time he played lead guitar in an Austrian bluegrass band, and he toured and recorded in a blues-jazz duo. He returned to the United States in 1991 and has recorded two albums for Rooster Blues.

Jerry Ricks is a versatile guitarist who sings traditional blues and his own songs as well. He currently tours in the United States and in Europe. He took the name Philadelphia Jerry Ricks to avoid confusion with another existing artist named Jerry Ricks.

"Right Next Door (Because of Me)"
(1986) blues hit by Robert Cray

Few blues songs have become hit pop records. Robert Cray's "Right Next Door," released in 1986, concerns a sex symbol blues man who has broken up another man's marriage by romancing the man's wife. The singer hears the couple fighting through the walls, since he lives in the apartment next door. The song is not in strict blues form, because it has a chorus that is repeated several times. The lyrics are also a bit different from most blues in that the singer takes responsibility for his actions and expresses his guilt in the song.

Rishell, Paul (b. 1950) guitarist and singer

Brooklyn-born Paul Rishell is one of the white revivalists who keeps the torch of traditional blues burning. He has toured and recorded for years with his partner Little Annie Raines, and both are currently members of John Sebastian's band, The J-Band.

Robillard, Duke (Michael Robinson)
(b. 1948) guitarist and record producer

Duke Robillard is a versatile guitarist whose music spills over from the blues into jazz, rockabilly, and rhythm and blues. He founded the band Roomful of Blues in 1967, staying with it until 1979. He then played with MUDDY WATERS, and started another band of his own in 1981. Robillard replaced JIMMIE VAUGHAN in the FABULOUS THUNDERBIRDS from 1990 to 1992 and has produced records by such artists as JOHN HAMMOND and JAY MCSHANN.

Robinson, Bobby (b. 1917) record label and record store owner

Bobby Robinson was a record store owner in New York City's Harlem who started a number of labels in the 1950s until the mid-1960s. He recorded blues and R&B records. Some of his labels were Fire, Fury, Whirlin' Disc, Robin, and Red Robin. Among the blues artists whom Robinson recorded were BIG BOY CRUDUP, LIGHTNIN' HOPKINS, BROWNIE MCGHEE and SONNY TERRY, and ELMORE JAMES. Robinson's biggest hits were Wilbert Harrison's recording of "Kansas City" and Lee Dorsey's "Ya, Ya," which Robinson recorded in New Orleans.

Rockin' Sidney (Sidney Semien) (1938–1998)
zydeco artist

Rockin' Sidney was a swamp blues–zydeco artist who had a million-selling record, "My Toot Toot", in 1986. Before then Sidney had been a local artist, performing for Lake Charles, LOUISIANA, audiences and recording on small labels. He started out performing mostly rhythm and blues but added zydeco music to his set because he enjoyed the work of zydeco artist CLIFTON CHENIER. After his one major hit, Sidney returned to working on the local scene.

Roderick, Judy (1941–1992) *singer and guitarist*

Judy Roderick was a talented singer and guitarist who never became lucky during her musical career. She started playing professionally while she was a student at the University of Colorado, moving to NEW YORK and signing a record contract with Columbia Records. Roderick was a small person with a big voice, and Bobby Scott, the piano player-songwriter who produced her records at Columbia seemed to want to turn her into a BILLIE HOLIDAY. He surrounded her with excellent jazz accompanists and took her out of the folk-blues music categories in which she had been performing. The second Columbia album was never released, when Scott and Roderick could not agree on the musical direction of the recording.

Roderick then recorded an album for Vanguard called *Woman Blue.* This recording was a combination of blues and folk-oriented material, but the timing of the record was unfortunate, because it was released in 1965, when the folk boom had waned and British rock groups were dominating the music scene. Roderick used the recording to play folk festivals and clubs, especially on the East Coast.

Roderick then formed a partnership with lyricist Bill Ashford, and they formed a folk-rock band called 60,000,000 Buffalo. The band recorded for ATLANTIC but the record did not have much success. The two wrote a song called "Floods of South Dakota," which was later recorded by Tim and Mollie O'Brien. Roderick then moved to Montana, where she continued to play music, but finally succumbed to diabetes, which she had fought since childhood.

Rodgers, Jimmie (1897–1933) *singer*

Jimmie Rodgers was known as the Singing Brakeman, a tribute to his years working on the railroad. Rodgers was discovered by RALPH PEER when Peer was doing field recordings in 1927. In six years of recording Rodgers recorded 110 songs. Rodgers was considered a country artist, but he recorded a number of blues songs and 13 songs that he called "blue yodels." The yodels used the format of blues songs, repeating lines, but Rodgers added a sort of cowboy yodel at the end of each verse. He also recorded with jazz musicians, including LOUIS ARMSTRONG, blues guitarist Clifford Gibson, and the Louisville Jug Band. It was unusual at the time for white and black musicians to record together.

Long after his death Rodgers's recordings continued to sell well. Rodgers influenced many country singers, including Lefty Frizzell and Merle Haggard. Haggard even recorded an entire album of Rodgers's songs, called *Same Train, Different Time.* Biographies and interviews with numerous blues singers have revealed that they were familiar with Rodgers's work.

Rogers, Jimmy (James A. Lane) (1924–1997) *multi-instrumentalist*

Jimmy Rogers is probably best known for early 1950s work with the MUDDY WATERS band. Rogers played rhythm guitar for Waters, often using bass lines to connect the chords. Like so many other blues artists, Rogers's first instrument was the HARMONICA, which he learned as a child growing up in ATLANTA. He played guitar with ROBERT LOCKWOOD Jr. and ROBERT NIGHTHAWK, and played with pianist Sunnyland Slim in St. Louis and East St. Louis before coming to CHICAGO in 1941. Before he joined Waters's band, Rogers played with MEMPHIS MINNIE, Sunnyland Slim, and other blues artists.

While he was in the Waters band, Rogers made solo records of his own for CHESS RECORDS. He had one hit, his 1957 recording of "Walkin' by Myself." It reached number 14 on the R&B charts. Rogers then continued to work as a sideman for HOWLIN' WOLF and SONNY BOY WILLIAMSON II (Rice Miller). He also performed with his own band.

In 1960 Rogers left music to open a clothing store. His store burned down during the 1968 Chicago race riots, and Rogers returned to performing in 1971. He recorded several albums, toured Europe, and played in Chicago clubs.

Rogers, Roy (b. 1950) *slide guitarist*

Roy Rogers has the reputation of being an excellent slide guitarist, and he made a number of albums, several of them with HARMONICA player Norton Buffalo. He also recorded an instructional video on SLIDE GUITAR. Rogers played in bar bands in the San Francisco area during the 1980s, and played in JOHN LEE HOOKER's band from 1982 to 1986. In addition to his guitar work, Rogers sang and also produced records. He produced John Lee Hooker's *The Healer* in 1990 then won a Grammy for producing Hookers's 1991 album, *Mr. Lucky.*

Roland, Walter (c. 1900–?) *pianist and singer*

Walter Roland was born around 1900 in Pratt City, Alabama, but no one is certain when he died. Roland was a piano player and singer who accompanied singers Lucille Bogan and JOSH WHITE. Roland's recordings reveal that he played boogie-woogie, blues, and ragtime-influenced music. He was popular around Birmingham, Alabama, and also played guitar. There is no record of his activities after 1935.

Rolling Stones, The

Most of the members of the Rolling Stones were blues fanatics who hung out in London clubs. Charlie Watts, the drummer, was more of a jazz fan. Early recordings by the Stones included cover records of such artists as CHUCK BERRY, WILLIE DIXON, and JIMMY REED. In 1964 the band actually recorded an extended-play 45 rpm record at CHESS RECORDS in CHICAGO. (Extended-play records were 45 rpm recordings that usually contained four songs, as opposed to singles, which had only two songs.) Since singer Mick Jagger and guitarists Brian Jones and Keith Richards idolized many of the Chess artists, this was a big thrill for the Stones. After all, the name of the band had come from of a MUDDY WATERS recording. The Stones also insisted on touring with blues artists during the early part of their career. Jagger also borrowed a lot of his performing personality from rhythm and blues artists.

Over the years the Stones began to write all their own songs and moved in more of a rock than blues direction.

See also LEONARD CHESS.

Roomful of Blues

Many instrumentalists and singers have passed through this band, which continues to perform. The band's founder was guitarist DUKE ROBILLARD. He was in the band from 1969 to 1979; others who passed through the band include vocalist Lou Ann Barton, and guitarist RONNIE EARL. Songwriter DOC POMUS helped the band get their record deal with Island Records in 1977. The band continues with nine pieces today.

Ross, Doctor (Charles Isaiah Ross) (1925–1993) *one-man band and radio show host*

In the 80-odd years that the blues have been recorded, there are only a few examples of one-man bands. JESSE FULLER and, earlier, Daddy Stovepipe come to mind. Another was Doctor Ross, who played HARMONICA and guitar at the same time and also rigged up a bass drum and high hat cymbal that he also used. Ross played the guitar left-handed but upside down, so that his thumb was playing the higher strings, and his other fingers the lower ones. This is the opposite right-handed guitar playing. Ross tended to strum percussively as though he were playing a BANJO or a 12-STRING GUITAR. He got his nickname because he carried his harmonica in a doctor's bag.

Ross had a radio show in MEMPHIS and he recorded for CHESS and SUN RECORDS. He spent most of his adult life in Flint, Michigan, where he worked as a janitor at General Motors, performing on the weekends or at night. There is a video available of Ross's final performance, five months before his death.

See also LEONARD CHESS.

Rounder Records

Founded in 1970 in Cambridge, Massachusetts, Rounder has become one of the most successful independent labels of all time. Ken Irwin, Marian Leighton-Levy, and Bill Nowlin, the original founders, still operate the label.

For blues fans the most significant part of the extensive Rounder catalog is the release of 140 albums by folk music scholar ALAN LOMAX. Although a number of the albums represent music collected in different parts of the world, many of the releases are newly issued and reissued artifacts of Lomax's many collecting trips in the southern United States. The label has also reissued albums recorded by Lomax and others for the Library of Congress, and many of these albums contain blues and other African-American music.

Rounder has achieved great commercial success with a few of their artists, notably white blues artists GEORGE THOROGOOD and the Destroyers in the late 1970s, and much more recently with bluegrass artist Alison Krauss. The label has also recorded cajun music and New Orleans blues artists.

Rush, Bobby (Emmett Ellis Jr.) (b. 1940)
"chitlin' " artist

Dozens of musicians work the so-called chitlin' circuit in the South, playing in black clubs often for older audiences. One of these artists is Bobby Rush, who featured in the Blues Legacy series about MEMPHIS. His story, the long bus tours and performances in small clubs, was compared in the Memphis video to the way in which B. B. KING became a worldwide star. Rush is from LOUISIANA, but he moved to CHICAGO with his family when he was 13 years old. He played in the West Side clubs but gave that up to tour the southern states.

Rush has recorded for a number of labels. Many of his songs are about romantic or sexual situations, and he uses dancers in his club act. In 2001 Rush's tour bus had an accident, and one band member was killed and Rush injured. Bus tours are part of the life on the chitlin' circuit, because there is not enough money to afford airplane tickets and the venues are regional.

Rush, Otis (b. 1934) *Chicago guitarist and singer*

Otis Rush has been a strong influence on other musicians, including rock group LED ZEPPELIN, but he has not been fortunate in his music career. He has consistently had problems with record labels. In 1971 he obtained a record deal with Capitol, and it appeared that he was finally going to get his big break. Instead the company paid all the costs of making an album, then decided they did not want to put it out. It took five years for Rush to get the record back and have it released on a small label. Earlier he recorded for Cobra Records, CHESS, DELMARK, ATLANTIC, and MCA, among others. Rush became disillusioned with record companies and walked out on a Rooster Blues Records session when he complained that his amplifier did not sound right.

A left-handed guitarist, Rush was one of the inventors of the West Side blues style and is considered to be one of the best Chicago blues performers both as singer and guitarist. He continues to perform and to record today. Among his songs are "I Can't Quit You Baby" and "My Love Will Never Die."

Rushing, Jimmy (1903–1972) *singer*

Jimmy Rushing—"Mister Five by Five," as he was called in reference to his small height but large body—was a jazz and blues singer. Rushing sang with the Count Basie swing band from 1935 to 1950. As a child he studied PIANO, voice, and music theory. He sang with JELLY ROLL MORTON at West Coast house parties, and went to Kansas City, where he played with Bennie Moten. After Moten's death, Rushing joined Basie.

After Rushing left the Basie band, he sang at various jazz festivals, did a few reunions with Basie, and worked with piano players Dave Brubeck and Earl Hines. He also appeared in several movies, including *Brussels Blues* and *The Learning Tree*.

Saffire—The Uppity Blues Women

Saffire is a feminist blues trio, started by three women who were all fond of the blues. They write original songs and also cover songs by such artists as MEMPHIS MINNIE, BESSIE SMITH, MA RAINEY, and IDA COX. The band features piano, guitar, and bass, and all three women sing. The original members were Ann Rabson on piano, Gaye Adegbolola on guitar, and Earlen Lewis on bass. Lewis left the group in 1992 and was replaced by Andra Faye McIntosh. The band has an acoustic sound, and their songs tend toward the sarcastic. A couple of titles of their original songs are "Even Yuppies Get the Blues" and "Middle Aged Boogie." The trio all gave up other careers to make music full time, and they tour in the United States, Canada, and Europe.

Sahm, Doug (1941–1999) *multi-instrumentalist*

It is difficult to pinpoint the style of Doug Sahm's music. He played, variously, cajun, rock and roll, western swing, and Tex-Mex music—the music of the TEXAS-Mexico border. Sahm started his musical career on the steel guitar, playing on San Antonio radio at the age of nine. He made recordings for the legendary record producer Huey Meaux, who was known as the "crazy Cajun." In the 1960s Sahm formed the Sir Douglas Quintet, and had some recording success with the song "She's About a Mover." He then moved to northern California, formed the Honkey Blues Band, then brought Sir Douglas back together and recorded the hit song

"Mendocino." Sahm made an album for ATLANTIC RECORDS in NEW YORK. The producer was the famed Jerry Wexler, and the personnel included BOB DYLAN, DR. JOHN, and the Tex-Mex accordion player Flaco Jimenez. Sahm sang, played guitar and violin and was a musical arranger and bandleader.

"St. Louis Blues" (1914) *early blues by W. C. Handy*

W. C. HANDY was a bandleader and songwriter who quickly grasped the commercial possibilities of blues music. He published his "St. Louis Blues" in 1914, and it quickly became a blues-jazz standard, recorded by many singers and bands. Artists who have recorded the song include the Mills Brothers, ETHEL WATERS, bandleader Cab Calloway, jazz artists LOUIS ARMSTRONG, Earl Hines, blues singer BESSIE SMITH, and swing-jazz musician Benny Goodman. Smith's only movie appearance was made in a short film named after the song.

Handy wrote the song while living in MEMPHIS. When music publishers expressed little interest in picking it up, he formed his own music publishing company in partnership with Harry Pace.

The form of the song is unusual. The verses are straightforward blues, with the first line of each verse repeated. The third verse is in tango form. The tango was an Argentine dance in vogue at the time. The Tango section is startling the first time the listener hears it, because it seems so uncharacteristic of the blues. Another uncharacteristic part of the song is a musical bridge that follows the tango section. This section has a lyric that contains three separate lines, with no repeated section. Possibly because of the tango section and the bridge, many jazz musicians were intrigued enough with this song to record their own versions of it.

Salgado, Curtis (b. 1954) *harmonicist and singer*

HARMONICA player and singer Curtis Salgado is one of the more important blues artists in the northwest. He was the lead singer in the ROBERT CRAY band from 1980 to 1982, joined a ROOMFUL OF BLUES from 1981 to 1984, and had his own band, Curtis Salgado and the Stilletos, in 1981. Salgado is a soulful player and singer, reflecting blues and R&B influences. He has recorded solo albums about every two years from 1995 to the present, often playing in the northwest, close to his Portland, Oregon, home.

"San Francisco Bay Blues" (1954) *popular folk blues by Jesse Fuller*

JESSE FULLER was a one-man band, playing guitar, bass (with his feet), and HARMONICA. He came up with this ragtimey song in 1954, and it became a staple of the folk music revival. It has been recorded by ERIC CLAPTON, the Journeymen, Peter, Paul & Mary, and JANIS JOPLIN. The song is about a woman who has gone away, and the singer dreams of getting her back, and "walking with my baby by the San Francisco Bay." The catchy melody sounds distinctively different from most blues-flavored material.

Satan & Adam (Sterling Magee) (b. 1936) (Adam Gussow) (b. 1958) *harmonicist and guitarist*

White HARMONICA player Adam Gussow met black guitarist and singer Sterling Magee on a Harlem streetcorner where Magee was playing his guitar and singing. Gussow started to sit in on harmonica, and soon the duo was born. It was an unusual combination of talents—an interracial, cross-generational, and social class combo.

Magee played PIANO growing up in Florida and MISSISSIPPI and, during the 1960s, played on recording sessions with JAMES BROWN, King Curtis, and George Benson. Gussow was a recent college graduate living in NEW YORK. The duo made three albums, but Magee moved to Lynchburg, Virginia, in 1998, and Gussow became a college professor. Gussow documented the story of their collaboration in a book called *Mr. Satans Apprentice,* and he has also written a recently published book on violence and the blues.

Satherly, Art (Uncle Art) (1889–1986) *record producer*

Art Satherly had a long and amazing career in Europe. Born in England, he moved to the United States around 1910 and became inventor Thomas Edison's secretary, He then worked as a promotion manager and record producer for Paramount Records during the 1920s, when their major artists were BLIND LEMON JEFFERSON and MA RAINEY. Satherly was one of the early commercial record producers to become involved in field recording, taking the studio to the artist instead of bringing the artist to the studio.

Next Satherly went to work for Columbia Records, where he recorded BLIND BOY FULLER and BLIND GARY DAVIS, but he achieved his biggest fame recording country music artists Roy Acuff, Carl Smith, Lefty Frizzell, cowboy singer Gene Autry, Marty Robbins, and many other artists. Satherly retired from Columbia in 1952 and was elected to the Country Music Foundation Hall of Fame in 1971.

Savoy Brown

The British band Savoy Brown has had several dozen personnel changes but continues today, after nearly 40 years. The only original member is founder and guitarist Kim Simmonds. The band has experienced varying degrees of success over its lengthy career, and was a popular touring band in the United States during the 1970s. More than a dozen of their blues-rock albums are available, such as *Live in Central Park*. Unlike some of the other British blues bands, no superstars have passed through Savoy Brown.

saxophone, trombone, trumpet, and clarinet

The classic blues singers were the first blues artists who performed with horn players—trumpet, trombone, clarinet or saxophone players. Singers like MA RAINEY and BESSIE SMITH often featured one or more horn players in their bands. These were jazz musicians for whom the blues were an ingredient in their musical stew but not the main course. Certain musicians, like trumpet players LOUIS ARMSTRONG, Tommy Ladnier, and Joe Smith; clarinetists Johnny Dodds and Jimmy Noone; and trombonist Charlie Green were known as particularly good blues players. Bessie Smith was fond of Joe Smith and sang a song that mentioned Green's trombone playing ("Charlie Green—play that thing, I mean that slide trombone").

Since many of the classic blues were vaudeville-like songs, sometimes with relatively sophisticated chord changes, jazz musicians were appropriate performers. Saxophone was not as common in the backup for early blues singers, but it appeared on some of BIG BILL BROONZY's records during the period 1935–40.

Seals, Son (Frank Seals) (b. 1942) *multi-instrumentalist*

Drummer, guitarist, and vocalist Son Seals got his record deal with ALLIGATOR RECORDS by auditioning over the phone for Alligator president BRUCE IGLAUER. He recorded eight albums for the label and switched to Telarc in 2000. Seals lived in the back of the juke joint run by his father in Oscela, ARKANSAS. A versatile musician, Seals played second guitar with EARL HOOKER and drums with ALBERT KING.

Seals's records vary between CHICAGO blues and a more R&B sound that includes horns.

"See That My Grave Is Kept Clean" (aka "Six White Horses," "One Kind Favor") (1926) *Blind Lemon Jefferson song*

BLIND LEMON JEFFERSON wrote this song in 1926. It is the lament of a dying man, afraid that he will not be remembered. In the lyric the singer gives directions as to how he should be buried. This song has been particularly popular with white revivalists. It was recorded by BOB DYLAN, JOHN HAMMOND JR., DAVE VAN RONK, and Australian blues artist Jeff Lang. There is also a recording by the white southern mountain instrumentalist and singer Hobart Smith.

Seward, Alec (1901–1974) *guitarist*

Alec Seward was a Piedmont musician who settled in NEW YORK. He recorded with SONNY TERRY and with Woody Guthrie, making two now out-of-print albums under his own name. Though a capable musician, Seward never established much of a music career.

sharecropping

After the end of the Civil War, few African Americans were able to realize their dreams and own their own land. Although many left the plantations where they had been slaves, many had no place to go and lacked the financial resources that would have enabled them to leave. This led to the development of a new labor system called sharecropping. Sharecropping literally meant sharing the ownership of crops. A black farmer would work part of a large farm owned by a white planter. The owner would provide the sharecropper with "furnish," meaning that he would lend money for basic necessities like food, provide farm equipment, furnish seeds and other necessities, and they would share the cost of fertilizer. The farmer usually shopped at a store operated by the large plantation owner, where prices were often marked up.

If the sharecropper ran out of money before the end of his monthly stipend, he would have to borrow money from the planter.

The sharecropper's working year began in March, and by the end of November the cotton, which was often the crop involved, would be picked. Before Christmas the sharecropper settled up in boss's office. The boss would pay anything left over between the monies advanced and the sales of the crop.

Many sharecroppers were only partly literate at best, and they had to take the owner's word for what monies were owed to them. Disputes might prompt the farm owner to call the sheriff, who was invariably white and took the side of the farm owner. Even if the farm owner did not overestimate the advance money he had paid to the sharecropper, between the interest that the owners charged and the inflated prices charged at the commissary, there was not likely to be much left for the sharecropper. In fact many owners claimed that the sharecroppers owed *them* money. This forced the cropper to stay on the farm until he could work himself out of debt, if that was ever to become a possibility.

Yale anthropologist Hortense Powdermaker, who spent a year studying the sharecropper system in the 1930s in Indianola, MISSISSIPPI, estimated that three quarters of sharecroppers were cheated by farm owners. (Indianola was the birthplace of B. B. KING and is about 60 miles from Delta blues center Clarksdale.)

The disgruntled sharecropper had a limited number of alternatives to staying on the farm. He could remain and hope the next year would be better. He could also try to find a farm where the owner might treat him better. If the sharecropper owed the owner money, leaving would be like attempting a jailbreak. It required packing up in the middle of the night and moving far enough away that the

owner could not trace him. The last alternative was to leave the area entirely and go north.

By the 1960s the sharecropper system had drastically declined, and what black workers were still working on the farm served as day laborers. In 1967 the federal government expanded the minimum wage program to include farm workers, and the farmers had to raise their wages to $1.15 an hour. According to Nicholas Lemann's book *The Promised Land,* the prevailing wage at the time had been $3 a day. The use of chemicals and machinery then largely eliminated the need for black farm workers in the South.

Shaw, Robert (1908–1985) *pianist*
Robert Shaw was one of a group of pianists who made a living during the 1920s playing at various railroad stops along the Santa Fe Railroad. Shaw also sang, and he played at the work camps where railroad workers lived. By the 1930s he was playing in Oklahoma City saloons, and in 1935 he moved to Austin, TEXAS, where he opened a grocery store, Shaw's Market & Barbecue.

Semiretired from music because of his business, Shaw was rediscovered by Houston playwright-folklorist Mack McCormick. He recorded an album for ARHOOLIE RECORDS that demonstrated his complex technique. He performed occasionally during the 1970s in the United States and Europe.

Shepherd, Kenny Wayne (b. 1977) *guitarist*
Kenny Wayne began his career by figuring out some of MUDDY WATERS's guitar licks at the age of seven. Managed by his father, Shepherd had a record deal with Giant Records, which was distributed by a major label. His first album sold over 500,000 copies. Shepherd's band uses lead vocalist Corey Sterling, because Shepherd himself does little singing. His band is a loud, closer to rock volumes than to a blues band. Shepherd finds some of the same kinds of fans that liked STEVIE RAY VAUGHAN.

Shines, Johnny (1915–1992) *guitarist*

Johnny Shines was so identified with ROBERT JOHNSON that in a sense he never had the chance to demonstrate his own talents. Wherever he appeared, blues fans knew that he and ROBERT LOCKWOOD JR. were among the only two living musician associates of Johnson, and they repeatedly pestered him with questions about the Delta blues legend. Shines had traveled with Johnson from 1934 until about 1938, and he did indeed have stories to tell.

In 1941 Shines moved to CHICAGO, where he recorded for CHESS and other smaller record labels. In 1958 he felt his career was going nowhere, so he sold his guitar and gave up music. A 1965 opportunity to record for NEW YORK's Vanguard Records revived Shines's career, and he pursued the opportunity by playing at festivals and recording for Testament. In 1969 he moved to Tuscaloosa, Alabama, then spent the next 10 years touring intensively; he taught guitar as well. He and Lockwood teamed up to make a couple of albums and to perform together. In 1980 Shines had a stroke, and though he continued to perform, his ability to play the guitar was limited. Some of his students traveled with him to help him.

Johnny Shines played many of Robert Johnson's tunes, but he was not limited to Johnson's repertoire, and he was a much more powerful singer than Johnson.

See also LEONARD CHESS.

Siegel-Schwall Band

Jim Schwall and Corky Siegel's band, like the PAUL BUTTERFIELD band, was a young white revivalist blues band. Their style was more subdued than Butterfield's group, and they recorded an album of a piece written by composer William Russo for rock band and the Chicago Symphony Orchestra.

After the band broke up in 1974, Siegel became more interested in combining the blues with classical music. He now plays keyboards and HARMONICA with a chamber group that includes a string quartet and a musician who plays the tabla (Indian drums). Siegel has performed with this group at the Aspen Music Festival and various concert series in major cities. Occasionally the Siegel-Schwall band plays together, but Schwall teaches music at the University of Wisconsin, and Siegel continues to pursue his experiments combining chamber music and the blues.

"Sittin' on Top of the World" (1930) *oft-covered blues song*

A widely circulated song first recorded in 1930 by the MISSISSIPPI SHEIKS, this was written by the duo of fiddler Lonnie Chatmon and guitarist WALTER VINSON. The song is unusual in having a chorus that is repeated after each verse: "Now she's gone, and I don't worry, 'cause I'm sittin' on top of the world." The verses invariably refer to the singer's woman leaving him. One of the most popular blues, it has been recorded by the Grateful Dead, BOB DYLAN, CARL PERKINS, Bob Wills and his Texas Playboys, Bill Monroe, HOWLIN' WOLF, CREAM, and Jack White on the soundtrack of the movie *Cold Mountain*. In the various versions the verses are noticeably modified. TAMPA RED recorded the identical melody with different lyrics in his "Things About Comin' My Way." It had a chorus as well, although the lyric was different: "After all my hard travelin', things about comin' my way."

slide guitar

"Slide guitar" can be played with a knife or a bottleneck as well as a metal, glass, or ceramic slide. The mystery of slide guitar is how a technique identified with Hawaiian guitar music could have become such a powerful force in the music of the MISSISSIPPI Delta.

Stephen Calt's introduction to guitar player Woody Mann's useful instructional folio *Bottleneck Guitar* traces the development of the style to a Hawaiian musician, Joseph Kekuku, who was a student at the Oahu Boys' School in 1893. Around that time he started experimenting with fretting the guitar. Initially he used a comb, then he found he could get a better sound with a knife or a solid steel bar. Kekuku created a fretless guitar, raising the strings by "wedging a thin piece of metal beneath the fretboard." By sliding the knife or bar he could play notes between the pitches at which he started, and his end note. He could also play the frets of the guitar, beyond where the fingerboard was joined to the body of the instrument. He played the guitar in his lap, and according to Mann, he held the bar either between his left thumb and forefinger or between the forefinger and middle finger.

Kekuku tuned the guitar to an open chord, that is, he did not have to use his other left-hand fingers to play, for example, the G chord in G tuning.

By the turn of the 20th century guitars were becoming popular in the southern United States, partly owing to their sales through Sears & Roebuck catalogs. They were sold through the catalog in 1900 for as little as $2.70, and the most expensive models were priced at $18.00.

It quickly became apparent to blues singers that the guitar was a great accompaniment vehicle for singers, better than either the BANJO or the FIDDLE. The fiddle could not play chords, and the banjo had a harsh sound and lacked the bass notes of the guitar. The six-string banjo had that range, but the sound in the low register tended to be muffled.

Slide guitar spread like wildfire in Hawaii, and it came into this country either because American sailors brought it home or because of the performances of a Hawaiian guitarist at the Columbia exposition in CHICAGO in 1893.

Another possible explanation for the introduction of American slide technique is the notion of "independent invention," an anthropological term used to describe the situation when two different people or groups come up with the same idea at the same time in different places. W. C. HANDY reported seeing a guitarist playing guitar with a knife in 1903 in Mississippi. It is difficult to believe that the style could have wandered into Mississippi from

Hawaii during the same year that Kekuku was experimenting with it.

Blues guitarists used the slide techniques to create two very different sounds. TAMPA RED, for example, played slide in a Hawaiian style. He used the technique to get a sweet sound, holding out and emphasizing single notes and he played only on the treble strings. Delta players like SON HOUSE or ROBERT JOHNSON were intrigued with slide because it could create a driving beat, and also because it could help to create a dialogue between the guitar and the singer where the slide echoed a voice. In fact the slide almost sounded like someone crying.

The slide guitar player holds the slide on top of the fret, rather than just behind it, as is the case in usual playing styles. If the player fingers behind the fret, the note will be flat. If the player fingers above the fret, the note will be sharp. It takes skill to play consistently on the frets, so that everything is in tune.

The early slide guitarists used the slide (or medicine bottle or knife) in one of two ways. One way was simply to hold it between two fingers of the left hand. When the player used the slide in this way, the other left-hand fingers could not be used to play chords. The other way of using the slide was to wear it like a ring on a left-hand finger. The player could then use the other left-hand fingers to play chords. Since chords in open tunings are easier to finger with the left hand, this meant that they could either use the slide with or without the left-hand fingers. Besides its use in blues, gospel evangelist guitarists like BLIND WILLIE JOHNSON and the Reverend Edward Clayborn also used the technique in their music.

Slide playing was effective for imitating sounds, especially the sort of train effects that BUKKA WHITE, for one, employed. Players who favored the Hawaiian approach would usually also adopt the technique of playing the guitar flat on the lap, as opposed to the Delta guitarists, who held the guitar upright. CASEY BILL WELDON used this technique, and today Ben Harper sometimes does. Blues musicians also started using glass slides, breaking off pieces of a bottle then smoothing them out. From that use the term "bottleneck guitar" developed. KOKOMO ARNOLD, who was left-handed, picked the strings with his left hand and wore his slide on the little finger of his right hand.

Among white country musicians slide playing was usually relegated to the dobro. It had raised steel strings and was played with a metal bar. It remains in use in bluegrass bands, but in many ways it was replaced and overwhelmed by the pedal steel guitar, a more complex instrument that lies outside blues territory. Country banjoist Doc Walsh used a knife in his blues banjo playing.

After World War II, MUDDY WATERS and ELMORE JAMES adapted slide technique to the electric guitar, and many rock and blues guitarists use the technique. It is virtually a staple of post–Muddy Waters Chicago style electric playing, with EARL HOOKER generally regarded as one of the masters of the style. BONNIE RAITT made her instrumental reputation through her slide guitar work, and the technique has particularly fascinated many younger white blues revivalists. RY COODER, KELLY JO PHELPS, and BOB BROZMAN have taken slide technique to many new musical areas, in their own compositions, Cooder's film scoring, especially for the film *Paris, Texas,* and Brozman and Cooder's experiments in integrating slide with various world music styles.

Smith, Bessie (1894–1936) *singer and songwriter*

Books and plays have been written about Bessie Smith. Her music career began with MA RAINEY's Rabbit Foot Minstrels, where Rainey employed her as a chorus girl. Smith got to record before her teacher, and she recorded more than 160 songs from 1923 to 1933. She received no royalties for the songs but initially was paid $125 per song, which was raised to $200, before falling back down to $125 toward the end of her career. Recent information has revealed that she signed away her songwriting royalties in a similar way to a Columbia Records executive. There was a guarantee that the company

Bessie Smith (Bettmann/Corbis)

would record a certain number of sides each year, but the records were so successful that until the end of her career Smith recorded more than that number. She made lots of money for Columbia—her first record sold over 780,000 copies in the first six months of its release.

Smith was a unique singer, with a powerful voice that she used in a very musical way. She could shout with the loudest singer, but often she preferred to let the lyrics tell the song's story. She rarely recorded with a drummer, which would be unheard of today or even among blues singers of the 1950s. Many of her most interesting songs, like "Young Woman's Blues" and "Back Water Blues," were her own compositions, although she also recorded many songs by other writers. In "Young Woman's Blues" a woman expresses her independence by saying "I'm a young woman, and I ain't done running round." "Backwater" is about a flood that someone described to Smith. She worked with accomplished jazz musicians, including LOUIS ARMSTRONG, but her favorite accompanist was cornet player Joe Smith. She even recorded a song about one of her accompanists, whom she called Trombone Cholly. The song was about Charley Green, who played on many of her records.

Smith had a dramatic, complex life, with an up-and-down relationship with her husband, Jack Gee. She had a huge appetite for life and drank heavily at times. Smith died in an automobile accident in MISSISSIPPI. For years it was rumored that she had been taken to a white hospital and turned away. Somehow that story got to record producer JOHN HAMMOND, and he spread the news in an article in the jazz magazine *Downbeat*. Smith's main biographer, Chris Albertson, interviewed a number of people involved, and it turned out that the story was not true.

Smith was buried in a cemetery in Philadelphia, with no stone to commemorate her life. A black housewife named Barbara Muldow wrote a letter to the *Philadelphia Inquirer* discussing this lack of appreciation for Smith's contributions to American music. In 1970, blues singer and Smith fan JANIS JOPLIN offered to bear the $500 cost, as did Juanita Green, a registered nurse and civil rights leader in Philadelphia. The two shared the cost of the headstone, and a ceremony was held where Columbia Records, which had hardly been generous to Smith during her lifetime, managed to get into the photos and publicity.

Smith, George "Harmonica" (1924–1985)
harmonicist

George Smith was one of the first bluesmen to amplify the HARMONICA. He was a member of the MUDDY WATERS band, and also toured and recorded with OTIS SPANN and BIG MAMA THORNTON. He traveled between CHICAGO and the West Coast during the 1950s and recorded under several different names.

ROD PIAZZA was a student of Smith's, and they formed a West Coast band called Bacon Fat. Smith also toured briefly with Waters again, and toward the end of his career was in a band with his student William Clarke. Smith used a technique of playing in octaves, which he apparently picked up from classical and jazz harmonica player Larry Adler. This technique was also used by jazz guitarist Wes Montgomery. Clarke has stated that Smith was particularly generous about sharing his knowledge with other harmonica players.

Smith, Huey "Piano" (b. 1934) *pianist and songwriter*

Huey Smith typified the happy PIANO sound of New Orleans. He got his start accompanying GUITAR SLIM from 1950 to 1954. Smith excelled at writing upbeat, humorous songs, such as "The Rocking Pneumonia and the Boogie Woogie Flu." Smith was a piano player and bandleader who hired others to do the vocals. "Rocking Pneumonia" was a number five R&B hit in 1957, and he followed it up with another hit, "Don't You Know," a year later. His biggest hit of all was a top 10 pop hit "Don't You Just Know It," backed up with "High Blood Pressure." This double-sided hit record reached number 10 on the pop charts.

That was the end of Smith's big successes, but he continued to do studio work in New Orleans, playing on records by such artists as rock and roll performer Little Richard and LLOYD PRICE. He tried to write songs about medical conditions, but none of his later songs proved to be successful. Eventually he converted to the Jehovah's Witness faith and gave up his music career.

Smith, Pine Top (Clarence Smith)

(1904–1929) *boogie-woogie pianist*

Another of the pioneers of boogie-woogie, Pine Top Smith was raised in Birmingham, Alabama, where he was a self-taught pianist. After relocating to Pittsburgh, Pennsylvania, he accompanied MA RAINEY. In 1928 he moved to CHICAGO, living in the same apartment building as boogie-woogie performer Albert Ammons and MEADE LUX LEWIS. During the same year he recorded his classic "Pine Top's Boogie," the first record that mentioned boogie-woogie in the lyrics.

Smith's career ended when he was killed by a stray bullet fired in a dance hall dispute. He was only 25 years old.

Smither, Chris (b. 1944) *singer and guitarist*

Born in New Orleans, Chris Smither moved to Boston and became part of the folk and blues revival scene in the mid-1960s. Smither is an excellent fingerpicking guitar player with a pleasing baritone voice. His musical arrangements are tasteful and interesting. He sings blues and rhythm and blues songs and is also an excellent songwriter. BONNIE RAITT has recorded two of his songs, "Love You Like a Man" and "I Feel the Same."

Smither had a long battle with alcohol and, after tough times in the 1970s and 1980s, returned to an active touring and recording career. He still plays blues by such artists as HOWLIN' WOLF, BLIND WILLIE MCTELL, and John Hiatt as well as his own songs.

social history and the blues

The first slaves brought to the United States came to Jamestown, Virginia, in 1619. At that time there was also a group of whites referred to as indentured servants. Indentured servants were brought to the United States in a position of temporary slavery—they were obligated to work for a set period of time for a master, in return for which they were provided with passage to the United States, housing, and all living expenses. After the set period ended, the servant then became free.

Initially black slaves and indentured servants were not treated very differently. Both groups were used as domestic servants and farmworkers. John Hope Franklin, an outstanding black historian writing with Alfred A. Moss Jr. in *From Slavery to Freedom: A History of Negro Americans,* maintains that indentured servants were often kidnapped, that some of them were prisoners and drunks, that the group included women and children, and that the ocean voyages that took the servants from England to Virginia were every bit as horrible as those that brought slaves to the Americas. Franklin also writes that for about the first 50 years that the slaves were in Virginia, they were simply listed as indentured servants, and many of them eventually became free.

Initially slavery was not limited to the South, but the northern United States became less and less focused on farming, while large farms developed in the South, especially after the labor saving invention of the cotton gin in 1793. Also, certain groups in the North, like the Quakers, were opposed to slavery and began to agitate for its abolition.

Singing, dancing, and religion were all viewed ambivalently by slave owners. Any gatherings or development of solidarity represented a possible threat to plantation owners, because such gatherings might lead to revolts or refusals to obey orders. On the other hand, music and religion could prove useful in diverting slaves from their immediate problems or the injustices they faced. Religion in particular could give slaves faith that their service would be rewarded by God after their death, rather than leading them into political agitation during their lifetime. One form of social control exercised by the masters was a rule that no more than five slaves were allowed to assemble without the presence of a white man. Slaves who came from the same tribe and spoke the same language were sometimes separated to keep them from plotting together.

Music was generally seen as harmless. Slave musicians were utilized to play at the masters' social

Slave auction house during the Civil War period (Library of Congress Films and Photographs Division)

functions. Advertisements seeking the return of escaped slaves often mentioned their musical talents on the FIDDLE or BANJO, the instruments most often used by slaves.

During the mid-18th century, before the American Revolution, there was a religious revival called the Great Awakening throughout the American colonies. It involved blacks as well as whites, both as participants and later as preachers. A certain amount of social integration occurred at these awakenings, though the races were usually segregated at the large camp meetings. The first licensed black preacher was George Leile Kiokee, who set up an African Baptist Church in Savannah, Georgia, in 1780.

Musicologist Dena Epstein has come to the reasonable conclusion that there was probably musical interchange between whites and blacks at the early 19th-century camp meetings that both groups attended. African Americans probably contributed the call and response lining out of spoken phrases found in spirituals, where a song leader sings a phrase and a congregation answers him. Improvisation is another musical trait often found in African-American folk music, but it is unusual in the performance of white folk performers. Finally the more extreme emotive aspects of performance in much black music is rarely utilized in white religious singing.

The blues and spirituals are for the most part quite different in terms of subject matter. However, there are some similarities. Structurally there are repeated lines in both forms, where a line can be repeated two or three times, or where there is a short refrain—a passage that repeats a phrase. Compare the religious:

In that great getting up morning, fare thee well, fare thee well

with the secular:

How long, how long, has that evening train been gone
How long, baby how long, baby tell me how long.

Another similarity is the use of coded messages, or phrases with double meanings. In spirituals one meaning might offer a call to run away, while seeming to talk about the North Star, as in the song "Follow the Drinking Gourd." In the blues the coded messages might be double entendres, phrases with more than one meaning. By the time the blues developed, slavery was ended. Nevertheless, singing about social or political events or open references to sexual situations might be considered inappropriate for a black musician singing in the South. Being "inappropriate" could lead to trouble for the black singer in a world where whites controlled virtually everything.

Although the blues may not be primarily a form of social protest, they often contained material that commented against prevailing social or economic conditions. In the years before the blues emerged there were a number of open slave rebellions, all suppressed. In 1810 slaves rebelled in Lexington, Kentucky; in 1815 there was a slave rebellion in Virginia; in 1822 Denmark Vesey, a former slave, led a rebellion in Charleston, South Carolina; and in 1831 slave Nat Turner, led an insurrection in Virginia. Add to this the slaves that ran away, some to the Florida swamps, some to various unpopulated areas of the South. There was also the Underground Railroad, which enabled hundreds of slaves to escape from the South to the North and to Canada. Both white antislavery advocates, called abolitionists, and former slaves and free blacks from the North participated in the Underground Railroad. Southern slave owners protected themselves against this opposition by utilizing Slave Codes. These codes punished slaves for all sorts of infractions, limiting their rights and also providing for imprisonment or beatings for violators. Slaves were used not only for farming, but in tobacco and textile factories, and some were skilled workers in such fields as carpentry.

Besides the economic domination of slave owners over their slaves, another important aspect of slavery was the use by white masters of slave women for sexual purposes. Any attempt by their husbands or families to prevent this sexual slavery put a black man at risk for beatings or death. By 1850 there were 246,000 mixed-blood (mulatto) slaves out of a total slave population of 3.2 million. By 1860, just before the Civil War, there were 411,000 mulatto slaves out of a total of 3.9 million slaves (over 10 percent.)

Another form of control exercised by slave owners was breaking up slave families by selling off husbands, wives, or children. Such behavior wreaked havoc on the structure of the black family. Many owners felt no obligation to keep slave families intact, and inevitably some families never got back together. This practice was based on the will or whim of the owners, not the moral rights of the slaves.

To understand the culture in which the blues developed, it is important to realize that there were

8 million white people in the South in 1860, of whom only 384,000 owned slaves. According to Franklin, 338,000 of these owners had 20 slaves or fewer and of this group over 200,000 owners had 5 slaves or fewer. Although more than one quarter of the slaves *did* work in such environments, the majority did not. These major players in the plantation system dominated the political life of the South. In the southern mountains, for example, farmers did not own large and profitable tracts of land, so slaves were of no use to them.

There were 488,000 free blacks in the United States in 1860, of whom 46 percent lived in the South, 44 percent in the North, and the remainder in the West. Southern free blacks were often tradesmen in southern cities. The slaves codes restricted their activities in regard to such things as owning firearms, schooling, or voting rights.

White Southerners responded to the social changes of the post–Civil War era with anger and violence. In 1866 a Tennessee social club evolved into a racist organization called the Ku Klux Klan.

Unidentified musicians playing the blues (Library of Congress Films and Photographs Division)

Its purpose was to intimidate the newly freed black population, through various acts of violence against them, including murders, floggings, cross burnings, and lynchings. The latter tactic involved a mob hanging a black person from a tree, often in a public place. In 1869 the Klan "officially disbanded," but the violence against blacks escalated and the Klan carried on in secret.

In the 1930s the Works Progress Administration (WPA) conducted a large number of interviews with ex-slaves. More than 65 years since the end of slavery. Therefore the youngest people interviewed with actual memories of slavery would have been in their seventies. The interviews revealed that the freed slaves had seen the end of slavery as a time of hope and possibility. When they realized that they would not receive any land, that their lives were endangered by senseless acts of violence, and that their right to vote was eroded by literacy or property requirements, their dreams turned to bitterness. Many of the northern states also had stringent voting restrictions. Nonetheless, schools were established for the freedmen, and the emergence of the church and establishment of more stable family units provided the base for the modern civil rights movement. This climate immediately preceded the creation of the blues.

Most scholars feel that the blues were born sometime during the 1880s or early 1890s. This period also corresponded with the most severe oppression of African Americans in the South. Besides formidable literacy tests, southern states instituted laws requiring registration months in advance of actual voting. Poll taxes were instituted, and some states passed the so-called Grandfather Clause, which stipulated that a voter needed to have served in the U.S. or Confederate Army before 1867, or be a descendant of someone who had served.

The sharecropper system kept blacks virtually imprisoned on the land, in debt to the landowner whose land they were working for what was often an illusory share of the crop. By 1900 African Americans made up half the population of the South, but they owned 158,479 farms, while whites owned 1,078,635 farms, or about six times as many.

Scholars generally rank the period 1880–1910 as the most oppressive period in the South. Whites passed a number of oppressive laws against black citizens. In 1896 the U.S. Supreme Court ruled that segregation did not violate the 14th Amendment of the U.S. Constitution. The case of *Plessy v. Ferguson* established the concept of "separate but equal." As long as blacks were provided with "equal" facilities, then segregation—the separation of races—was deemed to be legal. This segregation applied to schools and to virtually every other aspect of daily life from seats on buses and trains to drinking fountains in town squares. The equal part of the equation was a joke, because less money was spent on facilities for African Americans, whether in terms of lesser requirements for people to be licensed to teach school to paving streets in the white section of town, but not in the black section.

To reinforce the notion of racial inferiority, violence also escalated. Between 1883 and 1899 there were 2,500 lynchings, mostly of blacks. MISSISSIPPI, Alabama, Georgia, and LOUISIANA led the nation in this barbaric practice. In 1900, 100 blacks were lynched, and over 1,100 in the period 1900–1914. Of these 1,100 deaths, only 315 actually were the result of alleged rapes, over 500 concerned homicides, and the rest involved robberies or various disputes and insults. There were also race riots—violence directed against the entire black population—in Statesboro, Georgia, in 1904; Elaine, ARKANSAS, in 1906; and Brownsville, TEXAS, in the same year.

Not all these race riots were in the south. Springfield, in southern Ohio, was the site of a race riot in 1904, followed by riots in Greensburg, Indiana, in 1906 and in Springfield, Illinois, in 1908.

During the darkest days of racial oppression the African-American population invented and developed the musical genres of blues, ragtime, and jazz. Each of these genres was a reaction to what was happening to African Americans. Ragtime demonstrated that black popular music was a

Greyhound rest-stop facilities, 1941 (Library of Congress Films and Photographs Division)

highly developed form that required considerable skill to compose and play. The blues were an expression of sadness and continual repression, showing that out of these terrible social conditions could come a rich, expressive musical style that spoke frankly about every aspect of black American life. Jazz combined European harmonic sophistication with African improvisation and spontaneity to create a unique style whose innovations are still being absorbed almost 100 years after their beginnings.

The United States entered World War I in 1917, and 367,000 African Americans served in the armed forces. Many of them served in Europe and returned in 1918 to find that the country for which they had risked their lives to serve continued to treat them like second-class citizens. In the South, black students still went to separate schools, and black citizens, for the most part, still ate in separate restaurants, and earned less money than whites working at dead-end jobs.

By this time a considerable black middle-class was developing. In New York City's Harlem there was a Black Renaissance, with poets, playwrights, musicians, and artists all working in their art forms, and white admirers like Carl Van Vechten throwing legendary parties, bringing these creative people together with white critics and intellectuals. Paul Robeson was regarded as a celebrated actor and singer, and a series of successful all-black Broadway shows and musical reviews were produced, like *Shuffle Along* and *Runnn' Wild*. Black composers like Eubie Blake, Noble Sissle, and James P. Johnson wrote these shows, which played for white audiences. It became fashionable for such "progressive" or "avant-garde" whites as Van Vechten or JOHN HAMMOND to listen to BESSIE SMITH and other blues artists, and many whites became tourists to Harlem, where much of the population was black, and where there were numerous nightclubs and rent parties (parties at which a door charge was collected to raise rent money).

But despite these pockets of racial enlightenment, the denial of equal rights for blacks continued. The Ku Klux Klan was revived in the South in 1915, and soon after the end of World War I it had a membership of over 100,000. It extended its racist activities to include opposition to Jews, Roman Catholics, and Asian Americans, and it flourished in New England and in the Midwest. Southerners were afraid of the returning blacks who had been armed and fought in the war. As a result of these tensions the year 1919 saw a string of race riots, which spread across the country. One of the worst riots was in CHICAGO, where racial segregation prevailed. More than 70 blacks were lynched in 1919, including soldiers still in uniform. Black citizens were also burned publicly. There were 25

race riots in 1919, not only in the South but in Tulsa, Oklahoma, and Omaha, Nebraska.

Some blues scholars like SAMUEL CHARTERS have denied the importance of political factors in the writing and recording of blues songs. However, black blues artists were as aware as anyone of the country's racial climate, and they began to sing and write about it. CHARLES "COW COW" DAVENPORT sang the "Jim Crow Blues" in 1927, and various singers including TAMPA RED, PEETIE WHEATSTRAW, and Bessie Smith complained about hard times during the Great Depression of the 1930s. And just as the sharecropper was cheated out of his share of the crop, black blues artists were robbed of royalties for their creative contributions to the popular music scene.

Signs of the Great Depression appeared in the southern states in the middle 1920s, but by 1929 it had spread to the entire nation. Republican Herbert Hoover was president at the time, and he was defeated in his 1932 bid for reelection by Franklin Delano Roosevelt. By the time Roosevelt took office in January 1933 unemployment had become a serious problem everywhere, but it was particularly acute for African Americans. In large urban centers 25 to 40 percent of the black workforce was on relief. This rate was three to four times higher than for whites. Roosevelt instituted a number of measures that gained him near legendary status among blacks. He started the Civilian Conservation Corps (CCC), jobless paying citizens to work in the national forests and parks and to build roads, and he initiated the Works Progress Administration (WPA). This program employed people in all sorts of capacities, including the arts. Theater people, musicians, and writers were all paid to do their art, and some of them, such as novelist Richard Wright, were black. Roosevelt also consulted with black leaders, and some of the white members of his cabinet, notably Secretary of the Interior Harold L. Ickes, were sympathetic to the plight of black Americans. Roosevelt's wife, Eleanor, did many things that endeared her to the black community. She became friendly with blues-folk artist JOSH WHITE, who performed at the White House, and employed his brother Bill as her valet.

Toward the end of the Roosevelt administration, the president's programs saw cuts in their budgets, and several blues singers wrote and recorded songs begging the government not to cut these public works programs, complaining that they could no longer pay their rent as a result.

Although President Roosevelt sponsored the social legislation mentioned above, he did not make changes in the areas of racial segregation, nor did African Americans succeed in gaining voting rights in the South.

In 1941 the Japanese attacked the U.S. naval base at Pearl Harbor, Hawaii, and the United States entered World War II, which had begun in 1939 in Europe. Almost 900,000 black Americans served in that war, although they still fought in segregated units, usually commanded by white officers. World War II differed from the first world war in that German dictator Adolf Hitler was an avowed racist who endorsed "Aryan" superiority. African Americans were already familiar with his snubs of renowned black track star Jesse Owens at the Berlin Olympic Games of 1936, together with his condescension toward American heavyweight boxer Joe Louis, when the German Max Schmeling defeated him in 1936. More than half the African Americans in the armed forces saw service overseas, and in January 1945, the first efforts at integration took place when black platoons fought side by side with white platoons in Germany.

World War II brought about a number of changes in American life. Women entered the labor force in large numbers, including black women. This was a necessity because few men were available for factory jobs. Many black women whose prior work experience had been in domestic service were brought into the mainstream labor market, and many of them also became union members.

Josh White made a number of recordings openly protesting against racial discrimination during the 1940s, as did other blues artists. Many other blues songs discussed the war in nonpolitical terms, focusing on the question of lonely women left at home while their husbands or lovers went overseas. BROWNIE MCGHEE, who had had polio and thus did not have to serve, recorded "Thousand Lonesome Women," a song reassuring the soldier that McGhee would be "wearing your coat, carrying your business on."

It was only during the Korean War in 1951 that the armed forces finally were integrated. But once again black soldiers came home to the same racism that had greeted them at the end of World War II. But this time it had become apparent the situation could not continue in the same way. Thurgood Marshall, counsel for the NAACP and later a justice of the U.S. Supreme Court, argued the *Brown v. Board of Education* case, which overturned *Plessy v. Ferguson* and ended de jure school segregation in the United States.

HOW THE MUSIC EVOLVED

The songs collected by LAWRENCE GELLERT in the 1920s and 1930s reflected the African Americans' reaction to oppression. The songs of the classic blues singers were more concerned with the romantic situations between men and women than with social or political ideas. Black popular music of all kinds—blues, ragtime, or jazz—was meant to be danced to.

By the time World War II broke out, the blues had evolved into a more upbeat, positive kind of music. LOUIS JORDAN's jump-blues were often humorous novelty tunes meant above all to entertain. They were also the first black music recordings to "cross over," finding a mass white audience as well as a black one. The addition of a rhythm section and horns were suitable to the more modern, urban black audience. Middle-class blacks in particular began to feel that the blues was too "country-ish" and not sophisticated enough. This new audience was not eager to be reminded of slavery days or the racial injustices that accompanied them.

Part of the disinterest of young African Americans in the blues was subject matter, and part was musical structure. For younger listeners the blues seemed to be repetitious and they did not usually have choruses. Urban listeners wanted something closer to pop songs—songs with a beginning, middle, and end. The combining of verses that had little to do with one another, so common with singers like BLIND LEMON JEFFERSON, had lost its appeal. In the same way most blues had a single melody and no choruses. For many listeners the chorus of a song made it stand out from similar compositions.

In the same way, gospel music succeeded spirituals as the religious music important in the black church community. Gospel was newly composed music, and it was closer to the form of pop music than spirituals had been. It was also very emotional, personal music, often performed with passion. Music that was halfway between gospel and R&B was a big part of the civil rights movement. The most well-known song of the civil rights movement was "We Shall Overcome." It was sung at sit-ins, on marches, and when civil rights workers were jailed.

By the 1960s the black R&B audience, for the most part, was not interested in the blues. A few artists, like B. B. KING and JOHN LEE HOOKER, maintained and even increased their popularity, but even these artists were relatively unknown compared with the soaring popularity of RAY CHARLES and Aretha Franklin. Meanwhile a whole new audience of younger white people, most of them of college age, were fascinated by the blues. A market developed for the older black blues singers with this audience, so that an African-American folk art became part of the overall American folk revival. Meanwhile, except for country-blues artist TAJ MAHAL, virtually no younger black artists were performing and writing blues.

During the 1960s, R&B was succeeded by soul music. Soul featured vocal performances that had the passion of gospel music, and in fact many soul artists came out of the church. Almost all the recordings of that period conveyed strong emotion, although the instrumental backgrounds varied greatly. The soul records produced by Stax Records in MEMPHIS, or the recordings made in Muscle Shoals, Alabama, had strong rhythm tracks with powerful bass and drum lines, while the "Philly soul" recordings made by Gamble and Huff in Philadelphia featured slick, heavy string and brass arrangements in contrast to the rhythm section.

In this period the civil rights movement peaked. When the assassinations of major political figures—black and white—occurred, the songs reflected these events. CURTIS MAYFIELD, songwriter, producer and lead singer of the Impressions, wrote a number of hit songs like "People Get Ready" and "Keep on Pushing." Like traditional spirituals these songs employed coded messages whose lyrics could be taken lightly or could be symbolic of the situation of African Americans. "Keep on Pushing" is a good example of this writing style. Other soul artists, like the O'Jays, sang lengthy songs about slavery and the oceangoing passage to America, such as "Ship Ahoy." Even commercial performer JAMES BROWN exhorted his audience with the words "Say it loud. I'm black and I'm proud."

In the 1970s a whole new style called disco evolved. Disco was dance music meant to be played at dance clubs. The songs were entirely escapist in the sense that they avoided any mention of social issues but talked about such subjects as sex, dancing, and fashion. Disco also made use of modern recording technology, and in that sense it was more of a producer's music than a performer's music, with the use of electronic sampling and drum machines instead of live musicians. The music reflected the cynicism of the times. The civil rights movement had come to an end, and gangs, drugs, and violence had become features of black urban life.

The end of the decade saw the first rap records. Rap began with a strong social component, and an early record by Grandmaster Flash and the Furious Five, "The Message," used a largely electronic musical track, but it described the problems of ghetto life in considerable detail. Other rappers like Ice T, Public Enemy, and N.W.A. also discussed serious issues, but eventually rap was overcome by gangster styles and messages. Periodically artists mix rap with soul music, and some of these artists, like

Luther Vandross, who sings soul ballads, seem to have great crossover marketing appeal.

Despite some ups and downs, the demand for blues among white audiences has continued to grow. Possibly for the white listener of the 21st century, blues have the same appeal that they had to the white country blues singers of the 1920s and 1930s. The songs reflect real-life situations with a good deal of emotion and have an air of rebellion against conventional life styles. Moreover, many fans enjoy the guitar parts.

During the mid-1990s a group of younger black folk-blues artists appeared, like GUY DAVIS and KEB' MO'. Current younger white artists seem more influenced by rock blues and the harder-edged CHICAGO blues styles, but these artists are closer to the older black blues styles.

The future direction of the blues is difficult to predict. In the foreseeable future there will probably always be a demand for the blues, because of its expressiveness and intensity. As the black audience for blues grows older, and the older black blues artists like B. B. King or LITTLE MILTON retire or die, the blues may well become simply a musical niche in American roots music. That niche may well be more appealing to white audiences than to black. In some distant future when racism will have evaporated, or at least largely diminished, younger African Americans may view the blues as significantly representative of the troubled 20th century and the artistic way in which African-American musicians responded to the challenges that accompanied the end of Reconstruction, two world wars, and the Civil Rights movement.

Artists are always combining musical styles and looking for new approaches to old patterns. A 2004 album called *Alan Lomax's Southern Journey Remixed* took ALAN LOMAX's field recordings and combined them with electronic samples. The blues have always been considered an important component in jazz, and a few composers like Virgil Thomson attempted to utilize blues songs in extended classical music compositions. Country and rock musicians now consider blues to be a

working part of their musical arsenals, and blues can be heard in Broadway shows, in movie and television scores, and in commercials. Some younger black musicians playing the blues have become interested in tracing the blues back to African music, and they have performed and recorded with some of these musicians. Some of this experimentation may also come from the other direction, with African musicians arriving in the United States to perform and record music with American blues musicians.

Quite a few European musicians are blues artists today. In David Dicaire's book *More Blues Singers,* his biographical sketches include blues musicians from Spain, Sweden, Holland, Italy, Switzerland, France, and Russia, as well as Japan. Michael Urban's recent *Russia Gets the Blues* is entirely devoted to the advent of the blues in Russia and the development of an original Russian version of blues style. Urban discusses the period from the late 1960s to the present; in writing the book he interviewed more than 40 blues musicians, fans, and venue owners.

The American white slide guitarist, multi-instrumentalist, and composer RY COODER has always enjoyed experimenting with different musical colors, combining SLIDE GUITAR with Tex-Mex accordion music, or playing his music, which is steeped in the country blues, with Cuban and Indian musicians. With so much music accessible anywhere in the world through recordings and videos, it seems inevitable that these kinds of fusions of musical styles will proliferate, just as in any kind of blues performances or recordings, the music will inevitably vary in quality and interest.

Spand, Charley (c. 1900–?) *pianist and recording artist*

There is speculation that Charley Spand was born in Georgia around 1900, but that is not certain. The lyrics of his recorded songs indicate that he grew up in Alabama, and that he spent time on Hastings Street in DETROIT. Spand, who was a talented if obscure blues pianist who recorded 25 cuts for Paramount Records from 1929 to 1931, disappeared, then recorded an additional eight more sides. Among his early recordings are duets with ragtime guitarist BLIND BLAKE, and the last recordings feature BIG BILL BROONZY and MEMPHIS MINNIE's husband, Little Son Joe.

Spann, Otis (1930–1970) *pianist*

Otis Spann is considered one of the best blues pianists that ever lived. His most famous recordings were made with MUDDY WATERS during the 1950s and 1960s. Spann could play solos, and he excelled at playing rhythm parts without getting in the way of the guitar. Because pianists can play many chords or add notes to chords, pianists and guitarists often do not play well together.

Spann's father was a minister, and it was at his father's house that he started to play the PIANO. Spann was not only a professional boxer but also a semiprofessional football player. He turned to music as a career after his 1946–51 army service ended.

Besides working with Waters, Spann also played on recordings by HOWLIN' WOLF, and he had a brief solo career in 1960 playing piano with guitarist ROBERT LOCKWOOD JR. He also made recordings with members of the rock band FLEETWOOD MAC in CHICAGO and New York. Not until 1969 did Spann give up performing with Waters. He died only a year later and had no opportunity to launch a solo career.

Speckled Red (Rufus Perryman) (1892–1973) *musician and performer*

Rufus Perryman's trademark was the song the "Dirty Dozens," the sort of insult song that later became typical of rap music. The dozens was a kind of street sport in which two people would insult each other's family, especially their mothers. Perryman was a pianist and singer who played at CHICAGO rent parties, parties that charged an admission fee to pay for house rentals, with JIM JACKSON and TAMPA RED. He went on to record with Jackson and played with various Dixieland jazz bands. Toward the end of his life he played at blues festivals in the United States and Europe.

Speir, H. C. (1895–1972) *record store owner and talent scout*

H. C. Speir owned a record store in Jackson, MISSISSIPPI. From 1925 to 1935, he functioned as a talent agent, finding blues artists and taking them to record companies. Practically all the major singers in the Mississippi Delta got their deals through Speir, either because he arranged for the recording or, as in ROBERT JOHNSON's case, Speir simply recommended that someone else take them on. Among the artists Speir brought to recording studios were SON HOUSE, CHARLEY PATTON, WILLIE BROWN, TOMMY JOHNSON, SKIP JAMES, and ISHMON BRACEY—practically all the major Mississippi artists. Speir received no royalties from the record companies, but he was paid a small fee for each discovery. Sometimes Speir held auditions at his store.

"Spike Driver Blues" (1928) *blues variation on folk ballad "John Henry"*

John Hurt was one of many artists who appeared on the FOLKWAYS reissue albums, the six-LP set called *The Anthology of American Folk Music*. Many folk revivalists were intrigued by Hurt's wonderfully gentle guitar fingerpicking and quiet vocals. "Spike Driver" is a variation of the folk ballad "John Henry." Hurt half sings and half talks the lyric. The guitar part is a masterpiece of simplicity, because the entire piece is played on a G chord. There are so many subtle variations on the chord that the listener never tires of it. The original recording was made in 1928. Revivalist DAVE VAN RONK and the incredible country guitarist Doc Watson also recorded this song. Both of them learned it from Hurt's version.

Spivey, Victoria (1906–1976) *singer, songwriter, and record company owner*

Victoria Spivey was a good businesswoman. She started out in music as a contract songwriter for a St. Louis music publisher. At the age of 19 she was singing and playing blues and ragtime PIANO in tough clubs in Dallas and Houston, TEXAS. One of the musicians with whom she performed with was BLIND LEMON JEFFERSON. Spivey wrote and recorded the "T. B. Blues," and claimed that she wrote "Black Snake Moan." Jefferson also recorded "Black Snake," and they had a feud about who had actually written it.

During the 1930s Spivey appeared in films. After her recording career died down in the late 1930s, Spivey stayed in NEW YORK. By the 1950s she had left show business, but the 1960s folk-blues revival brought her back. She formed her own record company in 1962, recording some of her old friends, like Lucille Hegamin and younger people including a very raw BOB DYLAN. Not a great singer, Spivey will be remembered for the songs she wrote and the artists whom she recorded on her label.

Spoelstra, Mark (b. 1940) *guitarist and singer*

Few white blues revivalists took up the 12-STRING GUITAR. Mark Spoelstra was an exception to the rule, and he was also unusual because he fingerpicked the 12-string, favoring the lighter Piedmont style, rather than the more intense, heavy-strummed LEAD BELLY style. Spoelstra also had an attractive, light voice that matched his guitar style.

During the 1960s Spoelstra recorded for Elektra and FOLKWAYS, and after he moved to CALIFORNIA, he recorded for Fantasy and Kicking Mule. For a number of years he did not play music professionally, but he reemerged in 2001, recording an album for Origin Records, and started to tour again.

Stackhouse, Houston (1910–1980) *singer and guitarist*

Houston Stackhouse was heavily influenced by MISSISSIPPI singer TOMMY JOHNSON, and performed

his songs "Big Road Blues" and "Cool Water Blues." In the late 1920s he performed with Johnson around Jackson. During the mid-1940s he performed with SONNY BOY WILLIAMSON II (Rice Miller) on Helena, ARKANSAS, radio. He also toured with Miller.

Stackhouse taught ROBERT NIGHTHAWK how to play guitar. He chose not to go to CHICAGO, but stayed in Mississippi and in Arkansas. He recorded during the mid-1960s and played at various festivals. During the 1970s he often performed with the band JOE WILLIE WILKINS' King Biscuit Boys, touring the United States and Europe. These band members, like Stackhouse had been associated with Miller.

"Statesboro Blues" (1929) *blues song by Blind Willie McTell*

"Statesboro Blues" was written and recorded by BLIND WILLIE MCTELL in 1929. It is an unusual blues in that it has four distinct melodies but no chorus. The first part of the lyric complains about an unfaithful woman, but then McTell reverses himself and talks about loving a woman who was "better than I ever seen." He then talks about riding on a train, and he ends humorously, explaining that not only do his mother, father, sister, and brother have the blues, but so do his grandparents. McTell cleanly fingerpicked "Statesboro Blues" on his 12-STRING GUITAR. The Allman Brothers, who covered the song, treated it like a straight blues, not varying the different sections that distinguish it from most blues. TAJ MAHAL, DAVE VAN RONK, folk-rock group the Youngbloods, and rock band the Black Crowes, among others, have also recorded it.

Stokes, Frank (1888–1955) *recording artist and street singer*

Tennessee artist Frank Stokes was a street singer who often played in a duo with guitarist Dan Sane. They recorded as the Beale Street Sheiks, an obvious way to capitalize on the popularity of their well-established competitors, the MISSISSIPPI SHEIKS.

Stokes recorded 38 songs, for Paramount and Victor, some with Sane, and others with fiddler Will Batts. Stokes's style was the Piedmont light blues, which showed influences from minstrel shows and ragtime. Much of the music was good natured, like his song "T'Aint't Nobody's Bizness."

"Stormy Monday" (1947) influential blues first recorded by T-Bone Walker

"Stormy Monday" is one of the most performed blues songs of the post–World War II era. It was written and recorded by Aaron Thibeaux "T-BONE" WALKER, who was the first well-known blues artist to play electric guitar. Walker recorded the song several times over the years, but the first recorded version appeared on West Coast record label Black and White in 1947. Walker was a skilled acrobatic guitarist whose Oklahoma City teacher Chuck Richardson also taught Charlie Christian, the brilliant jazz guitarist.

The song itself is in standard blues format, with repeated lines in the verses. The lyric describes a week in the life of an average working man who spends his weekdays depressed, parties on Saturday, then goes to church on Sunday. The tension between the bluesman's life and religion has been a continual tug of war, with some religious African Americans feeling that the blues are the "devil's music."

Walker improvises on the melody in the third verse, singing a full octave higher to bring more tension into his performance. He mentions his romantic situation for the first time in the third verse. Walker pleads for an unnamed person to "send her back to me." Walker also used unusual, jazz-oriented chords in this song, including ninth chords (C ninth is C E G B-flat D), augmented chords (C augmented is C E G-sharp), and other chords that are part of the jazz vocabulary but are not found in folk blues.

Practically every electric blues guitar player of any significance has covered this song, along with some of the important blues-rock artists. This list includes ALBERT KING, B. B. KING, FREDDIE KING; BOBBY "BLUE" BLAND. Junior Wells, Boz Scaggs, MUDDY WATERS; folksinger-songwriter Eva Cassidy; rockers Mountain, Jethro Tull, ERIC CLAPTON, the ALLMAN BROTHERS; and jazz guitarist Kenny Burrell.

Strachwitz, Chris (b. 1931) founder of Arhoolie record label

Chris Strachwitz was born in Silesia, then part of Germany, now part of Poland. He moved with his family to CALIFORNIA in 1947 and became an avid record collector. He was mentored in record production by longtime Oakland producer–record company owner Bob Geddins.

In 1959 Strachwitz decided to record LIGHTNIN' HOPKINS. He went to Texas but discovered that Hopkins had moved to California. Strachwitz ended up finding songster-bluesman MANCE LIPSCOMB and started his ARHOOLIE label with a Lipscomb album.

Since that time Strachwitz has recorded all sorts of music. He bought LOUISIANA folklorist Harry Oster's label, Folk Lyric, and has released dozens of albums of Tejano music—the music of the Texas-Mexico border, as well as other world music recordings. In addition to recording Mance Lipscomb, Strachwitz has issued a large number of blues recordings. Most recently he recorded a newly recognized musical style called sacred steel—black gospel music in southeastern churches featuring the lap steel guitar as a lead instrument.

Strachwitz operated a well-stocked record store near Berkeley, California, with a mail order service, but he eventually left that end of the business.

Strehli, Angela (b. 1945) singer

During the early 1970s Angela Strehli was in the middle of the Austin, TEXAS, blues scene that centered around Clifford Antone's nightclub. She is often associated with Lou Ann Barton and MARCIA BALL, who were also active then in the same place, as were the Vaughan Brothers and Kim Wilson, who later became the lead singer of the FABULOUS THUNDERBIRDS. For a while Strehli stopped performing music and worked at the club, but she resumed playing music and moved to the San Francisco Bay Area. Strehli is a singer who originally played HARMONICA and bass before she started to sing. Her repertoire varies from blues to R&B covers.

Strehli was the first artist to record on the Antone's Records label, releasing an extended play album in 1986.

string bands

String bands had a broad repertoire of songs and styles. They also were as apt to play for white as black audiences. The repertoire of a black string duo like the MISSISSIPPI SHEIKS ranged from square dance tunes, waltzes, ragtime and vaudeville songs, pop songs, ragtime pieces, and even to jazz. The Sheiks consisted of fiddler Lonnie Chatmon and guitarist and singer WALTER VINSON. Although only the two of them recorded together, in live performances the band included a number of Chatmon's brothers. A brief listing of the Sheiks' recorded titles gives a glimpse of their repertoire: "Sittin' on Top of the World," "Honey Babe Let the Deal Go Down," "I've Got Blood in My Eyes for You," and "Sweet Maggie." The Sheiks recorded from 1930 to 1936.

Another string band that recorded in 1927 was the Dallas String Band, whose instrumentation was MANDOLIN, bass, and guitar. In their most famous song, "Dallas Rag," the acoustic bass was played with a bow. The trio of Carl Martin, Ted Bogan, and HOWARD ARMSTRONG, under assorted band names, was also well known. They probably had the broadest repertoire of any group, including polkas and such ethnic material as German and Italian songs. Sometimes called Louie Bluie, Armstrong spoke seven languages, so that the band could actually perform Italian songs in Italian, for example. Both Martin and Armstrong had played in bands that consisted of members of their own families. Martin played guitar, mandolin, and string bass; Armstrong played mandolin and violin, and Bogan played both fingerstyle and flat-pick guitar. The band first got together in Knoxville, Tennessee, in 1934 and ended up in CHICAGO. The band broke up during World War II and resumed activities 30 years later.

There were similar bands of white country players during this period, but they did not usually play for black audiences. Their white bands usually had a less varied repertoire, focusing more on southern mountain music and occasionally drifting over into the pop area. Sometimes jug band music was referred to as "hokum" music, indicating that it was novelty music with a fun-loving spirit.

Sumlin, Hubert (b. 1931) *lead guitarist*

Hubert Sumlin spent at least 20 years playing lead guitar for HOWLIN' WOLF. He played on most of Wolf's important recordings, including such songs as "Smokestack Lightnin'," "The Red Rooster," and "Spoonful." Sumlin started his career as a drummer, before he took up the guitar. He played with HARMONICA player JAMES COTTON, then worked with Howlin' Wolf. When he started with the band he played rhythm, but he soon moved to lead guitar. His playing was explosive and unpredictable, varying between fiery lead lines and choppy rhythm chords. Two years after he joined Wolf, they had a dispute and Sumlin left to play lead for MUDDY WATERS for a year. He then returned to the Howlin' Wolf band.

Since Wolf died in 1976, Sumlin's career has not gone so well. He is an adequate singer but he cannot match the power of Howlin' Wolf, and he has not been able to hook up with another powerful singer. Still, he has toured and recorded widely.

Sunnyland Slim (Albert Luandrow) (1907–1995) *piano player and singer*

Barrelhouse PIANO is raw blues piano that was played in rough saloons. Sunnyland Slim was a master of barrelhouse, and he made about 250 recordings for over a dozen record companies during his long musical career. Born in MISSISSIPPI, Slim moved to MEMPHIS during the late 1920s, then in CHICAGO in 1939. He served as a go-between for various musicians, bringing MUDDY WATERS to the attention of Aristocrat Records (the company that later became CHESS RECORDS). Slim played Chicago clubs with BIG BILL BROONZY, ROBERT LOCKWOOD JR., and other artists. He toured Europe during the 1960s, and in the 1970s he started his own label, Airways Records. Toward the end of his life he played every Sunday night at a North Side club.

Sun Records

Sun Records was started by Sam Phillips as the Memphis Recording Service in 1950. Phillips started out producing records and leasing them to other companies. After he became frustrated at not receiving what he felt was proper compensation, he started his label in 1952.

Phillips loved black music, and among the first artists whom he recorded were B. B. KING, HOWLIN' WOLF, and LITTLE JUNIOR PARKER. Phillips quickly came to the conclusion that if he wanted to be successful, he needed to "find a white boy who could sing the blues." ELVIS PRESLEY, then an unknown, went to the studio, using it to make a cheap recording for his mother. One thing led to another, and Phillips enlisted guitarist Scotty Moore and bass player Bill Black to rehearse with Presley. As if to hedge his bets, Presley's first release was "THAT'S ALL RIGHT MAMA," written by blues artist BIG BOY CRUDUP, backed up with "Blue Moon of Kentucky," a waltz written by Bill Monroe, often referred to as the father of bluegrass. Presley and his accompanists transformed the waltz into a 4/4 rocker, and soon the singer was the hottest artist in the area. All of Presley's Sun recordings had a blues or R&B song on one side. He had listened to country, gospel, and blues equally during his childhood, and

Phillips had finally found his white boy who could sing the blues.

Within a year Phillips sold Presley's contract to RCA for $35,000. While this may seem in hindsight like a foolish decision, Phillips needed the money to expand his company. In the next few years he recorded budding rock stars Jerry Lee Lewis, Johnny Cash, Charley Rich, and CARL PERKINS. They all had big hit records, and Sun had in effect invented a style called rockabilly, a blend of blues and country music. Sun's studio band played on most of the records, and Phillips used an effect called slapback echo on many of the recordings. This was a form of tape delay that lent excitement to the sound of the music.

By 1966 many of the hit artists had left, so Phillips sold his company and retired from the record business. With his rockabilly artists he had changed the direction of American popular music.

Swamp Dogg (Jerry Williams) (b. 1942)
musician. record producer. and engineer
Long before Snoop Dogg, there was Swamp Dogg! Swamp Dogg, aka Jerry Williams is a pianist, singer, record producer, and recording engineer who crosses the musical lines between swamp blues, rhythm and blues, and soul music. Dogg is an unpredictable performer whose songs range from romantic subjects to social criticism. The titles of two of his albums tell the story: *Surfin' in Harlem* and *Total Destruction to Your Mind*.

His vocal performances are raw. Swamp Dogg yells and writes outrageous songs that differs greatly from the smoother soul stylings of so many other artists.

Early in his career Swamp Dogg got to work with Jerry Wexler from ATLANTIC and Phil Walden, who managed Otis Redding and started Capricorn Records in Macon, Georgia. Swamp Dogg has referred to himself as a "genius," but his music has never been marketed very successfully. His record making is just as erratic as his music, and he may go five years or more without releasing a new album.

"Sweet Home Chicago" (1937) *traditional blues first recorded by Robert Johnson*

Writer and musician Elijah Wald has traced "Sweet Home Chicago" to KOKOMO ARNOLD's "Old Original Kokomo Blues" and then further back to Indianapolis guitarist FRANCIS "SCRAPPER" BLACKWELL. ROBERT JOHNSON's main contribution to the song seems to have been in substituting the name of CHICAGO for Kokomo. Johnson recorded his version of the song during the first day of his initial recording session, on November 23, 1937. In Johnson's recording, the lyric does not make geographic sense. He combines Chicago and CALIFORNIA in the same sentence as though they were related areas. The song seemed to catch on with many blues artists. TOMMY MCCLENNAN recorded it in 1939 and WALTER DAVIS in 1941. The song is in the *Blues Brothers* movie and has been recorded by Ben Harper, FLEETWOOD MAC, LONNIE BROOKS, LUTHER ALLISON, Magic Sam, and MUDDY WATERS, among others. It seems to be practically compulsory for any Chicago-based artist to sing the song at least once during a performance.

Sykes, Roosevelt (The Honeydripper) (1906–1983) *pianist*

Roosevelt Sykes was one of the most influential blues pianists. He started playing PIANO at the age of 12, and moved with his family to St. Louis in the early 1920s. In 1929 he recorded the "44 Blues" for Okeh Records. Sykes started out playing juke joints and lumber camps, but by the late 1930s he was leading a 10-piece band. He was so popular that he continued to record during World War II, when the production of records was extremely limited due to a shortage of shellac.

Sykes's piano technique was more harmonically sophisticated than that of many of his fellow blues pianists. His use of bass lines and more modern chords enabled him to play jazz as well as blues.

During the 1950s he moved to CHICAGO, then went on to play in Europe in 1961. All during this time he was recording, and more than two dozen Sykes CDs are available today. In addition to his own records, he also accompanied other artists. After Sykes returned from Europe he settled in New Orleans and played in the French Quarter. At the end of his life he became involved in the Baptist Church and played very little. Among his dozens of compositions are the "32-20 Blues" and "The Honeydripper."

Taggart, Blind Joe (unknown) *singer and guitarist*

JOSH WHITE led Blind Joe Taggart around the streets of the Carolinas. According to White, Taggart was mean and vicious, and a bit of a fraud because he had partial vision. Taggart recorded in 1926 in CHICAGO, the first "guitar-evangelist" to do so. He also recorded duets believed to have been accompanied by his wife.

Taggart recorded blues sides, many under different names, like Blind Joe Amos. Some of his recordings were reissued on CD during the early 1990s and are considered to have traces of some of the earliest musical styles to have ever been recorded.

talent scouts

Talent scouts were intermediaries employed by record companies during the 1920s and 1930s. Their job was to find artists for the record companies to record. Many scouts were based in towns in the southern United States, where they would find an artist, in some instances cut a recording, and accompany the artist to the recording studios in NEW YORK, CHICAGO, or Grafton, Wisconsin. Sometimes the recording studio was located wherever the headquarters of the company was situated, but a number of companies also either owned recording studios in southern cities or set up temporary headquarters to record artists in a particular area. Sometimes record companies would advertise in local newspapers to announce that they were coming to town to audition local artists.

When a record company agreed to record an artist found by a talent scout, they paid the talent scout. Some scouts, like H. C. SPEIR, worked on a flat-fee basis. Others tried to manipulate the artists and sometimes the record companies as well, so that they received songwriting royalties that properly should have been paid to the artist. The talent scouts often felt that they were underpaid, and therefore sometimes they "sold" the same artist to more than one record company, convincing the artist to use a pseudonym. Since artists were generally paid a fee per song, it was to their advantage to record as much as possible. Sometimes an artist even recorded the identical song for more than one company. Talent scouts also were paid for their travel expenses, (and some of them manipulated their expense accounts to increase their income). Some of the talent scouts had a hand in record production as well. Most of them left that work to record producers on staff of the record companies.

Blues talent scouts were either African Americans with direct access to the black community or they were white men willing to circulate in black neighborhoods and communicate with black musicians.

Some of the talent scouts were themselves professional musicians. WALTER DAVIS, Richard M. Jones, Will Shade, and ROOSEVELT SYKES were paid by record companies to bring in other musicians. Other musicians functioned as more informal talent scouts. Artists like BIG BILL BROONZY and TAMPA RED recommended their friends to record companies and thus constituted a pipeline for new talent that had recently arrived in Chicago. In turn the musicians might use their sponsors to play on their recordings. Sometimes the sponsor might put in a word with his or her record company for a protégé or simply give the musician a name, address, or phone number. New musicians could also break into the recording world when an established musician like MUDDY WATERS asked his record company to use them on his own recordings.

Companies used talent scouts for a number of reasons. Most record companies had only a limited understanding of blues music. Record companies felt that living in a town like Jackson, MISSISSIPPI (as Speir did), a scout would have continual access to available talent and could establish relationships with artists who would then recommend their friends and associates to the label. Scouts were not paid for the time they invested in forging such relationships, so it was a cost-effective way for the record companies to do business.

Other prominent scouts looking for blues talent include J. B. LONG in the Carolinas, Harry Charles in Birmingham, Alabama, Dan Hornsby in the Piedmont region, Ralph Lembo in MISSISSIPPI, and P. C. Brockman in ATLANTA.

Blues artist SLEEPY JOHN ESTES wrote a song about talent scouts, "Special Agent," in which he says "now I got to do recordin', ought to be recordin' right now."

Tampa Red (Hudson Whittaker) (1904–1981)
recording artist

Tampa Red was one of the most recorded early blues artists. He cut 335 songs for Okeh and Bluebird Records. Georgia-born Hudson Whittaker got his nickname when his family moved to Tampa, Florida. He first learned how to play guitar from his brother Eddie. Tampa arrived in CHICAGO in the mid-1920s, to become not only a recording artist, but a one-man blues machine. His house had two pianos, and he would house and feed blues artists when they first came to town. There were constant rehearsals at the house.

Tampa paired up with T. A. DORSEY, known as Georgia Tom, and they recorded a bunch of happy, almost silly blues songs, until Dorsey left the blues to start his gospel music career. Tampa then hooked up with PIANO player BIG MACEO.

During the late 1930s J. Mayo Williams supervised the so-called Bluebird sound, a slightly smoother blues sound that included drums and bass. Tampa played on many of these recording sessions as a guitarist, in addition to recording songs under his own name. He played SLIDE GUITAR, but he did not produce the intense, emotional sound of the Delta slide guitarists; his sound was more like Hawaiian guitar. Tampa played single-note passages on his steel-bodied guitar that were easy to recognize. He had a light, smooth voice, much more suited to happy blues or pop songs than to the deeper slow blues of the Delta. Tampa was known as "the guitar wizard," and used a variety of accompaniments, ranging from a jug band, to guitar duets, to small bands. Not satisfied with just singing and writing the blues, Tampa made many records in the late 1930s and 1940s that are closer to pop songs, which he crooned like a pop singer. Some of the blues that Tampa wrote have become standards, especially "It Hurts Me Too" and "Tight Like That."

By the mid-1950s the sound of the Delta had taken over Chicago blues, and Tampa Red was pushed into the background. His recording sessions slowed down and then stopped. Although he recorded a little during the folk revival of the 1960s, his career did not take off again. Tampa suffered from his drinking habit, his wife died, and he spent the last few years of his life in a mental hospital, with no money to his name.

Tarheel Slim (Alden Bunn) (1924–1977) *singer*

Tarheel Slim was one of many Piedmont musicians who ended up in New York City around 1950. He started his musical career under the influence of Carolina guitarists BLIND BOY FULLER and BLIND GARY DAVIS. Slim pursued several different musical avenues. He was a gospel singer who sang in vocal groups, he became a rhythm and blues singer in a group called the Larks, he made hit rhythm and blues records with his wife, Little Ann, and he used the Tarheel Slim name to record blues. Toward the end of his life producer Pete Lowry recorded an album of blues with Slim.

Tarlton, Jimmie (1892–1979) *guitarist and songwriter*

Jimmie Tarlton was a white musician who fell in love with the blues. During the late 1920s and into the 1930s he hooked up with Tom Darby. Their biggest hits were the songs "Cumberland Mountain Blues" and "Birmingham Jail." Like most of the black blues artists of the time, they received a grand total of $75, with no royalties, for this record.

Tarlton played SLIDE GUITAR, sometimes using glass and sometimes a knife. In addition to his work with Darby, Tarlton performed with JIMMIE RODGERS, Hank Williams, the Delmore Brothers, and the Skillet Lickers, all important figures in country music.

During the folk music revival of the 1960s Tarlton and Darby reunited briefly, and Tarlton played at the folk club Ash Grove in LOS ANGELES. By that time he was too old to want to pursue his musical career.

Tate, Baby (Charles Henry Tate) (1916–1972) *vocalist and guitarist*

Vocalist-guitarist Baby Tate was a Piedmont product heavily influenced by BLIND BOY FULLER. Tate taught himself guitar and hooked up with Fuller, who taught him more guitar techniques. He appeared on Greenville, South Carolina, radio in 1932, and spent a number of years working outside the field of music around Spartansburg, South Carolina. He also played in a duo there with guitarist PINK ANDERSON. In 1962 Tate made an album for Prestige/Bluesville under his own name, which has been reissued on CD.

Just as many of the Delta artists were heavily under the sway of SON HOUSE, CHARLEY PATTON,

and ROBERT JOHNSON, Fuller seems to have been the artist who affected most of the Carolina blues musicians of the 1930s.

Taylor, Eddie (1923–1985) *recording artist*

Eddie Taylor played an important role in JIMMY REED's successful career, but Taylor also made records for Vee-Jay under his own name. Taylor was a much more versatile musician than Reed. He could play Delta blues and everything from dance beats to rhythm and blues grooves. Taylor's records did not sell well, so his career at Vee-Jay turned more toward playing on the recordings of other artists, such as JOHN LEE HOOKER, ELMORE JAMES, SNOOKY PRYOR, and of course Reed.

Taylor, Hound Dog (Theodore Roosevelt Taylor) (1915–1975) *vocalist and guitarist*

Hound Dog Taylor was responsible for the launch of BRUCE IGLAUER's ALLIGATOR RECORDS, when Iglauer's boss, BOB KOESTER, refused to record Taylor. MISSISSIPPI-born Taylor moved to CHICAGO in 1942 and soon began to play in the South and West Side clubs.

Taylor had a three-piece band with guitarist Brewer Phillips and drummer Ted Harvey. They were called The House Rockers, and that described their music. Taylor played SLIDE GUITAR and sang, Phillips played "buzzing bass lines" on his guitar, Harvey pounded the drums, and the three of them did indeed rock the house. Taylor played loudly and was not afraid to make mistakes. Alligator Records took its motto, "genuine houserocking music," from the name of Taylor's band.

Taylor, Koko (b. 1935) *blues shouter*

A strong blues shouter, Koko Taylor had a million-selling record in 1965 with WILLIE DIXON's song "Wang Dang Doodle." Taylor is an energetic performer, who like so many blues and rhythm and blues artists started her career singing in church before she went on to sit in with CHICAGO blues artists HOWLIN' WOLF, MUDDY WATERS, and BUDDY GUY. She made two albums for CHESS and played jazz festivals, including the Montreux jazz festival in Switzerland in 1974. Taylor has won a closet-full of W. C. HANDY Blues Awards and a Grammy. She appeared in the David Lynch film *Wild at Heart,* and she survived a serious auto accident and the death of her husband. She continues to record and tour today.

Taylor, Montana (Arthur Taylor) (1903–1954) *pianist*

Arthur Taylor's nickname Montana comes from his birthplace, Butte, Montana where his father ran a bar. Taylor's family moved to CHICAGO, then to Indianapolis when he was a child. Taylor was a self-taught pianist who played house-rent parties, in which patrons paid a fee to attend, and bars in Indianapolis. He was a boogie-woogie player whose style was upbeat, happy music somewhat resembling that of MEADE LUX LEWIS. Taylor recorded for Vocalion Records in Chicago in 1929, then moved to Cleveland, giving up his music career. Rediscovered in 1946, he recorded both as a soloist and playing behind classic blues singer BERTHA "CHIPPIE" HILL. This resulted in some performances playing for Hill, but then Taylor once again disappeared. Taylor is best known for his compositions "Indiana Avenue Stomp" and "Detroit Rocks."

Taylor, Otis (b. 1948) *singer and songwriter*

Taylor grew up in CHICAGO, but his family moved to Denver, Colorado, after his uncle was murdered. As a teenager, Otis hung around a Denver music store, Denver Folklore Center. The Folklore Center was a magnet for folk and blues musicians during the 1960s. It sold acoustic instruments, had a staff of teachers who taught blues and folk music, and operated a concert hall where visiting artists performed. Otis studied guitar, BANJO, and HARMONICA at the store, hung out there with owner Harry Tuft,

and absorbed a large number of musical influences. He started several bands by his mid-teens, and a trip to London, England, in 1969 almost landed him a record deal with Blue Horizon Records.

Taylor returned to Denver and from 1977 until 1995 he operated a successful antique business and kept music as a hobby. He was encouraged by bass player Kenny Passarelli to resume playing music. He began to play in Denver-Boulder coffeehouses and recorded a series of albums, first for Canadian company Northern Blues, and most recently for Telarc.

Taylor's music is unlike that of any other blues artist. He writes openly about social and racial injustice, and his albums have thought-provoking titles, like *White African* and *When Negroes Walked the Earth.* His songs are just as intense; one describes the lynching of his great grandfather. Taylor developed a unique banjo style that is part southern Appalachian, part JOHN LEE HOOKER. He plays electric and acoustic banjo and electric and ACOUSTIC GUITAR. His records have gotten an increasing number of favorable reviews, he has won a Handy Blues Award, and he has played a growing number of concerts and folk festivals in Europe as well as the United States. Performing with a band that includes his daughter singing and playing bass, Taylor is a commanding presence, and he is perfectly capable of doing powerful shows without any help.

Tedeschi, Susan (b. 1970) *singer and electric guitarist*

Susan Tedeschi represents the new generation of young white women who are not afraid to play aggressive ELECTRIC GUITAR and who lead their own band. She studied guitar at the Berklee College of Music in Boston and sang in a gospel ensemble. Tedeschi formed her own band in 1991 and played on the local blues scene.

Her recordings are a blend of blues, original tunes, and rhythm and blues covers. She also covers songs by contemporary writers, like John Prine's "Angel from Montgomery."

Temple, Johnny (Geechie) (1906–1968)
guitarist, singer

Johnny Temple was born and raised on a MISSISSIPPI farm. His first instrument was MANDOLIN, and his stepfather taught him to play the guitar. He worked with SKIP JAMES and other Mississippi musicians at local house parties. During the early 1930s he moved back and forth between CHICAGO and Jackson, Mississippi. He often worked with the McCOY brothers in Chicago, playing not only blues but everything from pop songs to polkas.

Temple recorded for Decca in 1935 in Chicago, and in 1937 with the McCoys' band, Harlem Hamfats, in NEW YORK. He played with various jazz musicians in New York as well during the late 1930s, then returned to Chicago.

Temple developed the kind of boogie-woogie bass figures that ROBERT JOHNSON played. Temple's use of the bass notes influenced ELMORE JAMES. Temple's records sold well enough to enable him to keep recording through the 1940s. When the blues started to go electric in Chicago in the mid-1950s, Temple returned to Mississippi, playing around Jackson.

Terry, Sonny (Saunders Terrell) (1911–1986)
harmonicist

Sonny Terry's father played dance tunes on the HARMONICA, and Sonny was first taught how to play by his father, who did not play blues. Sonny Terry is a North Carolinian who hooked up with BLIND BOY FULLER. Fuller encouraged his move to Durham from his home in Greensboro. In 1937 he went with Fuller to NEW YORK, recording for Vocalion and the American Record Company (ARC). Terry was one of the artists who performed at JOHN HAMMOND's From Spirituals to Swing concert at Carnegie Hall in 1938. He also recorded for the Library of Congress in 1938.

Terry had met BROWNIE McGHEE in Durham in 1939, and they played together on a record date that McGhee had in 1941. By this time Terry was living in New York, and in 1942 McGhee moved there and the two formed their long-lasting musical partnership.

Though Terry and McGhee had a joint career, Terry performed without McGhee as well. He appeared in the hit Broadway show *Finian's Rainbow,* which had a run of over a thousand performances. The partners appeared in Tennessee Williams's *Cat on a Hot Tin Roof,* and Terry made a number of recordings on his own. He also taught his nephew J. C. Burris to play harmonica, played with calypso performer Harry Belafonte, and wrote an instruction book on the harmonica for New York's Oak Publications.

Terry's harmonica style included train imitations and making the instrument "talk." One of his favorite devices was to make the harmonica say "I want my mama." Terry also had a deep, powerful voice, and he could alternately sing and play harmonica. He also would launch into "whooping," which was almost like the harmonica talking back to the singer.

Sonny Terry (Larry Sandberg)

McGhee and Terry broke up in 1975. In 1984, Terry made an album with guitarist JOHNNY WINTER and bass player WILLIE DIXON, but age started to slow him down, and he was not able to take advantage of that recording, as he died in 1986.

Texas

Texas is the largest state in the continental United States, and it has a rich blues tradition as well as a continuing presence on the contemporary blues scene. Although the two most prominent styles of blues are the southeastern Piedmont style of the Carolinas and Georgia and the Delta style found in MISSISSIPPI and adjoining states, Texas blues has its own musical history and style. The difference between the Texas blues and the other two styles is that there is not a single dominant strand of blues that can be identified with the Texas blues.

AUSTIN

Austin got a late start in blues history because it had a relatively small African-American population in the early days of the blues. Austin played an important role in the folk music revival of the 1960s through a club called Threadgill's, and in the late 1960s and early 1970s several other clubs, notably the Vulcan Gas Company and Armadillo World Headquarters, featured rock bands and some of the older black blues artists and songsters, like Texan MANCE LIPSCOMB. JANIS JOPLIN played at Threadgill's before moving to San Francisco and a meteoric career as a rock-blues singer.

In 1975 Clifford Antone opened a club called Antone's. It became Austin Blues Central, and a whole corps of young white blues artists performed and developed there. Among these artists were a group of young white women that included Lou Anne Barton, MARCIA BALL, and ANGELA STREHLI. They all performed at the club and recorded for the record label that Antone set up. Antone also helped to develop the careers of STEVIE RAY VAUGHAN, JIMMY VAUGHAN, and the FABULOUS THUNDERBIRDS, with Kim Wilson. Some of these artists, notably the

Vaughan Brothers and the Thunderbirds, went on to successful and lucrative careers, moving beyond the scene that had nurtured them.

Threadgill's still exhibits various souvenirs of Joplin's career. Near the club is a statue of guitarist Stevie Ray Vaughan. It is also possible to see the store and home of blues pianist ROBERT SHAW, a barrelhouse musician who had retired from music to become a successful owner of a store and barbecue restaurant. He was rediscovered by blues scholar Mack McCormick and resumed his musical career, recording and touring in the 1970s and 1980s until his death in 1985.

There are many venues for live music in Austin, particularly in the Sixth Street area, and they feature blues musicians from time to time. Waterloo Records, one of the outstanding independent record stores in the United States, is located near the University of Texas. Waterloo has an excellent selection of blues recordings, and Antone also operates a record shop with a large collection of blues albums.

DALLAS

During the 1920s the Deep Ellum section of town along some abandoned railroad tracks was the major center for black musicians. Deep Ellum was a rough area, with violence a regular feature on Saturday nights. BLIND LEMON JEFFERSON roamed the streets with a tin cup, playing for tips. Around 1912 he was joined by LEAD BELLY on the streets. Today the area features art galleries, music clubs, and restaurants.

Later pioneering electric guitarist T-BONE WALKER played in Dallas before he moved to LOS ANGELES, and pianists ALEX MOORE and SAM PRICE held forth. On the R&B side, Dallas boasted FREDDIE KING and Z. Z. HILL, and ANSON FUNDERBURGH and the Rockets.

Blind Lemon Jefferson's grave is 45 miles south in his hometown of Wortham.

HOUSTON

When classic blues artist SIPPIE WALLACE was a child, she played organ at a local church, while her younger brother Hersal was developing into an accomplished blues pianist. A group of blues and barrelhouse pianists known as the Santa Fe Group gathered around West Dallas Street, playing there and hoboing all over the Southwest to play in lumber and turpentine camps. They took the name Santa Fe from their trips on the Santa Fe Railroad, the rail line stretching from Lamy to Santa Fe.

Other blues and R&B musicians like BIG MAMA THORNTON and ELECTRIC GUITAR virtuosos ALBERT COLLINS and JOHNNY COPELAND gravitated to Houston, and pianist-singer Katie Webster was born there. Don Robey operated Duke and Peacock Records during the 1950s. It was one of the few successful black-owned record companies, recording a number of gospel music acts and blues and R&B artists like CLARENCE GATEMOUTH BROWN, BOBBY "BLUE" BLAND, and JUNIOR PARKER.

Possibly the most renowned of the Houston blues artists was LIGHTNIN' HOPKINS, who played on the streets and in local bars, and after his "discovery" during the folk revival of the 1960s recorded many albums and played at colleges and coffeehouses.

PORT ARTHUR

Port Arthur was the birthplace of Janis Joplin. An exhibit of the Museum of the Gulf Coast honors her and other blues and pop musicians from southeastern Texas and nearby southwestern LOUISIANA. Thirty musicians are included, with statues, photos, and other souvenirs on display.

Tharpe, Sister Rosetta (Rosetta Nubin)
(1915–1973) *holy blues singer*
Rosetta Tharpe's mother was a traveling evangelist and gospel shouter, and Tharpe's childhood resembled the life of a touring gospel singer. By the age of six she could play like BLIND GARY DAVIS, the guitar, and she sang at the meetings and conventions that her mother attended. Tharpe was a singer of holy blues. The words were spiritual and religious, but the music was pure exuberant blues. Throughout

her life Tharpe went back and forth between religious and secular music, at times offending her gospel fans who did not think the two musical styles should be mixed.

Tharpe was a flamboyant singer and guitarist at a time when few women played the guitar at all, let alone in her flashy and powerful way. She recorded some of T. A. DORSEY's songs for her first records, which proved to be very successful. She then started to perform with such jazz musicians as Cab Calloway and Benny Goodman. She developed a strong white audience as well by rearranging such spirituals as "Down by the Riverside" in up-to-date, up-tempo musical arrangements.

During World War II Tharpe and the Golden Gate Quartet were the only black gospel acts chosen to record V-Discs for soldiers serving overseas. (The V-Disc program was a special government operation to provide military personnel with music despite a strike by the American Federation of Musicians during the war that ended in 1949.) She also recorded with pianist SAMMY PRICE, and their recording of the song "Strange Things Happening Every Day" was one of the rare gospel records that hit the top-10 on the Billboard race records chart. (Race records were black pop records; later Billboard changed the name to rhythm and blues.)

In 1946 Tharpe joined forces with gospel shouter Madame Marie Knight, and they made hit records and played to large audiences. In the early 1950s they recorded some blues, which offended their gospel music fans. Knight stayed in the pop field, but Tharpe toured in Europe and returned to the gospel fold. A 1960 appearance at the Apollo Theater in Harlem featured her along with gospel stalwarts James Cleveland and the Caravans.

"That's All Right" (1954) *Elvis Presley's first hit, written by Arthur Crudup*
Some musicians are better songwriters than performers. Blues historian Richard Waterman, writing in his book *Between Midnight and Day, The Last Unpublished Blues Archive*, describes ARTHUR "BIG

Boy" Crudup in those terms. Crudup wrote this song, which was Elvis Presley's first hit. As with a number of the most popular blues, the song has a catchy chorus that sets it apart from many other blues. The verses contain no repeated lines, and the song is like the older folk blues in the sense that it does not tell a coherent story. It is simply a series of comments about the singer's girlfriend. His parents warn the singer that she is not good for him, and after Elvis asserts that she can do anything she wants, the singer decides to leave town before she breaks his heart. Presley's quavery vocal caught on quickly with the public.

The song was originally published by Lester Melrose, but his publishing company was sold to Hill & Range. Waterman, acting as Crudup's representative, negotiated a settlement with Hill & Range through a songwriter's protective organization called the American Guild of Artists and Composers. Waterman describes how Crudup drove to New York from Georgia with his four children, thinking that he would receive a $60,000 check as a settlement for royalties due to him. After a half-hour wait, the president of the company refused to sign the check, and Crudup and his family returned home. Crudup died not long after this meeting, and Waterman pursued the rights for his estate. Meanwhile Hill & Range was bought by Chappell Music, and the sale was delayed until the Crudup matter was settled. The estate's first check was for $248,000, far more than the previous settlement stipulated. Over the last 30 years the estate has earned over $3 million in royalties from the song.

Thomas, Henry (Ragtime Texas) (1874–1930)
singer, songwriter, and guitarist

Henry Thomas wrote songs, sang, and played the guitar and also the quills, a homemade reed instrument that makes a shrill, whistling sound. Many ethnomusicologists feel that they are an African instrument that survived slavery.

Thomas was a songster, with a repertoire of songs that includes dance music, spirituals, ragtime tunes, dance tunes, and blues. He is believed to have been one of the oldest African-American artists to record (he was 53 years old when he made his first recordings). Thomas used a capo on the guitar on the high frets, and he strummed across the strings so that it sounded as much like a banjo as a guitar. This gave his songs a bright, happy-go-lucky feel.

Henry Thomas recorded 23 songs between 1927 and 1929. Very little is known about his life, other than that he spent most of it in east Texas, possibly playing at the Columbian exposition in Chicago in 1893 and the 1904 World's Fair in St. Louis.

Between the high strummed guitar, the quills, and Thomas' light but high-pitched voice, listening to his music is like walking into a museum. The rock band Canned Heat scored a major hit record retitling Thomas's "Bull Doze Blues" as "Goin' Up the Country," and imitating the quills on the flute. Another Thomas classic, "Fishing Blues," was later recorded by the Lovin' Spoonful and Taj Mahal.

Thomas, Hociel (1904–1956) *singer*

Hociel Thomas came from a highly musical family. Her father, George, recorded the first boogie-woogie solo on a record, and her nephew Hersal was a brilliant pianist. Hociel herself played the piano and sang. Hociel's aunt was classic blues singer Sippie Wallace.

Thomas moved from her native Houston to New Orleans at the age of 12 to live with her aunt Sippie. She worked at private parties and in the Storyville district as a teenager, sometimes performing alone, sometimes with her aunt. By 1924 both Wallace and Thomas were in Chicago, where Thomas made her first record. The band was led by her nephew Hersal. Another session produced a minor hit record, and Okeh Records asked her for more material. Her next recordings featured most of Louis Armstrong's Hot Five band.

Thomas had relied heavily on her nephew for musical support, and after he died from food poisoning in 1926, she moved to Detroit and began to sing gospel music. After World War II jazz critic

Rudi Blesh discovered Thomas living in Chicago, and she recorded seven songs for him. This time she played her own piano parts, including one boogie-woogie tune. After the recording session Thomas performed with jazz musician Kid Ory's band in San Francisco.

In 1948 a fight with her sister left Thomas blinded and her sister dead. This marked the end of her musical career, and two years later her life ended as well.

Thomas, Jesse (Babyface) (1911–1995), and Rambling Thomas (Willard Thomas)

(1902–c. 1943) *guitarists, singers, and musicians*
Jesse Thomas was the younger brother of Willard. Jesse moved to Dallas in 1929. Although he recorded blues songs for a number of labels, none of his recordings was successful. His early recordings were influenced by the guitar work of BLIND BLAKE and LONNIE JOHNSON, but later he attempted a variety of vocal styles, ranging from crooning to shouting. He also spent time on the West Coast, recording for BOB GEDDINS in LOS ANGELES. Jesse also began to play ELECTRIC GUITAR, combining country blues with a modern approach that was influenced by T-BONE WALKER. His last records, made at the age of 84, were for his own label.

Jesse's brother Willard played SLIDE GUITAR as well as the normal instrument. He played on the streets of Shreveport, LOUISIANA, and Dallas, TEXAS, and worked as far north as Oklahoma. Yet another brother, Joe, also played guitar. Their father was an old-time fiddler who played in string bands. Rambling Thomas bought his slide guitar from a Sears catalog. His brother reported that like Jesse, he was influenced by guitarist Lonnie Johnson. He recorded for Paramount and Victor.

Thomas, Rufus (1917–2001) *singer and songwriter*

Rufus Thomas was a throwback to vaudeville days. He wrote and recorded a number of hit songs, all of them revolving around dances and humorous subjects. MISSISSIPPI-born, he moved to MEMPHIS at the age of one. He toured with the Rabbits Foot Minstrels as a comic, and later he ran talent shows in Memphis and was a disc jockey. Thomas's first big record was his answer to BIG MAMA THORNTON's "Hound Dog," which Thomas called "Bear Cat." He sometimes recorded with his daughter Carla, known as the "Queen of Memphis Soul."

Thomas's biggest hit was "Walking the Dog." It hit the R&B top-10 in 1963 and was then covered by the ROLLING STONES. Thomas's records were basically dance grooves with humorous words, which he wrote and performed. In the 1970s he had more R&B hits with his songs "Do the Funky Chicken" and "Push and Pull." Thomas recorded for Memphis-based Stax Records. The label went bankrupt in the mid-1970s. Thomas continued to record and perform into the late 1990s.

Thomas was often interviewed for books and videos about the Memphis music scene.

Thornton, Big Mama (Willie Mae Thornton) (1920–1984) *blues shouter*

Thornton's mother sang in church, and Willie Mae joined a traveling review in 1941. She then moved to Houston, singing and playing drums and HARMONICA. At Houston's PEACOCK RECORDS she hooked up with JOHNNY OTIS. She continued to make powerful records, but she did not achieve commercial success. During the blues revival of the 1960s, Thornton performed in Europe.

Big Mama Thornton was a powerful blues shouter. Her moment in the sun came with her recording of "Hound Dog." It reached the number-one spot on the R&B charts in 1953, and it stayed there for seven weeks. Three years later Elvis Presley recorded the song, and it became such a huge hit that Thorton's version was forgotten. Thornton was eclipsed again when she wrote "Ball and Chain," only to see it covered and popularized by white rock-blues singer JANIS JOPLIN before she herself recorded it. This was a source of frustration and bitterness for Thornton, who felt that she never received the fame and money due her.

Thorogood, George (b. 1950) *recording artist, guitarist, and singer*

A semiprofessional baseball player in Wilmington, Delaware, George Thorogood rejected any major-label record deal, because he believed that a large record company would expect him to promote his records year round. This would have required him to quit playing baseball. Instead Thorogood record-ed an album for a small Boston-based company called ROUNDER. Supposedly the cost of producing the album was about $600, and it sold over 500,000 copies. Thorogood was an energetic and accessible blues man, popular with women audiences.

Rounder was pleased to have a successful album, but they were not prepared to deal with the promo-tional aspects of the popular music marketplace in the 1970s. So Rounder farmed out Thorogood's contract to Capitol Records. During the 1980s, Thorogood got lucky again, this time with his song "Bad to the Bone." MTV programmed the video, the song became a hit, and Thorogood found him-self enjoying four more gold albums.

Thorogood's good-time party music bar band features guitar, bass, drums, and a SAXOPHONE player, who was added in 1980. Thorogood does not make gold records anymore, but he still tours, performs, and records. More than a dozen of his albums are available on CD.

"The Thrill Is Gone" (1951) *1970 hit for B. B. King*

B. B. KING may be more identified with the blues than any other artist. For many years King played almost exclusively for black audiences and was relatively unknown to whites. During this period King had enjoyed a number of R&B hits but never made a pop hit. In 1970 ABC Bluesway Records paired King with young record producer Bill

Szymczyk and they recorded "The Thrill Is Gone," a song written in 1951 by Rick Darnell and Roy Hawkins. King had thought about recording the song for several years. They recorded the song, and Szymczyk decided to add string parts to it, calling in arranger Burt de Coteaux. The song rose to number 15 on the pop charts and it became King's trademark.

The song's form is a straight blues, with repeated lines. However, the title is used in three of the four verses. This is typical of pop songs but a bit unusu-al for a blues.

Titon, Jeff Todd (b. 1944) *author and music professor*

Jeff Titon teaches in the music program at Brown University. He is one of the leading blues authors who is currently active. Also a musician, he spent two years playing in PIANO player Lazy Bill Lucas's band. Titon has written a number of books, but the ones that discuss the blues are his detailed survey, *Early Down Home Blues,* and his collection of blues lyrics entitled *Downhome Blues Lyrics: An Anthology from the Post-World War II Era.* He has also pro-duced records and written or edited books about Kentucky FIDDLE tunes and world music styles.

Toussaint, Allen (b. 1938) *musician, arranger, and record producer*

Pianist, songwriter, arranger, singer, record produc-er, Allen Toussaint has done it all. He has produced records for R&B performers Ernie K-Doe and Irma Thomas, rock and roll performer Lee Dorsey, the NEVILLE BROTHERS, and outside the blues field, for-mer Beatle Paul McCartney. Toussaint was born in New Orleans and still operates a recording studio there. He recorded the first album under his own name in 1958 and has continued to record occasion-ally under his name. A soft, understated singer, his own albums have been the least part of his commer-cial success. That has come from his productions and from the recordings of his songs by the ROLLING STONES, the YARDBIRDS, BONNIE RAITT, the Band, trumpet player Al Hirt, and Glenn Campbell, singer of "The Rhinestone Cowboy." Toussaint's PIANO work follows in the New Orleans tradition of PROFESSOR LONGHAIR.

Townsend, Henry (b. 1909)

Raised in southern Illinois, Henry Townsend left home at the age of nine to go to St. Louis. He started to play guitar at age 15 and soon played for artists like WALTER DAVIS and ROOSEVELT SYKES. Townsend spent time with ROBERT JOHNSON not long before Johnson's death. Johnson had come to St. Louis and ended up taking over a job from Townsend. Townsend played on many records of other musicians, including such artists as ROBERT NIGHTHAWK, SONNY BOY WILLIAMSON I, Walter Davis, BIG JOE WILLIAMS, and Roosevelt Sykes.

Townsend also taught himself to play PIANO, he found making a living difficult, so he gave up playing music during the 1950s. He was periodically rediscovered by folklorists and record companies and made several albums under his own name. In addition to his gentle country blues side, Townsend had picked up the ELECTRIC GUITAR as well. He also wrote a number of his own songs. His autobiography, *Henry Townsend: A Blues Life,* was recently published by the University of Illinois Press.

Artie Traum (Larry Sandberg)

Traum, Artie (b. 1943), and Happy Traum
(b. 1939) *guitarists*

Artie Traum is a talented guitarist whose work spills over from blues to folk guitar and has jazz aspects as well. He played blues guitar on Judy Roderick's *Woman Blue* album. Traum has been over a good deal of the musical map. He recorded with a folk-rock band called Bear in the late 1960s; he recorded duet albums with his brother Happy; and he has made albums of his own songs, as well as instrumental albums that fall into the New Age category.

He has also written guitar instruction books and made instruction audio and videotapes.

Happy Traum studied guitar with BROWNIE McGHEE, edited folk magazine *Sing Out* for three years, played on some BOB DYLAN recording sessions, and has made his own albums. Happy owns a business called Homespun Tapes in his hometown of Woodstock, NEW YORK, the premiere company for guitar instructional audio and videotapes. Happy has recorded some of the tapes himself and has written several best-selling folk and blues guitar instruction books.

"Trouble in Mind" (1926) *blues standard first recorded by Bertha "Chippie" Hill*

"Trouble in Mind" is a blues standard composed by bandleader Richard M. Jones. A native of New Orleans, Jones was well known in CHICAGO as a bandleader and pianist, appearing in theaters and playing on recording sessions. The first recording of this song was made by BERTHA "CHIPPIE" HILL with LOUIS ARMSTRONG in 1926. Dozens of other artists have recorded the song over the years, ranging from JANIS JOPLIN, Sam Cooke, the Everly Brothers, and LOUIS ARMSTRONG to Johnny Ray, country artists Red Foley and Bob Wills, Aretha Franklin, and folksingers JOSH WHITE and Ronnie Gilbert, of the Weavers.

Like the song *Key to the Highway,* the song goes from the I chord to the V chord before going to the IV (in the key of G, the progressions is G, D7 to C). The song also has a somewhat more sophisticated harmonic pattern in the rest of the tune, using both minor and diminished chords. (G diminished has the notes G B-flat D-flat.)

The format of the song is four verses. There are no repeated lines as such, but the phase "trouble in mind" occurs several times, and the one verse that does not contain that phrase does use the word "trouble." Some of the artists who have recorded this song have incorrectly assumed that it was a traditional song, because the lyric seems so typical of the folk blues.

Trucks, Derek (b. 1980) *guitarist*

The nephew of Allman brothers drummer Butch Trucks, Derek Trucks began to play guitar at the age of nine. By the time he was 12, he was sitting in with the ALLMAN BROTHERS Band and BUDDY GUY. Currently Trucks has his own band, which has released three CDs. He plays SLIDE GUITAR and shows both jazz and blues influences. He replaced Dickie Betts in the Allman Brothers Band in 2000. His most recent solo album explores music from different parts of the world, including India. Trucks does not sing; his recordings use other artists to do vocals.

tunings

The most typical guitar tuning is E A D G B E, reading from the sixth string to the first string. Blues guitarists have experimented with a number of other tunings. Most of these experiments have involved "open tunings." An open tuning tunes the guitar to an actual chord, so that the player can simply strum the open strums to get that chord. Guitarists use open tunings for a number of reasons. The first is to explore what sounds can be created. The G tuning, for example, uses the notes D G D G B D. Compare these notes with the normal guitar tuning of E A D G B E. The distance between the strings is greater in some notes in the G tuning, and it is smaller in others. This distance (the intervals between the notes) also varies much more in the G tuning. In the normal tuning, the guitar is entirely tuned in fourths, except for the distance between the third and second strings, which is only a major third. In the G tuning the intervals are, respectively, a fourth, a fifth, a fourth, a third, and a minor third. This tuning is sometimes called "Spanish" tuning. Interestingly, this tuning is similar to the way the five-string BANJO is tuned; in fact the top fourth, third, second, and first strings are identical in the two instruments. Guitarist Woody Mann has transcribed a number of slide solos in various tunings. In the G tuning he has included BARBECUE BOB's "Yo Yo Blues," SON HOUSE's "Dry Spell Blues," and ROBERT JOHNSON's "Crossroads Blues."

Another common open tuning is the D tuning, with the guitar tuned D A D F-sharp A D. Once again the intervals are in a different order—a fifth from the sixth string to the fifth string, a fourth from the fifth to the fourth, a major third from the fourth to the third, a minor third from the third to the second string, and a fourth from the second string to the first. This is sometimes known as "Sevastopol," "slack key," or "Hawaiian" tuning. "Sevastopol" was a popular piece at the beginning of the 20th century. Mann has transcribed a number of pieces in the D tuning, by such artists as

KOKOMO ARNOLD, BUMBLE BEE SLIM, and BLIND WILLIE MCTELL.

These were the most popular alternate tunings, but some artists experimented with others. JOHN CEPHAS plays the ballad "John Henry" in D minor tuning, D A D F A D. This is quite similar to D tuning, with the F-sharp lowered to a D. SKIP JAMES was fond of using an open E minor tuning, E B E G B E.

A number of other artists who are not blues players have experimented with open tunings. Among them are Joni Mitchell, renowned folk singer and songwriter, singer-songwriter David Wilcox, and Shawn Colvin, adult contemporary singer and songwriter. Rock bands have also broken new ground with guitar tunings, notably the Seattle grunge band Soundgarden.

Some artists use tunings to write new musical compositions. When a musician plays in an unfamiliar tuning, her fingers do not automatically go to places where they have been before, and sometimes this results in new and interesting music. This is particularly obvious in Joni Mitchell's music. Other open tunings include those that use the notes E A C# E A E and C tuning, with the notes C G C G C E. The tuning D A D G A D is often used to play Celtic music and has been extensively explored by guitarist Pierre Bensusan.

Turner, Big Joe (1911–1985) *singer*

A classic blues shouter, Big Joe Turner started out singing in church. Working in his native Kansas City, Missouri, he developed the ability to shout over a horn-filled orchestra. He was a bartender in a Kansas City club, where he met PETE JOHNSON. Johnson was playing the PIANO at the club, and soon the two started a musical partnership. In 1938 Turner recorded his first hits, "Roll 'Em Pete," "Piney Brown Blues," and "Rebecca." He sang at the 1938 JOHN HAMMOND From Spirituals to Swing concert, then performed all over the United States, including performances with Count Basie. In 1954

he recorded "Shake, Rattle and Roll" for ATLANTIC RECORDS. It did well, but the song was covered by Bill Haley and the Comets in what is considered to be one of the first rock and roll records. Turner also wrote many songs, including the blues classic "Cherry Red."

Turner continued to tour and record, usually with jazz players accompanying him. He was respectfully called "the boss of the blues."

Turner, Ike (Izear Lester Turner) (b. 1931) *musician, record producer, and talent scout*

Multitalented Ike Turner is probably best known to the general public as the ex-husband of singer Tina Turner. Ike is a pianist, songwriter, guitar player, record producer, and record talent scout. In 1951 he made what many consider the first rock and roll record, "Rocket 88." The artist credited was Jackie Brensten & the Delta Cats. Turner played PIANO on the song.

Turner helped move the blues toward a more modern and commercial rhythm and blues sound. He played on sessions with B. B. KING, BOBBY "BLUE" BLAND, OTIS RUSH, and WILLIE DIXON. He worked for countless record companies, including SAM PHILLIPS's SUN RECORDS in MEMPHIS.

In 1956 Turner met Annie Mae Bullock. She became Tina Turner, and the two made many hit R&B records. During the mid-1970s their marriage broke up, and Tina's widely read autobiography detailed a long history of Ike's abusive treatment, his drug use, and jail time. Since that time Ike has been musically active but has not drawn much attention in the music world, while Tina has become a major star in her own right.

Turner, Othar (1909–2003) *fife player*

Othar Turner represented the fife and drum band tradition from northern MISSISSIPPI which dates back to the early 1800s. Turner played the fife, which he took up at the age of 14. The fife is a hollow instrument with a bamboo reed, and Turner was one of the last to take it up seriously. Later he taught his children to play the fife. He played the music on his farm in Gravel Springs, Mississippi, with the Rising Star Fife and Drum Band.

None of his music was recorded until MEMPHIS record producer Jim Dickinson recorded his first album between 1992 and 1997. Turner was almost 90 years old by the time the record came out. Another album followed a year later.

Many trace this music to the traditions of African music, and it sounds unlike anything else that was being played in Mississippi.

12-string guitar

Twelve-string guitars are set up with six pairs of strings, with each pair quite close together. The usual tuning is E E (tuned an octave apart) A A (tuned an octave apart) D D (tuned an octave apart) G G (sometimes tuned an octave apart, sometimes tuned the same) B B, and E E. The octave strings produce an unusual sound quality, and when played well the instrument sounds almost like an orchestra. Certain players, notably LEAD BELLY, tuned the instrument lower than normal pitch, producing an extremely heavy bass sound.

In the history of blues only a handful of players played 12-string guitar as their primary instrument. Lead Belly, the most famous of these artists, had several trademark playing techniques. He often started a song on a seventh chord; in other words, if the song were in the key of A, he would play A7 as his first chord. Lead Belly also liked to play heavy bass runs, somewhat similar to the way a boogie-woogie pianist would play.

ATLANTA was home to a number of 12-string players. BLIND WILLIE MCTELL was there, and so were the Hicks Brothers, "BARBECUE" BOB and Charlie. All three were high-voiced singers whose voices and guitar styles were much lighter than what Lead Belly was doing. All these players used a slide on some of their recordings. McTell's broad repertoire extended to religious songs, ragtime and vaudeville-influenced material, blues, white country songs, and songs that were as much recitations as tunes. Although the Hicks' guitar styles were not nearly as rhythmic and powerful as Lead Belly's work, McTell's guitar technique was the most fluid of the group, with a good deal of his music so accurately fingered that it is difficult to believe he is playing a 12-string instrument.

During the folk revival there was a brief vogue for the 12-string when the Rooftop Singers had a number one pop record in 1963 with two 12-string guitars playing on "Walk Right In." Many of the pop-folk groups used a 12-string from time to time in their shows and on their recordings. During this period it was common to hear 12-string guitar on commercials or movie soundtracks.

One of the black music performers who also toured widely during that time was JESSE FULLER. Fuller was a 12-string player, but most people focused on the fact that he was a one-man band, playing bass with a foot pedal, 12-string with his hands, and adding HARMONICA to the mix, with the harmonica placed on a rack above his guitar.

Some of the white revivalists have taken up the 12-string, notably PAUL GEREMIA, FRED GERLACH, Mike Russo, Tracy Moore, and Dave Ray. Many others play 12-string as a diversion from their normal six-string guitar playing. Although today's instruments are much better made than those of the 1900s, they are still difficult to master. Instrumentalist and singer Leo Kottke plays quite a bit of 12-string in his shows, but blues are only part of his extensive repertoire, and folk artist Judy Collins features 12-string in her shows.

Roger McGuinn, the leader of the Byrds, played electric 12-string guitar on their records, many of which became major hits. BOB DYLAN's "Hey Mr. Tambourine Man" and Pete Seeger's "Turn, Turn, Turn" are two of these songs. Today McGuinn tours and records as a solo artist, still playing electric 12-string.

The main difference between playing the 12-string guitar and the six-string is that the former requires considerable strength in the left hand to press the strings of the guitar. Until the 1950s, many 12-strings were cheaply made and the neck was set poorly, leaving the strings high above the fingerboard. This made it even more remarkable that Blind Willie McTell, for example, was able to pick the strings so cleanly and accurately. Another difference between the two instruments is that because of the doubled strings, there are loud overtones when open chords are played. Overtones are the sound that notes leave when played and before the sound diminishes into the next note or chord.

Van Ronk, Dave (1936–2002) *musician*

Born in Brooklyn, NEW YORK, Dave Van Ronk lived for years in the same apartment building in New York's Greenwich Village. One of the many students of BLIND GARY DAVIS, he had a jazz background as well and made a few recordings with jug bands. Most of his recordings centered around the blues, and a lifelong asthmatic condition gave him a gruff sound that was particularly appropriate for singing the blues. A bear of a man, Van Ronk could also howl quite convincingly.

Van Ronk was an important musician in a number of ways. He transcribed rags, and his guitar style could be delicate and intricate. He also liked to introduce songs by young singer-songwriters, interpreting them in his own way. For example, he is the last person the casual listener would expect to find singing a Joni Mitchell song, but in fact he interpreted her music in an interesting and creative way.

Van Ronk was also a teacher. Not only did he teach guitar for many years, but he was an informal teacher to BOB DYLAN and many of the folk revivalists and songwriters in Greenwich Village. He recorded for many record labels and even made children's records.

Though he was never a big star, Van Ronk was a big influence on many people active in the folk and blues revival, some of whom did become stars.

Vaughan, Jimmy (b. 1951) *guitarist*

Jimmy Vaughan was the older brother of STEVIE RAY VAUGHAN. An accomplished guitarist himself, he was deeply involved in the Austin, TEXAS, music scene in the early 1970s and was a founding member of the FABULOUS THUNDERBIRDS. Vaughan was born and raised in Dallas, Texas, and was heavily influenced by B. B. KING and FREDDIE KING. He played in a few garage bands and moved to Austin at the age of 19. In 1972 he formed the Storm, which backed up FREDDIE KING and other traveling blues acts.

In 1974 Vaughan met singer and HARMONICA player Kim Wilson; adding a bass player and a drummer, they formed the Fabulous Thunderbirds. The group was an outstanding rock-blues band, seemingly able to please both purist blues fans and much younger rock audiences. Their fifth album, *Tuff Enough,* broke them onto the national scene in 1986. It also helped Vaughan to receive some proper attention and to emerge from his brother's long shadow.

In 1990 Vaughan left the band to play with Stevie Ray. They completed an album together and were planning to tour when Stevie Ray was killed in an airplane accident. In 1996 Vaughan, assembled an all-star cast in a tribute album to Stevie Ray, and since then he has continued to record and tour on his own.

Vaughan, Stevie Ray (1954–1990) *guitarist*

Stevie Ray Vaughan was a virtuoso guitar player who added the wild guitar inventions of JIMI HENDRIX to TEXAS and CHICAGO blues to create his own guitar style. He was able to bring the blues headlong into rock and roll.

Like his brother Jimmy, Stevie Ray played in high school bands. When Jimmy left Dallas to move to Austin and become a professional musician, Stevie Ray did the same. He formed a band with Austin singer Lou Ann Barton under the name the Triple Threat Review. Later Barton left and in 1978 the band became Double Trouble. It was just Vaughan, a bass player, and a drummer. In 1980 a keyboard player was added.

The band toured internationally as well as nationally, and Vaughan was asked to play on records by such major rock stars as David Bowie. Legendary record producer and talent scout JOHN HAMMOND SR. convinced Epic Records to sign the band. Jackson Browne offered the band free recording time at his studio, and the band recorded the album *Texas Flood* in one week. It reached number 38 on the pop album charts in 1983, and a second album followed entitled *Couldn't Stand the Weather* that reached number 31 on the chart in 1984, and sold over a half million copies. The band's third album peaked at number 34 in 1986, called *Soul to Soul*.

Vaughan then fought off persistent problems with alcohol, checking himself into a rehabilitation clinic. The band made a fourth album, his biggest-selling record, reaching to number 33. In his 1989 album Vaughan did much more songwriting than he had ever attempted before, co-writing with his keyboard player Reese Wynans. He even wrote a song about his drinking problem, "Wall of Denial."

Then came the album with brother Jimmy, and the airplane crash that cost Vaughan his life. The album was released after his death and entered the pop record charts at number 10. Since then brother Jimmy has carefully supervised the issuing of additional CDs which have sold better than anything Stevie Ray did during his lifetime.

Vaughan will be remembered for his explosive guitar technique and for bringing the blues back to the rock scene during the 1980s. He remains an extraordinary influence on young guitarists.

Vinson, Eddie (Cleanhead) (1917–1998)
saxophonist and singer

Eddie Vinson's unusual nickname stemmed from his bald head. He spent his life bouncing between a career as a jazz alto SAXOPHONE player and a singing, sax-playing blues artist.

Born in Houston, TEXAS, Vinson played with guitarist T-BONE WALKER in his high school band. Vinson was influenced early in his career by the recordings of LOUIS JORDAN. Jordan's music was humorous and light, and he too played the saxophone. Vinson played in Milt Larkin's Band in 1935, hooked up for a while with guitarist BIG BILL BROONZY, and in 1941 played with Cootie Williams's orchestra. Vinson recorded "Cherry Red Blues" with the Williams band, and it became a big hit. In 1945 Vinson formed his own band and recorded his song "Cleanhead Blues."

Like Jordan, Vinson specialized in earthy, humorous songs, usually containing comments about romance. During the 1970s and 1980s Vinson toured Europe and became popular there. He always kept a hand in the jazz scene, and he wrote two tunes, "Tune Up" and "Four," that were recorded by the legendary jazz trumpet player Miles Davis. Toward the end of his career Vinson recorded an album with the blues-rock group ROOMFUL OF BLUES.

Vinson, Walter (Walter Jacobs Vinson)
(1901–1975) *guitarist and songwriter*

Walter Vinson was influenced early by the Delta blues. Living in Bolton, MISSISSIPPI, he took up guitar at the age of six, and soon he was playing with TOMMY JOHNSON and ISHMON BRACEY. He was the "adopted son" of the Chatmon Family, and he sang and played guitar with the influential Chatmon family band, the MISSISSIPPI SHEIKS. From 1941 to 1960 Vinson lived in CHICAGO and worked outside the field of music. The folk and blues revival brought him some festival and club appearances during the 1960s. Vinson is probably best remembered for having written "Sittin' on

Top of the World," which has been covered by a number of other artists.

vocal styles

Although there are some instrumental blues pieces, the great majority of blues songs contain lyrics. Over the approximately 110-year history of blues, a number of blues vocal styles have developed. ALAN LOMAX developed a theory called cantometrics, in which he separated world vocal styles into open- and closed-throat singing. Open-throat singers could sing without apparent vocal strain or restriction, while closed-throat singers sounded constricted and limited.

Piedmont vocal styles tend to be light and pleasant, using the voice almost as an extension of talking. Artists like FURRY LEWIS and MISSISSIPPI JOHN HURT (a Piedmont-style artist even though he came from Mississippi) use their voices in manner that is halfway between singing and talking. A MISSISSIPPI artist like SON HOUSE sings with much more passion and power.

Ideally a vocal performance should express the emotional content of a particular lyric, as expressed in a particular melody. This goal is likely to be modified, based upon the vocal equipment of the artist. What is there about a particular vocal performance that can be moving to the point of tears?

One of the elements involved in vocal performance is diction. The typical southern rural performer might be difficult for a white audience to understand. The folk-blues artist might also be an amateur or semiprofessional musician not used to performing in public. The player may also have a particular accent that makes it difficult for an audience in a different geographic region to understand.

Another vocal technique is vibrato. Vibrato involves a fluctuation in both pitch and intensity. Some folk-blues singers, like SKIP JAMES or WASHBOARD SAM (Robert Brown), used this device, but it became common in gospel music performance. Many of the soul singers of the 1960s were originally gospel singers who often used a great deal of vibrato, for example, Otis Redding. Some of today's pop singers, like Whitney Houston and Mariah Carey, use so much vibrato that it is sometimes difficult to know which note they are trying to hit.

The recitative style of performance in which artists half-talk a lyric has certain interesting qualities. If no melody has to be followed, the artists can omit some of the words, improvise phrases between the lines, and engage in spoken asides. These spoken asides are a common characteristic of duet music, where one artist talks to the other. It is usually fairly easy to understand the words in semispoken performances.

The first recorded blues were by such classic blues singers as Mamie, Clara, and BESSIE SMITH; MA RAINEY; IDA COX; and VICTORIA SPIVEY, among others. These were all professional singers accustomed to performing in public. In most cases it is not difficult to understand the words to their songs. Ma Rainey is the exception to the rule, possibly because she was accustomed to performing before southern rural audiences, and also because Paramount Records, the company that recorded her, made the worst-quality records of the group. Rainey's voice is more husky than voices of other artists, who, with some exceptions, sound more like vaudeville performers than blues singers. Rainey also had the habit of interjecting spoken asides, and it is as difficult to understand her speaking voice as it is to understand the words of her songs. Possibly because the companies that have reissued her recordings do not believe that they will sell in quantity, her recordings have not been as well served by technical reprocessing by audio engineers, as Bessie Smith's works have been, for example.

Smith's vocals stand out from any of the classic blues singers. Her voice is more powerful than that of any of the others and her diction is excellent. She also had the ability to bend tempo to suit her own needs. She often sings behind the beat, as though telling the backup musicians to slow down. Except for her final recordings, Smith did not use a drummer; this may have been because she was unwilling to get locked into someone else's tempo. Her diction is excellent, but the clarity of her words is not associated with a stiffness of performing style, which was typical of many other classic blues singers. Smith could also improvise, not necessarily singing each verse in the identical way. She did this by adding grace notes, using different accents and different rhythms for the notes, and in general acting more like an improvising horn player than a singer.

None of the classic blues singers had to play as well as sing, although some were capable of doing so. All the folk blues artists of the 1920 and 1930s, starting with PAPA CHARLIE JACKSON in 1925 and including such artists as BLIND LEMON JEFFERSON, BLIND WILLIE MCTELL, CHARLEY PATTON, MEMPHIS MINNIE, and ROBERT JOHNSON, played and sang at the same time. The challenges for an artist who has to play as well as sing are entirely different, but so are some of the musical opportunities. Solo folk blues artists could vary the tempo in the course of a performance. Since no one else (or in the case of Memphis Minnie only one other musician) was following the artist, he or she had the ability to speed up or slow down the beat, or even to vary the length of the verses. It is therefore not surprising that blues artists sometimes sang 11 1/2-bar blues, 12 1/4-bar blues, 11- or 13-bar blues, or whatever they attempted.

The style of Delta blues is more intense than any other kind of blues. The vocals follow the same pattern. Artists like Son House and Robert Johnson in particular sing in the high register in a way that almost indicates that they are suffering during the song. ISHMON BRACEY has one of the oddest vocal sounds of any of the Delta artists. Some of his vocals have an extremely nasal quality, as though he is singing through his nose. In other selections, notably "Woman, Woman Blues," he sings in the lower register with a buzzing bass sound, then jumps into the falsetto register. The overall effect is confusion rather than a coherent performance style. Mississippi artist TOMMY JOHNSON also is fond of jumping into the high register, but his vocal style is

much smoother than Bracey's. BUKKA (BOOKER) WHITE's vocals vary between the gruff voice that he uses on religious songs and the high-pitched vocals that he uses in his blues selections. The gruff religious vocals recall some of the holy blues artists, specifically BLIND WILLIE JOHNSON and the REVEREND GARY DAVIS, both of whom sang in extremely gruff voices, possibly partly because they worked mostly on the streets, playing for tips. White also performed a number of tunes about trains in which he uses the spoken word as a sort of dialogue between himself and his guitar. Robert Johnson tends to sing in the higher vocal register, and sometimes his voice almost breaks out of control, as in his performance in "Preaching the Blues." He is virtually shouting, and one wonders if he performed in this way on a regular basis, and if so, how he avoided hoarseness.

Singing in the high register gives voices dramatic quality particularly appropriate to the passion of the Delta blues. In Robert Johnson's case, listeners almost feel that he is involved in a battle between his voice and his guitar, each one egging the other on to greater extremes of performance.

Skip James is one of those artists who has developed his own individual style. His vocals start out in the high register, then drift into falsetto. No one else sounds much like him, except possibly Jack Owens, who is from the same area of Mississippi. Oddly on his album of piano-accompanied blues entitled *Greatest of the Delta Blues Singers,* which James recorded in 1964 after his rediscovery, he does not sing everything in the falsetto register. Whether he deliberately recorded in the high register because he originally thought such a technique would be identified with him is not known.

During the late 1920s and early 1930s LEROY CARR utilized more of a crooning and soft vocal style in his blues. Carr was enormously popular, and his work greatly influenced other musicians, though he was dead by 1935. One of those affected by Carr was St. Louis singer-pianist WALTER DAVIS. Davis sometimes sang with more passion than Carr, but many of his songs follow Carr's gentle delivery.

URBAN BLUES AND VOCAL STYLES

By the mid-1940s the ELECTRIC GUITAR was in common use, and bands were using bass players and drummers. Blues vocal styles had to change of necessity to be audible over the increased volumes of blues bands. Public address systems had also improved, so the microphone became the vocalist's ally. Delta musicians like MUDDY WATERS and ELMORE JAMES became blues shouters. Blues bands also had to compete with the early rhythm and blues bands, whose vocals varied from the crooning style of CHARLES BROWN to shouters like BIG JOE TURNER. A real dichotomy developed between the folk-blues revivalists, who performed at coffeehouses and college concerts, and the Chicago blues artists performing in the loud South Side and West Side clubs. Artists like Muddy Waters and BIG BILL BROONZY adjusted their vocal styles and instrumentation to suit the audience that was hiring them. The presence of the white revivalists complicated the situation. Should they imitate the older blues styles or the ones that actually were developing in Chicago? To complicate matters further, English rockers started to develop huge audiences, and they clearly were checking in on the side of the electric blues. The prevailing ideology among the rockers was that loud vocals were an indicator of deep emotion. They also seemed to get the attention of the audience.

WHITES, BLACKS, AND THE BLUES

There has been considerable controversy over the years about whether white performers can, or even should, perform the blues. For many years scholars and music critics gave readers the impression that white and black musicians operated in two different worlds. This notion was based on an examination of the segregated world that prevailed throughout the South. Because churches, schools, restaurants, and other facilities open to the public were not racially integrated, many assumed that musicians also did not have contact with one another across racial lines. Not all scholars of the subject accepted this picture.

In 1970 music scholar Tony Russell wrote *Blacks, Whites and Blues,* the only book specifically devoted to delineating connections between white and black blues musicians. He pointed out that despite the obvious fact that segregation in the South limited contact between the races, musicians also encountered songs from friends, in working environments like lumberyards, in performances by street singers, from religious gatherings, and from radio and phonograph records. Many white musicians grew up in households or farms that utilized black employees—yet another possible music connection. The brilliant white instrumentalist Hobart Smith, for example, learned some songs from Blind Lemon Jefferson, who had passed through Smith's hometown of Saltville, Virginia, and stayed for about a month around 1917.

Why did white singers, many of whom felt superior to African Americans, want to sing the blues, which were so closely identified with them? Russell theorizes that the blues offered a sense of freedom not found in white ballads. The blues was not bound by traditions of country music, like cabins in the wildwood, "gray-haired mothers," or religion. Russell feels that the blues "confers a license to break rules and taboos, to say the unsayable, create its own dark carnival." The blues talked about cheating women and unfaithful men, about jails and rambling. Certainly not all these subjects were forbidden in white country music, but they were not as freely discussed. The southern white has always been fascinated by the supposed sexual freedom practiced in the world of the African American; the blues talked explicitly about sex, as opposed to romantic love. It may seem ironic, but white performers may often have envied the freewheeling lives of the black folk-blues artist.

The work of early white blues singers, like FRANK HUTCHISON, Tom Darby, and JIMMIE TARLTON, and Cliff Carlisle, among others, makes obvious certain aspects of their performances. Many white performers, especially Hutchison, Darby, and Tarlton, absorbed black guitar styles. A number of white artists were fascinated by bottleneck styles, especially the sort of light bottleneck playing found among Piedmont black guitarists like TAMPA RED. Fingerpicking guitar may well have been a blend of white and black guitar techniques, and a number of these musicians, like Sam Magee, Roy Harvey, and Leonard Copeland, are fluent and accurate fingerpickers.

At the same time, what white artists *failed* to capture was the singing style of the blues, especially anything resembling that of black Delta musicians. White vocal styles are much closer to Piedmont blues, which have a much lighter texture, as close to talking as to singing. A few white musicians, like Roscoe Holcomb, had harsh, almost scratchy voices, but they lacked the volume and power of black Delta singers. Another factor missing from white vocalists was innovation. The single exception, perhaps, is the vocal style of JIMMIE "The Singing Brakeman" RODGERS. Rodgers sang 13 songs that he called "blue yodels." The blue yodels followed blues format, repeating the first line of each verse, but at the end of the verse Rodgers would break into a yodel. The yodel was not delivered in the pretty Swiss yodeling style, but had more of a western or cowboy feel. Other than the yodel the other performances on the Columbia reissues are based on African-American models of singing and playing, but they are not as powerful or as convincing as the originals, with the single exception of the so-called talking blues. The talking blues were first recorded in 1926, performed by a mandolinist named Chris Bouchillon. According to an article by folksong scholar Charles Wolfe, "A Lighter Shade of Blue: White Country Blues," which is a chapter in Lawrence Cohn's *Nothin' But the Blues: The Music and the Musicians,* Bouchillon auditioned for Columbia Records producer Frank Walker. Walker liked his speaking voice but thought that his singing was "the worst thing I had heard." Walker suggested that he simply talk the lyrics. The resulting "Talking Blues" turned out to be a big hit record, selling 90,000 copies. Wolfe suggests that this form already existed in black music, citing recordings by Talking

Billy Anderson and Coley Jones, and verses collected by folklorists.

The inability of white country artists to imitate black vocal styles may have been a difference in dialect and pronunciation in the two groups. Alan Lomax has theorized a difference between open- and closed-throat vocal styles, not only between black and white singers, but throughout the world. He has associated many other traits with these different vocal styles. The open-throat style is a freer, more open style of vocalizing, while the closed-throat is much more pinched and nasal. This is a good enough description of the differences between the early black and white blues singers.

Today the controversial question remains as to whether white artists can perform the blues in a convincing and significant way. Even before the revival had hit, Harry Smith's 1952 *Anthology of American Folk Music,* a six-album set on FOLKWAYS RECORDS, had introduced Hurt and many other blues and country artists to lovers of American roots music in 1952. Part of the folk music revival of the 1960s was the rediscovery of various blues artists, including Son House, Mississippi John Hurt, and Skip James. These artists performed at folk festivals, especially the giant Newport Folk Festival, and at clubs, colleges, and coffeehouses. They also re-recorded many of their songs, and even introduced new or unrecorded material.

A new generation of white American blues enthusiasts started to perform many of these songs and to write new ones of their own. Among these artists were DAVE VAN RONK, who began recording in 1959; and JOHN HAMMOND JR.; the Minneapolis trio KOERNER, RAY, AND GLOVER; and Boston artists Jim Kweskin and His Jug Band, which included GEOFF MULDAUR. NEW YORK spawned the Even Dozen Jug Band, which included blues guitar instructional specialist Stefan Grossman, HARMONICA virtuoso John Sebastian, later to start the LOVIN' SPOONFUL, mandolin virtuoso David Grisman, and Steve Katz, a founding member of jazz-rock band Blood, Sweat & Tears.

All these artists shared a reverence for traditional blues, but their approach to the genre was quite different. Van Ronk, a lifelong asthmatic, had a gruff voice that seemed to fit effortlessly into the blues idiom. Hammond was a proficient guitarist who initially tried to imitate black blues artists with varying degrees of success. Since jug band music itself is a blend of white and black musical styles, Kweskin's band seemed to fit comfortably into the style. It also included some accomplished musicians—Bill Keith was an inventive and talented BANJO player, and Muldaur's vocal style had little similarity to traditional blues singers, except possibly for Skip James. Koerner, Ray, and Glover were the first of the bunch to write original songs, and each of them explored different aspects of the blues, with Ray being a big fan of LEAD BELLY, Glover specializing in blues harmonica, and Koerner exploring more of the good-time storytelling aspects of the blues.

From the beginning all these musicians were suspect among white revivalist blues fans, many of whom felt that to sing the blues one had to be black, and preferably quite a bit older than these artists. However, by the early 1960s another group of young white artists were emerging in Chicago. PAUL BUTTERFIELD, MICHAEL BLOOMFIELD, and ELVIN BISHOP were more inclined to electric blues than the folk blues that the artists listed above favored. Furthermore, these three artists had learned their music by immersing themselves in the culture of Chicago blues, as opposed to learning from old records. All of them had, in particular, fallen under the spell of Muddy Waters.

The mid-1960s saw the emergence of such English rock groups as the Beatles and the ROLLING STONES. Both groups acknowledged the influence of African-American music in general and the blues in particular, especially the Stones, who even toured with Howlin' Wolf. At about the same time other British blues fans like Steve Winwood, Eric Burdon of the ANIMALS, and ERIC CLAPTON started touring in the United States. Unlike some of the American blues aficionados, they had voices that sounded black. Winwood and Burdon were probably the first white blues singers who had powerful voices. Rather than imitating specific singers, they came up with an identifiably "black" sound that mimicked no singer in particular. Van Morrison was another British singer for whom the blues idiom fit comfortably into his songwriting and performing style. Even pop sex-idol Tom Jones was something of a blues fanatic. Since the emergence of the British rock-blues artists, numerous American white blues artists have appeared, including BONNIE RAITT, JONNY LANG, STEVIE RAY VAUGHAN, and blues bands like CANNED HEAT, ROOMFUL OF BLUES, and many others. Raitt's voice seemed to be the most convincing blues voice of the group. Lang and Vaughan were much stronger at the instrumental end, like their American revivalist predecessors. Vaughan became accepted in the same way that JIMI HENDRIX had gained popularity—both artists were such compelling guitarists that their audiences tended not to focus on their vocal abilities.

Up until the mid-1990s there were only a handful of young American black blues artists. TAJ MAHAL was probably the most famous of the younger black Americans, but he also experimented with world music, among other things. Other American black blues artists like LARRY JOHNSON and JERRY RICKS were not well known. Johnson did little touring, and Ricks lived a number of years in Europe.

It is not possible to reach a simple conclusion about whether whites can sing the blues. From a literal point of view they obviously can. The issue has been further complicated by the emergence of black blues artists Eric Bibb, ROBERT CRAY, GUY DAVIS, Ben Harper, COREY HARRIS, ALVIN YOUNGBLOOD HART, KEB 'MO, and OTIS TAYLOR during the mid-1990s. Some of these artists come from a middle-class environment not unlike that of the young white blues artists of the 1960s. Does this mean that these artists are similarly unauthentic? Harper has moved into other musical avenues as well as the blues, and Taylor is one of the few blues artists to sing songs that deal with social and political issues. It may be worth mentioning that white blues artists other than the ones discussed here, like CHRIS SMITHER or PAUL GEREMIA, have not attempted to imitate black vocal styles but have tried to perform blues with their own vocal approaches.

Many current white blues players, like PAUL OSCHER, JOHNNY OTIS, BOB MARGOLIN, ROD PIAZZA, and CHARLIE MUSSELWHITE, have been playing blues with black musicians for a long time. It is possible to argue that they have had more direct contact with the blues than, say, a middle-class black musician who, in midcareer, develops a fascination with the blues.

Von Schmidt, Eric (b. 1930) *singer and songwriter*

Eric Von Schmidt's musical career has always taken a backseat to his painting. Von Schmidt's father did illustrations for the *Saturday Evening Post*. Von Schmidt learned to play guitar and BANJO, and after he received a Fulbright scholarship to paint in Italy in 1955, he settled in Boston. Von Schmidt was a fixture on the Boston folk scene in the 1960s, often performing at the Club 47 coffeehouse, occasionally recording, and hanging out with other folk musicians. He recorded an album with flamenco and blues guitarist Rolf Cahn, and some of the songs he sang, like "He Was a Friend of Mine" and "Baby Let Me Follow You Down," were performed, recorded, and sometimes rewritten by everyone from DAVE VAN RONK to BOB DYLAN and the Byrds.

Von Schmidt continued to perform from time to time, but most of his energy went into his painting. He also did album covers for such folk artists as Odetta, Joan Baez, and John Renbourn. With his friend Jim Rooney, Von Schmidt wrote a rambling history of the Boston folk and blues scene called *Baby Let Me Follow You Down*.

Von Schmidt currently suffers from throat cancer and can no longer sing following an operation in which his larynx was removed. Several of his albums have been reissued on CD.

Wald, Elijah (b. 1959) *musician and writer*
Elijah Wald is a musician who writes about music, especially the blues. He has written a biography of the underrated blues artist JOSH WHITE and a recent book that examinee the history of the blues, especially as it concerns the legendary ROBERT JOHNSON. In that book Wald analyzed each Johnson song in detail and pointed out where the song originated. A protégé of DAVE VAN RONK, Wald is currently compiling a book of Van Ronk's writings entitled *The Mayor of MacDougal Street,* released in 2005.

Walker, Blind Willie (1896–1933) *guitarist*
Blind Willie Walker recorded only four tunes, but he had a big reputation among Piedmont guitarists. JOSH WHITE called Walker the best guitarist he had ever heard, better even than the superb BLIND BLAKE. He compared Walker's mastery of the guitar to the PIANO playing of jazz great Art Tatum. BLIND GARY DAVIS was a harsh critic of other musicians, yet Walker is one of the few musicians that he described most favorably. Walker was blind, and JOSH WHITE claimed to have spent some time leading him around.

Because Walker recorded so little, his influence on guitar style cannot be determined.

Walker, Frank (1889–1963) *record producer*
Frank Walker was one of the pioneer record producers, recording in NEW YORK studios but also traveling through the South and recording in makeshift studios. He is noted mostly for his work with BESSIE SMITH, which started with her hit recording of "Down Hearted Blues" in 1923. Walker produced all of Smith's records, except for her last session.

Many of the artists whom Walker recorded in his field trips were country musicians, like Charlie Poole, Riley Puckett, and Gid Tanner. He later worked for RCA Records and recorded a number of jazz artists, including Duke Ellington, Coleman Hawkins, and the sweet-swing bandleader Glenn Miller.

Walker, Joe Louis (b. 1949) *slide guitarist and singer*
Joe Louis Walker combines Delta blues, ballads, and rock-tinged performances and songwriting on his records. Walker's parents were migrant farmers, and he was born in San Francisco after they settled in California. He took up guitar at the age of 14 and became part of the San Francisco blues scene. He lived with white blues guitar virtuoso MIKE BLOOMFIELD for a while, and in the 1980s he sang in a gospel group. He also went back to school, completing both high school and college.

Walker plays SLIDE GUITAR and sings, and his music can vary from raw and direct blues to smoother rhythm and blues tunes.

Walker, Phillip (b. 1937) *guitarist*
As a teenager Walker moved from his native LOUISIANA to Port Arthur, TEXAS. At the age of 16 he

played guitar in zydeco king CLIFTON CHENIER's band, staying with Chenier for three and a half years. In 1959 Walker moved to LOS ANGELES. Among his other credits are playing behind ETTA JAMES, JIMMY REED, and LOWELL FULSON, and touring during the 1960s with Little Richard.

In the mid-1970s, Walker began recording under his own name, singing, and playing. His records have appeared on a number of labels, including ROUNDER, HighTone, ALLIGATOR, an English release on JSP, and Black Top. Walker is considered to be an outstanding Texas guitar stylist, and in 1999 he recorded with guitarists LONNIE BROOKS and Long John Hunter in a guitar shootout album.

Walker, T-Bone (Aaron Thibeaux Walker)
(1910–1975) *father of modern electric blues*
T-Bone Walker is usually considered to be the father of modern electric blues. His stepfather played bass with the Dallas String Band, a folkish-jug band group. BLIND LEMON JEFFERSON was a friend of the family, and from the age of 10 until 13 Walker led Lemon around the streets of Dallas and collected money for him. Lemon rewarded him by giving him tips on how to play the guitar.

Walker was a friend of pioneering jazz guitarist Charley Christian, and both were among the first musicians to play ELECTRIC GUITAR. Walker is thought to be the first bluesman to do so, playing electric guitar in 1939 with the Les Hite jazz band. Walker played lead lines on his electric, but he could also play excellent shuffle rhythms. He was the first lead guitar player, and as such he influenced virtually every blues artist who turned to the electric instrument. B. B. KING always mentioned Walker as one of the most important influences on his music, and FREDDIE KING said the same thing.

In 1947 Walker recorded his most famous song, "Call It Stormy Monday (but Tuesday's Just as Bad)." It has been recorded by many other artists, including the ALLMAN BROTHERS. Walker went on to

make many more records for Imperial, ATLANTIC, and other companies, and he performed widely. During the 1960s he toured in Great Britain and in France and he also recorded in France.

More than any other single musician, T-Bone Walker was the father of the electric blues. A biography of him is available, written by Helen Oakley Dance. It is called *Stormy Monday: The T-Bone Walker Story,* published in 1987.

"Walk Right In" (1930) *jug band blues by Gus Cannon and Hosea Woods*
GUS CANNON and Hosea Woods wrote this jug band classic in 1930. In 1963 folk artist Erik Darling recorded it with his trio, the Rooftop Singers. Only a handful of the folk-pop records of the 1960s folk revival became pop hits, but this recording was the number-one record in the United States in 1963. The Rooftop Singer's arrangement featured two 12-STRING GUITARS, something not found in the original version. The record was so popular that it briefly brought the 12-string into broad popularity.

The piece itself is more of a ragtime-flavored song rather than a blues. The lyric is a simple, good-time call for the listener to have fun. Darling and his playing partner Bill Svanoe made changes in the original lyric. The song became so popular that Cannon, already in his eighties, got to record an album for Stax Records in his hometown of MEMPHIS. The song enjoyed something of a revival when it was featured in the soundtrack to the movie *Forrest Gump.*

Wallace, Sippie (Beulah Thomas)
(1899–1986) *singer*
A member of the musical Thomas family, Sippie relied on her older brother George and her younger brother Hersal to help her with her classic blues recordings. Wallace herself played PIANO but not on her early recordings. She worked TEXAS tent shows and New Orleans bars, and moved on to CHICAGO,

Warren, Baby Boy **237**

where she recorded more than 40 songs for Okeh Records. She wrote more than half the songs, either alone or with her brothers. The recordings were made during the period 1923–27.

Wallace suffered a series of personal tragedies, starting in 1926. In that year Hersal died from food poisoning. In 1936 George and her husband, Matt Wallace, both died. Wallace moved to DETROIT, gave up her career as a blues singer, and spent the next 40 years singing and playing organ at the Leland Baptist Church. She was coaxed back into the blues by her old Texas friend VICTORIA SPIVEY in 1966. Wallace recorded an album with her and played many folk festivals from coast to coast. She then recorded an album with Jim Kweskin's Jug Band. In 1982 BONNIE RAITT arranged for Walker to do an album for ATLANTIC RECORDS, and Raitt sang on the recording. By that time Wallace was 83 years old, and because she had suffered a stroke she was no longer able to tour. Wallace's song "Women Be Wise (Don't Advertise Your Man)" is a blues classic that has been performed and recorded by a number of other artists.

Walls, Van (Piano Man) (1918–1999) *studio pianist*
Van Walls was a studio pianist who recorded on dozens of other people's records, especially for ATLANTIC RECORDS. He played on NEW YORK sessions by RUTH BROWN, the Drifters, the Clovers, and BIG JOE TURNER, but he also did sessions with blues guitarist BROWNIE MCGHEE. In 1963 Walls moved to Montreal, Canada, where he remained until his death.

Walton, Mercy Dee (1915–1962) *recording artist and songwriter*
In 1950 Mercy Dee Walton recorded his hit song, "One Room Country Shack." That song was covered by jazz-blues pianist MOSE ALLISON and is still part of Allison's performing repertoire. Walton moved from TEXAS to CALIFORNIA in 1940 and did farm work and played solo PIANO in bars. He was a hard-edged blues player whose music crossed over into rhythm and blues.

Walton was mostly forgotten until CHRIS STRACHWITZ recorded him for ARHOOLIE RECORDS in 1961, also producing another album for Prestige/Bluesville Records the following year. Walton died in 1962 and unfortunately was not able to take advantage of these recordings.

Ward, Robert (b. 1938) *guitarist and singer*
Robert Ward's trademark sound is an ELECTRIC GUITAR with a peculiar vibrato, based on his use of a particular amplifier. White blues-rocker LONNIE MACK liked the sound so much that he bought a similar amp, which he used on his hit records "Wham" and "Memphis." Ward moved to Dayton, Ohio, in 1960 and started a band called the Ohio Untouchables. After he left, the band changed its name to the Ohio Players and had some major pop hits. Walker played on sessions at Motown Records in DETROIT during the 1970s, including records by the Temptations. In recent years he has recorded for Black Top and DELMARK RECORDS.

Warren, Baby Boy (Robert Warren) (1919–1977) *guitarist and songwriter*
One of the founders of DETROIT blues, Baby Boy Warren is associated with EDDIE KIRKLAND, JOHN LEE HOOKER, and Bobo Jenkins. Living in MEMPHIS, Warren had an older brother who taught him how to play guitar. He played for tips on streetcorners and wherever he could, learning from ROBERT LOCKWOOD JR. and HOWLIN' WOLF.

During the early 1940s Warren moved to Detroit and got a job working at General Motors. From then on he was a part-time musician who did little touring, although he made it to Europe in 1972. Although Warren recorded for a number of labels, there have not been any CD reissues of his work. As a songwriter his songs, like "Taxi Driver," often discuss life in the ghetto.

Washboard Sam (Robert Brown)
(1910–1966) *washboard player*

Washboard Sam may be the only person who made a living as a session musician playing the washboard. He was part of the so-called Bluebird sound during the late 1930s. His half brother BIG BILL BROONZY threw work his way. Before he moved to CHICAGO, Sam played for tips on the streets of MEMPHIS, and he continued to do so in Chicago.

Among the recording artists that Sam accompanied were Broonzy, BUKKA WHITE, and JAZZ GILLUM. Sam also made records under his own name. He was an average singer, but some of his songs, like "Digging My Potatoes," were sung by other artists. The Bluebird sound was intended for the most part as party music, and Sam's humorous lyrics fit right in. When the Chicago blues started to go electric in the middle 1940s, the washboard did not fit into the new sound, and Sam faded from the Chicago blues scene.

Washington, Dinah (Ruth Lee Jones)
(1924–1963) *singer*

Dinah Washington was a versatile singer of gospel music, pop, and jazz, as well as the blues. Her family moved from Alabama to CHICAGO when she was three years old, and she played PIANO in church. She sang with jazz bandleader Lionel Hampton by the time she was 18. Musician and jazz critic Leonard Feather liked Washington's work, and he wrote a series of blues with a jazz influence that she recorded with Hampton.

She cut records for Apollo before switching to Mercury, where she stayed from 1946 to 1961. During that time she had a number of hits. In 1959 she crossed over into pop music with the song "What a Difference a Day Made." After that, most of her songs were in the pop vein, with large orchestras. As if to prove that she could still do it, she recorded a blues album in 1962. Many CD reissues of her work are available.

Washington, Walter (Wolfman) (b. 1943)
bandleader, composer, and vocalist

Walter Washington has lived all of his life in New Orleans. He is a bandleader, composer, and vocalist. He spent time as the bandleader for vocalist Johnny Adams after touring with Lee Dorsey and then Irma Thomas. Later he formed several of his own bands and during the 1970s made several European tours.

Washington started putting out records under his own name in 1981. Currently he has a half dozen of them. His music varies between cover tunes and his own originals. The music varies between blues and R&B covers of other people's songs.

Waters, Ethel (1896–1977) *singer*

Ethel Waters had a lengthy career that started in music but moved into the theater. During the 1920s she was a big-voiced blues singer. In the 1930s she leaned more toward pop and influenced many singers, especially Mildred Bailey. She appeared in a number of NEW YORK musical revues and moved toward a career as an actress. She was in the Broadway show *Cabin in the Sky* and acted in a number of films. As time went on she started to get dramatic, nonmusical roles in film, on Broadway, and on television. She won many awards for her acting skills. On one episode of the TV show *Route 66,* she played a dying singer who tried to reunite the original members of her band who had scattered across the country.

During the last 20 years of her life Waters turned to religion and toured with evangelist Billy Graham. She also wrote her autobiography, *His Eye Is on the Sparrow.*

Waters, Muddy (McKinley Morganfield)
(1915–1983) *legendary blues artist*

More than any single person, Muddy Waters is responsible for the evolution of CHICAGO blues. Before he came to Chicago, the scene was dominated

Muddy Waters (center) flanked by two fans (Bruce Polonsky Photography)

by the Bluebird sound, a polite rhythm and blues version of the blues. Waters was a tractor driver on a cotton plantation in MISSISSIPPI when ALAN LOMAX recorded him in 1940. He had picked up HARMONICA and guitar during his childhood but lacked confidence in himself. He recorded two sides for Lomax, who liked the music well enough to return the following year. Waters made solos of his blues and also recorded with a string band featuring his friend fiddler Son Simms.

Waters was encouraged by the sound of what he had done for Lomax, and he decided to try his luck up north. By 1943 he was in Chicago. He did a recording session for MAYO WILLIAMS in 1946, but the records were not released until 1971. Next he recorded for Leonard Chess for his Aristocrat

Records (later, CHESS RECORDS). Chess released his "I Can't Be Satisfied" in 1948. Most of Waters's songs were either written by him or by Chess producer–bass player WILLIE DIXON. Many of these songs made it onto the R&B charts. This pattern continued from 1951 until 1956, when the rise of rock and roll seemed to make the blues decline in popularity.

Waters toured England in 1958 and young British rockers idolized him. By the 1960s the folk and blues revival caught on in the United States, and suddenly there was a great demand for real blues singers. For the rest of his life Waters played many folk festivals and clubs, and reached an audience that was very different than the South Side Chicago clubs where his career had begun.

A number of things about Muddy Waters make him particularly important in the history of the blues. By turning to ELECTRIC GUITAR and adding drums and electric harmonica, he transformed the folk blues into the city blues. The louder, more intense sound was more suitable to the tension of life in the big city. His band was also important in blues history. Many performers who went on to solo careers and became well known in their own right passed through Waters's band. These include harmonica players LITTLE WALTER and JAMES COTTON, piano players PINETOP PERKINS and OTIS SPANN, and guitarists EARL HOOKER and JIMMY ROGERS.

Record producer Jim Rooney wrote the book *Bossmen,* which compares Muddy Waters to Bill Monroe, the father of bluegrass. Rooney calls them "bossmen" because so many talented musicians passed through their bands and went on to pursue their own careers. In 1969 Waters made an album called *Fathers and Sons,* where MIKE BLOOMFIELD and PAUL BUTTERFIELD paid their musical tribute to the master. Both of them were young white bluesmen who had listened to Waters when they were teenagers. In 1977 Waters left Chess Records and signed with Columbia Records. His next four albums were produced by rock guitarist JOHNNY WINTER, who was a big fan.

Waters's music will be remembered because of his powerful, intense vocals, biting slide guitar work, his own songwriting and the songs of Willie Dixon, and the many brilliant contributions by the musicians who played on the records. Currently more than four dozen Muddy Waters albums are available, including one that contains the first recordings that he did for Alan Lomax. So far two biographies have been written about him, entitled *Can't Be Satisfied: The Life and Times of Muddy Waters* by Robert Gordon, and *Muddy Waters: The Mojo Man* by Sandra B. Tooze.

Watson, Johnny (Guitar) (1935–1996) *guitarist*
Johnny Watson followed the example of LIGHTIN' SLIM, who had played some shows with him. He had a very long guitar cord and wandered into the audience as he played. He also played the guitar behind his back. A TEXAS bluesman, Watson moved to the West Coast during the 1950s. He had two rhythm and blues hits. "Those Lonely, Lonely Nights" reached number 10 on the charts, and "Cuttin' In On," released in 1962 got to number 6. After that time he had no success with blues, so he turned to jazz, and later to superfly-style funk music. Periodically he experienced success, especially with his 1994 album *Bow Wow*. Watson died in the middle of his comeback tour in Japan.

Weaver, Curley (1906–1962) *guitarist*
Known as the "Georgia guitar wizard," Curley Weaver justified that name, working with BLIND WILLIE MCTELL, BARBECUE BOB, and others. His mother played guitar and sang gospel music, and he hooked up with HARMONICA player Eddie Mapp. Later Weaver formed a trio called the Georgia Cotton Pickers, which also included harmonica player BUDDY MOSS and Barbecue Bob. Weaver also

recorded sides under his own name. Barbecue Bob died in 1931, and Moss went to jail, leaving Weaver to spend the rest of his musical career playing and occasionally recording with Willie McTell.

Weaver, a lead guitarist, was considered one of the best Piedmont guitar players.

Weaver, Sylvester (1897–1960) *guitarist*
A talented guitarist, Sylvester Weaver recorded two instrumental solos in 1923, as well as playing for classic blues singer Sara Martin. One of Weaver's tunes was "Guitar Rag." Later Bob Willis turned it into the "Steel Guitar Rag." All told Weaver recorded 26 sides under his own name and almost as many accompanying Martin. He also sang on some of his solo cuts. A versatile musician, Waver played SLIDE GUITAR and recorded one piece on BANJO, although it was not issued. Weaver also recorded guitar duets with saxophonist Walter Beasley.

Webster, Katie (Kathryn Jewel Thorne) (1939–1999) *singer and pianist*
Katie Webster was a strong boogie-woogie PIANO player and R&B singer. Her father was a ragtime pianist as a child, but he quit to go into the ministry. She played on sessions with LOUISIANA swamp blues artist Lazy Lester, and guitarists LONNIE BROOKS, LIGHTNIN' SLIM, and Phil Phillips. She also did solo recording for swamp blues producer Jay Miller. Webster played pop, R&B, and country and western music in addition to blues. She opened shows and played for soul singer Otis Redding for two years. During the 1970s she went to Oakland, CALIFORNIA, to take care of her parents, resuming her music career in 1979. She did some touring and recording, traveling to Europe in 1982. In 1993 her career came to an end when she suffered a stroke. In addition to playing the piano, Webster played HARMONICA and sang. Her nickname was "The Swamp Boogie Queen."

Weldon, Casey Bill (Will Weldon) (b. 1909)
musician

Casey Bill Weldon played with the MEMPHIS JUG BAND in the 1920s, recording with them in 1927. He also worked as a solo artist on Memphis's Beale Street at that time. He was MEMPHIS MINNIE's first husband, and as she continued to with her later husbands, they recorded together. During the early part of the 1930s he worked outside of music but came back to record for Vocalion Records in 1935. In CHICAGO Weldon started to use the name Casey Bill. He changed his country blues style a bit to stay current, playing Hawaiian steel guitar and writing songs that commented on the times, such as the "WPA Blues."

No one knows what became of Weldon. He is believed to have gone to the West Coast and is rumored to have played on some film scores. Others reported him in DETROIT during the 1960s. The end of his story may never be known.

Wells, Junior (Amos Blackmort) (1934–1998)
harmonicist

Junior Wells was one of the most important musicians in the evolution of CHICAGO blues HARMONICA. As a child he learned the basics of the harmonica from singer and musician JUNIOR PARKER in MEMPHIS. In 1946 he was in Chicago, sneaking into clubs and absorbing the music. He hooked up with guitarists David and Louis Myers and formed a band called the Three Deuces, and later the Three Aces. When they added drummer FRED BELOW, they changed that number to Four.

His band was considered one of the hottest bands in Chicago. It often competed in clubs against other bands. Wells then played with TAMPA RED and MEMPHIS SLIM, before joining MUDDY WATERS and, later, BUDDY GUY. From 1958 to 1978 Guy and Wells had a musical partnership, recording, and touring in Europe with the ROLLING STONES in 1970.

Wheatstraw, Peetie (Wm. Bunch, also "The Devil's Son-in-Law," and "The High Sheriff from Hell") (1905–1941) *pianist, guitarist, singer, and songwriter*

Peetie Wheatstraw took his nickname from a black folk tale. He played PIANO and guitar, and wrote songs, as well as singing. His records usually included the phrase "well, well, well," as though he were having a conversation with himself. He delivered the phrase almost like a yodel. Born in St. Louis, Wheatstraw went to CHICAGO in 1935. He became extremely popular in the late 1930s, recording more than 150 titles for Decca under his own name. Among his accompanists were KOKOMO ARNOLD, Charley Jordan, and ROBERT NIGHTHAWK.

In addition to his own recordings, he played on records by CASEY BILL WELDON, LONNIE JOHNSON, and BUMBLE BEE SLIM. His songs dealt with everything from the supernatural to the difficulty of getting jobs during the Great Depression. Wheatstraw's car was hit by a train at a railroad crossing and he was killed while he was still quite popular.

White, Bukka (Booker T. Washington White) (1906–1977) *guitarist, singer, and songwriter*

Bukka White learned FIDDLE tunes from his father, who bought him a guitar. He met CHARLEY PATTON and probably learned some of his music from him. In 1930 he recorded for RCA in MEMPHIS, singing both religious songs and blues. In 1937 he shot a man and was sent to prison. White jumped bail and went to CHICAGO, where he recorded "Shake 'Em on Down," which became one of his most famous songs. He was caught and sentenced to the brutal Parchman Farm in MISSISSIPPI. White recorded two songs for ALAN LOMAX, who visited the farm. In 1940 he got out of prison and recorded 12 highly regarded songs for Okeh and Vocalion Records.

Like many of the older bluesmen, White was mostly forgotten until JOHN FAHEY and Ed Denson tracked him down in Memphis in 1963. They had written a postcard to White, addressed to "Bukka

White, Old Blues Singer, Aberdeen, Mississippi." The postcard was forwarded to White's new address in Memphis, Tennessee, and Fahey and Denson then made contact with him. Through their auspices White played at festivals in the United States and Europe, and during the remaining 14 years of his life recorded more songs than he had done in his original career.

Bukka White played a resonator guitar with a steel back, and he sang in the intense Delta style. His song "Fixin' to Die" became a standard in the blues repertoire. White made one album of songs called *Sky Songs,* because they were improvised. Like MISSISSIPPI JOHN HURT, White had more of a career after his rediscovery than when he was earlier trying to have a career.

White, Josh (Joshua White) (1915–1969)
guitarist and singer

Josh White started his career though just a child, by leading blind musicians around the streets of Greenville, South Carolina. Among them were Blind WILLIE WALKER, BLIND JOE TAGGART, BLIND WILLIE JOHNSON, and Blind Man Arnold. At the age of 13 he went with Taggart to CHICAGO to record. In 1932 he recorded as a soloist, using the name "Pinewood Tom." He recorded blues under that name and gospel music under the name "The Singing Christian." Soon after this, he moved to NEW YORK, where he lived for the rest of his life.

White's early recordings found him playing in the light Piedmont fingerstyle. In New York, he developed an entirely original style that no one else played. He bent the strings with his left hand, altering notes in the same way that B. B. KING did later. The difference was that White was playing an ACOUSTIC GUITAR, which required a lot more effort to achieve the bend. He also developed unusual right-hand strums, some of them so percussive that they sounded like the work of a drummer.

He also encountered the New York folk community and became friendly with Pete Seeger, LEAD BELLY, BROWNIE MCGHEE, and SONNY TERRY. White sang in a clear, high voice, with excellent diction, so he had no trouble getting white audiences to pay attention to him. He played college concerts and nightclubs and toured everywhere. He also had an acting career, appearing in two plays on Broadway with actor-singer Paul Robeson.

White was an outspoken foe of racism, and he recorded a number of chain-gang songs and songs protesting racial conditions in the United States. This got him into trouble during the early 1950s, when entertainers were being questioned about their loyalty to the United States. White would not back down from his opposition to racism, but he explained to the House Un-American Activities Committee (HUAC) that he had been young and did not always know what organizations he performed for.

He made many recordings, and was contracted to Elektra Records from 1954 to 1962. He had two musical children. His daughter, Beverly, born in 1939, is a singer, and his son, Joshua Donald, born in 1940, plays guitar and sings. Josh Jr. can play some of his father's guitar parts note for note, although his voice is softer than his father's.

It is hard to understand why more people did not learn Josh White's guitar style and repertoire. Possibly it was too individualistic and too difficult to execute. There is a Josh White songbook and a guitar instruction book, and recently ELIJAH WALD wrote a biography about him, entitled *Society Blues.*

"Wild Women Don't Get the Blues"
(1924) *classic blues by Ida Cox*

IDA COX was one of the several classic blues singers who wrote a good deal of her own material. "Wild Women" was recorded in 1924 and has become something of a feminist anthem in the blues revival movement. Besides Cox's own version, the song has been recorded by white blues singer Nancy Harrow, folksinger Steve Goodman, SAFFIRE—THE UPPITY BLUES WOMEN, blues revivalist Danny Kalb, and New Zealand blues singer Marg Layton. The song is halfway between a blues and a pop song, with a strong jazz flavor. The chorus "wild women don't worry, wild women don't have the blues" recurs in every verse. The song makes fun of men who want to control women and states that the singer will kick out any man if he "doesn't act right."

Wilkins, Joe Willie (1923–1979) *guitarist*

Joe Willie Wilkins played HARMONICA, FIDDLE, and accordion as a child. His father was a bluesman who was a friend of Delta artist CHARLEY PATTON. He appeared with SONNY BOY WILLIAMSON on the King Biscuit Radio Show from Helena, ARKANSAS, during the 1940s. Wilkins was a guitarist who played for other people, rather than a soloist. He was equally capable of playing single-string lead lines or rhythm chords. Wilkins was a good enough guitarist that B. B. KING took lessons from him during the late 1940s.

Wilkins toured and recorded with Williamson, and he also did many recording sessions at Trumpet Records and at SUN RECORDS in MEMPHIS as well. In the early 1970s he formed a group called Joe's King Biscuit Boys, and they worked in and around Memphis.

Wilkins, Robert (1896–1987) *guitarist*

Robert Wilkins started out as a bluesman in MEMPHIS as a young man. His stepfather taught him how to play the guitar. In 1915 he moved to Memphis and played on the streets for tips. After serving in World War I, Wilkins returned to Memphis and resumed his street singing career. In 1928 talent scout Ralph Peer recorded him for RCA Victor, and he recorded in 1929 and 1930 for Brunswick Records. Wilkins also taught guitar to MEMPHIS MINNIE.

In the 1940s Wilkins became an ordained minister in the Church of God in Christ, singing gospel music while still playing the guitar. He said that the places that he had played when he was a blues singer were dangerous, and had caused him to stop living that sort of life. Besides his work as a minister, Wilkins sold healing and herbal remedies.

When Wilkins played gospel music, he played his guitar exactly the same way as he had years earlier, but now he sang religious songs instead of worldly ones. Wilkins was rediscovered by folklorists, and he played at folk festivals and recorded a couple of albums. He was a superb guitarist, capable of fingerpicking in the Piedmont style. He played the guitar flat on his lap, did not use a slide, and sometimes played more than one bass note at a time.

The ROLLING STONES recorded his "The Prodigal Son." At first Wilkins received no credit, and when that got rectified, he never received any royalties, according to guitarist and music researcher Eugene Chadbourne, because they went to the music publisher.

Williams, Big Joe (1903–1982) *recording artist and traveling bluesman*

Big Joe Williams was a traveling bluesman who played in the streets, at house parties, on porches, and wherever else anyone would hire him. He wandered back and forth between New Orleans and CHICAGO and other far-flung places, making many records. He played a nine-string guitar, set up so that the bass strings were separate from each other, but the higher strings were in pairs. This enabled him to create the effect of a twelve-string without the guitar being quite as clumsy to play as twelve-strings were.

Williams went to St. Louis in 1934, performing with his cousin J. D. Short. He met producer and talent scout LESTER MELROSE through his cousin, and Melrose recorded Williams singing his song "Baby Please Don't Go," which became a hit in 1935. Williams was a rough person, and his raw vocal and guitar style went over well during the folk music revival. He played many festivals, toured Europe, and made more records.

Williams, Clarence (1898–1965) *songwriter*

Clarence Williams and Perry Bradford were both songwriters with good business sense. Williams wrote songs for BESSIE SMITH and vaudeville singer SARA MARTIN during the 1920s, and he often played PIANO, not particularly well, on Smith's recording sessions. William's "Gulf Coast Blues" was on one side of her first recording. He continued to write songs for Smith and other blues singers during the 1920s, and later he recorded jazz, and led several bands of his own.

Williams, J. Mayo (1894–1980) *talent scout, music publisher, and record label owner*

J. Mayo Williams was a professional football player. He was in the recording business for 35 years, working for Bluebird and at times operating his own publishing companies. He recorded BLIND BOY FULLER, BLIND LEMON JEFFERSON, TAMPA RED, MA RAINEY, and LOUIS JORDAN. He was also a talent scout and ran Paramount Records' music publishing company, owning several labels himself. Like some of his white contemporaries, Williams was notorious for not paying royalties to his artists.

Williams, Joe (Joseph Goreto) (1918–1999) *blues shouter*

Joe Williams was a blues shouter who was influenced by big-band blues singer JIMMY RUSHING. He sang gospel music in church at the age of four. Later he became a blues and jazz singer, working with the big bands of Count Basie, Lionel Hampton, and others. He had a big hit in 1952 when he sang "Every Day I Have the Blues," backed by the Basie band. After he left Basie in 1962, Williams continued to perform jazz and pop tunes as well as blues, touring all over the world.

Williams, Robert Pete (1914–1981) *songwriter*

Robert Pete Williams was serving time at the Angola penitentiary in LOUISIANA when he was discovered by folklorist Harry Oster. Williams was illiterate but he turned out to be a brilliant songwriter. He had never been a full-time professional musician, but when Oster and jazz fan Richard Allen helped him to get a pardon in 1959, he started playing music full time. The terms of his parole confined him to Louisiana until 1964, then he played the Newport Folk Festival, and the New

Orleans Jazz and Heritage Festival, and he toured Europe and recorded.

Williams's music was very spontaneous, and he was capable of making up songs on the spot. He and slide blues guitarist Fred McDowell are the two previously unknown major talents discovered during the blues revival of the 1960s.

Williamson, Sonny Boy (John Lee Williamson) (1914–1948) *harmonicist and singer*

There were two HARMONICA players who used the name SONNY BOY WILLIAMSON. John Lee was named Williamson, and he is generally referred to as Sonny Boy Williamson I. John Lee played harmonica and sang, although he had a slight speech impediment. Self-taught, he went to CHICAGO at the age of 23. He was signed by producer and talent scout LESTER MELROSE, and recorded with BIG JOE WILLIAMS. His song "Good Morning, School Girl," became well known to other blues artists, and many of them recorded it. He recorded more than 125 tracks and was considered the most influential harmonica player before World War II. Williamson played harmonica for a number of other artists, and he also performed with many Chicago blues artists.

Williamson never got to play amplified harmonica or to play the later, tougher Chicago blues. He was murdered in 1948, coming home from a club where he was working.

Williamson, Sonny Boy II (Aleck Miller, also Rice Miller) (1910–1965) *songwriter and recording artist*

Sonny Boy Williamson was a man of many names. It was never clear why he chose to adopt the name of an existing blues star when he had a name of his own. Miller traveled briefly with ROBERT JOHNSON, taught HOWLIN' WOLF how to play, and was the star of the live King Biscuit Radio Show.

From 1950 to 1954 he recorded for the Jackson, MISSISSIPPI, label Trumpet, and later he recorded for CHESS RECORDS's subsidiary Checker. His songs

"Nine Below Zero," "Eyesight to the Blind," and "Fattening Frogs for Snakes" became well known in the blues repertoire, and "Eyesight to the Blind" was used by the Who in their rock opera *Tommy*. Miller traveled to England and recorded two albums with rock and roll bands, one with the YARDBIRDS and the other with the ANIMALS.

Williamson was a showman who could put the whole HARMONICA in his mouth and play it without using his hands. He was also one of the first harmonicists to use it as a lead instrument, not one that accompanied other musicians.

Willis, Ralph (1910–1957) *guitarist*

Born in Alabama, guitarist Ralph Willis met BUDDY MOSS, BLIND BOY FULLER, and BROWNIE MCGHEE in the 1930s in North Carolina. He relocated to NEW YORK in 1944 and did some recording, some of it with McGhee and SONNY TERRY. He did not live long enough to participate in the folk and blues revival.

Winter, Johnny (b. 1944) *guitarist*

In 1968 Johnny Winter received a reported half a million dollar advance to record for Columbia Records. Winter was a spectacular guitarist, but that kind of money was remarkable for a blues musician, even a white one. He made several successful records before turning to more of a rock and roll approach, the direction that Columbia hoped to see him pursue. Johnny is an albino, and Columbia probably assumed that his unusual appearance together with his rock-tinged guitar style would transform him into a superstar.

By 1977 Winter returned to the blues, tiring of the rock and roll lifestyle. He also produced four albums for MUDDY WATERS that earned him a lot of respect among blues fans. He continues to play, sing, and record today.

His younger brother Edgar (b. 1946) is a SAXO-PHONE and keyboard player who plays blues and jazz. Edgar had a number-one pop hit with his instrumental composition "Frankenstein" in 1973.

He moved to LOS ANGELES from NEW YORK to do some film scoring work.

Witherspoon, Jimmy (1923–1997) *blues shouter*

Jimmy Witherspoon was a blues shouter who sang the blues and jazz. He had his first break sitting in with guitarist T-BONE WALKER at a show in the Watts section of LOS ANGELES in 1944. Witherspoon was a cook in the merchant marine during World War II, and after the war he sang with Jay McShann's band for four years.

On his own, Witherspoon had a number-one R&B hit with the song "Nobody's Business, Parts I and II" in 1949. As rock and roll became popular and the demand for blues lessened, he once again turned to jazz, playing many jazz festivals, recorded, and performed on television. During the early 1970s, Witherspoon retired from performing and became a disc jockey in Los Angeles. By 1973 he went back on the road with jazz-blues guitarist ROBBEN FORD, and he recorded in England while on tour there. During the early 1980s he was diagnosed with throat cancer, and although he continued to perform, the effects of the disease were obvious.

"Women Be Wise (Don't Advertise Your Man)" (1966) *recording by Sippie Wallace*

SIPPIE WALLACE was one of the dozen or so classic women blues singers. A series of family tragedies drove her away from the blues during the period 1936–66. At that time her old friend VICTORIA SPIVEY convinced her to start singing blues again. This led to her meeting BONNIE RAITT, who helped her get a recording contract with ATLANTIC. Raitt also recorded this song on her own album. Beside Wallace's own work, Rosa Henderson had also recorded a similarly titled song in 1924. Henderson's song had different lyrics but the same key phrase. The vaudeville-oriented song has basically one theme in the lyrics: don't tell anyone else about your wonderful romantic partner, because she might try to take him away from you.

Yancey, Jimmy (1898–1951) *pianist*

A deep and reflective blues PIANO player, Jimmy Yancey probably played the blues on the piano as well as anyone. He also was a pioneer of boogie-woogie. Yancey was an inventive player but not a fast or spectacular one, like Albert Ammons or MEADE LUX LEWIS. He was the first pianist to record an album of boogie-woogie solos, in 1939 called *The Piano Blues of Jimmy Yancey.* Some of Yancey's pieces, like "35th and Dearborn," "Yancey Stomp," and "State Street Special," are part of the basic boogie-woogie repertoire.

Yancey lived in CHICAGO where his father was a vaudeville performer, and his brother was a ragtime pianist. Yancey had a regular job outside of music, working for 25 years as a groundskeeper for the Chicago White Sox baseball team.

Although Yancey did not sing a great deal, his recorded selections reveal a thoughtful if subdued singer. He sometimes accompanied his wife, Mama Yancey (Estella Harris, 1896–1986). After her husband died, Mama continued to perform and record, working with such excellent pianists as LITTLE BROTHER MONTGOMERY and Art Hodes.

Yardbirds, The

The Yardbirds were a British blues-rock band that turned away from the blues as their career unfolded. The original guitar player for the band, Anthony "Top" Topham, was soon replaced by ERIC CLAPTON. Clapton dropped out when the group's recording of "For Your Love" became a big hit. Clapton felt the band was moving in too commercial a direction. He was replaced by two guitarists—Jeff Beck, who later became a star on his own, and Jimmy Page, who became a founder of LED ZEPPELIN. During their five-year history the band included three of the top guitar players in England. Their first recording was as a backup band for visiting bluesman SONNY BOY WILLIAMSON II.

Young, Johnny (1918–1974) *mandolinist, singer, and guitarist*

Johnny Young was one of the few artists who specialized in playing the MANDOLIN, although he also played guitar and sang. Born in Vicksburg, MISSISSIPPI, Young moved to CHICAGO in 1940. His music came out of the Mississippi string band tradition, although he often played electric mandolin. He played in clubs, on the streets, and at the Sunday Maxwell Street market.

Young recorded a few tunes in the late 1940s, but as the Chicago blues sound got tougher and more electric, the demand for string band music declined. During the 1960s white blues revivalists found Young's mandolin playing intriguing, and he recorded an album for Testament Records, and two more for ARHOOLIE.

Young, Mighty Joe (1927–1999) *vocalist and guitarist*

Vocalist-guitarist Mighty Joe Young was the first black CHICAGO musician to carry the blues to the white North Side of Chicago. Originally from LOUISIANA, Young grew up in Milwaukee, Wisconsin, and passed through several Chicago bands, including HOWLIN' WOLF's band. He made solo recordings and also played behind guitarist OTIS RUSH.

The rest of his career veered between fronting his own group and backing up artists like Jimmy Dawkins, MAGIC SAM, and ALBERT KING on their recording sessions. From 1986 to 1988 Young was inactive when a pinched nerve in his neck prevented him from playing. He resumed his career in 1988, singing but not able to play anymore.

young black country blues artists
By the decade of the 1960s, there was very little interest in folk blues on the part of either black audiences or musicians. CHICAGO blues continued to be a force in the world of rhythm and blues, but this music was basically an electric form of blues that utilized bass players, drummers, keyboard, and SAXOPHONE players. The country blues practitioners that remained were either rediscoveries, like SKIP JAMES or MISSISSIPPI JOHN HURT, or artists like JOHN LEE HOOKER and LIGHTNIN' HOPKINS, whose performances varied from electric R&B to the "folk" performances that they felt their white audiences expected. Furthermore, almost all these artists were fairly old, with Hooker, born in 1920, being the "young man" of the group.

There were a number of reasons that African-American musicians and music fans were no longer especially attracted to country blues. The blues was identified with an older generation, and country blues, in particular, was thought of rural and primitive, compared to, say, the music coming out of Motown Records in DETROIT or Stax in MEMPHIS. Not only were performers of country blues old in comparison with the young R&B crossover artists like Smokey Robinson, but they were "old" in the way they dressed and their performances did not involve slick choreography or staging. Furthermore, the blues was identified with an era that younger African Americans did

not consider relevant. The hard times of the Great Depression were over, and the blues did not speak to younger black audiences in terms of the musical structure of the songs or the content of their lyrics. Many of the images presented in BLUES LYRICS were countrified and, to a young audience, had elements of minstrels and white stereotypes of African Americans.

Another problem was that performing blues was not remunerative. The big money was in following the Motown model and making records that appealed to both black and white audiences, especially teenagers. Blues, with its emphasis on trouble and hard times, had little appeal to younger audiences. The music was also too loose—it did not have the compelling beat that rhythm and blues offered, with its pounding bass and drum parts.

The artists were also old and unglamorous, at least by the standards of younger audiences. Someone like CHUCK BERRY could generate sex appeal and amusement, cavorting around the stage with his duck walk. This was not possible for older blues artists, many of whom were not in the best of health. As strong an artist as B. B. KING, with many hit R&B records to his name, felt his audience slipping away by the end of the 1950s. Limited to performances in black clubs and theaters, the older blues artists found their income shrinking as their audiences diminished.

Several factors contributed to a change in this situation. First, the folk revival had gathered steam by 1960. The folk audience was a white audience of college age, and it opened the door to the development of a whole new audience for the blues. The first successful pop-folk act was the Weavers, whose performers included a few blues, like "Easy Rider," and other black songs like "The Midnight Special" and "The Rock Island Line," songs that they had learned from band member Pete Seeger's friendship with LEAD BELLY. The Weavers' pop career ended after only two years, but it was followed by Harry Belafonte's success. Originally a jazz singer, Belafonte hit it big with calypso music in 1956, but although he was essentially a ballad singer, he also included blues as part of his repertoire, recording an album of blues in 1958.

During the years 1958–65, the folk explosion grew. Starting with pop-folk groups like the Kingston Trio, artists like Joan Baez, Peter, Paul & Mary, the Limeliters, and many others sold hundreds of thousands of albums, performed widely, especially at colleges, and occasionally had hit singles. At the same time, a folk music movement headquartered in NEW YORK was involved in the early days of the civil rights movement.

In both the folk revival and the political folk-song movement, there was a relatively small number of black performers. What performers there were did not specialize in the blues, although in some cases it formed a part of their repertoire. Among the African-American artists in the folk-song revival were Odetta (Odetta Gordon), who began recording in 1958, and Leon Bibb, father of current blues artist ERIC BIBB. Both were trained singers with a strong background in theater as well as music. Odetta sang some blues, but she was more of a songster, performing spirituals, work songs, and folk songs. She continues to perform and record today.

During the 1970s a number of younger black folk artists emerged. Len Chandler was a singer-songwriter heavily involved in the civil rights movement. Chandler had a master's degree in oboe performance. Jackie Washington was a Boston folksinger, and musician writer Julius Lester was also quite involved in the civil rights movement. Elmerlee Thomas had performed with a Weaver-like group called the Gateway Singers, and Stan Wilson was a folksinger who performed blues but was basically a songster. Other black artists played a number of coffeehouses and folk clubs, like West Coast–based Don Crawford; Walt Conley, who moved between Los Angeles and Denver; Bill McAdoo, who had a brief career as a protest singer in New York; and Chicago artist Terry Callier. All these artists made records, but none of them was especially successful, and few of them did much in the way of blues. Almost all the artists had relatively

brief performing careers during the heyday of the folk music revival. Chandler had a radio news show in which he wrote two songs a day for several years, then he went on to cofound the Songwriter's Showcase, a songwriter's aid organization. Conley continued to alternate between acting and performing, Washington and Callier reemerged after a long performing hiatus, Lester became a well-known writer and college professor, and some of the others seem to have dropped out of music.

Two other black music folk groups of the period were the Freedom Singers and the Phoenix Singers. The Freedom Singers were formed in 1962 by four members of the black civil rights organization Student Non-Violent Coordinating Committee (SNCC). The group, including Bernice (Johnson) Reagan, was formed to sing the freedom songs of and for the movement. Their musical emphasis, consequently, was closer to gospel than to blues. The group disbanded in 1964, but in 1975 Reagan formed the ensemble Sweet Honey in the Rock. They sang without accompaniment, and although they branched out into other musical styles, the ensemble focuses on gospel music and traditional spirituals. Reagan, who earned a reputation as a black music scholar, has taught and written several books on the subject.

The Phoenix Singers were three black male singers who had sung in Harry Belafonte's backup group, the Belafonte Singers. They were trained singers with strong voices who made two albums for Warner Brothers and were songsters, performing a broad repertoire of African-American folk songs. JOSH WHITE had a son named Donny, who uses the professional name Josh White Jr., born in 1940, Donny is a ballad singer who performs in a variety of musical styles, including folksongs, standards, and blues. He has mastered his father's guitar style, although he does not especially focus on blues. Josh Jr. is one of the few black folk performers who has maintained a steady musical career from the 1960s to the present.

The folk revival opened the door to a blues revival, but the blues revival was sparked by white performers, including JOHN HAMMOND JR., KOERNER, RAY AND GLOVER, and DAVE VAN RONK. The only African-American blues artist to emerge during this period was TAJ MAHAL, although New Yorker Richie Havens enjoyed success as a folksinger and singer-songwriter. Another musician who worked primarily in the recording studios was Bruce Langhorne, an innovative black guitarist who played on everything from BOB DYLAN records to Gordon Lightfoot sessions. Langhorne is an unusual finger-style guitarist with a very personal touch. Finger-style involves using one guitar to do the work of two by placing a treble-string melody over a bass-string accompaniment. He played on many recording sessions during the 1960s but since that has spent most of his energy in writing a half dozen film scores, including the Peter Fonda underground classic film *The Hired Hand.*

Initially, the white blues revivalists did not use the ELECTRIC GUITAR, probably because of a combination of audience expectations and their own taste. Neither did the early black country blues players. Taj Mahal was not only a rare young black performer in the idiom, but he also played BANJO and MANDOLIN. The banjo in particular was identified by black audiences as a remnant of the minstrel era with whites, and even blacks, blacking their faces and performing music that often ridiculed African-American culture. Taj Mahal ignored such stereotypes and has always crossed musical boundaries at will. He later recorded albums that fit more into the category of world music than blues. The few other young black musicians playing folk blues at that time included LARRY JOHNSON, a protégé of GARY DAVIS, who lived in New York and did not tour widely, and JERRY RICKS, who left his native Philadelphia for Europe during the late 1960s, for the most part staying there until 1990. Ricks performed widely, but mostly in Europe. He is a versatile guitarist, and his performances ranged from playing lead guitar in an Austrian bluegrass band to playing in a jazz duo.

In the middle of the white blues revival music, the English rock bands came onto the scene and dominated American pop music during the mid-1960s. Several of the bands, notably the ROLLING STONES, the ANIMALS, the YARDBIRDS, and LED ZEPPELIN, worshipped the blues. Unlike some of the white revivalists, they made no distinction between country blues and rhythm and blues. Musicians like ERIC CLAPTON and the Stones were equally enamored of ROBERT JOHNSON and B. B. King. The British musicians played rock and roll for teenagers, so they played electric guitars, and they played loud, but they were self-contained small bands and they made it clear in interviews that they identified with American blues artists.

The success of the British groups had several effects. First, some of them toured with black blues artists; second, many of the rock bands recorded songs by blues artists like Skip James or blues songwriters like WILLIE DIXON. Because many of these rock albums sold in the millions, the songwriting royalties were by far the most money these writers had ever earned. Suddenly it became possible to think of the blues as leading to big-time income. Meanwhile a young white New York record producer, named Bill Szymzyck, overdubbed some string parts on a B. B. King record, and King had his first pop hit. He went on to become not just an R&B artist, but an international star who owns nightclubs, makes commercials, and commands healthy fees for live appearances.

The British also broke down the resistance of blues fans to the electric guitar, and that process was accelerated when JIMI HENDRIX, a little-known American blues and R&B guitarist, moved to England and transformed himself into an electric guitar superstar. Hendrix played the blues, but he mixed in all sorts of electronic sounds, and he dressed like a hippie rock musician.

During the 1970s a variety of British and American acts broke open the market for electric blues guitar, and some of the black guitar heroes like ALBERT and FREDDIE KING could at least share in the financial windfall generated by the ever-increasing demand for more and more spectacular guitarists. During this decade rock gave way to heavy metal, punk became a factor, and the first rap records were made. None of these styles had much to do with blues, and even rhythm and blues and soul music started to be regarded as old-fashioned by young black audiences. The folk revival gave way to the singer-songwriter movement, which, for the most part, also was further from anything that connected to the blues.

As records and performances became more technologically sophisticated, and as the recording process became increasingly impersonal, it was almost inevitable that a fresh connection to acoustic music and the country blues would come into play. Suddenly a group of (mostly) younger black country-blues artists appeared on the scene. JERRY RICKS returned from Europe in 1991 and began touring, and in 1997 his first American CD was released. His albums were already available in Europe, especially a number of duet albums with his European playing partner Oscar Klein, as well as a solo release in Hungary.

But Ricks was, relatively speaking, an old-timer compared with the half dozen black country blues artists who appeared shortly after his return from Europe. Ben Harper's first widely distributed album came out in 1994, along with KEB MO's first solo project. In 1995 actor-singer-guitarist GUY DAVIS's first CD was released, as was COREY HARRIS's first album. ALVIN YOUNGBLOOD HART's 1996 album followed, and in 2000 Denver-based OTIS TAYLOR entered the scene. Fruteland Jackson, another black blues performer, also recorded several albums that are less widely distributed than the ones listed above.

The social conditions that prevailed in 1995 were very different from the life of a blues singer in 1925. All these artists had attended high school, and some had attended, or graduated from college. They were all products of urban life, although Jackson was born in MISSISSIPPI, and Hart spent time there with relatives.

Davis and Eric Bibb came from artistic family backgrounds. Bibb's father was a folksinger of some renown during the folk music revival, and his family friends included Paul Robeson and Pete Seeger.

Davis is the son of Ruby Dee and Ossie Davis, both of whom had amassed major theatrical credits during their long and distinguished careers. Many of these artists were heavily involved in theater as well as music. Guy Davis played on Broadway in *Mule Bone,* a play based on the writings of black folklorist Zora Neale Hurston, with music by Taj Mahal. He too had played ROBERT JOHNSON, in Davis's case in the off-Broadway play *Trick the Devil.* He also had a one person off-Broadway show in 1994. Keb Mo' played the part of Robert Johnson in the video *Can't You Hear the Wind Howl?* He also wrote the music for the play *Thunder Knocking on the Door.* Otis Taylor won a fellowship to study film scoring at Robert Redford's prestigious Sundance Institute.

Possibly one of the reasons these artists were interested in the blues was because of the contrast between their upbringing and that of the blues artists. The blues afforded them an opportunity to recapture the roots of African-American culture.

Eric Bibb lives in Sweden and has featured Swedish musicians on his recordings, which were issued initially in Europe. He has written a considerable amount of his material, and his performance style is more like the Piedmont blues artists—relatively low-key and calm. Bibb comes from a musical family. Besides his father, folksinger and theater performer Leon Bibb, his uncle was the late John Lewis, pianist, composer, and leader of the Modern Jazz Quartet. Bibb's latest recording is a trio effort with white blueswomen RORY BLOCK and Maria Muldaur.

Guy Davis, like Eric Bibb, comes from a rich artistic background. With his two famous parents involved in movies and theater, it is natural that Davis has been involved as an actor and director, as well as a composer and performer. His work includes a collection of short stories, film scores, plays, and performances with his parents. A talented, self-taught guitarist, most of Davis's guitar arrangements lean toward the Piedmont style, but his vocal style is more Delta.

Ben Harper's music started out in the blues category. At the age of six he picked up the guitar with the help of his maternal grandparents, who owned the Folk Music Center near Los Angeles. Harper worked at the shop as a guitar repairman. His trademark instrument is the Weissenborn lap slide guitar. He spent one year in college, playing music professionally at the same time. He did a stint in Taj Mahal's band, and was the opening act for John Lee Hooker. Harper is one of several younger bluesmen with a major label contract. Keb Mo' records for Columbia subsidiary Okeh, and Harper records for Virgin Records.

Harper has been successful in France, Italy, Australia, and New Zealand, where his records have sold heavily. Of all the younger blues artists his records lean more toward rock than folk blues. As such he has appeared on programs with the Beastie Boys and Radiohead.

Corey Harris is the kind of artist who is sort of a modern-day literate Robert Johnson. Born in Denver, Colorado, he played trumpet and tuba in junior high school. Harris attended Bates College in Maine, then wandered into Africa, returning to teach school in rural Louisiana, spending his weekends singing on the street of New Orleans. Harris's travels to Africa are reprised in Martin Scorsese's blues movie series entitled *Martin Scorsese Presents the Blues,* where he is seen visiting various African musicians and performing with them. Harris has featured New Orleans keyboard player Henry Butler on several of his albums and has used a New Orleans horn section. Like Ry Cooder, Harris seems to be interested in integrating the blues with his other musical interests and explorations. His album *Greens from the Garden* includes "Lynch Blues," one of the few songs by this younger group of artists that concerns social issues.

Alvin Youngblood Hart is a self-taught guitarist born in Oakland, California. He made his way to the Maxwell Street market in Chicago, then to his grandmother's home in northern Mississippi. Originally involved in the electric blues scene in Los Angles, Hart became increasingly interested in the folk blues. He joined the Coast Guard in 1986 and developed a musical relationship with JOE LOUIS WALKER in the Bay Area. He opened for Taj Mahal in 1995, and through these performances he gained a record deal with Sony.

Since then Hart has made several albums, appeared in the Scorsese-produced *Legacy of the Blues* videos, and toured at American folk festivals and in Australia and Norway. Equally comfortable on acoustic and electric guitar, Hart is closer to the Mississippi and Chicago blues styles than to anything else.

Fruteland Jackson has not attracted as much attention as some of the other artists in this listing. Born in Mississippi in 1953, he attended Columbia College in Chicago, where he studied musical theater, and to Roosevelt University, where he studied voice. Working as a private investigator and then operating a wholesale seafood company took him to Biloxi, Mississippi. He has actively performed in the Blues in the Schools program, and has made several instructional videos and albums.

KEB MO' came at the blues from the commercial music business. He had been a staff songwriter for A&M Records's Almo Music, playing with violinist Papa John Creach. Of all the younger artists, Keb Mo' comes off as the most accessible to listeners who know little or nothing about the blues. He writes humorous, lighthearted songs, it is easy to understand their lyrics, and his recordings border on the easy-listening category. His original songs have pop music formats, with verses and catchy choruses and in that respect, they are closer to pop songs than to folk blues. On the other hand, he has mastered mandolin and banjo as well as various guitar styles. He is perhaps best thought of as a songster and entertainer, rather than a bluesman.

Jerry Ricks is the oldest of this group of artists. He was not well known in the United States, except in his native Philadelphia, because he spent most of the 1970s and 1980s in Europe, playing and recording in a duo with Austrian Oscar Klein. Upon his return to the United States in 1991, Ricks played at clubs, coffeehouses, and folk festivals, occasionally returning to Europe to play.

Ricks changed his name to "Philadelphia Jerry Ricks" to avoid confusion with another artist named Jerry Ricks. Although Philadelphia Jerry Ricks had periodically recorded as a backup musician for various artists, including rock stars Hall and Oates, his first solo recordings appeared in 1998.

Ricks mastered countless blues styles because of his personal relationships with LONNIE JOHNSON, BROWNIE MCGHEE, Skip James, Mississippi John Hurt, BUDDY GUY, and numerous other blues artists. His recordings reveal traces of all of them, but his vocal style is low-key and more like such Piedmont artists as FURRY LEWIS than Chicago or Mississippi artists.

Of all the younger African-American country blues artists, OTIS TAYLOR may be the most original and the one who deals with the most social and political issues. Taylor was born in Chicago in 1948, but his family moved to Denver in the early 1950s. He spent his teenage years hanging out at a music store, the "Denver Folklore Center." There he began to play music, starting out on a ukulele, then graduating to banjo and harmonica. At the Folklore Center he met musicians who played country music, folk music, and blues, and all these styles became part of his musical toolbox. By 1964 he formed his first band, the Butterscotch Fire Department Blues Band. This led to a recording contract in London five years later, with Blue Horizon Records. Artistic differences ended that deal without the release of a record, and Taylor returned to Denver, performing with rock guitarist Tommy Bolin, who later played in Deep Purple and the James Gang.

By 1977 Taylor had left the music business and worked in antiques. He resumed performing in 1995 and has recorded a half dozen albums, which received considerable critical acclaim. Although Taylor is well schooled in folk music and the blues, his style owes little to anyone else, except for the occasional John Lee Hooker influence. He is a creative traditional banjo player but also plays electric banjo, harmonica, and various guitars.

What stands out about Taylor is the subject matter of his songs. He sings about lynchings, black cowboys, civil rights workers called Freedom Riders, cars, and racial injustice. He is the only one of these artists to sing so many songs about social issues. Even the titles of some of his albums—*White African,* or *When Negroes Walk the Earth*—are provocative.

During the 1930s, African Americans lost their domination in jazz because so many of the swing bands featured white bandleaders and vocalists. By the mid-1940s black jazz musicians had invented the style called bebop, which restated the music as an expression of African-American culture. In the blues, a generation of Chicago black blues artists continued the notion that the blues are an expression of African-American culture. Yet it was British rock-blues artists, and such white Americans as JOHNNY WINTER and STEVIE RAY VAUGHAN, who enjoyed large record deals and whose records sold in quantity. Although none of the African-American country blues revivalists have become superstars at this time, the young audience for blues can now hear performers who have a personal relationship with the issues that are part of the blues repertoire.

Another interesting development in today's blues is the continuing strength of the Chicago blues, and the presence of the sons and daughters of the older, and in some cases, deceased artists. This group includes Lurrie Bell, son of CAREY BELL; Bernard Allison, son of LUTHER ALLISON; Big Bill Morganfield, son of MUDDY WATERS; and Shmekia Copeland, daughter of JOHNNY COPELAND. All these artists are contemporary black Chicago blues performers who show strong soul influences and play electric instruments. They do not fall into the category of younger black country blues musicians. Among white blues revivalists, two of the three musicians in the North Mississippi All Stars, a contemporary blues group, are sons of Jim Dickinson.

Zephyr

Zephyr was a hard rock blues band started by married couple David and Candy Givens. The band also included Tommy Bolin, who went on to fame as a rock lead guitarist, later playing with the James Gang and also gaining a reputation as a jazz-fusion player during his brief career. Candy was an explosive singer with a sound that drew comparisons to JANIS JOPLIN. The band achieved a degree of commercial success with their first album, released in 1969, but succeeding albums did not do as well. Candy and David split up, Bolin left the band in 1971, and the band has occasionally reassembled in one form or another to play in the Denver-Boulder area, without Candy Givens, who died in 1984.

ZZ Top

A blues-rock band, the emphasis of the band has varied at different times and on different albums. All three original members of the group are still together, which must be a record for a rock band, or almost any band for that matter. Billy Gibbons plays guitar, Frank Beard is the drummer, and Dusty Hill plays bass. Gibbons and Hill sing, and Gibbons is considered to be a good blues guitarist when not playing more rock-oriented tunes.

The band is a good-time party band, and humor is a big part of its repertoire. Two of the band members have long, flowing beards, which give them a sort of ancient appearance. They experienced considerable success during the early 1970s but took a three-year break, from 1973 to 1976, to recover from their exhausting tour schedule. When they came back they recorded two hit albums, *Eliminator* and *Afterburner*. Part of their success came from their funny, successful videos, which were played incessantly on MTV.

Although the band moved in more of a rock direction, their affection for the blues can be judged from one of their charitable acts. They were given a piece of wood from MUDDY WATERS's Clarksdale, MISSISSIPPI, shack, and they commissioned a luthier to make it into a guitar. The guitar was then sent on a national tour to raise money for the blues museum in Clarksdale.

Appendixes

Appendix I

Recommended Listening

This brief list of essential recordings includes a number of boxed sets and anthologies currently available at reasonable prices along with individual albums that are generally regarded as being important.

Boxed-Set Anthologies of Various Artists

The British label JSP has issued boxed sets of individual artists including Blind Blake, John Lee Hooker, Lightnin' Hopkins, Blind Lemon Jefferson, Memphis Minnie, and Blind Willie McTell. The Classic Blues label has issued double-CD sets of a number of artists, priced at less than the cost of most single CDs. The artists in the series include Kokomo Arnold, Barbecue Bob, Blind Blake, Big Bill Broonzy, Leroy Carr, Bo Carter, Bumble Bee Slim, Ida Cox, Arthur "Big Boy" Crudup, Cow Cow Davenport, Walter Davis, Georgia Tom Dorsey, Sleepy John Estes, Blind Boy Fuller, Bill Gaither, Jazz Gillum, Rosa Henderson, Lonnie Johnson, Charley Jordan, Willie McTell, Memphis Minnie, the Mississippi Sheiks, Buddy Moss, Tampa Red, Lucille and Walter Roland, Clara Smith, Mamie Smith, Victoria Spivey, Roosevelt Sykes, Washboard Sam, Johnny Temple, Casey Bill Weldon, Peetie Wheatstraw, and Josh White. Rounder Records (www.rounder.com) is in the process of releasing 150 CDs of material collected and/or recorded by Alan Lomax. Although a number of these recordings are of world folk music, a sizable number of them involve blue artists.

Getting' Funky: The Birth of New Orleans R&B. (Proper Box, 4 CDs, 2001)

The Kings of Blues: Blue on Blues. B. B. King, Albert King, Freddy King, and PeeWee Crayton. (Fuel Records, 2 CDs, 2002)

Legends of Country Blues: The complete prewar recordings of Son House, Skip James, Bukka White, Tommy Johnson, and Ishmon Bracey. (JSP, 5 CDs, 2003)

Rhythm & Blues Goes Rock 'n' Roll: The Birth of Rock and Roll. (International Music Co., AG, Volumes 1–15, Fuel Records, 2002)

Roots 'N Blues: The Retrospective 1925–1950. (Columbia, 4 CDs, 1992. Many artists; some white blues are included.)

Twentieth Century Blues. (Catfish Records, Volumes 1–4, 2001. This set includes many artists from most genres of the blues recorded before 1950.)

Individual Artists

Albert Ammons/Meade Lux Lewis. *The First Day.* (Blue Note, 1992)

Bobby "Blue" Bland. *I Play the Fool: The Duke Recordings, Vol. 1.* (MCA, 2 CDs, 1992)

Big Bill Broonzy. *Good Time Tonight.* (Sony/Legacy, 1990)

Charles Brown. *The Very Best of Charles Brown.* (Cleopatra, 2000)

Chicago: The Blues Today. (Vanguard, 1999, 3 volumes)

Eric Clapton. *Unplugged.* (Reprise, 1992)

Albert Collins, Robert Cray, and Johnny Copeland. *Showdown.* (Alligator, 1985)

Rev. Gary Davis. *Pure Religion and Bad Company.* (Smithsonian-Folkways, 1957)

Sleepy John Estes. *I Ain't Gonna Be Worried No More 1929–1941.* (Yazoo, 2004 original release 1992)

Blind Boy Fuller. *East Coast Piedmont Style.* (Sony/Legacy, 1991)

Buddy Guy. *The Very Best of Buddy Guy.* (Rhino, 1992)

John Lee Hooker. *The Ultimate Collection.* (Rhino, 1991)

Lightnin' Hopkins. *The Gold Star Sessions, Vol. 1.* (Arhoolie, 1991)

Howlin' Wolf. *Moanin' in the Moonlight.* (Chess, 1986)

Mississippi John Hurt. *1928 Sessions.* (Yazoo, 1988)

Blind Willie Johnson. *The Complete Recordings of Blind Willie Johnson.* (Columbia Legacy, 1993)

Tommy Johnson. *Complete Recorded Works in Chronological Order (1928–1929).* (Document, 1990)

Louis Jordan. *The Best of Louis Jordan.* (MCA, 1977)

Ray and Glover Koerner. *Blues, Rags and Hollers.* (Red House, 1963)

Lead Belly. *King of the 12 String Guitar.* (Sony/Legacy, 1991)

Little Walter. *The Best of Little Walter.* (Chess, 1958)

Brownie McGhee. *Complete Okeh Recordings, 1940.* (Sony/Legacy, 1994, 2 CDs)

Mississippi Sheiks. *Stop and Listen.* (Yazoo, 1992)

Charley Patton. *Founder of the Delta Blues.* (Yazoo, 1969)

Professor Longhair. *New Orleans Piano.* (Atlantic, 1972)

Ma Rainey. *Ma Rainey.* (Milestone, 1992)

Bonnie Raitt. *Nick of Time.* (Capitol, 1989)

Otis Rush. *Right Place, Wrong Time.* (Hightone, 1976)

Bessie Smith. *The Complete Recordings, Volume 1.* (Sony/Legacy, 1991, 2 CDs)

Tampa Red. *The Guitar Wizard 1932–1934.* (Sony/Legacy, 1975)

Otis Tayor. *Truth Is Not Fiction.* (Telarc, 2004)

Dave Van Ronk. *Inside Dave Van Ronk.* (Fantasy, 1989)

Stevie Ray Vaughan and Double Trouble. *Texas Flood.* (Epic, 1983)

T-Bone Walker. *T-Bone Blues.* (Atlantic, 1959)

Muddy Waters. *The Best of Muddy Waters.* (CHD, 1975)

Bukka White. *Complete Recordings.* (Sony/Legacy, 1994)

White Country Blues, 1926–1938. *A Lighter Shade of Blue.* (Sony/Legacy, 1993, 2 CDs)

Josh White. *Free & Equal Blues.* (Smithsonian Folkways, 1998)

Sonny Boy Williamson I. *Complete Recorded Works in Chronological Order (1937–1947).* (15 vols. Document, 1991, 5 CDs)

Sonny Boy Williamson II. (Rice Miller). *King Biscuit Time.* (Arhoolie, 1989)

Appendix II

Chronology

This brief time line notes major events in American history that are also relevant to the blues, including political events, race relations, and musical landmarks that note significant events or changes in African-American musical history.

1619

First enslaved Africans arrive in Jamestown, Virginia.

1750s

Great Awakening religious revival begins.

1755

Quakers found first antislavery society in Philadelphia.

1776

Declaration of Independence issued; American Revolution begins.

1783

British defeated; American Revolutionary War ends.

1800

First serious slave rebellion led by Gabriel Prosser in Virginia.

1807

Further importation of slaves prohibited.

1821

Nat Turner Rebellion, in Virginia.

1843

First public minstrel show presented in Virginia.

1850

Fugitive Slave Law passes, allowing owners to pursue slaves in free states.

1861

Civil War begins.

1863

Emancipation Proclamation frees slaves in Confederate States.

1865

End of the Civil War. Abraham Lincoln assassinated. The Thirteenth Amendment abolishes slavery.

1866

Founding of Fisk University in Nashville, Tennessee. Ku Klux Klan organized to terrorize African Americans.

1867

First printed collection of African-American spirituals, with a few secular tunes is released, entitled *Slave Songs of the United States,* by William Allen, Charles Ware and Lucy McKim Garrison.

1870

Fifteenth Amendment passed, giving voting rights to African Americans.

1871

First tour of the Fisk Jubilee Singers.

1877

Federal troops withdrawn from the South.

1890

Mississippi passes an amendment to the state constitution initiating literacy tests for prospective voters.

1891

Plessy v. Ferguson decision by the U.S. Supreme Court legalizes segregation.

1899

Scott Joplin's song "The Maple Leaf Rag" published.

1905–1908

Sociologist and folklorist Howard W. Odum collects blues songs in Mississippi and Georgia.

1909

Founding of the National Association for the Advancement of Colored People (NAACP).

1910

Four blues songs are published, including an instrumental version of W. C. Handy's popular "Memphis Blues."

1912

W. C. Handy's full song "Memphis Blues" is published.

1916

United States enters World War I. The armed services induct 367,710 men in segregated units. The first jazz band, a white group called the Original Dixieland Jazz Band, records.

1918

End of World War I.

1919

Race riots take place in Washington, D.C., and Chicago.

1920

Mamie Smith becomes the first black singer to record blues. Her record "Crazy Blues," is the first widely circulated blues record.

1921

Tulsa, Oklahoma, race riots. First all-black show, *Shuffle Along,* opens on Broadway.

1922

Marcus Garvey's Universal Negro Improvement Association at height of influence. Garvey advocates that all blacks return to Africa.

1923

Bessie Smith makes first record, "Down Hearted Blues."

Papa Charlie Jackson records first country blues.

1925–1926

Sociologists and folklorists Howard W. Odum and Guy Johnson publish two collections of African-American music, including blues lyrics.

1926

Blind Lemon Jefferson makes first recordings.

1927

Barbecue Bob makes his recording debut on Columbia Records with "Barbecue Blues"; Blind Wille McTell releases an album on Victor Records.

1929

Great Depression begins. Charley Patton records his first songs.

1930

Bukka White records his first album for Victor; Son House records three songs for Paramount.

1932

Franklin Delano Roosevelt elected president of the United States. Works Progress Administration (WPA) and Public Works Administration (PWA) established. Federal government employs thousands of workers, including many African Americans, to build roads, tend the national parks, and work in the arts.

1933

First Lead Belly sides are produced by the Library of Congress and supervised by John Lomax.

1936

Robert Johnson begins his recording career.

First From Spirituals to Swing concert presented at Carnegie Hall, featuring blues and jazz.

1937

After Daughters of the American Revolution (DAR) ban black singer Marian Anderson from singing at Constitution Hall in Washington, D.C., First Lady Eleanor Roosevelt resigns from the organization and Anderson gives a free concert on the steps of the Lincoln Memorial.

Bessie Smith dies from loss of blood after automobile accident in Mississippi. Sonny Boy Williamson I records for the first time.

1941

United States enters World War II after Japanese attack Pearl Harbor. Alan Lomax records Muddy Waters for the Library of Congress.

1943

American Federation of Musicians bans recordings of union-affiliated musicians.

1944

Mechanical cotton picker introduced, leading to end of hand-picked cotton.

1945

World War II ends.

1947

Jackie Robinson becomes first black baseball player in the Major Leagues. T-Bone Walker's recording of "Call It Stormy Monday (But Tuesday's Just as Bad)" is released.

1948

Long-playing records are introduced; John Lomax dies.

1950

President Harry Truman integrates U.S. armed forces during the Korean War.

1951

Sonny Boy Williamson II records for Lillian McMurry's label, Trumpet.

1954

Supreme Court declares segregation illegal in *Brown vs. Board of Education.* Elvis Presley records "That's All Right Mama." Ray Charles records "I Got a Woman" for Atlantic, marking the beginning of his successes in integrating blues, gospel, and pop music.

1955

Rosa Parks refuses to sit in back of bus in Montgomery, Alabama, starting the boycott of city buses by African Americans.

1959

Sam Charters's book *The Country Blues,* the first study of the blues, is published.

1961

First Motown hit record, "Shop Around," by the Miracles is released. Congress of Racial Equality (CORE) enlists civil rights activists to ride on buses in southern states. The activists become known as Freedom Riders. Robert Johnson's long-playing record is released.

1962

James Meredith becomes first black student at the University of Mississippi. First Stax hit record, "Green Onions," by Booker T. and the MGs.

1963

Medgar Evers, head of the NAACP in Mississippi, is murdered. Martin Luther King Jr. delivers his famous "I Have a Dream" speech at Washington, D.C., civil rights rally attended by 250,000 people. President John F. Kennedy assassinated.

1964

Civil Rights activists declare Mississippi Summer project to register black voters. Three activists are murdered—James Cheney, Andrew Goodman, and Matthew Schwerner. Son House and Skip James are featured at Newport Folk Festival. The Beatles begin the British invasion of U.S. pop music, followed by the Rolling Stones. Both cover R&B and blues songs in addition to their own material. United States passes Civil Rights Act of 1964, creating legal framework for enforcement of laws against discrimination and segregation.

1965

Black activist Malcolm X assassinated. Voting Rights act passed, prohibiting literacy and moral tests to qualify voters.

1968

Martin Luther King assassinated. Race riots follow in Newark, Detroit, and other cities.

1970

B. B. King has his first pop hit, "The Thrill Is Gone."

1971

Alligator Records launched in Chicago.

1972

Scott Joplin's opera, *Treemonisha*, premieres in Atlanta.

1979

First rap record, "Rapper's Delight," is released.

1980

The Blues Brothers movie is released, featuring a number of R&B artists.

1986

Robert Cray's *Strong Persuader* album is released, with the hit song "Right Next Door."

1989

John Lee Hooker has a hit album, *The Healer*.

1990

Blues artist Stevie Ray Vaughan is killed in a helicopter crash. Columbia releases Robert Johnson's complete works in a boxed CD set. It sells more than a million copies.

1993

Alan Lomax receives the National Book Award for *The Land Where the Blues Began*, his account of his work in the South from the 1930s to the 1980s.

2002

Alan Lomax dies.

2003

Martin Scorsese documentary series Legacy of the Blues caps a year that sees the U.S. Congress declare "the year of the blues." NPR also produces a set of blues radio shows.

Appendix III

Important Organizations and Festivals

Organizations and Schools

Virtually every state in the United States and many larger cities in Europe have some organization devoted to the blues. They generally publish newsletters, promote concerts, and sponsor major blues festivals. These groups can often be found through the Internet by searching their name, i.e., Beale Street Blues Society, but there is also a helpful list of organizations in David Dicaire's *More Blues Singers.* The two colleges most involved in academic programs studying the blues are the University of Mississippi in Oxford, Mississippi, which publishes *Living Blues Magazine,* and the University of Memphis in Tennessee, which offers a doctoral program in southern music studies.

Blues Foundation
49 Union Ave.
Memphis, TN 38103
(901) 527-2583
http://www.blues.org

Rhythm and Blues Foundation
14th & Constitution Ave., NW, Rm. 4603
Washington, D.C. 20560
http://www.rhythm-n-blues.org

University of Memphis
101 Wilder Tower
Memphis, TN 38152-3520
(901) 678-2000
http://www.memphis.edu/

University of Mississippi
University, MS 38677
(622) 915-7211
http://www.olemiss.edu

Festivals

Living Blues Magazine publishes a guide to international blues festivals in the spring issue. Many folk or jazz festivals feature blues along with other styles of music, like the Vancouver Folk Festival or the Newport Jazz Festival. A few of the largest American festivals are listed below:

Ann Arbor Blues and Jazz Festival (Michigan, http://www.a2.blues.jazzfest.org)
Chicago Blues Festival (Illinois, http://www.cityof chicago.org)
Memphis Music and Heritage Festival (Tennessee, http://www.southernfolklore.com)
Monterey Bay Blues Festival (California, http://www.montereyblues.com)
New Orleans Jazz and Heritage Festival (Louisiana, http://www.nojazzfest.com)
Portland Waterfront Blues Festival (Oregon, http://www.waterfrontbluesfest.com)

Glossary of Music Terms

a cappella Literally "in the chapel." Used generally to describe unaccompanied vocal music.

accent Extra emphasis given to a note in a musical composition.

alto (1) The lowest female voice, below mezzo-soprano and SOPRANO. (2) In musical instruments, an instrument with a range of either a fourth or fifth below the standard range; the viola is tuned a fifth below the violin, for example. (3) The alto CLEF (also known as the C clef) used for notating music for alto instruments and voices.

arpeggio A broken CHORD; the notes of the chord played in succession, rather than simultaneously.

ballad (1) In folk traditions, a multiversed song that tells a narrative story, often based on historic or mythological figures. (2) In popular music, a slow lament, usually on the subject of lost love.

bar See MEASURE.

baritone (1) The male voice situated between the BASS (lowest) and TENOR (highest). (2) Baritone is sometimes used to describe musical instruments that play an octave below the ordinary range.

barrelhouse An aggressive two-handed piano style suitable for a piano player working in a noisy room, a bar, or a brothel. The same word is used to describe such a venue.

bass (1) The lowest male vocal range. (2) The deepest-sounding musical instrument within a family of instruments, such as the bass violin. (3) The lowest instrumental part.

beat The basic rhythmic unit of a musical composition. In common time (most frequently used in popular music), there are two basic beats to the measure; the first is given more emphasis, and therefore is called the *strong* beat, the second is less emphasized and thus is called the *weak* beat.

bebop A form of jazz that developed in the late 1940s and 1950s played by small ensembles or combos, which emphasized rapid playing and unusual rhythmic accents. Many bebop musicians took common CHORD PROGRESSIONS of popular songs and composed new melodies for them, allowing the accompanying instruments (piano-bass-drums) a form that could be easily followed while the melody parts (trumpet, saxophone) improvised.

bending notes Technique used on stringed instruments where the musician pushes against a string with the left hand, causing the note to rise in pitch. On an electric guitar, which has light gauge strings, the pitch may rise as much as a whole tone (two frets).

big band jazz A popular jazz style of the 1930s and 1940s featuring larger ensembles divided into parts (brass, reeds, rhythm). Riffs, or short melodic phrases, were traded back and forth between the melody instruments.

"Blue Moon" progression A sequence of four chords associated with the song "Blue Moon," popularized in 1935 by Benny Goodman and others. The chords are I, VI minor, IV (or II minor), and V. In the key of C, they would be: C, A minor, F (or D minor), and G. Each chord might be held for two, four, or eight beats, but they appear in sequence. The progression is very common in doo-wop music.

blues An African-American vocal and instrumental style that developed in the late 19th to early 20th centuries. The "blues scale" usually features a flattened third and seventh, giving the music a recognizable sound. The classic 12-bar blues features three repeated lines of four bars each, with the first two lines of lyrics repeated, followed by a contrasting line. The chord progression is also fairly standardized, although many blues musicians have found ways to extend and improvise around these rules.

boogie-woogie Boogie-woogie is a way of playing BLUES on the piano that was first recorded in the 1920s. Its chief characteristic is the left-hand pattern, known as eight-to-the-bar (a note is played on every one of the eight possible eighth notes in a measure of four beats), which provides a propulsive rhythm that seems to have been influenced by the sound of trains. Boogie-woogie became a fad after the 1938 and 1939 From Spirituals to Swing concerts, and was adapted into big band swing, pop, and country music. From there it became part of ROCK 'N' ROLL. To boogie in general slang (as in "I've got to boogie now") means to leave somewhere in a hurry. In musical slang, to boogie means to maintain a repetitive blues-based rhythmic foundation, particularly one associated with the style of John Lee Hooker, similar to the figure in his song, "Boogie Chillen."

brass Traditionally, musical instruments whose bodies are made out of brass (although sometimes today they are made out of other metals). Usually used to refer to members of the horn family, including trumpets and trombones.

British invasion Popular groups of the 1960s that dominated the American pop charts. The Beatles led the charge in 1964, but were quickly followed by many soundalike bands, as well as more distinctive groups like the Rolling Stones, The Who, the Kinks, and many others.

cadence A melodic or harmonic phrase usually used to indicate the ending of a PHRASE or a complete musical composition.

capo A metal or elastic clamp placed across all of the strings of a guitar that enables players to change key, while still using the same chord fingerings as they would use without the capo.

CD (compact disc) A recording medium developed in the mid-1980s that enables music to be encoded as digital information on a small disc, and that is "read" by a laser. Various forms of CDs have been developed since to contain higher sound quality and/or other materials (photographs, moving images, etc.)

chord The basic building block of HARMONY, chords usually feature three or more notes played simultaneously.

chord progression A sequence of chords, for example in the key of C: C, F, and G7.

chorus Most commonly used in popular songs to indicate a repeated STANZA that features the same melody and lyrics that falls between each verse. Perhaps because members of the audience might "sing-along" with this part of the song, it came to be known as the chorus (a chorus literally being more than one voice singing at the same time). See VERSE.

clef The symbol at the beginning of a notated piece of music indicating the note values assigned to each line of the STAFF. The three most common clefs used in popular music are the G clef (or treble clef), usually used to notate the melody; the F clef (or bass clef), usually used for harmony parts; and the less-frequently seen C clef (or tenor clef), used for notating instruments with special ranges, most usually the viola.

country and western (C&W) A category developed by the music industry in the late 1940s to distinguish folk, cowboy, and other musical styles aimed at the white, rural, working-class listener (as opposed to R&B, aimed at black audiences, and pop, aimed at urban whites). Later, the *western* was dropped.

cover versions   The music business has always been competitive, and even before recordings were possible, many artists would do the same song, as can be seen by the multiple editions of the sheet music for certain hits, each with a different artists' photo on the front. In the 1950s the practice of copying records was rampant, particularly by bigger companies, which had more resources (publicity, distribution, influence) and which used their artists to cover songs from independent labels that had started to show promise in the marketplace. A true cover version is one that attempts to stay close to the song on which it is based. Interpretations of existing songs are often called covers, but when artistry is involved in giving an individual treatment to an existing song, that effort is worthy of being considered more than a cover version.

crescendo   A gradual increase in volume indicated in music notation by a triangle placed on its side below the STAFF, like this <.

crossover record   A record that starts in one musical category, but has a broader appeal and becomes popular in another category. For example B. B. King's "The Thrill Is Gone" started out as an R&B record, but crossed over to the pop category.

cut a record   Recording a record.

decrescendo   A gradual decrease in volume indicated in music notation by a triangle placed on its side below the STAFF, as in >.

Delta blues   Blues music originating in the Mississippi Delta and typically featuring the use of a slide, intense vocal performances, an aggressive, sometimes strummed guitar style with bass notes "popped" by the thumb for a snapping sound.

diatonic harmony   The CHORDs implicit in the major scale. The sequence of triads is I major, II minor, III minor, IV major, V major, VI minor, and VII diminished. Because the diminished chord is unstable, it is virtually never used in this context. Because major chords are more common, many songs use only them: I, IV, and V.

disco   A dance form of the 1970s developed in urban dance clubs, consisting of a heavily accented, repeated rhythmic part.

Dixieland jazz   Jazz style popularized in New Orleans at the beginning of the 20th century by small combos, usually including three horns: a clarinet, a trumpet, and a trombone. The rhythm section includes a banjo, a tuba, a simple drum set, and a piano, and occasionally a saxophone, string bass, or guitar is added.

DIY (Do-It-Yourself)   An emphasis on homemade music and recordings, which began with the PUNK movement but outlived it. The message was that everyone could make their own music, and record and market it on their own, using simple, inexpensive instruments and technology.

DJ (deejay)   The person who plays records at a dance club or on a radio station. DJs began to create musical compositions by stringing together long sequences of records, and then further manipulated them using techniques such as backspinning (rapidly spinning a turntable backward while a record is being played) and scratching (moving the turntable back and forth rapidly to emphasize a single note or word).

DVD (digital video disc)   A form of optical disc designed to hold video or film, but also sometimes used for higher-quality music reproduction. See CD (COMPACT DISC).

easy listening   See MOR (MIDDLE-OF-THE-ROAD).

eighth note   See NOTE VALUES.

electronic music   Music created using electronic means, including SYNTHESIZERS, SEQUENCERS, tape recorders, and other nontraditional instruments.

falsetto   A high register vocal sound producing a light texture. Often used in soul music.

finger-picking   A style of guitar playing that keeps a steady bass with the thumb while playing melody on the treble strings.

flat   A symbol in music NOTATION indicating that the note should be dropped one-half step in PITCH. Compare SHARP.

flat pick   A pick held between the thumb and first finger of the right hand that is very effective for playing rapid single note passages or heavy rhythm guitar.

flip side   The other side of a 45 rpm record, typically the nonhit song.

folk music   Traditional music that is passed down from one person to another within a family or a community. Often the original composer or songwriter is unknown.

45   A record that plays at 45 revolutions per minute (rpm). Developed in the 1950s by RCA, the 45 or "single" was the main way of promoting individual songs on the pop and R&B charts through the CD era.

gospel music   Composed black religious music.

half note   See NOTE VALUES.

harmony   Any musical composition with more than one part played simultaneously. In popular music the harmony is usually the accompanying part, made up of CHORDs, that complement the MELODY.

heavy metal   Rock style of the mid-1970s and later that emphasized a thunderous sound, simplified chord progressions, subject matter aimed to appeal to teenage boys (primarily), and flamboyant stage routines. Other variants (death metal, speed metal) developed over the coming decades.

hip-hop   The music (rap), dance (breakdancing), and visual expression (graffiti art) originating in urban areas in the mid-1970s.

holy blues   Songs that combine religious words with blues melodies and accompaniments.

hook   A recurrent musical or lyric phrase that is designed to "hook" the listener into a particular song or record. It is often also the title of a song.

interval   The space between two PITCHES. The first note of a SCALE is considered the first interval; the next note, the second; and so on. Thus, in a C major scale, an "E" is considered a third, and a G a "fifth." The I-III-V combination makes up a major CHORD.

jukebox   A machine designed to play records. Commonly found in bars (known as "juke joints" in the South), these replaced live music by

the mid-1950s, and were a major means of promoting hit records. Customers dropped a "nickel in the jukebox" to hear their favorite song.

key   Indicates the range of notes (or SCALE) on which a composition is based.

key signature   The symbol at the beginning of a piece of notation that indicates the basic KEY of the work.

looping   Repeating a short musical PHRASE or RHYTHM. SEQUENCERs can be programmed to "loop" or repeat these parts indefinitely.

LP   A "long-playing" record, playing at 33 revolutions per minute (rpm). Developed in the late 1940s, the LP enabled record companies to present more or longer compositions on a single disc (the previous time limit of 78s was 3 to 5 minutes, while an LP could hold 20 to 25 minutes per side).

major   One of the two primary SCALES used in popular music. The relation between the seven notes in the major scale is whole step (WS)-WS-half step (HS)-WS-WS-WS-HS. Each scale step has a related CHORD defining major harmony. Compare MINOR.

measure   A unit of musical time in a composition defined by the time signature. In 4/4 time, for example, each measure consists of four beats (and a quarter note is equal to one beat). The bar line (a vertical line across all five lines of the STAFF) indicates the beginning and end of a measure.

melody   Two or more musical tones played in succession, called the "horizontal" part of a musical composition because the notes move horizontally across the staff (as opposed to the HARMONY which is called the "vertical" part because the harmony notes are stacked vertically on the staff). In popular music the melody of a song is the most memorable part of the composition.

meter   The repeated pattern of strong and weak rhythmic pulses in a piece of music. For example, in a waltz, the oom-pah-pah meter is the defining part of the music's style.

MIDI (Musical Instrument Digital Interface) A common programming language that enables SYNTHESIZERS, computers, and SEQUENCERS to communicate with one another.

minor One of the two primary SCALES used in popular music. The relation between the seven notes in the major scale is whole step (WS)-half step (HS)-WS-HS-WS-WS. (There are two variations of this basic pattern found in scales known as the "harmonic" and "melodic" minor.) Each scale step has a related CHORD defining major harmony. Compare MAJOR.

minstrel Performance of African-American songs and dances by white performers in blackface, burnt cork rubbed on their faces beginning in the mid-19th century. Later, black minstrels appeared. Minstrel shows included songs, dances, and humorous skits. Many of these skits and songs made fun of African Americans.

modes A type of SCALE. The two common scales used today (the MAJOR and MINOR) are two types of mode. In the Middle Ages, a system of eight different modes was developed, each with the same intervals but beginning on a different note. The modes are sometimes still heard in folk music, some forms of jazz, and some forms of contemporary classical music.

MOR (middle-of-the-road) Pop music aimed at a wide audience, designed to be as inoffensive and nondisturbing as possible. This term is often used pejoratively by critics. Also sometimes called "easy listening."

movement A section of a longer musical composition.

notation A system developed over many centuries to write down musical compositions using specific symbols to represent PITCH and RHYTHM.

note values The time values of the notes in a musical composition are relational, usually based on the idea of a quarter note equaling one beat (as in 4/4 time). In this time signature, a quarter note fills a quarter of the time in the measure; a half-note equals two beats (is twice as long) and a whole note equals four beats (a full measure). Conversely, shorter time values include an eighth-note (half a single beat), a sixteenth (¼ of a single beat), a thirty-second (⅛ of a single beat), etc.

octave An INTERVAL of eight notes, considered the "perfect" consonance. If a string is divided perfectly in half, each half will sound an octave above the full string, so that the ratio between the two notes is expressed as 1:2.

opus A numbering system used in classical composition to indicate the order in which pieces were composed. Some composers only give opus numbers to works they feel are strong enough to be part of their "official" canon.

percussion Instruments used to play the rhythmic part of a composition, which may be "unpitched" (such as drums or cymbals) or "pitched" (such as bells, chimes, and marimbas).

phonograph A mechanical instrument used to reproduce sound recordings. A phonograph consists of some form of turntable, needle, tone arm, amplifier, and speaker. A record is placed on a turntable, a disc that is set to revolve at specific speeds. The needle "reads" the grooves cut into the record itself. The vibrations then are communicated through the tone arm (in which the needle is mounted) into an amplifier (which increases the volume of the sound). A speaker projects the sound out so that it can be heard.

phrase A subsection of the MELODY that expresses a complete musical thought.

Piedmont blues A form of blues from the Carolinas, Georgia, Florida, and Alabama that uses a restrained style of fingerpicking and soft vocal performances. It also often uses ragtime CHORD PROGRESSIONS.

pitch The note defined by its sound; literally, the number of vibrations per second (of a string, air column, bar, or some other vibrating object) that results in a given tone. Pitch is relative; in most tuning systems, a specific note is chosen as the pitch against which others are tuned. In modern music, this is usually A above middle C, defined as vibrating at 440 vps.

pop music Any music that appeals to a large audience. Originally, the pop charts featured records aimed at white, urban listeners (as opposed to R&B, aimed at blacks, and C&W or country, aimed at rural, lower-class whites). Today, "pop" is applied to any recording that appeals across a wide range of listeners, so that Michael Jackson or Shania Twain could equally be defined as "pop" stars.

power chords Played on the low strings of an electric guitar, power chords use only the root and the fifth (and often a repeat of the root an octave higher) of a triad, leaving out the third of the CHORD. With no third, the chord is neither MAJOR or MINOR. With only two notes, it is technically not even a chord, but an interval. The use of power chords was pioneered by Link Wray ("Rumble") and the Kinks ("You Really Got Me"), and used extensively in hard rock (Deep Purple's "Smoke on the Water"), heavy metal (Metallica), and grunge (Nirvana's "Smells Like Teen Spirit").

power trio Three instruments—guitar, bass, and drums—played at loud volumes.

psychedelic Popular ROCK style of the late 1960s-early 1970s that featured extended musical forms, "spacey" lyrics, and unusual musical timbres often produced by synthesizers. Psychedelic music was supposed to be the "aural equivalent" of the drug experience. See also SYNTHESIZER; TIMBRE.

punk A movement that began in England and travelled to the United States in the mid-1970s emphasizing a return to simpler musical forms, in response to the growing commercialization of ROCK. Punk also encompassed fashion (including spiked hair, safety pins used as body ornaments, etc.) and sometimes a violent, antiestablishment message.

quarter note See NOTE VALUES.

race records Music industry name for African-American popular music recorded in the 1920s until around 1945.

ragtime Music dating from around the 1890s and usually composed in three or four different sections. The most famous ragtime pieces were for piano, but the style was also adapted in a simplified form for the banjo and the guitar.

record producer The person in charge of a recording session.

register The range in notes of a specific part of a musical composition. Also used to define the range of an individual musical instrument or vocal part.

resonator guitar Guitars with a metal front and back, often used in playing slide guitar, and prized during the 1930s for their volume.

rhythm The basic pulse of a musical composition. In 4/4 time, the 4 beats per measure provide the pulse that propels the piece. Compare METER.

rhythm and blues (R&B) Black popular music that emerged around 1945 and peaked in popularity in the 1960s. It usually included gospel-influenced vocal performances, and a rhythm section of piano, bass, and drums. The lead instruments were often guitar and saxophone.

riff A short, recognizable melodic phrase used repeatedly in a piece of music. Commonly heard in big band jazz or in electric guitar solos.

rock An outgrowth of ROCK 'N' ROLL in the 1960s that featured more sophisticated arrangements, lyrics, and subject matter. The BRITISH INVASION groups—notably the Beatles and the Rolling Stones—are sometimes credited with extending the style and subjects treated by rock 'n' roll. Rock itself has developed into many different substyles.

rockabilly Mid-1950s popular music that combined BLUES and COUNTRY music.

rock 'n' roll The popular music of the mid-1950s aimed at teenage listeners. Popular rock 'n' roll artists included Elvis Presley, Chuck Berry, Little Richard, and Carl Perkins. Compare ROCK.

royalties Payments to recording artists based on the sales of their records.

salsa Literally "spice." A form of Latin dance music popularized in the 1970s and 1980s.

scale A succession of seven notes. The most common scales are the MAJOR and MINOR.

score The complete notation of a musical composition.

sequencer An electronic instrument that can record a series of pitches or rhythms and play them back on command.

78 The first form of recorded disc, that revolved on a turntable at 78 revolutions per minute (rpm). The first 78s were 10 inches in diameter and could play for approximately three minutes per side; later, 12-inch 78s were introduced with slightly longer playing times.

sharp A symbol in a piece of music indicating that a pitch should be raised one half-step in PITCH. Compare FLAT.

side One side of a recording disc.

slide guitar Style of guitar in which the player wears a metal or glass tube on one finger or uses a bottle neck to play notes. It creates a distinctive crying sound. Also called bottleneck guitar.

songster A turn-of-the-20th-century musician with a varied repertoire that included different styles of music.

soprano The highest female voice, or the highest pitched instrument in a family of instruments.

soul A black musical style developed in the 1960s that combined elements of GOSPEL MUSIC with RHYTHM AND BLUES.

spirituals Traditional religious music found in both white and African-American traditions.

staff The five parallel lines on which the symbols for notes are placed in a notated piece of music. The CLEF at the beginning of the staff indicates the pitch of each note on the staff.

stanza In poetry, the basic lyrical unit, often consisting of four or six lines. The lyrics to both the VERSE and CHORUS of a popular song follow the stanza form.

strings Instruments that produce musical sound through the vibration of strings, made out of animal gut or metal. Violins and guitars are stringed instruments.

suite In classical music, a group of dances played in succession to form a larger musical composition.

symphony In classical music, a defined form usually consisting of three parts, played Fast-Slow-Fast.

syncopation Accenting the unexpected or weaker BEAT. Often used in RAGTIME, jazz, and related styles.

synthesizer An electronic instrument that is capable of creating different musical pitches and timbres.

tempo The speed at which a piece of music is performed.

tenor The highest male voice.

theme A recognizable MELODY that is often repeated within a musical composition.

thumb picks and finger picks Guitar picks made of metal or plastic worn on the player's right hand fingers and thumb in order to play louder.

timbre The quality of a PITCH produced by a musical instrument or voice that makes it distinctive. The timbre of a guitar is quite different from that of a flute, for example.

time signature In notation, the symbol at the beginning of each STAFF that indicates the basic metric pulse and how many beats are contained in a measure. For example, in 4/4 time, a quarter-note is given one beat, and there are four beats per measure; in 6/8 time, an eighth-note is given one beat, and there are six beats in a measure.

Tin Pan Alley The center of music publishing on West 28th Street in New York City from the late 19th century through the 1930s (so-called because the clatter from competing pianists working in different buildings sounded to passersby like rattling tin pans). Used generally to describe the popular songs of this period.

tone See PITCH.

tremolo The rapid repetition of a single note to give a "quivering" or "shaking" sound. Compare VIBRATO.

turnaround   A musical phrase at the end of a verse that briefly outlines the CHORDs of the song before the start of the next verse.

12-bar blues   A 12-bar BLUES has 12 measures of music, or bars, and is the most common blues format, though eight bars and 16 bars are also used.

vamp   A short segment of music that repeats, usually two or four CHORDs. Two chord vamps are common in GOSPEL and ROCK, especially the I and IV chords (C and F in the key of C).

vanity records   Recordings that are conceived and financed by the artists involved. They are called "vanity records" because the motivation comes from the person or group themselves, not from a record company. The reason is to realize a creative project, to promote a career, or just to boost the ego. Previously, singers and musicians would pay to go into a studio and to cover the costs of backup musicians, mixing, mastering, and manufacturing. This continues, but with the rise of home studios, these steps can be done at home, with computerized recording and CD burning. Vanity records now represent perhaps the majority of recordings being made and are more likely to be called independent productions.

verse   The part of a song that features a changing lyric set to a fixed MELODY. The verse is usually performed in alternation with the CHORUS.

vibrato   A rapid moving up and down slightly in PITCH while performing a single note as an ornament. Compare TREMOLO.

walking bass   A style of bass playing that originated in jazz on the upright bass. The bassist plays a new note on every beat, outlining the CHORDs as they pass by in a CHORD PROGRESSION. Chord notes are primary, but passing notes and other decorations enliven the bass line, as well as brief rhythmic variations enliven the bass line. A rock example is Paul McCartney's bass part in the Beatles' "All My Loving" (1964).

whole note   See NOTE VALUES.

woodwinds   A class of instruments traditionally made of wood, although the term is now used for instruments made of brass or metal as well. Clarinets, flutes, and saxophones are usually classified as woodwinds.

Further Reading and Research

A. Books

I. African Roots

Kubik, Gerhard. *Africa and the Blues.* Oxford: University of Mississippi Press, 1999.

Oliver, Paul. *Savannah Syncopators; African Retentions in the Blues.* New York: Stein and Day, 1970.

II. Autobiographies and Biographies

There are currently biographies and autobiographies in print by or about Dannny Barker, Willie Dixon, David (Honeyboy) Edwards, Buddy Guy, Earle Hooker, JOHN LEE HOOKER, Alberta Hunter, SKIP JAMES, ROBERT JOHNSON, B. B. KING, LEAD BELLY, MANCE LIPSCOMB, Little Walter, MEMPHIS MINNIE, CHARLEY PATTON, MA RAINEY, BESSIE SMITH, MUDDY WATERS, JOSH WHITE, and HOWLIN' WOLF. The works listed below are a sampling of suggested titles or books of particular importance.

Davis, Angela. *Blues Legacies and Black Feminism: Gertrude "Ma" Rainey, Bessie Smith, and Billie Holiday.* New York: Pantheon Books, 1998.

Harris, Sheldon. *Blues Who's Who: A Biographical Dictionary of Blues Singers.* New York: Da Capo Press, 1993.

Santelli, Robert. *The Big Book of Blues, A Biographical Encyclopedia.* New York: Penguin Books, 1993.

Wald, Elijah. *Escaping the Delta: Robert Johnson and the Invention of the Blues.* New York: Harper-Collins Books, 2004.

III. Blues Histories

Bastin, Bruce. *Red River Blues: The Blues Tradition in the Southeast.* Urbana: University of Illinois Press, 1986.

Cohn, Lawrence. *Nothing but the Blues: The Music and the Musician.* New York: Abbeville Press, 1993.

Evans, David. *Big Road Blues: Tradition and Creativity in the Folk Blues.* Berkeley: University of California Press, 1982.

————. *The NPR Curious Listener's Guide to Blues.* New York: Perigee Books, 2005.

Harrison, Daphne Duval. *Blues Queens of the 1920s.* New Brunswick, N.J.: Rutgers University Press, 1998.

Jones, Leroi. *Blues People.* New York: HarperCollins Perennial, 2002.

Keil, Charles. *Urban Blues.* Chicago: University of Chicago Press, 1968.

Oliver, Paul. *Blues Fell This Morning: The Meaning of the Blues.* Cambridge: Cambridge University Press, 1990.

Titon, Jeff Todd. *Early Downhome Blues: A Musical and Cultural Analysis.* Urbana: University of Illinois Press, 1994.

Wardlow, Gayle Dean. *Chasin' That Devil Music: Searching for the Blues.* San Francisco: Miller Freeman Books, 1998.

IV. Country Blues and the Delta and Piedmont Styles

Charters, Samuel. *The Bluesmen.* New York: Da Capo Press, 1991.

Charters, Samuel. *The Country Blues.* New York: Rinehart, 1959.

Lomax, Alan. *The Land Where the Blues Began.* New York: Pantheon Books, 1993.

Oster, Harry. *Living Country Blues.* Detroit: Folklore Associates, 1969.

V.   Discographies

Bogdanov, Vladimir, Chris Woodstra, and Stephen Thomas Erlewine, editors. *All Music Guide to the Blues: The Definitive Guide, Third Edition.* Ann Arbor, Mich.: All Media Guide, 2003.

Rucker Leland, ed. *Music Hound Blues: The Essential Album Guide.* New York: Schirmer Trade Books, 2002.

VI.   Miscellaneous

Bernard, Shane K. *Swamp Pop: Cajun and Creole Rhythm and Blues.* Jackson: University of Mississippi Press, 1996.

Brunning, Bob. *Blues: The British Connection.* London: Helter Skelter, 2002.

Gussow, Adam. *Seems Like Murder Here: Southern Violence and the Blues.* Chicago: University of Chicago Press, 2002.

Lomax, John A. and Alan. *American Ballads and Folk Songs.* New York: MacMillan, 1934.

Nicholson, Robert. *Mississippi the Blues Today!* London: Blandford, 1998.

Tisserand, Michael. *The Kingdom of Zydeco.* New York: Arcade, 1998.

VII.   Musical Backgrounds of the Blues

Allen, William, Charles Ware, and Lucy Garrison. *Slave Songs of the United States.* New York: Peter Smith, 1867.

Blesh, Rudi, and Harriet Janis. *They All Played Ragtime.* New York: Oak, 1971.

Cockrell, Dale. *Demons of Disorder: Early Blackface Minstrels and Their World.* Cambridge: Cambridge University Press, 1997.

Conway, Cecilia. *Africa Banjo Echoes in Appalachia: A Study of Folk Traditions.* Knoxville: University of Tennessee Press, 1995.

Epstein, Dena J. *Sinful Tunes and Spirituals: Black Folk Music to the Civil War.* Urbana: University of Illinois Press, 1977.

Heilbut, Anthony. *The Gospel Sound: Good News and Bad Times.* New York: Simon and Schuster, 1971.

Kelley, Norman, ed. *R&B: Rhythm and Business, the Political Economy of Black Music.* New York: Akashic Books, 2001.

Odum, Howard, and Guy Johnson. *Negro Workaday Songs.* Chapel Hill: University of North Carolina Press, 1925.

Southern, Eileen. *The Music of Black Americans: A History,* 3d ed. New York: W. W. Norton, 1997.

Scarborough, Dorothy. *On the Trail of Negro Folk Songs.* Hatboro, Pa.: Folklore Associates, 1963.

White, Newman I. *American Negro Folk-Songs.* Hatboro, Pa.: Folklore Associates, 1963.

VIII.   Music Business

Weissman, Dick. *The Music Business: Career Opportunities & Self Defense,* 3d rev. ed. New York: Three Rivers Press, 2003.

IX.   Photo Collections

Waterman, Dick. *Between Midnight and Day: The Last Unpublished Blues Archive.* New York: Thunder's Mouth Press, 2003.

X.   Protest Songs and the Blues

Gellert, Lawrence. *Negro Songs of Protest.* New York: Hours Press, 1939.

Greenway, John. *American Folksongs of Protest.* Philadelphia: University of Pennsylvania Press, 1953.

Van Rijn, Guido. *Roosevelt's Blues: African-American Blues and Gospel Songs on FDR.* Jackson: University of Mississippi Press, 1997.

———. *The Truman and Eisenhower Blues: African-American Blues and Gospel Songs, 1945–1960.* London: Continuum Press, 2004.

XI.   Record Labels

Cohodas, Nadine. *Spinning Blues into Gold: The Chess Brothers and the Legendary Chess Records.* New York: St. Martin's Press, 2000.

Kennedy, Rick, and Randy McNutt. *Little Labels—Big Sound.* Bloomington: University of Indiana Press, 1999.

XII.   Songbooks and Collections of Blues Lyrics

Sackheim, Eric. *The Blues Line: A Collection of Blues Lyrics.* New York: Grossman, 1969.

Taft, Michael. *Blues Lyric Poetry: An Anthology.* New York: Garland, 1983.

Titon, Jeff Todd. *Downhome Blues Lyrics; An Anthology from the Post–World War II Era.* Urbana: University of Illinois Press, 1990.

Shirley, Kay, and Frank Driggs. *The Book of the Blues: The Music and Lyrics of 100 Songs.* New York: Leeds Music Corp., 1963.

XIII.   Social History

Lemann, Nicholas. *The Promised Land.* New York: Alfred A. Knopf, 1991.

Levine, Lawrence. *Black Culture and Black Consciousness.* New York: Oxford University Press, 1979.

XIV.   Urban and Electric Blues, and R&B and Soul Music

Bowman, Rob. *Soulsville, USA: The Story of Stax Records.* New York: Schirmer Books, 1997.

George, Nelson. *The Death of Rhythm & Blues.* New York: Pantheon Books, 1998.

Gurlanick, Peter. *Sweet Soul Music: Rhythm and Blues and the Southern Dream of Freedom.* New York: Harper & Row, 1986.

Keil, Charles. *Urban Blues.* Chicago: University of Chicago Press, 1991.

Pruter, Robert. *Chicago Soul.* Urbana: University of Illinois Press, 1991.

Rowe, Mike. *Chicago Blues: The City and the Music.* London: Eddison Books, 1981.

Shaw, Arnold. *Honkers and Shouters: The Golden years of Rhythm & Blues.* New York: Collier Books, 1978.

B.   Magazines

Many blues magazines are published in various languages around the world, and many local and regional blues societies publish periodical newsletters. The following three magazines are good places for beginners to start.

Blues Review
Loose Leaf Music Corp.
P.O. Box 234
Deal, NJ 07723

Juke Blues
c/o Dick Sherman
3 South 321 Winfield Road
Warrenville, IL 60555-3145

Living Blues
301 Hill Hall
University of Mississippi
University, MS 38677

C.   Instructional Books and Videos

An overwhelming amount of instructional material about the blues is available. The most useful instructional books are accompanied by CDs or DVDs. Relatively few music publishers produce instructional materials, and they can be easily accessed via the Internet or through their catalogs. They are as follows:

Alfred Music Publishing
16380 Roscoe Blvd.
P.O. Box 1003
Van Nuys, CA 91410
http://www.alfred.com

Mel Bay Publications
#4 Industrial Drive
Pacific, MO 63069
http://www.melbay.com

Hal Leonard Publications
7777 W. Bluemound Road
P.O. Box 13819
Milwaukee, WI 53213
http://www.halleonard.com

Music Sales Corp.
222 Park Avenue South
New York, NY 10003
http://www.musicsales.com

Stefan Grossman Guitar Workshop and Vestapol Videos
P.O. Box 802
Sparta, NJ 07871
http://www.guitarvideos.com

Homespun Tapes
P.O. Box 325 BU
Woodstock, NY 12498
http://www.homespuntapes.com

Arlen Roth Hot Licks Productions
4601 SW 128th Avenue
Southwest Ranches, FL 33330
http://www.hotlicks.com

D.   Films and Videos

I.   Feature Films
Blues Brothers (dir. John Landis, Universal, 1980)
Blues Brothers 2000 (dir. John Landis, Universal, 2000)
Crossroads (dir. Walter Hill, Columbia, 1986)
Lead Belly (dir. Gordon Parks, Paramount, 1976)
St. Louis Blues (dir. Dudley Murphy, RKO Pictures, 1929)

II.   Documentaries
Alan Lomax's American Patchwork (series, prod. Alan Lomax, Vestapol Video)
Cajun Country—Don't Drop the Potato (1998)
Dreams and Songs of the Noble Old (1998)

The Land Where the Blues Began (1998)
Les Blues de Balfa (dir. Yasha Aginsky, Vestapol Videos, 1983)
Blues Story (dir. Jay Levey, Sony, 2003)
Last of the Mississippi Jukes (dir. Robert Mugge, BMG Video, 2003)
Legacy of the Blues (series, Vulcan Productions, 2003)
Feel Like Going Home (dir. Martin Scorsese, 2003)
Godfathers and Sons (dir. Marc Levin, 2003)
Piano Blues (dir. Clint Eastwood, 2003)
Red, White and Blues (dir. Mike Figgis, 2003)
The Road to Memphis (dir. Richard Pearse, 2003)
The Soul of a Man (dir. Wim Wenders, 2003)
Warming by the Devil's Fire (dir. Charles Burnett, 2003)

E.   Mail-Order Sources
Many mail-order companies sell specialty books, recordings, and videos about the blues. The following three are known for their deep stock of blues-related items:

Down Home Music
10341 San Pablo Avenue
El Cerrito, CA 94530
http://www.downhome.com

Elderly Instruments
1100 N. Washington
P.O. Box 14210
Lansing, MI 14210
http://www.elderly.com

Jazz Record Mart
444 N. Wabash
Chicago, IL 60611-3538
www.jazzmart.com

Editorial Board of Advisers

Richard Carlin, general editor, is the author of several books of music, including *Southern Exposure, The Big Book of Country Music, Classical Music: An Informal Guide,* and the five-volume *Worlds of Music.* He has also written and compiled several books of music instruction and songbooks and served as advisory editor on country music for the American National Biography. Carlin has contributed articles on traditional music to various journals, including the *Journal of Ethnomusicology, Sing Out!, Pickin', Frets,* and *Mugwumps.* He has also produced 10 albums of traditional music for Folkways Records. A longtime editor of books on music, dance, and the arts, Carlin is currently executive editor of music and dance at Routledge Publishers. He previously spent six years as executive editor at Schirmer Books and was the founding editor at A Cappella Books, an imprint of the Chicago Review Press.

Barbara Ching, Ph.D., is an associate professor of English at the University of Memphis. She obtained a graduate certificate in women's studies and her doctorate in literature from Duke University. Dr. Ching has written extensively on country music and rural identity, and she is the author of *Wrong's What I Do Best: Hard Country Music and Contemporary Culture* (Oxford University Press) and *Knowing Your Place: Rural Identity and Cultural Hierarchy* (Routledge). She has also contributed articles and chapters to numerous other works on the subject and has presented papers at meetings of the International Association for the Study of Popular Music.

Ronald D. Cohen, Ph.D., is professor emeritus of history at Indiana University–Northwest (Gary). He obtained a doctorate in history from the University of Minnesota–Minneapolis. Dr. Cohen has written extensively on the folk music revival and is the coproducer, with Jeff Place, of *The Best of Broadside: 1962–1988: Anthems of the American Underground from the Pages of Broadside Magazine* (five-CD boxed set with illustrated book, Smithsonian Folkways Recordings, 2000), which was nominated for a Grammy Award in 2001. He is also the author of *Rainbow Quest: The Folk Music Revival and American Society, 1940–1970* (University of Massachusetts Press) and the editor of *Alan Lomax: Selected Writings, 1934–1997* (Routledge). He is also the editor of the Scarecrow Press book series American Folk Music and Musicians.

William Duckworth is the composer of more than 100 pieces of music and the author of six books and numerous articles, the most recent of which is "Making Music on the Web" (*Leonardo Music Journal,* vol. 9, December 1999). In the mid-1990s he and codirector Nora Farrell began *Cathedral,* a multiyear work of music and art for the Web that went online June 10, 1997. Incorporating acoustic and computer music, live Web casts by its own band, and newly created virtual instruments, *Cathedral* is one of the first interactive works of music and art on the Web. Recently, Duckworth and Farrell created Cathedral 2001, a 48-hour World Wide Web event, with 34 events streamed live from five continents.

Index

Entries in **bold** denote main treatment of a topic; *italics* indicate a picture. Page numbers followed by *c* indicate an entry in the chronology; those followed by *g* denote an entry in the glossary.